YOUNGHUSBAND

YOUNGHUSBAND

*The Last Great
Imperial Adventurer*

PATRICK FRENCH

HarperCollins*Publishers*

HarperCollins*Publishers*
77–85 Fulham Palace Road
Hammersmith, London W6 8JB

Published by HarperCollins*Publishers* 1994
3 5 7 9 8 6 4

A catalogue record for this book is
available from the British Library

ISBN 0 00 215733 0
Maps by Leslie Robinson

Photoset in Linotron Meridien by
Rowland Phototypesetting Ltd, Bury St Edmunds, Suffolk

Printed in Great Britain by
HarperCollinsManufacturing Glasgow

The legal seal that seals documents,
Is not able to utter a word in witness.
It is better to mark your heart,
With the seal of justice and truth.

His Holiness the Sixth Dalai Lama, c.1700

CONTENTS

LIST OF ILLUSTRATIONS

ACKNOWLEDGMENTS

I would like to thank the following people for their help: Janet Adam Smith, Alexander Andreyev (who supplied rare information on Dorzhiev), Anthony Aris, Michael Aris, Jennifer Armstrong, Mike Baddeley, Frederica Barkley, the Bedis, David Blake (who catalogued the monstrous volume of paper in the Younghusband Collection at the India Office Library), Chris Bonington, Michaela Bosquet, Louisa Bouskell, John Bray, John Burke, Sue Byrne, Edward Carpenter, Nirad Chaudhuri, Terry Coleman, Tim Concannon, Roger Croston, Olive Dalrymple, Willy Dalrymple, Julian Daly, Richard Davenport-Hines, Dawa Norbu, Hubert Decleer, Michael Dillon, Bill Dolby, Donkar Topden, Jerome Edou, Nona Countess of Essex, Gerald Evered, Jerry Fisher, Michael Fishwick (that incomparable editor), Zara Fleming, Lionello Fogliano, Dave French (no relation), Lavinia French (for advice on psychological matters), Maurice French (for advice on military matters), Alan Furness, Elizabeth Furness, David Gilmour, Gyurme Dorje, Lady Hallifax, Duff Hart-Davis, Sir Rupert Hart-Davis, Pat Heron, James Hill, Michael Holroyd, Kath Hopkirk, Peter Hopkirk, John Hunt, Robin Huws Jones (Eileen Younghusband's executor, who saved many papers from the shredder and gave me much help), Fredrick Hyde-Chambers, Samuel Hynes, Lois Wyse Jackson, Jamyang Norbu, Greta Jansen, Jetsun Pema, Jigdol Densapa, Kathleen Jones (for essential insights into the Younghusband family), Tamio Kaneko (who revealed the workings of the Fight for Right), Karma Topden, Pat Kattenhorn, John Keay, Nikolai Kuleshov, Tessa Lambourne, Sir Thomas Lees, Gennady Leonov, the late Sir Jack Longland, Mary Lutyens, Parshotam Mehra, Jan Morris, Andrew Macdonald, Dominic Martin, John Michell, Naomi Mitchison, Robert Morrell, the late John Grey Murray, Joseph Needham, Miss Neema, Peter Newbolt, Pamela Nightingale, Maggie Noach (my literary agent), Christina Noble, Norbu Sangpo (who interpreted some crucial conversations), Alex Norman, Penny Olsen, Pushpa Pandya, Bill Peters, Ahmed Rashid, Katherine Rawlinson, Emma Reeves, Hugh Richardson, Rinchen Kazi, Rinzin Wangmo, Isabelle Ritchie, Annie Robertson, Kenneth Rose, John Rowley, the late Sir Algernon Rumbold, Kit Russell, Peter Seaver, Sioban Shirley, my multifarious siblings (Emily and Hugh in particular), Clive Stace, John Stewart, James Symington (for information on the Gilgit Agency), Tashi Densapa, Mary Anne Taylor, Tenzin Geyche Tethong, Thinly Woser, Thondup Kyibuk, Dorothy Thorold, Geshe Thubten Jinpa,

Betty Townsend, Sir George Trevelyan, Tsering Shakya (who shared his remarkable knowledge of Tibetan history with me, time after time), Tsewang Topgyal, Frank Tuohy, Richard Wheaton (a comparably incomparable editor) and Richard Wingfield.

I would also like to thank the Society of Authors for enabling my research in India and Sikkim to take place by kindly awarding me a Travelling Scholarship, and all the staff of the India Office Library; Edward Smyth of the Alpine Club, Chitrabhanu Sen of the Asiatic Society of Bengal, Neil Somerville of the BBC Written Archives Centre, the Bodleian Library, the British Library, Cambridge University Library, Janet Johnstone of Cheltenham Ladies' College, Robin Barton and Derek Winterbottom of Clifton College, Mrs M. B. Nicholson of the Dartington Hall Trust, the Fitzwilliam Museum, Lambeth Palace Library, Lobsang Shastri and Norbu Choephel of the Library of Tibetan Works and Archives, Rebecca Lang and Fiona Philpott of Liverpool Museum, Mrs E. Sandwell of the Men of the Trees, Mr C. P. Mathur of the National Archives of India, Giustina Ryan of the National Institute for Social Work, the National Library of Scotland, Jennifer Scarce of the National Museum of Scotland, the National Sound Archives, Jean Kennedy and Freda Wilkins-Jones of the Norfolk Record Office, the Public Record Office, Charlotte Evans, Gwen Hawkins and Helen Clarke of RADIUS, Michael Bott of Reading University Library, Lady de Bellaigue of the Royal Archives, Thom Richardson of the Oriental Collection of the Royal Armouries, Frances Devereux and George Pettifar of the Royal Fusiliers Museum, Christine Kelly, Nicky Sherriff and Peter Clark of the Royal Geographical Society, Kate Thaxton of the Royal Norfolk Regimental Museum, Marinel FitzSimons of the Royal Society for Asian Affairs, the Royal Society of Literature, the School of Oriental and African Studies Library, the Society for Psychical Research, the West Bengal State Archives, Trinity College Cambridge Library, the monks of Tse Chok Ling monastery in Dharamsala, John Clarke of the Victoria and Albert Museum, Hiren Chakrabarti of the Victoria Memorial Hall in Calcutta, the West Sussex Record Office, and Marcus Braybrooke and Helen Garton of the World Congress of Faiths.

My greatest thanks are reserved for Jane Brian, Kunsang Chodon, Adrian Moon and Tashi Tsering, without whose help it would have been hard to write this book, and Abigail Ashton-Johnson, my closest friend, wife and occasional travelling companion.

Younghusband: The Last Great Imperial Adventurer is dedicated to the memory of Dzonga Tadhey Tsering Palzom.

PATRICK FRENCH, December 1993.
Chelsea Rectory – Lachung Chu – Salisbury Plain.

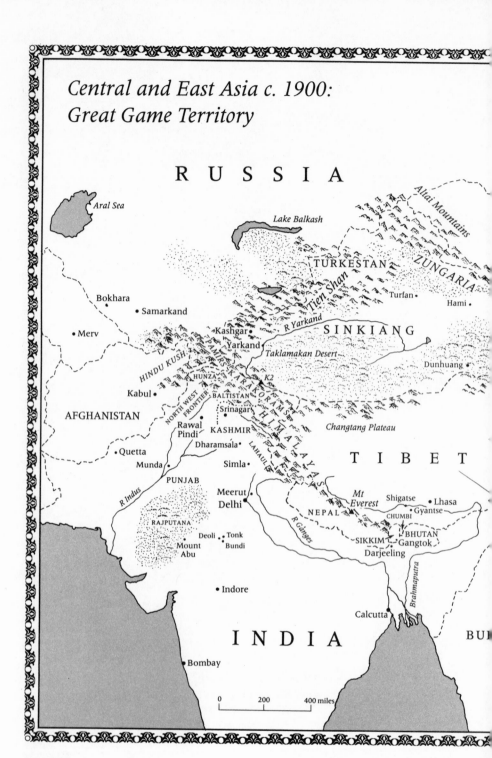

Central and East Asia c. 1900: Great Game Territory

RUSSIA

Aral Sea

Lake Balkash

Altai Mountains

ZUNGARIA

TURKESTAN

Tien Shan

Turfan

Hami

Bokhara

Samarkand

R Yarkand

SINKIANG

Merv

Kashgar

Yarkand

Taklamakan Desert

Dunhuang

HINDU KUSH

PAMIRS

KARAKORAM

HUNZA

K2

Kabul

BALTISTAN

NORTH WEST FRONTIER

Srinagar

HIMALAYAS

Changtang Plateau

AFGHANISTAN

Rawal Pindi

KASHMIR

TIBET

Dharamsala

LAHAUL

Quetta

Munda

Simla

R Indus

PUNJAB

Meerut

Delhi

Mt Everest

Shigatse

Lhasa

NEPAL

Gyantse

CHUMBI

RAJPUTANA

Deoli

Tonk

R Ganges

SIKKIM

BHUTAN

Mount Abu

Bundi

Gangtok

Darjeeling

Indore

Brahmaputra

Calcutta

INDIA

BU

Bombay

0   200   400 miles

MAP 1

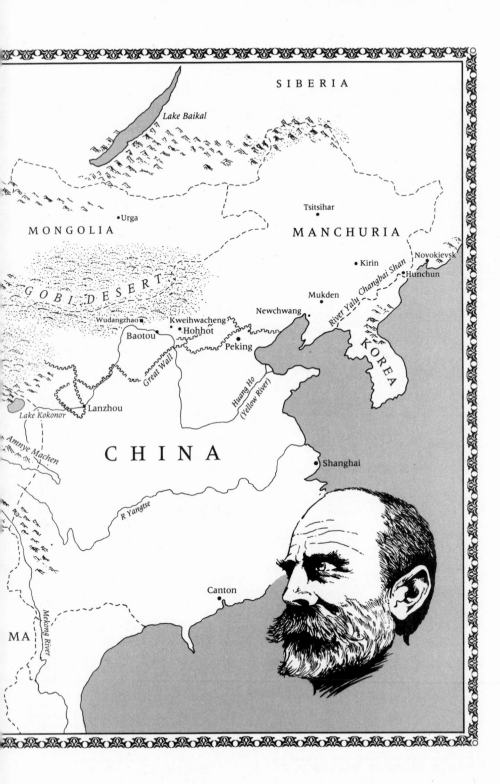

SIBERIA

Lake Baikal

MONGOLIA

Urga

MANCHURIA

Tsitsihar

GOBI DESERT

Kirin

Novokievsk

Hunchun

Mukden

Newchwang

KOREA

Wudangzhao

Kweihwacheng

Hohhot

Baotou

Peking

Great Wall

Huang Ho
(Yellow River)

River Yalu Changbai Shan

Lanzhou

Lake Kokonor

CHINA

Amnye Machen

Shanghai

R Yangtse

Canton

Mekong River

MA

The North West Frontier of India, and Beyond

TURKESTAN

RUSSIA

Lake Rangkul

PAMIRS

AFGHANISTAN

Taghdumbash Pamir

Kugiar •

HINDU

Bozai Gumbaz

Mintaka Aksai

Wakhan Corridor *Kilik Pass*

Baroghil Pass

HUNZA

R Yarkand

Khaian Aksai •

Shahidula

KUSH

Mastuj • • Chizr

Darwaza•

Shimshal Pass

Mustagh Pass

CHITRAL

Gilgit •

KARAKORAMS

▲ K2

Askoli •

TIBET

NORTH WEST FRONTIER

Karakoram Pass

BALTISTAN

Saser Pass

LADAKH

R Indus

R Indus

K A S H M I R

• Gulmarg

• Leh

Murree •

• Srinagar

Rawal Pindi •

R Jhelum

LAHAUL

Khokser • Palchan

R Chenab

McLeod Ganj • *Rhotang Pass*

Dharamsala • Manali • Vashist

Baijnath • • Kulu

SIND

Lahore •

P U N J A B

Kasauli • 0   50   100 miles

MAP 2

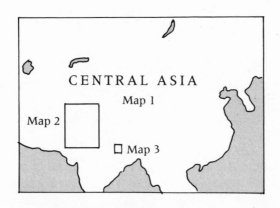

CENTRAL ASIA

Map 1

Map 2

☐ Map 3

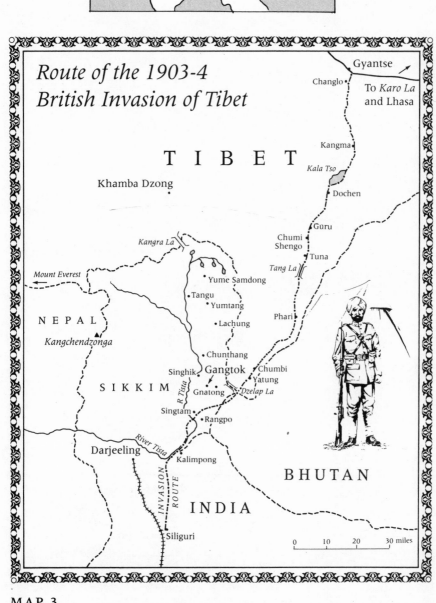

Route of the 1903-4
British Invasion of Tibet

Gyantse

Changlo• To *Karo La*
and Lhasa

TIBET

Kangma•

Kala Tso

Khamba Dzong
•

Dochen

Guru

Kangra La

Chumi
Shengo

•Tuna

Tang La

Mount Everest

Yume Samdong

•Tangu

•Yumtang

Phari

NEPAL

•Lachung

▲Kangchendzonga

•Chunthang

Singhik• Gangtok •Chumbi
Yatung

SIKKIM

Gnatong •*Dzelap La*

Singtam• •Rangpo

River Tista

Darjeeling
Kalimpong

INVASION ROUTE

BHUTAN

INDIA

•Siliguri

0   10   20   30 miles

MAP 3

Introduction

While travelling through Central Asia at the age of nineteen, seeking some elusive land where childhood dreams and present realities might come face to face, I heard that Tibet was being opened up to outsiders. Taking the chance, I headed down towards the snow mountains of Amdo, through grey-green valleys and over rickety wooden bridges to the edge of the Amnye Machen range.

On reaching the remains of an ancient Buddhist monastery, I found I had acquired a memorable illness of the stomach, and so lay for days on end in a brightly painted room reading books. The more that I read about the 1904 British invasion of Tibet, the more it came to fascinate me. Soldiers and porters and beasts had crossed the Himalayas in their thousands, marching to the forbidden city of Lhasa, marching through wild, unfeasible terrain in pursuit of some forgotten imperial dream. Most intriguing of all was the character of the expedition's leader, Francis Younghusband.

Despite being a colonialist colonel, with the obligatory walrus moustache, he had apparently had a revelatory experience on a Tibetan hillside, abandoned militarism on the spot, and ended his days as a mystical visionary. His life seemed to reflect the West's fascination with the East, conquest and wonder dancing hand in hand. There was an emblematic quality to his transformation which stuck in my mind.

The maroon-robed Tibetan monks could tell me little about him or his exploits. It was clear that the Chinese invasion of 1950 was a more pressing piece of history: the excesses of the Cultural Revolution had left many of them hollow-eyed and wary of questions. But I did gain two bits of information: that Younghusband's army had used sorcery to overcome the Dalai Lama's troops, and that somehow, somewhere a British army pith helmet had found its way into a Tibetan Buddhist temple, where it still sits today as an offering alongside sweet biscuits, white silk scarves and yak-butter sculptures.

When I got back to Britain I tracked down the only biography of Younghusband. It was a dreary example of neo-Victorian hagi-ography, long out of print, and it failed to offer a believable portrait. There were other mentions of him in various books, but nothing that caught him as a full person. The reason for this soon became apparent. His daughter, Dame Eileen Younghusband, had guarded his papers and his reputation keenly, shooing off inquisitive histori-ans. When she died, her father's huge collection of letters, notes, documents and journals passed to the India Office Library in London. By the time that I came to investigate, these papers had just been catalogued into 680 bulging boxes.

A wide variety of Sir Francis Younghusbands were to be found. He was a journalist, spy, guru, geographer, writer, staunch imperial-ist, Indian nationalist, philosopher and explorer; his friends ranged from Sir Henry Newbolt to Shri Purohit Swami. Peter Fleming praised him as 'a thruster', Kenneth Mason judged him 'the father of Karakoram exploration', while Peter Hopkirk considered him 'a member of the Great Game elite' whose exploits managed 'to thrill a whole generation of Englishmen'. He was, according to taste, the promoter of 'a religion of atheism' (Bertrand Russell), 'a devout Christian' (D.N.B.), a prophet of 'Anti-Christ himself' (the *Tablet*) or 'a visionary of rare radiance' (Baron Palmstierna). To the *Herald Tribune* he was nothing less than 'a legendary hero . . . like Ulysses'.

At the age of only twenty-four he found a new land route across the Gobi Desert, descending the impassable Mustagh Pass wearing nothing on his feet but a pair of worn leather stockings. His sup-posed death in the Pamirs at the hands of Russian agents almost caused an Indo-Russian war. As a prominent Great Gamer he mapped swathes of Central Asia and tried to tame the Mir of Hunza ('no doubt he was impressed by my bearing,' Younghusband recorded at the time).

Yet after retiring from frontier life he began to preach free love to shocked Edwardians, and set up a strange patriotic movement during the First World War with 'Jerusalem' as its specially composed rallying song. He wrote over thirty published books, founded numerous outlandish societies, attempted to start a new world religion and organized the first four expeditions up Mount Everest. He took cold baths at very low temperatures, had great faith in the power of cosmic rays, and claimed there were extra-terrestrials with translucent flesh on a planet called Altair.

It was the very incongruity of his interests and achievements that so fascinated me. How had a blimpish colonialist managed to end up as a premature hippy? Each piece of information drew me closer into his orbit. For a time I was deterred by the news that previous attempts to write his life had ended in failure. One person had died in the process, two had given up, while another had suffered a mental collapse after three decades of research. It would be imposs-ible, I was told, to understand and reconcile the different phases of his career. The military explorer could never be united with the saintly mystic. A certain obstinacy drove me onwards. I wanted to track him down, to create a travelling biography, a living biography, a bio-biography – which allowed my journey to become part of the story. I was almost twenty-one when I conceived this vain aspiration.

Francis Younghusband was to colonize nearly five years of my life. My original intentions altered as I came to realize that definitive biographies could never be written, and that only in specific instances could the story of my own adventures help to elucidate his. I also saw that the subject I was dealing with went far wider than one person. I had to try to make sense of a generation – and eight decades of rapidly changing history. The age of imperialism and the age of anti-imperialism formed no part of my direct or indirect personal experience: the British left India twenty years before I was born.

The pursuit took me from chaotic archives in Calcutta to the cold snows of the western Himalayas and the blank expanse of the Gobi Desert. I sought out Tibetan material in an effort to understand the response of a Buddhist theocracy to the appearance on its borders of Colonel Younghusband's invading modern army. Risking dis-appointment and blind alleys, I followed the leads and clues that I could see before me, chasing the elusive shadows of history, seeking the perfect information that would make the story complete. In the end I came closest to him not in Asia, but in a dusty attic in Dorset. Tumbling out of ancient cardboard boxes came passionate, mystical letters between Younghusband and Madeline, Lady Lees. At the age of seventy-six, after a sad and sexless marriage, he had met the great love of his life, with whom he could share his remarkable prophecies.

Younghusband proved to be a more coherent personality than I had expected. There was no sudden change of character, no Jekyll and Hyde adjustment: the seeds of the mystic were there in his earliest years, and the traces of the imperialist remained to his death. In his own mind, his actions were never contradictory. There was an absurd sincerity and idealism within his most offensive pronouncements, and a clear unpredictability that maintained my attention to the end. I came to realize the complexity of each person: a character who is abominable one year might be oddly endearing the next. I learned the need for scrupulous research and selection, as well as intuition, empathy and compassion. I saw the difficulty of trying to judge another era or condemn an individual's motivation, preferring to expose the subject with ruthless clarity to the calm eye of the reader.

PART ONE

ONE

Younghusband: 'Damned Rum Name'

Although he always took pride in his Anglo-Saxon roots, it was in Asia that the course of Francis Edward Younghusband's life was decided. He was born on 31 May 1863 at Murree, a hill station on the North West Frontier of India, the son of Clara Jane and John William Younghusband. His mother's family, the Shaws, were moderately rich Evangelicals from Somerset. In 1842, after her husband's premature death, the formidable Martha Shaw (Francis's grandmother) shocked her relations by setting off from Bath on a Grand European Tour. With her four daughters and one son in tow, together with a clutch of maids and a French governess, she swooped through France, Switzerland and Italy. Each morning her daughters executed drawings of Venetian palaces, or wrote essays on the history of landscape painting, while in the afternoon Mademoiselle instructed them in French and Italian. Robert, the youngest child and only boy, was tended by a nurse and plied with broth in an effort to improve his weak constitution.

Martha Shaw's leather-bound notebooks show that the purpose of these journeys was essentially moral rather than aesthetic. Amidst the descriptions of French chateaux and Renaissance paintings are frilly-edged religious pictures, and extracts from the stricter sections of the Bible. She was a fervent Evangelical, viewing Continental travel as a means to self-improvement and ethical instruction. Conscious perhaps of the growing revolutionary fervour in Europe, her notes mention the Sinfulness of Man, Temples of Lasciviousness, the Papists (who are 'inflated with pride'), and contain frequent reminders that 'the wages of Sin are death'. There are neat columns on opposite pages recording income and expenditure, and details of the spiritual development of her children. Each year her daughters were issued with 'a review of your conduct since your last birthday'.[1]

Martha's writings reveal a mixture of vision and repression. She had a wide knowledge of European culture, while remaining suspicious of its possibilities, and of the risk that Art might lure her towards decadence and corruption. She passed on this ambivalence to her solemn daughter Clara, who had substantial ability as an artist. Clara remained wary of her own talent, limiting herself to sketches and pale landscapes. The pictures she drew were fluent and accomplished, but never developed beyond a formal style; she would not allow her proficiency to be contaminated by originality or exuberance. When Clara Shaw was in her late teens she met a short but respectably dashing young officer who had been sent home from the Indian frontier with a fever. All of Somerset had heard of his adventures among the Wild Tribes, and he was called John Younghusband.

The name Younghusband is the most striking feature: imperious, unlikely, teetering on the edge of absurdity. It has been rendered variously as Young, Husband, Houngbushand, Young-Husband, 'Young' Husband, Youngblood, House-husband, Loving-husband, Yang-ta-jen and (in the case of a Manchu official) Yang-hasi-pan. 'Younghusband? Damned rum name that is,' observed Sir Charles Macgregor when he first met Francis Younghusband.[2] The name came originally from Osban (a variation on Oswald); Osban's son was known as Young Osban, which in turn transmuted into Young-husband. The family could trace itself through many years of Northumbrian history, including a fifteenth-century Sheriff of Newcastle and an assortment of local dignitaries.

John Younghusband was born in 1823, spending his childhood in Italy and Wiltshire before joining the army at the age of seventeen. His father had been a Major-General in the Royal Artillery, and his uncle had captained a ship in the Battle of the Nile. John fought in the First Afghan War, before acting as aide-de-camp to Sir Charles Napier during the conquest of Sind. After the capture of Hyderabad in 1843 he was accused of involvement in the looting of the town and the sale of 'Prize Property'. It was alleged that he and other soldiers had held an auction of jewellery, tapestries and even clothing and undergarments looted from 'the Ladies of the Ameer of Sinde'.[3] Following the campaign, Napier made him a Lieutenant of Police, with responsibility for raising a new police force. Younghusband was apparently 'actively employed in Upper Sind, hunting down and chastising marauders and rebels, and the official records of the time contain frequent honourable mentions of his name'.[4]

An obituary in the Sind Gazette notes that John Younghusband 'was greatly loved and esteemed by a large circle of friends, and it is difficult to imagine his having ever made an enemy'.[5] References to him often stress his affability and capacity for friendship, but given the job he was doing he must have had a ruthlessly coercive streak. The police force he helped set up was full of rough paramilitaries who could be deployed to quell unrest in fractious territory, a tradition that has continued in India to the present day. The grainy photographs of John and his fellow officers capture the atmosphere of the time. Harsh men with mutton-chop whiskers sit with their knees open to the camera and scabby dogs at their feet. Occasionally there is a woman in the picture, sensuous in a dark bonnet. The figures have none of the ardent pomposity of the late Victorian period, looking more like adventurous American frontiersmen than stiff-necked imperial servants.

Clara Shaw and John Younghusband were aged twenty-three and thirty-three respectively when they married, in some considerable style, on 21 February 1856.[6] As the Crimean War came to an end they left Somerset and began a three-month sea-voyage to India, until finally, by horse, they reached the small Himalayan hill station of Dharamsala. In a clearing in the pine forest above the Church of St John in the Wilderness, local craftsmen built a bungalow with a wooden verandah. Dodging the bears, Clara climbed the ridges above the forest and painted watercolours of the mountainous landscape. Although few other European women chose to go to remote parts of India at this time, Clara seemed content with her isolated life. The house was idyllic, she was in good health, and at the end of 1856 she became pregnant. Then the Indian Mutiny broke out.

For the previous 250 years, the status of the British in India had fluctuated. During the first half of the nineteenth century they had expanded steadily from their base in Bengal, conquering territory and strengthening their political control. Having taken Sind and the Punjab, the East India Company had a firm control of the country's northern borders and significant influence over the princes of Rajputana. By 1857 the situation in parts of India had come close to breaking-point: conflict was finally sparked by British mistreatment of Indian troops. As unrest grew, John Younghusband and his men rode through the country stamping out any hint of revolt, and trying to ensure that insurrection did not spread to the Punjab. News came through that his brother Edward had been killed in the fighting, and shortly afterwards a letter from his friend Dighton Probyn revealed that another brother had been shot through the lungs during the siege of Delhi. Meanwhile Clara was left, heavily pregnant, in a remote village with scarcely a European in sight. Her mother sent cataclysmic letters on the flimsiest of writing-paper, bewailing 'the ardour of the insurgents ... Great God forgive such impiety – for who have we else to trust to and who besides can help us – with Thy help we are safe even when destruction itself seems inevitable and without Thee we are lost.'[7] In August 1857 their first child, Clara Emily (Emmie) was born, and after months of violence the British suppressed the Mutiny. The Punjab had 'held' throughout, but John Younghusband's fears about the dangers of lax discipline were confirmed.

Some historians now regard the Mutiny as India's first war of independence. In certain respects this is accurate: although it was never a co-ordinated revolution it was more than a sepoy's revolt, since it gave a voice to the mute resistance of many northern Indians. The Mutiny was old India's last attempt to stave off the Westernization of its culture, and marked a permanent change in the relationship between Britain and India. The power of the East India Company was transferred to the British Crown, and the governor-general took on the authority of a viceroy, guided by the Secretary of State for India back in Whitehall. The Viceroy was given immense power, and an influence that the government in London would have trouble controlling. When George Curzon became Viceroy, he would manipulate it to instigate his own forceful policy in Central Asia and the Persian Gulf.

Any mutual trust that had existed between Britishers and Indians was destroyed, and social contact was severed. The early envoys of the East India Company had worn Indian clothing, smoked hookahs and married Indian women, but after the Mutiny stiff collars, chota pegs and memsahibs took their place. More troops were sent out from Britain, and Indian regiments were put under strict control. The British stuck to their cantonments on the edges of settlements, or else restricted Indians to certain areas of the towns: dogs and Indians were barred from walking in the Mall at Simla until 1918. Trade – the bedrock of British involvement in India – had been superseded by an era of racial supremacy.

Clara and John Younghusband settled back into their old pattern of life, more wary than before. Another two children were born in rapid succession (George and Ethel) and then a baby girl called Gertrude who died after a few weeks. John investigated the possibility of buying a tea plantation, and was assisted by his brother-in-law Robert Shaw who had come out from England to improve his health in the Himalayan air. Realizing that the increasingly popular China tea would grow there, and that the planters were 'exclusively gentlemen', they purchased a plot of land in Dharamsala and went into partnership.[8] Robert Shaw soon became secretary of the Kangra Valley Planters Association. Clara and her brother enjoyed a good relationship, going on several expeditions together to the valleys beyond Simla. When John was promoted, Robert Shaw took on the business alone and the Younghusband family moved north to Murree.

The birth of Francis Edward in May 1863 was followed by a series of upheavals. At the end of the year Clara and her four children, including the rather sickly baby Francis, set sail for England. She tended her dying mother in Bath, and soon gave birth to another child, named Leslie Napier after the legendary conqueror of Sind. Two years of relative stability followed, until Clara and John had to return to India while their children were dispersed to various schools and relations. Francis, aged four and a half, was sent to live with his father's two unmarried sisters in Freshford near Bath. The Aunts were stringently religious; any hint of moral laxity in their young charge was beaten out of him with the aid of a leather strap. 'They were of the sternest stuff,' wrote Francis a year before his death, 'dressed in poke bonnets and living in the greatest simplicity. Strict teetotallers waging a war against drunkenness and teaching in the Sunday school.'[9]

Three years of severity and austerity followed until his parents returned. The reunited family moved back to Bath and Francis was sent to a local school, but the emphasis on discipline remained unchanged. There were family prayers at least twice a day, and frequent visits to church; any disobedience resulted in a beating. One day Francis was found stealing a coin from a servant's purse. The subsequent punishment, and its emphasis on his irredeemable wickedness, convinced him he had betrayed his family and his God. 'I lost my childhood's happiness, and became serious. Indeed I doubt if I ever completely recovered it till my old age.'[10]

In 1873 he travelled out to India with his parents. William Ewart Gladstone was coming to the end of his first term in office, and the Tsar's army was riding south through Uzbek territory, expanding the Russian Empire. The Suez Canal had just opened, reducing the journey time to three weeks, and many more women and children were now going to the subcontinent. The Younghusbands stayed at Lahore and Dalhousie before returning to Murree, but shortly after his twelfth birthday Francis was sent to England to be educated. Clifton College was the chosen establishment, an all-male boarding school in Bristol. Although it had been founded only a decade earlier, it had already caught the attention of many British officials serving abroad. Francis's elder brother George was there, as were several of his cousins. Clifton was to have a profound influence upon him for the rest of his life. Although his time there was not especially happy, he retained a traditional British loyalty to the alma mater, and an instinctive empathy towards other Old Cliftonians. During his schooldays he formed the social and racial philosophy which took him into adulthood.

Clifton was one of a crop of boarding schools to spring up in the wake of the celebrated Dr Arnold of Rugby. At the beginning of the nineteenth century Britain's public schools were, supposedly, the very seats and nurseries of vice. Arnold aimed to introduce a system of schooling based upon patrician ideals of morality, which would turn out 'Christian Gentlemen'. John Percival, who was appointed Clifton's first headmaster, endorsed Arnold's vision and spoke of 'a nursery or seed-plot for high-minded men, devoted to the highest service of the country, a new Christian chivalry of patriotic service'.[11]

When Francis Younghusband arrived at Clifton in 1876 he was immediately assailed by this ethos of stern athleticism. Percival had surrounded himself with a squad of earnest and enthusiastic assistant masters, many of whom were still in their early twenties. Rugby, cricket, running and athletics were the principal means of instruction; academic study was of secondary importance. There were lessons in military history and strategy, geography, classics, map-making, even rudimentary mathematics, but any hint of intellectualism or sentiment was scorned. Reverence for manly vigour and the doctrine of *mens sana in corpore sano* were the guiding principles. Fortunately for Francis he could move at great speed, so he won numerous medals for his running skills. When he was only sixteen he came third in the cross-country race, and received the ultimate accolade: 'There were lines of cheering boys all down the Avenue, and Reynolds the head of the house hugged me.'[12] Although physical contact was officially discouraged, sporting victory was clearly regarded as a suitable occasion for the display of emotion.

Francis developed the tough skin necessary for survival in this harsh, masculine environment, but underneath he had a tense sensitivity; the singing of the choir could move him to the brink of tears. Although he was 'good at games', he was too serious and withdrawn to be popular within the school. His religious sensibility was continually troubled by the notion that he was guilty of dreadful sins. 'I have been indulging bad thoughts and they have taken a root on me.' This fear was not helped by the books he was plied with by his parents and the Freshford Aunts. In his pocket he would carry a copy of Farrar's *Sermons*, detailing: 'The Courage of the Saints possible in Boyhood', 'The Evil of Depression' and 'The Need for Constant Cleansing from Constant Assoilment'. Although Francis enjoyed reading, his academic work was unremarkable. There were numerous studies of the Peninsular War, and essays with titles such as 'Discretion is the better part of Valour'.[13]

Clifton's ambition was to produce the sort of men who would run the British Empire; it was extraordinarily effective at this task. Over the years thousands of Old Cliftonians sallied forth – soldiers, sailors, political officers, box wallahs and colonial servants – to every country that was coloured red on the map. They were generally not the visionaries or the viceroys, but the middle-class stalwarts who formed the backbone of the imperial administration. Their training had given them the discreet arrogance and lack of self-doubt that was required to fight the Great War, or administer thousands of square miles of frontier territory with the aid of nothing but a clipped voice and a light rattan cane. Francis described them as 'men of moral and political integrity, men imbued with the qualities of administration and leadership, men unsparing and unstinting of themselves in their country's service'.[14]

His own year was unusual in that a remarkable number of his contemporaries and friends went on to become eminent in different fields. There was Jack McTaggart ('a limp, melancholy, asymmetrical figure', useless at games) who ended up a revered Hegelian philosopher; William 'Birdie' Birdwood, who was to command the ANZAC forces at Gallipoli and become a Field-Marshal; Arthur Quiller-Couch, the jingoistic Cornish writer and literary critic; Roger Fry, the art critic, who nourished an enduring hatred of Clifton; and Douglas Haig, Chief of Staff in India, architect of trench warfare and Commander-in-Chief of the British Expeditionary Force. Most significant of all was Henry Newbolt, the poet laureate

of High Imperialism, with whom Francis remained friends for life.
After the invasion of Tibet, Newbolt wrote an 'Epistle' honouring
their schooldays together and sent it out to Lhasa:

> The victories of our youth we count for gain
> Only because they steeled our hearts to pain,
> And hold no longer even Clifton great
> Save as she schooled our wills to serve the State.
> Nay, England's self, whose thousand-year-old name
> Burns in our blood like ever-smouldering flame.[15]

Although most of his poems were a substantial technical improvement on this one, Henry Newbolt was not only a poet. He had a
notable influence on the academic development of English literature and language, promoting its study as a means of encouraging
national pride and social cohesion. His famous poem *Vitai Lampada*
encapsulates the philosophy of Clifton. In the opening stanza, the
captain of the school cricket team rallies the players (with 'Ten to
make and the match to win') by appealing to their sense of honour.
In the next stanza he reappears in the thick of a battle, in some
far-flung outpost of the Empire:

> The sand of the desert is sodden red,–
> Red with the wreck of a square that broke;–
> The Gatling's jammed and the colonel dead
> And the regiment blind with dust and smoke.
> The river of death has brimmed his banks,
> And England's far, and Honour a name,
> But the voice of a schoolboy rallies the ranks,
> 'Play up! play up! and play the game!'[16]

The ethos of the Victorian public school extended far into public
life. At a dinner given in his honour after the invasion of Tibet,
Francis spoke of the Old Cliftonians who had accompanied him on
the expedition: 'They all have that trait so characteristic of Clifton,
and which has been so finely inculcated by Henry Newbolt, of
playing the game. They may have nasty jobs to do but it is the
game and they will play it through.'[17] The invasion of Tibet was
itself only an extension of that ultimate manifestation of imperial
game-playing, the Great Game. The players believed they had a
moral duty to propagate the ideas upon which their own civilization
was based. It would be many years before Francis began to challenge that philosophy, and play the game according to different
rules.

Before leaving England to follow Francis Younghusband's footsteps across the Himalayas, I went on a visit to Clifton College, searching for traces of the spirit that had animated him. To my surprise I found the school haunted by memories of past glory, twisting back into its own history.

'Park yourself here,' the Head of Classics said to me, 'while I see what I can find.' I sat at a long oak table in the Percival Library and looked out of a gothic window at the hordes of scurrying boys. They were dressed in rugby kit, whooping, jumping, throwing and running, just as they would have done a century before. 'Practising for Saturday's match,' said the Head of Classics, returning with a manuscript letter in his hand. 'Sirs,' it began:

> We are Old Cliftonians who left the School long ago, but are still, and more than ever, concerned for its lasting welfare . . . The present age is generally felt to be more chaotic than those which went before it . . . Life has become more controversial; controversy is more violent; the unintelligent are perverting science into a new form of superstition . . . We who now write are men of different character and experiences, but we have at least this in common . . . the desire to find God in the universe and to understand our relation to Him.

The letter was signed by Newbolt, Younghusband, Birdwood and Haig. It was the last will and testament of a fading generation, a desperate attempt to make sure their romantic, outdated brand of patriotism did not die with them. According to the 1928 copy of *The Cliftonian* in which it was printed, the letter was 'the outcome of a conversation between Lord Haig and Sir Francis Younghusband during the Prince of Wales's visit to the School last summer'.[18]

'I think we ought to head for Big School now,' said the Head of Classics, 'if we want to be on time for lunch.' He was a short man with craggy eyebrows and punctilious manners. 'You'll have to run the gauntlet, I'm afraid,' he announced, as we strode down flights of stone steps past archaic classrooms and the Newbolt Room. Running the gauntlet involved walking through rows of uninterested boys with loose ties and gelled hair, and a few girls in raunchy versions of the school uniform. I wondered what Colonel Younghusband and Field Marshal Haig would have made of them. 'Gave up formal meals a while back, I'm afraid,' said the Head of Classics apologetically. 'Cafeteria system now. Not the same thing at all.' We ate shredded turkey and lumps of stuffing and gravy off plastic plates.

I sat opposite the Head of History, a quick man with a slightly threatening manner and a pair of Philip Larkin spectacles. He was an expert on Henry Newbolt, I gathered.

'The thing about Newbolt,' I suggested, 'is that however ridiculous his ideas seem now, some of his poems are quite good. I mean from a technical point of view.'

This was clearly a mistake. His eyes narrowed behind the spectacles and he muttered, 'I think that depends on just what you mean by *ridiculous*.'

'Man's just done a book on Haig,' he said to me in the clubbish atmosphere of the Masters' Common Room after lunch. 'Said Haig didn't know what he was up to and falsified his journals. Ridiculous book.'

The Head of Classics took me to look at the Chapel. As he stood in the doorway he whispered, 'Did you ever read Newbolt's poem *Clifton Chapel*? "To set the cause above renown, to love the game beyond the prize." That one.' We marched past a memorial to the Old Cliftonians who were killed in the South African War. In front of the playing fields ('Chap from Clifton once scored 618 runs in one match. World record, you know') was a huge statue of Field Marshal Haig in a greatcoat with a map open on his knee. 'I ran the Clifton Cadet Corps for a long time,' said the Head of Classics. 'Old link between Greek and the Army. Used the Haig statue for Ceremonial Parades. Lined the boys up in front of it and let him do the work for me. Did the trick.'

We walked back to the front of the school. 'It's difficult for us to be dispassionate about this place and its history, you know,' he said, cocking his head a little to one side. 'I sometimes think about what it must have been like for Younghusband and his chums, the boys who were here a century ago. When Clifton had only just been founded. How they must have gone out into the world, so conscious that they were the first, that it was up to them to set the School's reputation. Did all right though, didn't they?'

Having toyed with the idea of going into the Navy, Francis followed his father's advice and took the exam for the Royal Military Academy at Woolwich. After failing twice he tried for Sandhurst instead. Despite some doubts about his shortness and feeble physique, they accepted him in February 1881. He spent a year there learning the intricacies of tactics, manoeuvres and boot polishing. Running continued to excite him, and he came first in a three-mile race between Sandhurst, Woolwich and several universities. Most of his spare time was spent alone, either reading biographies of eminent soldiers or going on long walks. He already had a sense that he would achieve remarkable things, that he had a special purpose of some kind. One day he plucked up his courage and decided to explain this feeling to his eldest sister, Emmie. After dodging round the subject for a while, he suddenly blurted out: 'I feel that one day I shall do something.' But Emmie did not grasp the significance of his proclamation and replied: 'Do your duty.'[19]

Emmie was the only person with whom he felt able to communicate on a personal level. In the absence of any sign of affection from his mother (who had taken to dressing in black and regarded the world as a 'vale of woe') or any softness at Clifton or Sandhurst, he was left emotionally stunted. His moment of contact with Emmie occurred almost by accident. When he was sixteen he fainted in church during the evening service and Emmie took him home to bed. Something unspecified then happened which enabled him to release a flood of emotion, and the suppressed feelings inside him found an outlet for the first time. 'I always felt rather ashamed of myself,' Francis wrote to her afterwards, 'and so my old darling you cannot know the joy I felt that night when you first showed that you loved me. I never could be happier because I had so loved you before that and longed to talk openly with you. But I never could get over my sensitiveness and was always afraid I had done something that you did not like.'[20]

Over the years that followed the link between them grew stronger, although always in an atmosphere of the greatest secrecy. In a family which regarded dancing as evil, they had to be careful to hide their intimacy. Francis would send Emmie letters using a code that was worthy of the Great Game. If the final word of the address was underlined on the envelope, it meant that there were two letters inside – one for public consumption signed 'Ever your affect. brother Frank', and another couched in the language of adolescent love. 'Now my darling,' he wrote in one, 'I got your note just as I was getting into bed so I had a jolly long think of you in bed. I did so long to see you, old horror.'

The period reticence of their correspondence makes it hard to establish the exact nature of the contact between them. Their letters are charged with a high sexual tension, but the passion is never made explicit. Certainly their relationship was emotionally incestuous, although to what extent it also had a physical dimension is open to question. For Francis it was significant primarily as a psychological breakthrough. He became able to articulate his worries and emotions, knowing that Emmie would sympathize. She was six years older than he was, and began to take on the role of his mother, lover, friend and confessor. 'I sometimes wish we had known each other sooner but I think it was God's will that we shd. not,' Francis told her. 'I would have been too young for such love as yours.'

At times Emmie was almost overwhelmed by the intensity of his passion. 'Oh darling how jolly that was when you stooped over me & kissed me. I shall never forget that night . . .' She could share his fears and his guilt. 'I have been awfully wicked, more wicked than I think you would think possible,' he had written to her during his final term at Clifton. 'O my Emmie you know my great sin though I can't say anything to you about it. You don't know how great it is and how hard to conquer; but I must and with God's grace I will conquer it.'[21] Throughout the correspondence his 'great sin' is never specified, but given the moral climate of the time there is little reason to suppose it was anything more heinous than masturbation or teenage eroticism.

In May 1882, with Tsar Alexander II dead from an assassin's bomb and the British busily advancing through Egypt, Francis was commissioned into the King's Dragoon Guards, having passed out of Sandhurst 'with honours'. The regiment was stationed at Meerut, near Delhi, and he made arrangements to sail immediately on a cargo ship. His elder brother George was already out in India, having just won a medal in the Second Afghan War. By this time his parents had returned to Britain to settle in Southsea, John Younghusband having retired as Inspector General of Police in the

Punjab. He gave Francis numerous instructions regarding appropriate conduct in India, and wrote letters to his friends in high places announcing the imminent arrival of his son.

John's opinions had changed substantially as the years went by. He had arrived in India as a soldier of fortune fighting on behalf of the East India Company, but departed a convinced imperialist. His experiences during the Mutiny had persuaded him that 'a few good men' could control India by the application of careful pressure at the appropriate points, and that the British had a duty to 'civilise' the races under their control. This sense of mission was reinforced, rather than challenged, by his strong Evangelical Christianity. John Younghusband also had an unshakeable belief (which he passed on to Francis) that the Russians were intent on annexing Afghanistan and northern India, and he gave several public lectures on this subject.

As a parent John was strict and formal, but he had a sparkle that his children admired. In old age, Francis would write that his father and George Curzon were the two people who had done most for him during his life. Clara Younghusband maintained a similar Victorian formality, but it was rarely tempered by any obvious signs of affection. The Bible ruled her actions, and she regarded 'sentimentality' towards her offspring as a weakness. When Francis left for India in July 1882, knowing that he was unlikely to see his parents for at least ten years, he was amazed by his mother's display of emotion. 'I was again astonished when I said good bye. She threw her arms round me and squeezed me to her . . . Never before had I seen her so demonstrative.'[22] Throughout his life he was conscious of his failure to establish a proper relationship with his mother, unfairly blaming himself for their mutual remoteness.

Francis sailed out of Liverpool Docks aged barely nineteen, the wispy beginnings of a life-long moustache sprouting from his upper lip. His opinions and his feelings were conditioned closely by the strictness of his upbringing, and the sense of mission that had been instilled into him at Clifton. He was solemn, intense, nervous, profoundly religious and somewhat shorter than he felt was appropriate. Like Henry Morton Stanley he claimed to be five feet five inches, and nurtured an intense but unrequited desire to grow taller. There were only three other passengers on the ship, so he paced the deck and sat in his cabin reading books about Jesus. Sea voyages were to play an important part in his life. He was to write books, set a chapter of a novel, discuss philosophy with Bertrand Russell and meet his wife on board ship, but on this occasion there was little excitement. Memories of his sister were always on his mind. 'Oh darling the parting was so hard I don't think I realised it at the time but now when I am all alone I feel what it is to be without my precious Emmie,' he wrote to her in a letter. 'I was so glad when you talked about keeping house for me because that is what I have always longed for.' By this stage he was justifying their closeness in spiritual terms. 'Oh my darling Emmie this love of ours is indeed a blessing as it brings us nearer to God and helps us realise what he is, the God of Love.'[23]

The ship steamed across the Mediterranean to Port Said, through the Suez Canal and the Red Sea and into the Indian Ocean. After three weeks it docked at Bombay, the trading port that was used for trips to and from Britain. 'Awfully rum sort of place is Bombay,' wrote Francis to his mother. 'Strange houses and wretched little ones all jumbled up together. The native houses not over clean.' 'May God bless you dear,' came the reply, 'and prosper you for this World and lead you on the bright happy way of true Peace and Holiness.'[24] Steam trains brought him to Meerut, the hot, dull town where the Mutiny had broken out. His father's string-pulling ensured he was given a good reception by the regiment, and he was quartered in the adjutant's bungalow. Within days he had employed a sweeper, a *khitmudgar* (to wait at his table), two *punkah wallahs* (to keep him cool) and a bearer. Francis had become Younghusband, Second Lieutenant in the 1st King's Dragoon Guards. 'I am awfully pleased with everything I have seen in the regiment so far,' he told his father. 'The officers seem an awfully good set of fellows doing their best to make me feel at home.'[25]

But before long Younghusband was feeling out of place. 'The talk in Mess is very bad at times,' he told Emmie, 'nothing but scandal about people in the station . . . the bad seem to have the upper hand.' He had arrived with great hopes, dreaming of martial glory and religious discussions, only to find his brother cavalry officers concerned principally with sins of the flesh. Most of them were rich, able to keep strings of polo ponies and hordes of servants. They drank and swore and visited the Rag (the regimental brothel, with a separate section for officers) which was staffed by Indian women and subsidized from the Canteen Fund. The officers rose at 4.50 each morning, did drill until 7.00 and then galloped their horses for a couple of hours before breakfasting off porridge and quails. During the blinding heat of the day they would retire to their bungalows, and at 6.00 reappear to play tennis or go shooting before dinner.

Younghusband felt bored and melancholic. There was only one officer with whom he felt relaxed, Captain Hennah the adjutant. He was horrified by the antics he witnessed all around him: 'It is more than I ever thought possible from so called ladies and gentlemen.'[26] Yet as the weather cooled and the months passed, life became easier. For all the talk of whoring and gambling, many of his colleagues were good natured and likeable. 'There is no doubt that as a young man I was a prig,' Younghusband wrote in the last year of his life. 'For some reason or other earnest Christians are inclined to be prigs. At school we were exhorted to be "examples", and there is nothing more awful than a young man trying to be an example to fellow young men.'[27]

Time went slowly, his mood going through dramatic swings. He felt stifled by the drill and the route marches, while he had a sense that his military training lacked any real purpose. In the spring of 1883 Hennah died of fever, which made Francis retreat further into loneliness. During his days on leave he went on excursions into the jungle, coming across members of the Baiga tribe. The wild animals delighted him. To the consternation of his companions, he would sit for hours peering through his field-glasses at parrots, monkeys and leopards; without raising his gun.

Towards the end of the year the King's Dragoon Guards were sent north to Rawal Pindi in response to growing fear about the Russian threat. Younghusband's excitement at moving to the edge of the Himalayas was compounded when he was appointed adjutant. Here at last was an opportunity for action; he would spread Clifton's ideas of athletic morality to those around him and infuse the regiment with esprit de corps. His strong personal ambition, which until then had been left stagnant in the face of military formality, found an outlet. He laid down plans for games and sports and exhibitions of fraternal unity, enlisting the support of senior officers. For as Peter Fleming observed in *Bayonets to Lhasa*, Younghusband 'was by nature a thruster'.[28]

In his novel *But In Our Lives: A Romance of the Indian Frontier*, Younghusband gives a vivid picture of his life as a keen young officer. It is directly autobiographical, with the exception of the ending when the hero, Evan Lee, dies a heroic death on the frontier. When the book was published in 1926 it was given good reviews. The *Madras Mail* wrote that it 'cannot be too highly commended', while *The Spectator* felt it was 'sincere and sometimes beautiful'. The *Pioneer* dissented, calling it 'verbose, ill-arranged, in certain directions verging almost upon platitude', although the *Sketch* insisted it was 'a capital book to give a boy of eighteen with his own way to make in one of the fighting services'.[29] Today the book seems stunningly naive and saccharine, but it gives an extraordinary insight into the priorities and outlook of the time, and contemporary military attitudes to women, sexuality and 'games'.

Evan Lee (the name presumably intended as a desperate pun on 'heavenly') is a two-dimensional, saintly character who is brought up in the west of England by strict aunts and sent to Sandhurst, where he resists lewd talk and leads 'a pure, healthy manly life'. His sister is 'almost religiously devoted to him and he to her'. On joining a cavalry regiment out in India he shares a bungalow with a major who 'was irreverently called "Tummy" by the subalterns on account of his ample waist measurement'. He soon feels that stronger emphasis needs to be placed on character and welfare. Fortunately the Colonel shares this view, and invites Lee to counter 'that eternal beer-swilling in the canteen'.

'The Colonel then referred to a matter which we would all rather shut our eyes to. But we cannot altogether blind ourselves to the brutal side of life . . . There before their eyes was the terrible fact that numbers of able-bodied men were incapacitated for active service through diseases contracted from women.' The Quartermaster is summoned to join in the discussion, and suggests that copulation is a consequence of human nature. '"I can quote high medical authority against that view,"' retorts the Colonel. '"Intercourse is not a necessity . . . We're playing the very devil if we lead men to think that yielding is manly . . .Containing themselves will be very good discipline for them. They'll be all the better for it. I won't have my men defiling themselves. I want you to look to it, Lee."'

Lee looks to it by enlisting the help of 'Tiger' Tennington, who 'has a good way with the men. He was brought up in the stables and with gamekeepers and such-like and knows how to deal with them.' Together they organize football, cricket, a regimental newspaper, 'games and sport of all kinds, and theatricals, sing-songs, and all the rest of it'. The soldiers are dragooned into line and forced to 'play up and make things go'. Tennington writes a farcical play about the regiment which is performed to great acclaim, and boxing matches are organized with the York Fusiliers. 'Regimental sports were held, too, and gymkhanas with competitions which both required skill and afforded amusement.'

As a result of the sporting activity the men thrive, and the incidence of VD declines. But, ever the thruster, Lee sees he must inspire the soldiers with spiritual fervour. Only then will they realize the true dangers of defilement:

> Every mother must be yearning that her own son should keep himself uncontaminated. And a son should think of his mother's feelings and of all she has gone through to bring him up. He should loathe to tarnish his purity. And besides this there should be as much care taken to keep his soul unspotted from the world as there is to keep his uniform and accoutrements clean. If religion could see to keeping his soul unspotted, his soul would keep his body pure.[30]

But In Our Lives ends with Evan Lee being killed by a huge Gulistani warrior. As the last post is sounded, the gallant British officer is buried in a shallow mountain grave – an apotheosis that Francis Younghusband was never to achieve, despite his reckless acts.

TWO

Two Journeys to the Mountains

After eight months of immersion in Younghusband's papers, I flew to India to follow his trail through the foothills of the Himalayas, to catch the sensations of the places he had known and try to encounter his experiences at first hand. I had tried to find a boat, tried for a serene journey through the Suez Canal and the warmth of the Indian Ocean, but such travel was no longer practical. Languid sea voyages from Britain to India had disappeared with ship's biscuits and deck quoits.

During a stop-over at Kabul I had my first taste of the wildness of High Asia. The airport was unconvincing, a scrubby expanse of huts and dust dotted with scavenging dogs and people, the product of many years of war. Its desolation was fringed by rigid khaki hills. In the distance sat towering snow mountains, and beyond them Gilgit, Chitral, the Pamirs: outposts that had been fought over by invading armies for centuries, the places where Younghusband went exploring. I caught my first sense of the audacity with which he and his generation had adopted this tough, uncompromising and deeply fractured region when the plane stopped on the runway and we were taken across the reddish soil to one of the huts. In this rickety terminal I sat down on the floor and awaited my connecting flight to Delhi. Outside in the dust were men in woollen cloaks and Pathan hats, and two brown-suited officials perched in a tinselly old Ford Cortina. Beside me was a young Afghan couple with a baby. The wife reminded me of Clara Younghusband, dressed utterly in black with a book of prayers in her hand.

The gunfire in the distance got faster: what had previously been a mild irritation now became an insistent thud that filled our hut. Then a shell exploded on the edge of the runway. The yellow grass and some straggly bushes went up in flames. The Ford Cortina and an ancient fire engine lumbered slowly towards it as the fire spread. So we sat, listening to history tearing into the present.

I tried to rationalize the dreamlike nature of this place of seemingly continual war as we were herded on to the plane for Delhi by frightened guards with simple rifles, but all my attempts to understand how people lived in such chaos fell in tatters after we took off. As we cleared Kabul the pilot fired off flares to confuse any heat-seeking missiles: we headed for India, a blaze of fireworks in our wake.

After two days of scrabbling confusion in New Delhi I took some buses to Dharamsala, where the pregnant Clara had waited during the Mutiny. I trudged up the hill through damp dark green trees until I reached the Church of St John in the Wilderness. In the graveyard were broken stones covered with patches of grass, and a huge marble mausoleum.

'He was one of our first Viceroys,' announced a keen voice from behind the tomb. 'He expired while executing his official duties here. His great son came to visit us once, the new Lord Elgin, and he made a donation for the upkeep.'

The voice emanated from a short, plump, beaming figure in a white robe, who clutched my hand in a lingering salutation. 'I am the pastor here, always happy to welcome a new friend. Will you be so kind as to make a reading for us tomorrow?' He was, he told me, a Dravidian from Kerala who had been educated by missionaries and sent north to minister to the occasional Christians in the Himalayas. 'Our congregation is small but cheerful. You see many visitors are preferring the Buddhist teaching.' The pastor pointed up the hill. When the Dalai Lama escaped from Tibet in 1959, it transpired, his exiled government had been established at Dharamsala. Since then the place had become an outpost of Tibetan refugees.

On Sunday morning when the mist was still down I walked through the pine forest to the church, and found the pastor in the company of two elderly hill-men and an Australian tourist. At the back of the church was a flock of cagouled evangelists from Düsseldorf, busily rehearsing 'Morning Has Broken'. It was a confusing service, conducted in Hindi and English alternately, with what I took to be occasional bursts of Tamil. The pastor enjoyed it hugely, his voice rising to a squeak during some of the prayers. Streams of sunlight shot through the high stained-glass windows behind him, and on to the stone tablets which remembered earlier members of the congregation; soldiers, traders and tea planters, dead from dysentery or fever. A lieutenant had been 'mauled by a bear', while a captain had died with his 'faithful servant' by his side. One man was defined not by his rank, his regiment or his manner of death, but simply with the bald words: 'A Wykehamist'.

The rustling and shuffling made me realize it was time for my reading, so I walked forward to the curling steps and up into the pulpit, only to notice the pastor semaphoring wildly. I wondered why, incuriously, as the floor of the pulpit splintered into a cloud of woodworm dust and I sank downwards. The whole edifice toppled slowly to one side. 'And he cried mightily,' I began finally, 'Babylon the great is fallen, is fallen, and is become the habitation of devils, and the hold of every foul spirit, and a cage of every unclean and hateful bird.' The pastor crossed himself repeatedly, swaying gently in the whistling draught.

After the service and several apologies I climbed up the slope behind the church to look for John and Clara Younghusband's house. I had one of her sketches showing its rough location. The most likely house seemed to be a picturesque old building with flowerpots set out along the verandah. It had a gabled slate roof above the doorway and sheets of corrugated iron by the chimney. There was no one at home, so I walked through the rhododendron bushes to the village of McLeod Ganj. Later I found out the house belonged to Jetsun Pema, the Dalai Lama's formidable younger sister. History had come full circle: Younghusband went to Tibet, and now the Tibetans had come to Younghusband's house.

I walked down the hill to the Dharamsala tea plantations.

In April 1884 Younghusband was given two months' leave from his regiment. He took a slow train from Rawal Pindi to the hills, heading in search of the memory of his Uncle Robert, his childhood hero. Robert Shaw had flourished out in India and become a successful Dharamsala tea planter, but his real interest lay to the north. A Muslim state had just been established in Turkestan by the redoubtable Yakub Beg, the self-proclaimed King of Kashgaria. Shaw thought this would offer a new market for his tea, since supplies from China had been curtailed. In 1868 he set off from Leh, accompanied by a caravan laden with gifts, guns and bundles of tea.

Three months later he reached Yarkand, and after a short delay was permitted to proceed northwards. Robert Shaw became the first European to enter the fabled city of Kashgar, with its huge mud walls bounded by the Pamirs and the Taklamakan desert. When the summons came, he was ushered through rows of archers and silk-robed courtiers into the august presence of Yakub Beg, descendant of Tamburlaine the Great. Trade was discussed, presents exchanged, and the celebrated Dharamsala tea sipped. Shaw thought his mission had succeeded, only to find he was under house arrest. Another British traveller, George Hayward, had reached Kashgar on a mission from the Royal Geographical Society. Yakub Beg felt threatened by these foreigners, and by his powerful neighbours, Russia and India. After a few months of waiting he decided to see if he could play off the British against the Russians. Shaw was released and given messages of goodwill for the 'Lord Sahib', the Viceroy Lord Mayo.

Upon return, Shaw and Hayward found they had become celebrated explorers, and the RGS awarded them gold medals. Hayward took the opportunity to set off on a solo mission to Dardistan, only to have his head chopped off by brigands, which later prompted Henry Newbolt to write the poem *He Fell Among Thieves*. Meanwhile Shaw forsook the tea trade for the life of a freelance government servant, being appointed Political Agent in Yarkand where he compiled a book on Central Asian linguistics. Later he visited Burma and became, so he said, the first human ever to enter the presence of a Burmese monarch without first 'taking off his shoes and assuming a crouching attitude'.[1] In 1879 Robert Shaw died of a rheumatic fever in Mandalay, aged only thirty-nine.

Here was the intrepid figure who inspired the early years of Francis Younghusband's life. Uncle Robert, with his flamboyant Yarkandi costumes and exotic tales of oriental potentates, was worth following over the Himalayas. Younghusband walked from the railhead at Pathankot towards Dharamsala, and after three days reached Robert Shaw's old house. It sat on the top of a small hill, surrounded by deodar trees and lush greenery. Although Shaw had died nearly five years before, the house was untouched. Younghusband pushed open the door to find crumbling mementoes and 'books too, and maps, and old manuscripts. I was among the relics of an explorer, at the very house in which he had planned his explorations, and from which he had started to accomplish them. I pored over the books and maps, and talked for hours with the old servants, till the spirit of exploration gradually entered my soul . . .'[2]

Bounding down the road with the traditional arrogance of the young army officer, Younghusband was heading for the Rhotang Pass. In Indian lore, the Rhotang marked 'the end of the habitable world' – the Himalayan division between India proper and Lahaul. By the end of the first day he thought he should be close to the village of Dadh. 'So I asked again how far Dadh was and the man said two miles. So I asked if I could see the village so he said yes and showed me a village behind me,' Younghusband wrote in his journal, adding that poor directions were 'the sort of thing one has to expect from these natives, & then people make a row if you lick them'.[3] When he wrote an account of the journey forty years later, he regretted his attitude. 'I rather think I said and did things of which I would now be heartily ashamed.'[4]

Accompanying him were two mules, a muleman, a servant and a dog. For nearly a fortnight Younghusband would march ahead each morning with a pocketful of chapattis, and meet up with his servants at nightfall. He slept in dak bungalows – government rest huts which were (and still are) dotted around remote parts of India. Along the route he met holy men and merchants, even 'an odd looking native dressed in yellow' who turned out to be a recruiter for the Salvation Army.[5] There were 'almost English hedges of wild roses, both white and pink, now in full bloom', a welcome change from the drabness of the plains. He 'stopped at Palumpur, one of the prettiest places I know – almost like a park – with a bazaar at one end, and the houses of the European tea planters dotted about among the deodar cedars, firs and pines; while above the tops of the trees rose the pure white outline of the Himalayan rampart.'

At Baijnath he found 'another witness to men's craving for satisfaction of their soul needs – a beautiful Hindu temple, centuries and centuries old, far older than Westminster Abbey'. He 'could not help being impressed by that temple at Baijnath, so ancient, so grand and simple in its general outline, so rich and fine in its detailed carvings'. Already he was developing a fascination with the antiquity and devotion of Eastern spirituality. Two nights later he found a dangerously ill man in a caravanserai, and had his feet kissed when he dosed him with chlorodyne. Breaking through a pine and flower forest, he passed an endless succession of waterfalls: 'I could lie flat down by the edge of a stream, and with my face on the running water gulp down mouthful after mouthful.' Mountains, and the Himalayas in particular, were to form an essential dimension in Younghusband's spiritual theories: his ideas combined the Romantic tradition of Wordsworth and Coleridge with Hindu and Buddhist faith in sacred mountains.

As he entered the Kulu valley he ran to keep warm until he reached Sultanpur. There 'I saw a fine Rampur Chudder which I bought for Rs.6 . . . It was of thick home-spun wool and twelve feet long, so could be doubled up,' he wrote many years later. 'That blanket I had with me on all my Himalayan journeys. And I have it to this day.' Towards the snow-line there were 'encampments of traders waiting for the Rotang Pass to clear of snow so that they could cross into Lahoul, and proceed thence to Ladak, and some, perhaps, even to Yarkand,' Younghusband recorded. 'They were tanned and hardy men, not over-clean, but genial and polite.' With them were flocks of sheep and goats laden with grain to sell in the mountain villages. 'The mountains, the men, and the animals all seemed extraordinarily close to each other.'[6]

The 'wonderful healing qualities' of the hot springs at Vashist detained him – 'some of them are too hot for your hand to bear' – but soon he was off again, following the Beas towards its source as it foamed through chasms 'as deep as the Avon from the suspension bridge at Clifton'. Two days of steep climbing across packed snow brought him towards the edge of the Rhotang Pass. The journey marked a turning point in his life. It made him see that he did not have to spend the rest of his days caught in drab regimental life. If he could only find a way into frontier work and surveying, he would be able to become a traveller; even an explorer. In the distance were the white peaks of the Pir Panjal range. His head was splitting from the effect of the altitude and he felt exhausted, but he kept on walking. 'A most frightful wind was blowing – intensely cold wh. pierced me through and through although I was wearing double kit,' he wrote in his journal that night.

'It was the coldest wind I have ever felt.'[7] There he stood, teetering on the crest of the Rhotang Pass.

Rattling along through the Dharamsala tea plantations in a maroon taxi, brimming with slightly feverish biographer's zeal, I was hoping that I would find Robert Shaw's old house. Perhaps somewhere in a mildewed trunk in the basement might be his old books, and maybe the remains of his maps and manuscripts. When we reached a small hill surrounded by tea plants, I got out and inspected a wobbly wooden building. Inside there was an elderly tea-drying machine, and a pair of loitering pickers. They took me to the owner of the plantation, an old man who seemed to be thriving on the commercial foresight of Uncle Robert.

Mr Mann had short eyelashes, a scrubby beard and a natty white turban. His eyes were uncontrollable. In attendance upon him was a boy servant, carrying a rug and a stick. After the appropriate greetings I told him I was searching for an old house called Easthome.

'It used to be owned by a planter called Robert Shaw a long time ago.'

'In the Britishers' time?'

'Yes.'

He took his stick from the attendant and leant forward on to it: 'I remember Shaw-sahib. He was a great man.'

Astonished, I asked him again: surely he could not have known Shaw? He insisted he remembered Shaw very well. But that would make him well over a hundred, I thought to myself, a hundred and twenty at least. He certainly looked very wrinkled, so perhaps it was true? After all, Younghusband had believed that highly realized spiritual practitioners could live for a very long time. I tried to remain calm, knowing that, at the very outset of my trip, I was about to uncover some solid historical evidence, perhaps find some clues that would bring my academic research in London to life. Maybe my whole journey in Asia would be littered with easy, tangible discoveries of this kind.

'Mr Shaw was a very reverenced man. His house . . .' At this point Mr Mann twirled his stick in the manner of a drum majorette, and finally settled on a decaying corrugated-iron shack '. . . is that one.' Inside I could find nothing but heaps of tea. There were no old foundations, or anything that indicated a proper building had once rested there. Mr Mann silenced my inquiries and took me round the plantation.

'My tea garden was bombed in the war by enemy planes,' he insisted. 'In the Blitz. And now we are menaced by tigers. You should see my tiger heads – last week I shot another one.' Given his physical state this seemed unlikely. We went on a lingering perambulation around the amphitheatre of dark green tea plants. There was no sign of tigers. Back at the taxi he shook my hand firmly. As I reclined into the back seat, which was upholstered in shag-pile carpet, he banged the roof of the car with his stick.

'We had losses here in the great earthquake,' he said solemnly. His eyes were flickering in every direction. 'Many cattle were killed by the Rolling Stones.'

'This guy is crazy,' said the Tibetan taxi driver, twirling his right index finger beside his temple as we trundled down the hill. It was true that Mr Mann was eccentric, and his conversation confusing. I was particularly troubled by a passing remark he had made about the great plays that Mr Shaw had written. I felt certain *High Tartary and Yarkand* was his only published work.

'What academic qualifications, please?'

'I've got a degree in English literature.'

'An honours degree?'

'Yes.'

'You are a scholar?'

I was sitting in the Judicial Complex in Dharamsala, a huge, grey multi-storey car park of a building. Across the desk was the Senior Sub Judge cum Chief Judicial Magistrate, Mr J. N. Barowalia MA (Eco.) Ll.B. HPJS. He wore a cricketing blazer and had a carefully groomed black moustache. Every so often our dialogue would pause while he signed documents with a long gold pen and a flourish. A flunkey glided in, bowed, and handed me a cup of sweet tea. Mr Barowalia, they said, had records on the provenance of local houses.

'This was the residence of Sir Younghusband?'

'No, of his uncle, Robert Shaw.'

The Judge banged a bell on his desk. More tea appeared.

'You are wishing to purchase this property?'

'No. No, I just want to go and have a look at it. Out of historical interest.'

'Oh my goodness,' he said slowly. 'You wish to see the house for historical purposes?'

'Yes, that's right.'

'In which case I understand, and am able to assist you.' He stood up. 'For historical information you must approach Mr Nowrojee.'

Nowrojee General Stores was a stately, decaying wooden structure in the hill village of McLeod Ganj. There were old-fashioned tin signs advertising Bovril and cough medicine, gargantuan glass jars of boiled sweets and every variety of biscuit. The proprietor was a composed Parsee in a tweed jacket, thin and distinguished, with a hint of a sneer. His family had owned the store for over a century. Concessions to the modern era were not going to be made.

'I don't know anything about it,' he sniffed, 'although I used to supply soda water to the barracks down that side. Now please excuse me.'

On my next visit I was more circumspect. After ten minutes of formal conversation I was ushered into the back of the shop. Mr Nowrojee produced a dusty book of photographs and a pair of quizzing glasses.

'Take this, for example,' he said, gesturing towards a photograph of a red stone pillar box. It bore the legend: 'G. R. Kaiser-i-Hind' and beside it stood a uniformed *havildar*. Mr Nowrojee led me to the door, and pointed through the sunlight at a heap of reddish stone. 'That is it now – smashed into pieces by miscreants during the summer. I tell you, these fellows have no sense of history,' he mourned, flicking his long fingers at a posse of young Hindus with a motorbike. They wore tight polyester trousers, and one had a T-shirt emblazoned in turquoise with the suggestion 'TRUST ME'.

Mr Nowrojee turned to the darkness of his shop. 'We had a severe earthquake in Dharamshala in 1905,' he muttered wistfully, handing me a glass of ginger beer. 'The spire fell off John in the Wilderness, and the buildings got knocked flat.' He fingered his tie, indicating dismissal. 'You won't find any old planters' houses; not here.'

I purchased a tin of kippered herring and departed for the Rhot-ang Pass.

I realized that the first part of the journey would be unlikely to evoke many echoes of 1884. Mountain tracks had made way for crumbling tarmac roads, while 'Palumpur, one of the prettiest places I know' was now a mass of chai stalls and reversing buses. The Shiva temple at Baijnath was still impressively simple and grand. A sadhu with glued hair and a gingery beard watched over it, accompanied by a squad of sharp-toothed monkeys. Although the ancient stone carvings were fine and delicate, some of them had been coated roughly with fluorescent paint. It was Holi, the Hindu festival when people celebrate the end of winter by throwing coloured powder and water over each other. The wrinkly sadhu pointed gleefully at a statue of Ganesh, the elephant-headed deity of wisdom. Great, orange globules were dripping down the elephant's trunk. Oblivious to the demands of the heritage industry, the sadhu did not regard Ganesh's unnatural brightness as the desecration of an ancient monument. Rather it was a reason for celebration, for joy.

I took a bus into the Kulu valley, where the air was thinner and the scenery was like the Scottish Highlands: huge rocks, bursting waterfalls, skeins of wild flowers and long sweeps of pine forest. The people looked different, fair-skinned and Himalayan. The women wore thickly woven tartan woollen dresses of pale green, orange and pink, held together by giant silver hatpins, while the men had rough grey coats with high collars and pill-box hats with a coloured band across the front. It was cold by the time I reached the town of Kulu (which Younghusband had known as Sultanpur) so I went to the bazaar to buy a shawl. One stall holder had a fine Rampur chudder which was priced at Rs 1400. He would make no profit at all, he said, if he sold it for any less, and his family would go hungry in winter. It was soft and smelt of kerosene and goat. He sold it for Rs 600. At the village of Vashist I found a gathering of Gaddi shepherds from Lahaul and Spiti, some Tibetan refugees, and Indians from the nearby town of Manali. They told me the Rhotang Pass was closed until May, but I was determined to try to cross it.

On a quiet March morning, sniggering slightly at the absurdity and impossibility of what I was trying to do, I put on a pair of ancient knee breeches, climbing boots, puttees, two shirts, and a thick coat. I felt it was important to catch the spirit of Younghusband's original journey across the pass, even if the damp woollen breeches did make my legs itch. In my rucksack was the long Kulu shawl with its beautifully coloured edges. At 3 a.m. I set off from the main street in Manali in a battered jeep with some silent old men and two goats. The goats wore elegant pouches of grain across each shoulder. I had a dull, heavy lump in the bottom of my stomach as we drove towards the mountains, turning corner after corner. The jeep dropped the men and the goats at Palchan and we carried on up the track until the beam of the headlights met a wall of packed ice. The driver warned me that I should be nearing the crest of the Rhotang by sunrise, or else . . . He mimed a person slithering down into a melting snow-drift, never to reappear. I began to walk through the crisp snow and the darkness.

It was easy at first, trudging onwards, leaping occasionally over holes in the curve of the ice, or up brief banks of rock. There was no vegetation, but silvery stone and packed brown earth sprouted from the blank whiteness of the snow. The air was so thin that the jagged peaks ahead of me looked miniature, as if I could hop over them one by one. Sometimes I ran a short distance, exhilaration surging upwards through my ankles. I felt that anything could happen, that all things were possible in this detached, mystical, mountainous world. Even Younghusband could happen, without any particular wonder. I half expected to see him, striding along in the distance with short steps and a determined gaze, gobbets of ice hanging from his moustaches.

The greyness of the night began to fade, but the wind was getting stronger. I met up with a Lahauli called Prem who was going to Kelong to see his mother. We walked together, developing a steady regularity of pace, the rhythm that comes from having another person moving beside you. At the crest of the Rhotang the noise of the wind was all about us. It threw random swirls of snow which collided like the spray of ocean waves. We stopped at a heap of boulders and drank some water. There was a mani stone and a string of prayer flags, and a painted metal sign to tell us we were 4000 metres above the level of the sea.

As we tramped onward towards Lahaul the squalling wind seemed to become colder, more intense and piercing. Although the sun was coming up, it was hard to see what lay around and ahead of us. At times I almost felt that there was a third person walking with us, an extra presence marching forward on the same cold trail.

'Rhotang La,' said Prem, 'means the Pass of Bones. The Rhotang Pass is the Bones Pass.' It would have been easy to stumble off the trail and go to sleep. My head felt compressed by the thin air and my legs were working slowly.

Gradually it became easier as we descended into the valley. The surface of the snow was starting to melt and we could slip and slide down the slope, avoiding the edges that jutted out to nowhere. The wind had dropped now, and Prem turned west towards Kelong. I carried on until I reached Gramphoo, a scrappy settlement of a few wooden shacks. After eating bread and dried apricots I followed the course of the iced-up river through the ravine towards Khokser. On either side were the steep, brown edges of the mountains, with their towering snow peaks. The view was monumentally bleak. There was a harsh, barren, depressing wonder about it. The people did not live off the land, they survived off it, born by chance into a dislocated valley between Tibet and India.

I watched a mother and son dig up a store of potatoes that they had buried deep in the soil the previous autumn. The digging was difficult because the earth was frozen at the surface. When they had broken through, the mother climbed into the pit and the potatoes ascended like precious stones. I pitched my tent nearby, next to a stream of icy water which was running off the glacier behind. I lit a fire and mixed dried soup with glacier water. Then I ate some chapattis and Mr Nowrojee's herrings. It was getting dark. I wrapped myself up in the Kulu shawl and faded into sleep, watching the moonlight on the snow, the moon on the mountains.

Climbing back over the Rhotang Pass the next morning, the sun was brilliant and the air was calm. It seemed incredible, watching the rays bounce off that placid white sea, to think the ground had ever been a flurry of swirling snowstorms and ear-shattering vortices of wind. I felt an elation at the unique beauty of the Himalayas, and rather pleased with myself for having followed Younghusband's route all this way. As I passed the stones and the prayer flags at the mid-way point, I could see figures in the distance. At first I thought it was a flock of displaced sheep, but then I saw there were people moving up the slope. There were men with crates of vegetables strapped to their backs, others with flour or sugar on their heads, even an old woman carrying what looked like a drum of kerosene. Two or three barely teenage children were scrabbling through the snow. They had cloth-wrapped bundles over their shoulders and their shoes were made of lacerated strips of car tyre. They were taking provisions to Khokser, one man said. They had to go while the weather was good. People needed food on the Lahaul side.

I trudged down towards Palchan, pensively. I had thought my journey was an achievement, but wondered now if it was anything more than a romantic stroll. In summer you could drive much of the way in a truck. People had been crossing the Rhotang Pass, the Pass of Bones, for thousands of years. They had crossed it because they needed to get to Leh or Yarkand or Kashgar to trade, to survive. The trails of the great explorers have usually been tramped for centuries by merchants and nomads, pilgrims and shepherds.

'It was the coldest wind I have ever felt,' wrote Francis Young-husband. He pushed on towards the Lahaul side of the Rhotang Pass, and 'slid nearly the whole way down. Once I tumbled over on my face and went down at a great pace but luckily I managed to stop myself with my alpenstock.' When he got to Khokser he found a rest hut lying under the winter snow. 'It is probably the coldest house on the face of this earth . . . I lit a fire but it had no effect. I made some Liebig's soup and had some kippered herring (tinned).' He ate some chapattis but still felt hungry, so he went for a disconsolate walk and, looking upwards, 'saw a sight that it would be worth while coming all the way for . . . One peak after another was lit up till at last the moon rose on the whole valley & anything more glorious you can never have seen.' 'For the air at this height . . . is clear like crystal; the snowy whiteness of the mountains' is 'insubstantial as a dream, and glowing with a radiance not of earth.'

Younghusband wandered around Khokser next day, and then began to climb again. 'The ascent from Lahoul back to the top of the Rotang Pass was fearfully steep and very slippery.' He crossed the pass and marched as quickly as he could towards 'something like civilisation, with plenty of food. I had had my little fling. I had caught just a glimpse of the other side of the Himalayan range. But I thirsted for more mountain beauty.' It had been enough to convince him that his destiny lay in travel and exploration. He formed brilliant plans inside his head, and imagined journey after journey to the unseen lands of Central Asia, to the source of the Indus. He would go to Tibet, he decided, and 'come to know the curious people of that secluded country, make a great name for myself, and be known ever after as a famous traveller'.[8]

THREE

Playing Great Games beyond Manchuria

Returning to the monotony of regimental life in Rawal Pindi, Younghusband determined to travel once more to the mountains. He wrote to the Secretary of the Royal Geographical Society in London for information about the forbidden lands beyond the Himalayas. 'In answer to your letter I am afraid I can give little information,' replied Bates of the RGS, 'almost all the knowledge we have received of late years regarding southern or western Tibet is from the surveys of the Pundits . . . If you succeed in crossing the frontier with the faithful servants who were with your uncle, you could not fail in making interesting discoveries and it would be a pity not to acquire knowledge of mapping before then.'[1]

Younghusband promptly learned the skills of mapping and surveying, and pestered senior officers to send him on reconnaissance work. At the end of the year he was seconded to the Divisional Staff, and sent north to explore routes and passages across the Indus from the frontier. Evidently impressed by his zeal, the Staff sent for him again at the beginning of 1885 to inspect sites for the location of mobilized regiments. Russian troops were moving towards Afghanistan, and under the terms of the Anglo-Afghan agreement an Indian army of 20,000 soldiers was being sent to the frontier to deter them. Following the assassination of Tsar Alexander II four years earlier, internal unrest in Russia had been deflected by eastern expansion. In 1884 the Turcomans of Merv had sworn allegiance to the new Tsar, giving the Russians a significant strategic foothold a few miles north of India's border. Younghusband's task was to work out in advance which areas would be suitable for military encampments, and to act as a 'galloper' for various generals. He felt excited by the action and the glamour of his new role, writing to Emmie, 'Everything is perfectly prepared out here – we have thoroughly good men at the head and if we don't give those Russians the jolliest hiding they have had for some time I will eat my hat.'[2]

On the last day of March 1885 the Russian army advanced and

seized the small Afghan town of Penjdeh (or Pandjeh). Gladstone obtained a vote of credit from the House of Commons and a major war between Russia and Britain looked set to break out. But following mediation the Russians withdrew a few miles, and a Boundary Commission was established which eventually handed over the town to Russia in exchange for Afghan control of a strategic pass. Although the British government maintained that the settlement was an example of wise diplomacy, it looked to Younghusband and other young officers like a humiliation. India had been left looking vulnerable, which strengthened the position of the 'hawks' in the administration. It was at this time that William Lockhart (who later became the Jang-i-Lat Sahib or Commander-in-Chief of the army in India) claimed to have spotted Younghusband's talents as a potential spy; but it was Sir Charles Macgregor who sent him on his first mission.

Macgregor was Quartermaster-General of the Indian army, and head of its new Intelligence Department. A firm proponent of the 'Forward Policy', which maintained that possible Russian designs on India could be checked only by military might and the creation of buffer states, Macgregor was the author of a controversial 'secret book' *The Defence of India*. This startling work was to become the bible of the hawks and the bane of a troubled government. It prophesied the invasion of Afghanistan, spotted Russians under every bed, and claimed that India would never be safe until Russia had been 'driven out' of Turkestan. During the previous two decades, he observed, Russia had managed to annexe the Central Asian khanates of Bokhara, Khiva and Khokand. A bluff, stern man of idiosyncratic disposition, Macgregor was the model for Colonel Creighton in Rudyard Kipling's *Kim*, and the effective instigator of the second phase of the Great Game.

When the Game began in the early nineteenth century, it was as a clandestine quest for information and power over unknown parts of Central Asia. There was a huge expanse of uncharted, mountainous territory caught between the empires of British India and Tsarist Russia which both sides wanted to control. At first the players had travelled in disguise and great secrecy. Captain Charles Christie traversed Baluchistan dressed up as a Tartar horse dealer, while Lieutenant Arthur Conolly of the 6th Bengal Native Light Cavalry (who coined the phrase 'the Great Game') passed himself off as a Persian merchant when trying to reach Khiva in 1830.

As European features became increasingly recognizable to the inhabitants of the frontier, the British began to train educated

Indians in the skills of espionage and surveying. The Pundits, as they became known, were taught how to use theodolites and altitude thermometers, and sent off for years at a time to unmapped regions, disguised as pilgrims or traders. They would take with them mercury sealed with wax inside cowrie shells (to provide a false horizon), prayer wheels containing trigonometrical charts and false-bottomed trunks packed with sextants and compasses. The Pundits were responsible for the first maps of western Tibet and southern Turkestan.[3]

Several Indian Pundits never returned from their expeditions, and it is unclear what persuaded them to face the risk of a violent death in the service of the Queen Empress. Their motives were not financial, since the rewards the British gave for their services were miserable. Kishen Singh, who spent many dangerous years secretly mapping Central Tibet, was rewarded with a small plot of land and a Royal Geographical Society gold watch. Kipling's Lurgan Sahib believed that the lure of London's learned societies lay behind the endeavours of his spies: 'Do you know what Hurree Babu really wants? He wants to be made a member of the Royal Society by taking ethnological notes . . . Curious – his wish to be an FRS. Very human, too.'[4]

Kipling gives the impression in *Kim* that the Great Game was a massive intelligence-gathering operation extending throughout India. This was never the case, and Macgregor's Intelligence Service often came into conflict with the Survey of India, the body responsible for producing accurate maps of India and neighbouring territories. By the time Younghusband appeared on the scene in 1885, the Great Game had entered its second phase. There was no longer the same emphasis on disguise and secrecy, and the rivalry with Tsarist Russia was more blatant. High Asia was becoming 'a vast adventure playground for ambitious young officers and explorers of both sides.'[5] The Tournament of Shadows, as the Russians described the Game, had begun.

Sir Charles Macgregor made use of his intelligence gatherers in a deliberately vague way. Very few were officially on secret government service; most of them were freelance adventurers, and the unsuccessful could be disowned where necessary. A potential Great Gamer might travel as a 'special correspondent' for *The Times*, as a representative of the RGS, or perhaps as a member of a shooting party in search of the Himalayan barking deer. The difference between intelligence work and private travel was never precisely defined, which had the effect of making the inhabitants of the

Central Asian khanates immediately suspicious of any British soldier on leave. The Great Game was alluring and dangerous, and to this extent at least Kipling's version was accurate. As the agent 'E23' tells Kim: 'We of the Game are beyond protection. If we die, we die. Our names are blotted from the book. That is all.'[6]

In May 1885 Francis Younghusband was called to the Intelligence Department at Simla to undertake the revision of the military gazetteer of Kashmir. This position gave him access to much classified information about regional geopolitics, as well as Macgregor's *The Defence of India* (marked CONFIDENTIAL on its title page) with its threats about Russian expansionism. Younghusband later wrote that he had learnt the book nearly by heart, and that it had confirmed his earlier thoughts on Russia's ambitions. Stimulated by the reports he was reading he wrote to his sister Emmie, 'I tell you I sometimes feel inclined to chuck the service altogether and go off and travel, unfettered by anyone, like Uncle Robert.'[7] He was particularly keen to go to Manchuria, an obscure part of the Chinese Empire caught between Mongolia, Siberia and Korea.

Younghusband's hypothesis was that the next Russian move would be made in that direction, and that the Department's knowledge of the region would be utterly inadequate. He had seen a report which claimed that Russia had established a protectorate over Korea. If this were true, Manchuria would have been effectively encircled. Younghusband resolved to write a paper on the subject and present it first to his immediate superior, the fierce war veteran Colonel Mark Bell VC, and then to Macgregor Sahib himself. 'I would somehow convince them that if the Indian Empire were to be saved, I must at once be sent on duty to Manchuria.'[8]

But even Sir Charles Macgregor had doubts over the logic of Younghusband's theory. There was no obvious threat to Manchuria, although it was true that information on its geography and defences was thin. Yet he had a certain faith in Younghusband, and thought this expedition would be a good way of testing his abilities. Although Macgregor must have been aware that the trip would take at least a year, he agreed only to six months' leave, and on the condition that Younghusband paid some of his own travelling expenses. H. E. M. James of the Indian Civil Service, a confirmed bachelor in his early forties, would lead the party. They would be provided with an interpreter on arrival in China.

Before departure Younghusband returned to his regiment and spent several months training for the journey. He practised his mapping skills and took part in endless running races, to the irritation of his fellow officers who resented his forthcoming jaunt, and had even tried to block it. One morning he ran the three-hundred-yard dash in under thirty-three seconds, which, according to George Seaver, constituted a world record.[9] Every evening he wrote and re-wrote detailed plans for his expedition. Nobody he spoke to seemed to have heard of Manchuria, so there was little advice he could take. He left Delhi at the beginning of March 1886, twenty-two years old and determined to make his name. 'Whatever you do,' Lieutenant Younghusband ordered his beloved sister, 'don't say a word about my having gone to China as I am on leave in India and Govt. will recall me if it gets into the papers where I am going to.'[10]

Younghusband sailed out of the docks at Calcutta aboard an opium steamer, accompanied by Mr James, a collection of strong wooden boxes, some tents and lanterns, several spare pairs of khaki breeches and an elegant portmanteau. In his inside breast pocket he carried a pale brown notebook which listed his vital equipment, including: telescope, sextant and horizon, prismatic compass, carbolic ointment, quinine, Eno, spectacles, dark glasses, cigarettes, boiling apparatus, one bottle of sherry, flint and steel, common watch for servants, revolver, and two cholera belts.[11] The young explorer also carried a hymn book, in which was inscribed: 'F E Younghusband from his loving sister Emmie "Endure hardness as a good soldier of Christ"'.

'My greatest ambition', he told her, 'is gradually being realized.'

At Canton he disembarked to inspect the forts. 'Colonel Bell, my chief, was there in '82,' he wrote to Emmie, 'and he says the best plan is to walk straight in in an innocent way and keep yr. eyes open till you are turned out, which of course will happen as soon as the sentry wakes up . . . you cannot use any instrument or make any notes in the fort, but directly you get outside you write on yr. shirt cuffs.'[12] Having noted the thickness of the parapets and the number of siege guns, the two men continued to Shanghai where they were entertained by a 'merchant prince of the old style, Mr. Keswick, the chief representative in the East of Jardine, Matheson and Co.'[13] Younghusband soon decided the Chinese were 'a rummy looking lot – going about naked to the waist with their pigtails screwed up behind wearing very wide straw hats'.[14]

By 1886 Britain and other foreign nations had succeeded in establishing powerful trading concessions and influence across China. Although the Manchu imperial court in Peking (the Ch'ing Dynasty) was still in nominal control, its rule was weakening and being replaced in many areas by the power of European 'foreign devils'. After a fortnight in Peking meeting diplomats, the two men headed for Newchwang, the main Manchurian treaty-port and home to a small European enclave. There they met up with Henry Fulford, an official in the Chinese Consular Service and ardent proponent of the new sport of bicycling. Each member of the party had a clear role. James was responsible for organization, Fulford for interpreting conversations with Chinese officials, and Younghusband for mapping, surveying and the collection of military intelligence.

Having hired mule carts and drivers, the party set off on May 19 in the direction of Manchuria's capital, Mukden. The weather was 'mild and soft' and the lush countryside was 'dotted over with well-built, pent-roofed farmhouses, not at all unlike those which one sees in England'. Manchuria was at this time under a process of colonization by the Han Chinese. Historically China's central government had exercised varying degrees of control over Manchuria: by the late nineteenth century the grip was being strengthened in an attempt to check the expansionist ambitions of Russia, Britain and Japan. Han Chinese were encouraged to settle in Manchuria, and ethnic Manchus and Mongols pushed back to the borders. Younghusband compared this process favourably to Britain's 'civilising mission' in India. He was glad to 'see the fresh young life of a colony pushing vigorously ahead', and 'impressed by the vigour and prosperity of these Chinese colonists breaking through the forest'.

In the evenings the expedition would stop at road-side inns, most of which were simply long rooms with low platforms or k'angs on either side, upon which visitors sat and ate, 'chatting volubly. At night the travellers sleep in long rows cheek by jowl along the platforms. The great drawback to these inns is their dirt, inside and around,' wrote Younghusband in his account of the journey in *The Heart of a Continent*. Occasionally they would manage to obtain a private room, but in Mukden itself they were pursued everywhere 'by a hooting, yelling crowd. A Chinaman has no regard for privacy ... Even when we had cleared our room, they did not desist from pestering us, but, while we were undressing, poked holes with their fingers in the paper windows of our room, and then applied their eyes to these easily made peep-holes. Looking up in the middle of our ablutions, we would see a mass of eyes . . . peering at us.'

Having rounded up 'a caravan of mules' the three men travelled towards the forests near the Korean border. Heavy rain had begun, and it proved difficult to cross the Yalu river. 'On such occasions we put up in some farmhouses near the river, and here out in the country, away from the crowds of the towns, we could examine John Chinaman at leisure.' Their destination was the 'Long White Mountain', the Changbai Shan, a mountain range several hundred miles south-west of Vladivostok. Although it had been surveyed by Jesuit priests in 1709, no European had been there since. According to Manchu legend, there was at the summit a huge lake of unfathomable depth. For several weeks the party pushed its way through bog and forest, staying in sable hunters' huts at night. Younghusband was stunned by the beauty: meadows of irises, tiger-lilies, ferns, columbines and deep blue gentians. But there were no human settlements, and their supplies were running low. 'I remember James, Fulford, and myself all sitting down to dine off one partridge between us; this, with a little palatable soup and a scone was all we had after our trying march.'

They abandoned the mules and pressed on with a single porter until they reached the mountain. The ascent proved easier than expected until the group reached the brink of the summit, 'and then, instead of the panorama we had expected, we looked down in astonishment on a most beautiful lake in a setting of weird, fantastic cliffs just at our feet. We were, in fact, on an extinct volcano, and this lake filled up what had once been its crater.'[15] Lieutenant Younghusband boiled a thermometer to establish the altitude and made various geographical calculations before, to the astonishment of the others, insisting on climbing higher.

'It was very steep, and not unaccompanied with danger,' wrote James afterwards, 'as the foothold was treacherous, and, had he slipped, he might have rolled over the edge and dropped five or six hundred feet.' Reaching the top, Younghusband began 'creeping out to the very edge of a peak of rock which projects over the lake like a bowsprit, and waving his hat at us. Far below it looked as if nothing but an eagle could find a resting-place in such a position.'[16] Throughout his book *The Long White Mountain* James recounts tales of his travelling companion's reckless daring, and his insistence on pushing himself to the limit. He comments on the way that every night, even in the bitter cold, Younghusband would doggedly spend several hours outside making notes and establishing their position by means of the stars and a sextant. As an experienced traveller James must have been used to hardship, but he seems to have been baffled by Younghusband's compulsive risk-taking and physical exertion.

It took them several weeks to reach Kirin, a large town in central Manchuria where rifles and field-guns were being manufactured. Younghusband spent several weeks snooping about in search of information on weapons production. When a new set of mule-carts had been procured, the men proceeded north to Tsitsihar, but winter was approaching so they travelled quickly on towards the Siberian border. After 'some excellent pheasant shooting' on the way they got to the ancient town of Sansing and 'fitted ourselves out with long sheepskin coats, reaching well down to the ankles'.[17] Younghusband was able to inspect the forts by the river and file a report: 'Chinese side: fort has been constructed on the Sungari 10 m. below Sansing wh. will mount 5.8 inch Krupp guns now lying inside fort . . . The troops are mostly armed with Enfield rifles with the Tower mark on them.'[18]

The weather and the roads were worsening, but as the party approached the Sea of Japan provisions grew more plentiful. At Hunchun they bought sweets, soap, canned fruits and other luxuries. Younghusband was amazed to find heavy Krupp guns in place, which the Chinese had hauled for hundreds of miles over frozen bogs on giant sledges. By now they were nearing Manchuria's eastern border with Russia, and James asked permission to visit the Russian port of Novokievsk. Colonel Sokolowski sent word that they would be welcome, and a Cossack escort guided them over the frontier. 'There was the same rough shaggy-looking grey sheepskin cap, long overcoat, high boots, whip, and rifle slung over the back, that we knew so well from pictures.'

A dinner was given in honour of the three Britishers, attended by the Russians and a Chinese interpreter. It consisted of sardines, salmon chips, soup, vodka and 'a very excellent sort of claret', but 'before that was finished, another officer would fill your glass – the same glass! – with sherry. Then the colonel would insist upon you trying the beer. Meanwhile course after course of the most substantial dishes were being served up.'[19]

The following day James, Fulford and Younghusband were allowed to visit Novokievsk. To their surprise the Russian officials did not treat them with suspicion, but spoke of their own country's lack of territorial ambition. Younghusband was able to make detailed intelligence notes for his controllers back in Simla. 'As regards Russian movements Possiet Bay is frozen for three or four months in the winter and it is only a few miles north of the Tumen R. so probably the bays for some distance further down are frozen ... The present garrison at Novakeyesk [Novokievsk] is head-quarters of a battalion. 1 battery (mountain) 300 cavalry. Possiet 200 inf. Corean frontier post 200. Chinese frontier post 134. The whole are Cossacks.'[20]

The temperature was now well below freezing, so the party headed back towards Kirin. The rivers they had crossed by boat a few weeks before were frozen solid, and they found one 'which was about one hundred and fifty yards broad and with a by no means slow current, now frozen over so completely that we could run our heavily laden carts over on the ice'. It was approaching minus 25° Centigrade, but Younghusband found that 'though it was so cold, I do not remember suffering very much from it'. Reaching Mukden in early December they made their way to the Scottish Mission, only to discover a genteel tea party 'of Scottish cakes and scones and muffins' in full swing. 'We had had many trials on the journey, but this facing a ladies' tea-party in a drawing-room in our disreputable condition was the hardest of them all.'[21] At Newch-wang James departed for Japan, while Fulford and Younghusband continued on to Peking. They arrived in late January 1887, and Younghusband was asked to stay in the British Legation by Sir John Walsham, Britain's envoy and minister plenipotentiary at Peking.

Relishing the cosmopolitan atmosphere of the diplomatic whirl in pre-Boxer Rebellion Peking, the young explorer had no urge to return to India. The foreign legations were keen to hear tales of his travels across Manchuria. One evening there would be a party hosted by 'Baron Clemens Ketteler, Secretaire de la Legation de SM l'Empereur d'Allemagne en Chine,' and the next a dinner with 'Alexis Coumany, Chambellan de SM l'Empereur de toutes les Russies, Son Envoye Extraordinaire et Ministre Plenipotentaire.'[22]

By day Younghusband would write the official report of the jour-ney. He had been allowed full access to the archives by Walsham who, despite being an opponent of the cold warriors of the Great Game, went out of his way to help his young guest. In the report Younghusband had to conclude, forlornly, that there were no signs of an immediate Russian threat to Manchurian territory. However, his original theory was to prove accurate: in 1900, under the pretext of restoring order, Russian troops would invade Manchuria. Later it would be taken over by the Japanese, who installed the last Chinese Emperor, Pu Yi, as a puppet ruler.

Just as the report was nearing completion, and the time had come for Lieutenant Younghusband to return to his regiment, Colonel Bell VC popped up in Peking. Throughout the previous year there had been grave doubts about imperial adventurism (following the loss of General Gordon at Khartoum), but the return of a Tory government in August of the previous year, under the premiership of the discreet Russophobe Lord Salisbury, had strengthened the position of the Intelligence Department. Having debriefed his agent about Manchuria, Bell announced that he was setting off across Chinese Turkestan to inspect military fortifications. Younghusband immediately asked if he could accompany him, but Bell, with characteristic brusqueness, declined on the grounds that it would be a waste of resources. However, he would permit Younghusband to follow a parallel route through the unexplored wastes of the Gobi Desert, providing that leave could be obtained. Walsham telegraphed directly to the Viceroy, who gave permission for the journey to take place. Younghusband set about procuring an interpreter, an elaborate Chinese passport and a guide. It did not take him long to discover that nobody in Peking had ever crossed the Gobi, 'and how a solitary European traveller would be likely to fare among the people, we knew not'.

On the evening of Sunday 3 April 1887, Francis Younghusband sat in the Walshams' drawing room sipping port. Lady Walsham leant over and asked to be shown his proposed route on a map of Asia. As he picked up a pencil and drew a line from Peking to Hami to Turfan to Kashgar to Yarkand to Srinagar, the enormity of the undertaking hit him. He was attempting a journey of several thousand miles across the breadth of the Chinese Empire, following an unknown desert and mountain route. 'All the terrible vagueness and uncertainty of everything impressed itself on me as I traced that pencil line on the map . . . Had but one traveller gone through before me,' wrote Younghusband, neglecting to mention Marco Polo, 'the task would have seemed easy in comparison.'

The following morning he rode out of the British Legation on a borrowed pony, to the cheers of the small crowd of Europeans that had assembled. Accompanying him was a Chinese servant who had been on the Manchuria trip (but was soon to disappear) and Liu San 'who eventually travelled with me the whole way to India, acting in turn as interpreter, cook, table-servant, groom and carter'.[23]

After less than a mile one of the mules 'thought he would prefer going the rest of the way backwards, so he coiled the traces several times round his legs and body, faced inwards towards the cart and commenced to pull the cart into booths and shops and every other suitable place', Younghusband wrote to Lady Walsham that night. 'The crowd was immensely pleased at all these proceedings and my own get-up (in which I had rather fancied myself) seemed to amuse them too.'[24]

At the age of twenty-three, Francis Younghusband was fulfilling every romantic's dream, setting off into the unknown on a quest for knowledge and self-discovery, risking his life for the chance of gaining fame and glory.

FOUR

Across the Gobi and Down the Mustagh

It took the young thruster a fortnight to reach the edge of the Mongolian steppe. Away from the dust storms of Peking 'an extraordinary bounding sense of freedom' engulfed him as he 'looked on that vast grassy plain, stretching away in apparently illimitable distance all around'.[1] He was glad to be getting away from central China. In his notebook he wrote how 'a Chinaman' had called him a 'western devil'. 'I had never been so riled before, calling me a devil to my very face . . . Thank goodness I am now getting into a country peopled by a dignified gentlemanly race and away from these nasty conceited Chinese. Compared with the races of Central Asia the Chinese are utterly despicable as far as manners go.'[2] He was flattered to be invited into a yurt, the dome-shaped felt tent used by Mongolian nomads. 'The whole family collected to see my things, and pulled my kit to pieces. The sponge was a great source of wonder; but what attracted them most of all was a concave shaving-mirror . . . It was a pleasure getting among these jolly, round-faced, ruddy-cheeked Mongols.'

On reaching Kwei-hwa-cheng, the last town before the Gobi Desert, Younghusband was able to find traders with huge fox-skin caps and dirty sheepskin coats who had crossed from Turkestan. He 'looked with the profoundest interest on men who had actually been to these mist-like towns of Central Asia'. Eight camels were procured with the help of a local missionary, as well as some water-casks and a Kabul-pattern tent. Younghusband bargained his way through the bazaar accompanied by his 'boy' Liu San. A letter of credit from the Hong Kong bank, which had been forwarded by Lady Walsham with a small loan, was his only source of finance. Dried beans, brick tea, potatoes and tins of beef were purchased, together with sacks of flour and rice and oatmeal. He also obtained such luxuries as a few tins of preserved milk, some dried apricots and a sack of dark Mongolian mushrooms 'which gave a most excellent relish to the soup'.

A Mongolian camel-man called Ma-te-la was employed, 'a care-less, good-natured fellow, always whistling or singing, and bursting out into roars of laughter at the slightest thing, especially at any little mishap'.[3] The miniature caravan set off into the unknown expanse of the Gobi Desert (home of dust, wind and dinosaur eggs) on what the astrologers deemed to be an auspicious day, 26 April. Younghusband thought fondly of the world he was leaving. 'Please remember me very kindly to Sir John,' he told Lady Walsham in his final letter to her, 'and all in the Legation and tell Johnnie and Percy I miss those kicks and bumps and side-splitters very much at my solitary meals. Believe me, yours very sincerely, F. E. Young-husband.'[4]

The guide was an elderly opium addict who used to sit fast asleep on the back of his camel. As night fell 'he would suddenly wake up, look first at the stars, by which he could tell the time to a quarter of an hour, and then at as much of the country as he could see in the dark. After a time he would turn the camel off the track a little, and sure enough we would find ourselves at a well.' Younghusband, after some hesitation, issued Liu San with a revolver to fend off bandits and raiders. The result was that when-ever they encountered other travellers Liu San would 'swagger about with the revolver' telling 'the most abominable lies about the frightful execution he could do with it . . . I used to see him buttonhole a grave old Turki, and tell him in a subdued whisper, with mysterious glances at me, that I was "Yang-ta-jen", an influ-ential envoy from Peking, and that the utmost respect must be shown to me.'

At first they passed Buddhist temples and monasteries, but soon human settlements petered out. Most of the time there was 'noth-ing to guide the eye – no objects, as men or trees'. The land was bleak, 'covered with a reddish clay, which supports a scanty crop of coarse grass and scrubby plants'. As they approached the heart of the Gobi streams and grasses disappeared. Water could be obtained only by digging down into the water-holes of previous caravans. The sun was so strong that they could not set off until the afternoon, and had to march until midnight. Younghusband's mind was numbed by the silence of the desert and 'the fearful monotony of those long dreary marches seated on the back of a slow and silently moving camel'.[5] But he found he was able to read on camel-back during the hours before the sun had finally set. At night he gazed up at the stars 'in unperturbed serenity'. Their 'enchanting influence both calmed me and yet drew my whole soul out to them . . . I had a sense of the wholeness of the universe and of being intimately connected with the whole.'[6]

After three weeks they had reached the Galpin Gobi, the bleakest part of the whole desert, which the Russian explorer Nikolai Przhewalski had called the 'Valley of Death'. Younghusband doggedly updated the map he was drawing. Some evenings they would not find water, and had to rely on the hot, brackish remains in their casks before moving off early in search of more. The sand was mixed now with grey gravel, and huge sweeps of flat rock stretching to infinity. The temperature was falling well below freezing at night, and often in the morning the wind was too violent for them to strike camp. Sometimes a sand and gravel storm would blow up unexpectedly as they walked, and they would have to lie on the ground until it had passed.

In the sixth week the party crossed the Hurku hills and the landscape changed again. Around them lay huge sandhills, constantly shifting as the wind blew. Younghusband heard rumours of whole cities being buried beneath the waves of grit and sand. They were approaching an area notorious for bandits, so removed their camelbells. During the night Liu San twice fired his revolver at the shadows. But there were no robbers; only a makeshift stupa marking the place where nine travellers had been robbed and murdered a few months earlier. On 11 June they reached the foot of the Altai mountains, and Younghusband quarrelled with the guide and Liu San over the slow speed at which they were progressing.

There was snow on the peaks of the Altai range, and in the distance they saw giant Marco Polo sheep and mobs of wild Przhewalski's horse, with their stubby necks and gingery manes. Finding a cluster of Mongol yurts, Younghusband managed to barter three bricks of tea for a sheep, and buy more camels to replace the lame and escaped. Two days later it began to rain heavily, turning the sand and clay into an impassable swamp. The camels were unable to move, and had to be beaten and dragged on to little hillocks of gravel. During their ninth week in the desert they came to a small oasis town called Ya-hu, where Ma-te-la's family lived. Younghusband was surprised to find that Ma-te-la had kept an assortment of rubbish that had been thrown out during the journey, 'such as bits of paper, ends of string, a worn-out sock, and numerous other trifles' to show to his family.

The expedition plodded along the lower slopes of the Altai mountains, weakened by thirst and exhaustion. The dark brown rock was becoming dusty and fragile. It crumbled to the touch. In the tenth week they crossed into 'the branch of the Gobi which is called the desert of Zungaria, one of the most absolutely sterile parts of the whole Gobi'. The sand-filled wind was as hot as that in the Punjab, and there was no vegetation or scrub. Younghusband and Liu San were plagued by swarms of virulent sandflies. 'Nothing we have passed hitherto can compare with it – a succession of gravel ranges without any sign of life, animal or vegetable, and not a drop of water.'[7]

I never reached the heart of the Gobi. The railway line from Beijing (Peking) curved down to Lanzhou, away from the barren sands of the desert, towards the Tibetan border. I was on Younghusband's trail once more, but with less chance of success than before. Great sections of the Gobi were being used for nuclear weapons testing or *laogai*, the euphemistically named 'reform through labour' camps, while synthetic factory cities had taken the place of the old oasis settlements on the eastern side. The Mongolian nomads had been urbanized and collectivized, their ancient system of trade and barter replaced by Chairman Mao's trail of economic dogma. I had to feel the Gobi from the smeared windows of a steam train as it cut its way through the vastness of rock and gravel. For two days I lay on the bunk of a 'hard sleeper' compartment, watching and wondering.

First came the Mongolian grasslands, rolling expanses of deep green turf which stretched for ever, inhabited only by occasional yurts and swerving ox-bow rivers. They gave on to a blankness of golden-grey desert, in which the simplest landmarks were magnified to gargantuan proportions. The colour and the texture of the distorted rock began to catch my eye; there was so little else to focus on that the texture of the dry yellowness jumped into life as it leapt into escarpments and hollows. Sometimes water would come into view, the bright, flat turquoise of Mongolia's lakes. Like the desert, the water shimmered into existence on a massive scale. The lake would stretch for miles into the distance, broken only by the spike of a mountain or the sweep of an escarpment. Then the train would cover another blank of epic formlessness until we reached buildings, all of which would be covered in the film of yellow dust.

The city of Baotou consisted of huge concrete lumps. A small oasis settlement a hundred miles to the west of Kwei-hwa-cheng, it had been transformed in the 1950s into a 'model worker's' city. Out of nothing a monstrous excrescence had sprouted, producing ton after ton of steel and coal and iron ore. The indigenous Mongolians had been driven to its edge, and it was now home to over a million Han Chinese. It had an air of dislocation, as if the dream of a central planner in Beijing had never become a human reality, merely a physical one. Baotou had houses and shops and factories, but no soul.

I spent the night in a *binguan*, one of the faceless state-run hotels which squat in every Chinese city. After eating a breakfast of spiced eggs in a spacious but deserted dining hall, I wandered out into the heavy, damp air of Baotou. Within minutes I was being followed by a crowd of loitering onlookers. Everywhere I walked I was stared at by astonished Chinese faces, who gawped at me as if I were sprouting supplementary limbs. I felt like an African in Elizabethan England; a focus more of wonder than hostility. It was a time when few Europeans had been to the fringes of northern China; and besides, there was little reason for a tourist to visit the bland wasteland of Baotou. I was probably the first white-faced, long-nosed, yellow-haired dog the inhabitants had set eyes on. That evening I stumbled across an improbable night-spot. It was a sort of improvised disco in the basement of a factory building, with a winking yellow light and young dancers wearing stacked platforms and pale purple flares. The band played a Sinicized rendition of 'Auld Lang Syne'. One man was blowing a saxophone, but when he caught sight of me the music ceased and I had to slip away.

Heading west into the Gobi the following day, I reached a Buddhist monastery called Wudangzhao. It had been desecrated, but there were still half a dozen elderly Mongolian monks living forlornly in the remains. I established that they had been imprisoned during the Cultural Revolution, and released in the early 1980s. Behind the monastery was a row of flimsy huts, and a brash metal pagoda beside which Chinese tourists were photographed. As time went by I realized that I was sharing – involuntarily – Younghusband's ethnic prejudice. The Han Chinese seemed so cold and conformist compared to the Mongolians. Although many Mongolians had been driven from their own land, they had a joy, even a freedom, that their oppressors lacked. One afternoon I sat in the shade of a tree

with a wrinkled man called Touhyin. He had a thin V-shaped moustache and sharp, flat eyes. 'Genghis Khan?' I enquired, tracing the
extent of the Great Khan's empire with my finger in the dust. He
seemed not to understand. But a minute or two later he looked
carefully over his shoulder before hissing, 'Jinghiz! Jinghiz Shan!'
He held his clenched fist in front of my nose while his eyes crinkled
into a triumphant smile.

During the desiccated afternoons in Wudangzhao I read Younghusband's account of his journey through the Gobi Desert. I was
struck again and again by his indifference to physical hardship.
Throughout *The Heart of a Continent* he is scarcely troubled by the
heat or the cold or the travelling, let alone by fleas or blisters or
diarrhoea. But reading his private journals later on, I found he had
sustained a bad fall from his horse after leaving Peking. This event
was not mentioned in his published account. Moreover in James's
account of the journey through Manchuria, another episode is
recorded as the party approaches Tsitsihar: 'Younghusband, who
was reclining on the *k'ang*, suddenly jumped off it, upsetting a pair
of scissors which were lying upon his bedding; his foot caught them
before they reached the ground and he ran the points, which were
slightly open, more than an inch perpendicularly into the sole of
his foot. He at once got on his back and we bandaged him up, but
it was a fortnight before he could put his foot to the ground.'[8]

Nowhere does Younghusband write about this accident. I began
to feel that his apparent hardiness was a sham, a literary convention
designed to evoke an impression of bravery and sprezzatura. But
as I read his other writings, I came to think that the reality was more
complex. He seems to have regarded physical debility as somehow
improper. The very idea of immobility or illness disturbed him,
and throughout his life he remained extraordinarily healthy. His
upbringing and the athletic philosophy of Clifton had made him
feel that disease or sickness was the result of some kind of moral
failing. This psychological determination was compounded by a
genuine physical ability to withstand pain; a trait that his colleagues
often remarked on.

Younghusband's physical isolation during his expedition across
the Chinese Empire made him withdraw more deeply into himself.
Although there is a sense of spiritual development as *The Heart of
a Continent* progresses, and the book ends on a broadly religious
note, it is matched by a mood of emotional atrophy. He gives no
indication of his feelings towards his European companions in Manchuria, while the guide and servants he travelled with for months

on end are scarcely characterized at all. Shukar Ali, a Ladakhi who escorted him on the second phase of the journey, is simply compared to a 'dear big faithful dog'. His characteristics as a fellow human being are not touched on. 'I loved him as men love their dogs, knowing that their fidelity can be counted on through every circumstance whatever.'[9]

One result of this withdrawn and simplistic approach to other people was that he misjudged their motivation. Younghusband never realized that his 'boy' Liu San, who is praised several times in the book as a 'faithful servant', was persistently defrauding him. William Rockhill in *The Land of the Lamas* writes of a meeting with Liu San, who boasted of Younghusband's gullibility. Liu San had given Younghusband false prices for carts and mules, and kept the difference. 'This was his start in business, and by the time he reached India (six months later), he had stolen over three hundred ounces of silver.'[10] Younghusband was also unaware of the external orchestration that lay behind the journey, and how close it came to being prevented. As he was leaving Peking the King's Dragoon Guards sent an order that he should return at once to India. But Sir John Walsham decided to pocket the telegram, and wired back that Lieutenant Younghusband had already departed for the Gobi.

One afternoon I walked down from the monastery to the dried-up river bed which had become a dust road. Twice a day a truck would drive along it piled high with stones. I made my way up the valley, the gravel and sand drifting away down the hillside in the twists of hot wind. When I crossed the mountain I had felt part of it, but I did not feel a part of the desert. There were a few scrubby brown bushes and ugly sprouts of halophyte. The sun was high and it glinted from the silver and the yellow of the rock. The air was parched but I kept on walking.

Younghusband's ragged party of men and camels trudged on steadily through the sand and gravel. At last they were nearing the end of their epic journey through the Gobi. Having crossed nearly a hundred miles of the desert of Zungaria with no water, they

found themselves in a cultivated area. There were crops and even
the first house that Younghusband had seen for a thousand miles.
They had reached a new land – Turkestan – and could drink water
until fit to burst. They continued to the edge of the Tien Shan, the
Celestial Mountains, and climbed higher to another cultivated ridge
where they found trees and birds and more flowing water. Following a non-stop twenty-four-hour march the party reached the town
of Hami. 'My desert journey was now over,' wrote Younghusband,
'and I had accomplished the 1255 miles from Kwei-hwa-cheng in
just seventy days.'

There was a letter from Colonel Bell waiting for them in Hami.
Bell had arrived there three weeks earlier and, after pausing for an
afternoon in case Younghusband happened to turn up, pressed on
quickly towards India. For several days the party stocked up on
stores, and Younghusband hired a covered mule cart to take him
across Turkestan. In early July they began the six-week voyage to
Kashgar. Sometimes they stopped for the night at simple road-side
inns, but usually Younghusband preferred to sleep in the privacy
of the cart. The journey was monotonous, but after a few weeks
they reached the old Silk Road trading post of Turfan, said by the
Chinese to be the hottest place on earth.

The inhabitants were Turkic and Han Chinese, together with
some Afghan merchants and a distinguished Arab Hajji with whom
Younghusband was able to converse in Hindustani. While he was
in Turfan he made the discovery that the town was, uniquely,
nearly three hundred feet below sea level. At the time he assumed
his barometer was faulty, but it was subsequently shown by surveyors to be a correct reading. Travelling through Kashgaria he
took the opportunity to continue the reconnaissance he had been
doing in Manchuria. The Intelligence Department was anxious to
know how quickly troops could move in and out, and what routes
they would be likely to take. But more immediate worries presented
themselves as he approached the city of Kashgar.

For several nights Younghusband had stayed in a Kirghiz
encampment, but on the third morning he found himself surrounded by a threatening mob. 'As I mounted to ride away, crowds
of these rough Kirghiz collected around me gesticulating wildly.' It
looked as if he was going to be dragged from his horse, beaten
and possibly killed, but a Pathan guide he had recently engaged
intervened. Rahmatula Khan, the Pathan, managed to convince
the mob that Younghusband was on a mission from the Emperor
of China, and that if he was harmed their land would soon be

swarming with Chinese soldiers. The Kirghiz argued that no foreigner had been allowed to pass through their territory before, but in the end were persuaded to let Younghusband proceed. 'Rahmatula Khan had successfully extracted me from what might have been a very awkward situation.'

Towards the end of August they reached Kashgar, the fabled Central Asian city where his uncle Robert Shaw had been held prisoner twenty years before. Yakub Beg, the self-proclaimed King of Kashgaria, had been overthrown, and the region was now administered by a Chinese Taotai. But in the upheaval Russia had managed to snatch a piece of western Turkestan, and secure the right to a consulate in Kashgar itself. Younghusband was amazed to find that Monsieur Petrovski, the Russian consul, had a precise knowledge of Indian affairs. 'The annual parliamentary report on the "Material and Moral Progress of India" was one which he took regularly.' He also kept 'an astronomical telescope, barometers, thermometers of all kinds, an apparatus for measuring the movements of earthquakes, and various other instruments. He was evidently a man of considerable attainments.'

As he made his way south towards the town of Yarkand, Younghusband felt refreshed by his stay in Kashgar. There had been fresh fruit in abundance, and he had found the Russian consul most interesting. One afternoon Younghusband had returned Petrovski's hospitality by inviting him to tea, but was surprised when he appeared accompanied by an escort of sixteen mounted Cossacks carrying the Russian flag. It may have given him an inkling as to the brand of diplomacy that Petrovski practised. Three years later Younghusband was to return to Kashgar on an official mission, and spend some of the most depressing months of his life trying vainly to out-manoeuvre the Russian.

In Yarkand he was entertained by a group of merchants who remembered his uncle 'Shaw Sahib'. They ate stews and rice and 'huge bunches of grapes and delicious melons and peaches . . . and we ended up with a pudding made of whipped egg and sugar and some other ingredients, which it would be hard to beat anywhere.'[11] Another letter from the ubiquitous Colonel Bell was waiting for him: '13th August 1887. Under the Kara Korum . . . Don't fail to try the Mustagh,' it insisted, 'it is your shortest route & wants to be explored.'[12] This bald order, so characteristic of Bell, gave little indication of what was to be expected. The Mustagh was a 19,000-foot pass on the edge of the mountain K2 which marked the watershed between India and Central Asia. It had been blocked by an avalanche twenty-five years before, and no European had ever tried to cross it.

Younghusband sprang into action. He engaged a Balti guide called Wali and three servants, together with a handful of pony men from Leh. The caravan was put under the control of a Ladakhi Buddhist known as Drogpa or 'Nomad', who later converted to Islam, changing his name to Mahmood Isa. He was to play a vital role in Younghusband's explorations over the next two decades. The men were equipped with sheepskin coats, fur caps and leather boots. Tea, sugar, rice and ghee were purchased, as were some sets of spare horseshoes, some Turkic robes, a length of rope and 'a pickaxe or two, to help us over the ice and bad ground'.[13]

Younghusband had no money, but succeeded in obtaining all his goods on credit. This was a source of great pride to him, and he was to mention the achievement for the rest of his life whenever he wanted to illustrate the virtues of being English. (He rarely described himself as British, since he saw Scotland, Ireland and Wales as countries in their own right.) At the outbreak of the First World War he made these notes for a speech he was giving at a 'Fight for Right' gathering: 'Relate how I, an unknown Englishman coming out of the void was, simply because I was an Englishman, offered this money. I had only a scrap of paper to give them (here I will produce the actual piece of paper signed by me in 1887) but that scrap of paper was worth hard cash to enable me to prosecute my journey because previous Englishmen had been honourable.'[14]

Bursting with excitement, the young patriot penned a letter to his mother in Southsea. 'I never was so proud of my country as on this journey. Afghans, Turks and Arabs whom I have met have all declaimed loudly in praise of English rule in India . . . they say the English are the only people who know how to govern a country.'[15] In his enthusiasm he made a foray into the slave market, purchasing a sturdy-looking man who had been captured by Kanjuti raiders. The expedition set off for the Mustagh Pass in early September. In his brown notebook he carried a Certificate of Ownership for his slave: 'Date of selling 23 Muharram 1303. Mirza Hakim of Sarikol . . . a man named Turgan 40 years of age for 800 tangas. This man is no other man's slave or servant.'[16] Perched on horseback, with a burnt face and flowing Yarkandi robes, Younghusband must have looked much like any other Central Asian traveller. But his headgear distinguished him from the rest.

At all times he wore a solar topi, 'in order to show I was an Englishman'.[17]

After collecting final provisions from the village of Kugiar, including some bags of doughcakes and a few sheep, they headed for the Kun Lun mountains. Younghusband was interested to meet members of the Pakhpu tribe, 'whom Dr Bellew, the skilled ethnologist who accompanied the Forsyth Mission, considered to be of pure Aryan stock'. The party followed the line of the Yarkand river, which narrowed into a gorge as it approached the tributary which led to the Mustagh Pass. Getting the ponies across the icy river was 'cruel work . . . They were constantly slipping and falling back, cutting their hocks and knees to pieces'. Climbing up the valley, the men reached a plain covered with scrub and dwarf birch. 'We were about fifteen thousand feet above the sea-level, and as soon as the sun set one could almost see the cold stealing over the mountains – a cold grey creeps over them, the running streams become coated with ice.' They sat around the camp fire in the biting wind while Wali told stories about the journeys he had made many years before.

As darkness fell 'we took up our beddings from the places where we had ostentatiously laid them out to mislead any prowling Kanjutis, and hurried off to deposit them behind any rock that would shelter us'. Younghusband was elated by the hardship. 'I recollect that evening as one of those in all my life in which I have felt in the keenest spirits.'[18] 'I thought to myself this – this really is living. Now I really am alive,' he wrote later. 'Deep, splendid inner satisfaction came upon me.' They spent the next two days following the valley of the Shaksgam river, Younghusband pressing on ahead of the main party in his excitement. As he approached the rise at the end of the pass, he ran forward through the ice and snow to see what lay on the other side.

'Beyond was the fulfilment of every dream I had had three years ago. There, arrayed before me across a valley, was a glistening line of splendid peaks, all radiant in the sunshine, their summits white with purest snow, their flanks stupendous cliffs . . . Where I had reached no white man had ever reached before.' Although he did not know it at the time, Younghusband was looking at K2, the second highest mountain in the world, 'a peak of almost perfect proportion . . . so massive, so firm and strong'. The twenty-four-year-old soldier was having the first of his mystical, mountainous experiences, enthralled by the sheer beauty of the snow peaks around him. He was giving full rein to a side of his character that had previously been suppressed, and allowing his natural impulses to develop in the remote privacy of the Karakorams. 'This world was more wonderful far than I had ever known before. And I seemed to grow greater myself from the mere fact of having seen it. Having once seen that,' demanded the diminutive explorer, 'how could I ever be little again?'[19]

The party began to ascend the glacier of black rocks and green ice which flowed down from the Mustagh Pass into the Shaksgam valley. It was Younghusband's first encounter with a glacier, and he was astounded by its size and depth. The men pulled and pushed the ponies, whose legs were being cut to ribbons as they stumbled up the ice. During the third day on the glacier it became apparent that the ponies could go no further. Wali suggested the pony men be sent back to Shahidula, where they could find the longer route across the Karakoram Pass which led to Leh. That night the Ladakhis, the Chinese, the Baltis and the Englishman held an anxious conference around the brushwood fire. It seemed unlikely that they could get much further. They were approaching 19,000 feet and some of the men were having difficulty breathing the thin air. Younghusband drifted into sleep, and when he awoke in the morning his beard and moustache were stuck to his face in a block of ice.

After eating some bread and drinking hot tea, Younghusband set off with Wali the guide, Turgan the slave, Shukar Ali, Drogpa the caravan leader and a spare Balti. Liu San was left in charge of the ponies. Fresh snow had fallen during the night, and the band of climbers could take only a few steps at a time before stopping to regain their breath. It took them six hours to reach the summit. But on the crest of the Mustagh Pass the ground dropped away. It had been splintered into the valley below by a series of avalanches. They were standing on the edge of a precipice. Younghusband's dreams and fantasies evaporated before his eyes. It would not be possible to cross the Mustagh Pass. It would not be possible to breach the watershed between the rivers of Central Asia and those of the Indian Ocean, the dividing line between China and India. He would have to return, ignominiously, to explain his failure to Colonel Bell.

Lieutenant Francis Younghusband stared forlornly over the edge of the frozen cliff. Wali, mistaking this solemnity for stoicism, began to edge his way out on to an ice ledge. It had not occurred to him to turn back. With a grim ardour, Wali 'hewed steps across the ice slope which led to the precipice,' Younghusband wrote afterwards in a private letter. Without boots, ropes, ice-axes or crampons, Wali was trying to descend an ice precipice. Younghusband decided to follow him. 'I freely confess that I myself could never have attempted the descent and that I – an Englishman – was afraid to go first.'[20]

The descent of the Mustagh Pass was to assume a mythic importance in Younghusband's career. I noticed that in old age, his daughter Eileen referred to a crucial turning point in her own life as 'my Mustagh Pass'. This rite of passage, the crossing of the watershed, the baptism of fire, the epiphany of ice, convinced him that he had a special purpose in the world, and was a key moment in the development of his own ambition; he was now an explorer.

Younghusband lectured about his pilgrimage across Asia on his return, and again and again whenever the opportunity presented itself. As time passed by the story was altered and embellished until the role of Wali in instigating this act of foolish bravery was largely obscured. 'I bound handkerchiefs round the instep of my smooth native leather boots to give me some hold,' the seventy-four-year-old Sir Francis Younghusband told a Royal Geographical Society audience in 1937. 'I supposed from what I had read in mountaineering books that the correct thing to do was to rope ourselves together; so we passed a rope round our waists and fastened ourselves together.'[21] 'Knotting turbans and reins for ropes,' wrote the historian John Keay in *The Gilgit Game*, 'hacking steps in the ice with a pickaxe and trusting to a grip from frozen, bootless feet, he managed what the great Swedish explorer, Sven Hedin, would call "the most difficult and dangerous achievement in these mountains so far".'[22]

A stream of mountaineers, writers and explorers have spoken of Younghusband's feat with admiration. One of the last Great Gamers, Kenneth Mason, wrote that his generation regarded Younghusband as 'the father of Karakoram exploration'.[23] The newspapers of the day were ardent in their praise, one saying that Younghusband had achieved more than H. M. Stanley had in Africa, but with considerably less bloodshed. The magazine *Nature* went so far as to write that the journey was 'one of the most remarkable ever made, considering its length, the time taken and the novelty and value of the results'.[24]

I found a peculiarly imperial view of the expedition in an old BBC recording. Peter Fleming, who wrote *Bayonets to Lhasa* and had himself traversed Central Asia with Ella Maillart in the 1930s, was being interviewed about his memories of Sir Francis Young-husband. In stirring, patrician tones, Fleming declared that Young-husband's success in crossing the Gobi Desert and descending the Mustagh Pass had, primarily, been a consequence of his 'superb manners' and social grace: 'Of course in those sort of regions on those sort of journeys – both in those days and in these – you are really fundamentally dependent on good manners ... Young-husband knew the importance of getting on with the often rather rough and unreliable people in whose hands, after all, your life really is.'[25]

Using a small axe they had brought from Yarkand, Wali began to hack chunks out of the ice. Inch by inch, the men followed in his footsteps. They were standing 'on a slope as steep as the roof of a house', roped loosely together, edging their way out towards a precipice. Had one of them slipped 'the whole party would have been carried away and lunged into the abyss below. Outwardly I kept as cool and cheerful as I could,' wrote Younghusband, 'but inwardly I shuddered at each fresh step I took. The sun was now pouring down on the ice, and just melted the surface of the steps after they were hewn, so that by the time those of us who were a few paces behind Wali reached a step, the ice was just covered over with water, and this made it still more slippery for our soft leather boots, which had now become almost slimy on the surface.'

Half-way across the slope, Drogpa panicked and lost his nerve. He began to scramble back across the ice. Younghusband 'was in a state of cold, horrible fear ... but I pretended not to care a bit, and laughed it off, *pour encourager les autres*'. Eventually they reached a projecting overhang of rock on the far side of the slope, where they crouched and took stock of the situation. With the wind buffeting him from every direction, Younghusband found that behind them lay an ice slope, ahead of them thin air, and below them a cliff face leading to another glacier. One by one they climbed down the cliff, with ice and rock tumbling over their heads, until they reached the head of the glacier. In the distance Younghusband could see the forlorn Drogpa, 'salaaming profusely'.

The face of the glacier was a smooth, sheer drop, but out of it jutted three shards of rock. Younghusband decided they could be used as stepping stones in the descent of the ice face. The men threw their bedding and equipment out into the void. Then by knotting together turbans, pony ropes and cummerbunds, they were able to fashion an improvised rope which was tied around the waist of the lightest Balti. They lowered him over the edge, and as he descended to the jutting rock, he cut rough steps in the ice with the axe. Each man then climbed down, gripping the rope for security. One of them slipped and fell backwards on the ice, but managed to grab the rope with one hand: 'when he reached the rock his hand was almost bared of skin, and he was shivering with fright.' The last man to descend, Turgan the slave, had to do so without the benefit of the patchwork rope. 'He reached our rock of refuge in safety, and we then in the same manner descended two more stages of the ice-slope, and finally reached a part where the slope was less steep.'

The descent had taken six hours, 'and when I reached the bottom and looked back, it seemed utterly impossible that any man could have come down such a place'. The sun was setting, and the ragged group of travellers trudged through the ice in search of shelter. Careless with exhaustion, they scarcely noticed when the Balti disappeared. 'We retraced our steps, and found the poor fellow had dropped down a crevasse, the mouth of which had been covered with a thin coating of ice and snow.' By lowering a rope through the glacier, they were able to pull him back up to the surface. It was approaching midnight when they found a small piece of bare ground, and made a feeble fire by breaking up two of their alpenstocks. Younghusband decided to open the present Lady Walsham had given him in Peking – a bottle of brandy. But he found it had been smashed during its flight over the Mustagh Pass, and glass remnants were now embedded in his sheepskin sleeping-bag. But Younghusband was glad to be alive and in India, and they all slept 'as if nothing could ever wake us again'.

The five men moved on early the next morning, passing the largest mountain glacier in the world, the Baltoro glacier. Younghusband was in constant pain 'for my native boots were now in places worn through till the bare skin of my foot was exposed, and I had to hobble along on my toes or my heels . . . I was always slipping, too, falling and bruising my elbows.'[26] That night they slept in a clump of fir trees, and had nothing to eat except dry biscuits. Although Younghusband does not say so in his published writing, it appears from his private diaries that he was almost delirious by this point. The next day he had to be carried across a river by Shukar Ali, who slipped over in the process. Both men were almost drowned, and Younghusband had difficulty in climbing out of the river. 'Soaked to the skin in the icy water I felt completely numbed. The only thing to do was to walk on hard till we could find some shelter.'[27]

Two days later they reached their first Balti village, Askoli, and Younghusband collapsed into bed with a bowl of rice and a stewed fowl. Baltistan was on the fringes of British influence, and the Baltis did not welcome the appearance of a sahib and his entourage.[28] Wali refused to leave Younghusband's side for fear of being killed, but after a few days the inhabitants were placated: a bullock was sacrificed to a mountain deity, and a group of villagers agreed to take supplies back to the stranded pony men on the top of the pass. Younghusband, meanwhile, had regained his health and was determined to explore the 'new' Mustagh Pass, an opening to the west of the one they had just crossed.

On the third day he found the pass blocked by massive chunks of ice, and turned back. He would now be able to report to Colonel Bell that no Russian military force could enter Baltistan (and hence India) by that route. Heading down through the Shigar valley towards Kashmir the weather improved. There were apricot trees and wild walnuts, and even a pony for Younghusband to ride. At Skardu he split up with his followers, feeling 'sincere regret'. Turgan was released from his bond of slavery 'and kissed my hands and feet', while Shukar Ali was given a favourable reference for future employers: 'He was always ready to do any amount of work and is a capital man to have on a rough journey. Though he is only a *kahar* [porter] he cooked for me and made himself generally useful.'[29] Younghusband was fond of Shukar Ali, referring to him in *My Debt To India*, the last BBC broadcast he made before his death, as 'always cheerful, always ready to meet any demand exploration made upon him, and as hard as the mountains themselves'.[30]

On the edge of the Zoji Pass, Younghusband met up with Nikolai Notovitch, the conspiracy theorist and adventurer whom Kipling is said to have characterized as a Great Game spy in *Kim*. He was glad to talk to the Russian, although 'sadly disappointed at not finding an Englishman'.[31] Descending through the Sind valley and then the Kashmir valley, he reached Srinagar on 30 October 1887. Younghusband had spent nearly twenty months in Manchuria, China, the Gobi and Turkestan: his beard was coarse and his face darkened by the sun. 'I was dressed, except for a European cap, entirely in native clothes – a long Yarkandi robe with a band round my waist, and with long, soft leather native boots.' He went to a tailor and obtained a 'knickerbocker suit' before reporting his presence to the Political Agent in Srinagar. 'It was very trying, therefore, when Captain Ramsay, almost immediately after shaking hands, said, "Wouldn't you like to have a wash?"'

A telegram of congratulations from Sir Frederick Roberts, the Commander-in-Chief in India, was waiting for him. Younghusband took a boat down the Jhelum river, and rejoined his regiment at Rawal Pindi. Soon he was wearing a 'scarlet and gold mess jacket and waistcoat', sitting in the mess eating a regimental dinner. But the food made him sick, and he seems to have had little pleasure in seeing his fellow officers again. Within days Colonel Bell summoned him to Simla to be debriefed. Younghusband produced maps of the areas he had explored, and began to write a detailed *Report of a Journey from Peking to Kashmir via the Gobi Desert, Kashgaria, and the Mustagh Pass*. Liu San, Drogpa and the ponies appeared six weeks later, having taken the long route round the Karakoram Pass. Liu San was suffering from pleurisy, and Younghusband arranged for him to have medical treatment before taking a ship back to China. Although he felt a strong debt of gratitude to Liu San, in *The Heart of a Continent* Younghusband dismisses him with the casual arrogance that was expected of colonial travellers. 'He was a Chinaman, and therefore not a perfect animal, but he understood his business thoroughly, and he did it.'[32]

In Simla Younghusband was in great demand as a new expert on China's empire, lecturing to the United Services Institute on 'China and the Chinese army'. Geographers and military tacticians wanted to make use of the unique insight he had into Manchuria and Turkestan. He was summoned to a private meeting with the Commander-in-Chief. In early 1888 the ultimate accolade appeared – an invitation to address the Royal Geographical Society in London. The young explorer took a ship from Bombay, and in April stepped back on to British soil. He was stronger than before, if no taller, and his moustache was now thick and well clipped. His family were desperately proud of him. Emmie was in a state of rapture, scribbling in her diary, 'My darling brother has just been home . . . What joy! I feel I can never forget it . . . May God bless and repay you for the exquisite joy your love has been.'

Yet their relationship had changed. They had corresponded consistently for six years, but Francis's letters had become increasingly distant. His perspective had widened as Emmie's had contracted, and he no longer used her as the outlet for his emotions. Back in Britain, he concentrated not on his sister, but on the glamour of being a renowned traveller. 'Others now claim a share in my darling boy,' wrote Emmie one night, 'and I must not expect the devotion he once gave me.' Yet her own charged passion was undiminished. Francis was the paragon through which this thirty-year-old Victorian spinster had her being: he was her reason for living. 'My devotion to him is unchanged. It seems to grow deeper and deeper as I see my darling's character developing so beautifully.' When he left for India again in June, Emmie's world caved in. She prayed and prayed, but her strict Evangelical God offered no answers. 'No words can say the blank and desolation it was to feel he was gone; the intense longing for him. Oh it is heart rending.'[33]

In the middle of May, Younghusband had held forth to the dignitaries of the Royal Geographical Society. Sir Richard Strachey, the esteemed Indian administrator and father of the essayist Lytton Strachey, presided over the meeting. Younghusband began with an unassuming burst of reticence, designed to suggest the whole operation had been a chance jaunt. 'In the summer of 1885 Mr H. E. M. James of the Indian Civil Service asked me to accompany him on a journey he was about to make into China.' He outlined the routes he had taken in Manchuria and Baltistan, implying that the purpose of the journey had been purely recreational. The military intelligence gathering was not mentioned. In conclusion Younghusband praised Liu San, Drogpa and Wali. 'That I was enabled to carry on this journey successfully is entirely due, under Providence, to the unfailing fidelity shown towards me by my staunch companions,' he announced, as the company dissolved into applause.[34] 'It was an evening never to be forgotten,' wrote Emmie later, her tears staining the paper, 'seeing my darling standing up among all those learned men, looking so young and handsome and simply telling the story of his travels.'[35]

The geologists, ethnographers, botanists and glaciologists of the RGS were all determined to have their say. Mr H. H. Howarth MP felt it was 'gratifying to know that the name of England had reached those regions,' while a Mr Allen reported that he could 'bear testimony to the filthy habits of the Mongols'. Sir Henry Rawlinson, the elderly Great Gamer and oriental scholar who had spent two years dangling from the end of a rope at Behistun deciphering inscriptions in the rock face, praised Younghusband whilst bemoaning the ease of modern travel. In his day, he felt, Samarkand had been 'almost a fabulous place . . . but now a person could book himself for Samarkand just as for Constantinople'. Lieutenant-Colonel Henry Godwin-Austen then stood up and declared that he too had visited the Himalayan region. In 1860 and 1861 he had been working for the Survey of India, and had tried unsuccessfully to reach the Mustagh Pass.

At this point General J. T. Walker intervened. He thought the second peak in the Karakoram Range, K2, was 'so lofty and eminent a peak' that it should be given a name. Why not call it after his old friend 'Godders' Godwin-Austen, 'who first surveyed the Mustagh Range and glaciers'?[36] The proposal was adopted by the meeting with enthusiasm, and K2 was renamed 'Mount Godwin Austen'. Thus are the great decisions of history made. Although the name was not formally adopted by the British government, most international bodies called the peak 'Godwin Austen' until the 1960s when 'K2' came back into fashion. Younghusband felt, with some justification, that it might more rightfully have been named after someone else. When Mrs Godwin-Austen wrote to him 'in great state of mind' asking why he insisted on referring to the peak as 'K2', he did not bother to answer her letter.

It was with a new sense of confidence and a rather awkward arrogance that he arrived back in Rawal Pindi in July. 'It is unfortunate for the young soldier that African travel is more fashionable than Asiatic at present,' declared the RGS on the subject of its newest and youngest Fellow. 'His exploit performed on African soil might well have gone near dimming the lustre of many a recent exploration.'[37] Younghusband revelled in his achievement and the opportunity it gave him for contact with distinguished people, but he still lacked the social ease of his contemporaries. Back with his regiment he spent much of the time walking alone or reading; Wordsworth, Scott, Tennyson, Darwin, Kidd's *Social Evolution* and Seeley's *Ecce Homo*. He longed to go exploring again, and was utterly bored by working for his military examinations. In the autumn he had an attack of cholera. More significantly, he became depressed by a hopeless romantic entanglement, the consequences of which were to reverberate through the rest of his life.

FIVE

'Impressed by My Bearing': Bearding the Mir

Francis Younghusband had first met May Ewart on his way back from the Rhotang Pass in 1884. She was young and ethereal, clad in white muslin, and lived in the fragrant hill station of Kasauli on the edge of the Himalayas. Colonel and Mrs Ewart were friends of his parents, and several times had invited him to stay. His relationship with May was formal and immature, his declaration of love being limited to a lingering handshake on departure from one of his visits. 'I remember one day at Kasauli,' he wrote afterwards, 'when I had been trying all I could to be cheerful and seemed to have pleased her and she gave me such a kind sweet smile.' Shortly after his return from Central Asia he had caught sight of her at Lahore railway station, but been too embarrassed to show his face. 'I really feared to go up and speak to her and I hid myself away in my carriage.' She was still on his mind when he returned to Kasauli in early 1889.

Sitting on the Ewarts' verandah in the cold January sunlight, he decided that May did not love him. He could not be certain, for he felt it would be 'ungentlemanly' to broach the subject with her. But the atmosphere was not encouraging. 'I wish to lead a new life thoroughly good and devoted to God's service,' he told his diary. 'The more I fight against my sins the easier it will become.' With Colonel Ewart he felt relaxed and fluent, chatting away about the frontier and the regiment and the Gobi. But whenever May was present he clammed up, sat to attention and tried hopelessly to strike a casual attitude. Looking back, he thought that 'if I had not restrained myself, but had gone on and spoken openly of my love much pain might have been saved both of us'.

In many ways Younghusband was an impressive figure; athletic, knowledgeable and adequately handsome. Senior officers had taken note of his abilities, and at twenty-five he already had a proven track record as an explorer. Yet he was too intense and serious, his emotions and capacity for self-expression stunted by his upbringing and education. 'In love I had none of the nerve I

had in exploring and in dealing with wild peoples,' he wrote sadly
many years later. 'I had very little social experience.' May seems
to have loved him, but a similar inability to communicate prevented
her from breaking down the social barriers between them.
Occasionally they went on walks together, chaperoned by Mrs
Ewart, marching stiffly along the paths of Kasauli.

Back in Rawal Pindi he vented his frustration on the soldiers,
finding fault wherever it could be spotted. He intervened to stop
two of his sergeants being promoted. 'I hope it will give them a
lesson and make them smarten up a bit. I want good men only at
the head of the N.C.O.'s in my troop.' The journey across China
had left him badly in debt, and every month two hundred rupees
were taken from his pay. The drill and military regulations continued to frustrate him, and he considered transferring from the
cavalry to an infantry regiment. He was unable to concentrate on
his work; his strangled cry for love could find no outlet.

In February he paid another visit to Kasauli, and Colonel Ewart
broached the subject of marriage. What were his intentions? Did his
parents want him to marry? Awkward and stammering, Younghusband confessed that he loved May, and that he was sure that once
his parents met her, 'they could not wish for me to be married to a
better little wife'.[1] There had been a proposal from another suitor,
Mrs Ewart intimated, but May was uncertain about her feelings. Con-
sultations were made, prospects assessed, and May rather reluctantly
cajoled into a decision. She wanted to marry him, she thought, perhaps. 'I was too much of a girl,' she told him a decade later. 'How
sorry I am that I was so cruel and unsympathetic in the days which I
think neither of us can really ever forget.'[2] Finally an engagement
was agreed upon, on the understanding that there would be no plans
for marriage until Younghusband was promoted.

'I feel just a perfectly different fellow altogether now,' Francis
wrote to Emmie back in England, 'and more happy than I can tell
you. Everybody up here is charmed with May . . . Try to write her
a line or two – all of you – call her May and be friendly to her.'[3]
Emmie was less than delighted, writing a frosty letter in reply. 'Old
Emmie must not think that my love for her is a bit the less,' Francis
reassured the pages of his pale brown notebook. He was experiencing a fragile sense of joy, knowing that she wanted to share his life.
Yet he still found it difficult being with May. His movements became
awkward and his palms began to sweat. He found that, however
strong the sensations in his heart, he could not 'show her any
feeling. I had to stifle all my ardent affection years ago and now I

cannot show it and I am losing my darling May . . . all the time I am cold & stiff & formal.'

Less than a month later May broke off the engagement.

'We never could break down the reserve there was between us and now we are parted,' wrote the desolate lover.[4] He jumped on his horse and galloped away from Kasauli, his mind in turmoil and his tentative love ground to ashes. Finding himself on a train to Simla, he tried, pathetically, to imagine his future without May. His one desire, his fantastic hope, had shrivelled away. Maybe he should return to the mountains, the only place where he had experienced true joy. His mind wandered to the beauty of the snow peaks, the Karakoram range and the glaciers and the snow as the sun glinted off the crest of K2. He glanced across the railway carriage, and found, by a remarkable twist of fate, that he was staring into the eyes of the most revered and elusive Great Gamer in the Indian subcontinent, Mr Ney Elias.

Elias was the spy's spy, so successful at covering his tracks that almost nothing is known about him. He was of unassuming appearance, unknown antecedents (though said to be a Sephardic Jew) and rarely published details of his journeys. To Younghusband he was simply 'the best traveller there has ever been in Central Asia'.[5] They fell into an ardent conversation as the train jolted towards Simla. Elias pulled some strings and disappeared into the ether, leaving Younghusband standing in the office of Sir Mortimer Durand, the Foreign Secretary to the Government of India.

It was the last, great, mysterious, unexplored country in the world, declared the young lieutenant: Tibet, the missing square on the imperial chess board. 'Durand was most sympathetic. He was amused at my enthusiasm and listened to my plans.'[6] Younghusband's proposal was that he should penetrate to the depths of Tibet, even to Lhasa itself, in the guise of a Yarkandi merchant and gather intelligence about the unknown region. After careful consideration Durand acquiesced, and, after consulting Ney Elias, agreed to give him five thousand rupees for the purpose.

But back at Rawal Pindi, Younghusband was met with a curt reprimand. On no account, said the Colonel, could permission be granted for him to leave his post in order to travel to Tibet. The King's Dragoon Guards had already been disrupted by his absence the previous year. Once again the Indian army was in conflict with the political administration, and Younghusband's ambition was the victim. He returned to the 'arid and meaningless' life of a cavalry officer. Through the heat of the summer he marched and saluted, 'spending hour after hour in looking out for microscopic atoms of dust on my men's uniforms', dreaming about the remote spectre of May Ewart.[7] Then at the end of June, a telegram arrived. Lieutenant Younghusband was to go to Simla at once.

Following the Russian take-over of Merv, the Penjdeh incident of 1885 and Petrovski's activities in Kashgar, there was growing Russo-phobia within the Indian administration. Most worrying of all was the knowledge that a railway line had now been extended through Merv, Bokhara and Samarkand. It was possible – in theory at least – for the Tsar's armies to encircle the North West Frontier of India within days of the order being given in Moscow. Opinion was sharply divided over the likelihood of this happening. To Liberals back in London such fears seemed a hysterical over-reaction; to young British army officers in Northern India, a Russian invasion was a realistic possibility. Even now, over a century later, the Russian nationalist leader Vladimir Zhirinovsky is insisting that his people will not be safe until Russia's soldiers have 'washed their boots in the warm waters of the Indian ocean'. Such talk can be construed as meaningless bluster; or as a serious threat to global security.

To the hawks in India's foreign office in the late 1880s, the pros-pect of Tsarist imperialism was deadly serious. The temperature of the Great Game was rising, and their position was being strength-ened by the stern views of the Tory government back in London. Morty Durand gave Younghusband a personal briefing. The Rus-sians were sniffing around the Hindu Kush and the Pamirs, and it was even said that the formidable Colonel Grombtchevski had got as far as Hunza and held talks with the ruler. Moreover raiders from the Hunza region were using a secret pass to plunder the caravan route between Leh and Yarkand. Younghusband had been chosen to tackle the problem. The success of the operation would be crucial in protecting British interests on the frontier. He would be given all the necessary equipment and an escort of six Gurkha soldiers. His mission was to locate the secret pass, seek out the skulking Grombtchevski and tame the Mir of Hunza. 'Could any-thing more delightful be imagined?' he wondered.[8]

Seventeen Kashmiri sepoys, fifteen ponies, six Gurkhas, two Balti guides, a Pathan surveyor from the 11th Bengal Lancers called Shahzad Mir, a Turki interpreter, some very sketchy maps, a stock of magnesium signalling wire, a box of ornamental soap and a portable goat-skin raft departed from Leh on 8 August 1889. Younghusband marched ahead with Shukar Ali, the Mustagh Pass veteran who had agreed to accompany him as personal cook and valet. Caught by a bout of mountain sickness, he was uninspired by the Ladakhi scenery: 'Its mountains, though lofty, are not grand or rugged, but resemble a monotonous succession of gigantic cinder-heaps.'[9]

Their initial destination was Shahidula, a Kirghiz settlement several hundred miles to the north of Leh. The Kirghiz were the principal victims of the Hunza raiders, two dozen of them having been kidnapped and held for ransom the previous autumn. Living in a barren stretch of land on the eastern edge of the Pamirs, trapped between China, Russia and British India, they had appealed in every direction for protection. The British moved in quickly to guard the trade route through Shahidula: Younghusband hoped to establish a direct link between the Kirghiz chief and officials in Simla. His government also thought it might provide a good opportunity to bring the people of Hunza into line – a vain hope as it turned out; the Pakistani administration is still trying to do so today, without much success.[10]

After a week among the apricot trees and Buddhist stupas of the Nubra valley, the expedition crossed the Saser Pass, on the far side of which a pack of transport camels was waiting. Younghusband was able to talk to a party of traders from Turkestan, who informed him that a group of Russians were said to be in the area. He pushed on quickly through 'a wilderness of barren rocky mountains' and across the drab gravel ranges of the Depsang Plains. After traversing the 'Valley of the Shadow of Death', which was littered with the skeletons of sheep and ponies, the travellers reached the freezing blankness of the Karakoram Pass, crossed it and marched on to Suget. There Younghusband met Jan Mohamed Khan, a 'cunning, intelligent man' who 'led me into a comfortable yurta and regaled me with tea, fresh milk and some excellent chuppaties of Kirghiz make'. Jan Mohamed had acted as interpreter to Ney Elias, and Younghusband soon realized he would make an invaluable assistant.

Towards the end of August they reached Shahidula where Younghusband was greeted by the Kirghiz chief, Turdi Kol, 'a thin care-worn looking man, rather over middle age, very grave and sedate in manner, but with a certain dignity about him'.[11] The settlement consisted of rough pasture, inhabited by a few hundred Kirghiz herders who lived in felt tents. Younghusband considered them to be 'timid, irresolute and shifty . . . a flabby lot, who, like parasites, preferred to hang on to some greater power rather than make any attempt at defence themselves'.[12] But he was impressed by Turdi Kol, who petitioned to transfer his allegiance from the Chinese (whose regional influence had waned with the death of Yakub Beg) to the British. Turdi Kol was at the end of his tether, having narrowly missed being killed by the Hunza raiders the previous year, and Younghusband saw the opportunity to enhance the prestige of the British Empire.

The following day he ordered a chair and a table to be placed on a carpet in the middle of the settlement. On either side of it stood Kashmiri sepoys and uniformed Gurkhas with fixed bayonets. Captain Younghusband (as he now was) prepared for his grand entrance:

> At the fixed time I myself appeared, proudly arrayed in my scarlet full-dress King's Dragoon Guards uniform. With me was Shahzad Mir, carrying a drawn sword. As I approached the assembly the Gurkhas fired a salute of three volleys, the Kashmir sepoys presented arms, and all the Kirghiz rose to their feet and salaamed deeply.[13]

With the help of the interpreter Jan Mohamed Khan, he told them that he would ask the Viceroy to give them protection. Meanwhile he would leave sepoys to guard them, and make his way to Hunza to find the raiders. He hoped several of them would accompany him, and show him the secret pass.

> All of them were in the most abject terror of the Kanjutis [the Kirghiz name for the Hunza people], and assured me that the first man who entered Hunza territory would be killed without a doubt . . . I turned round and said in chaff to the corporal of the Gurkhas, 'All right, you shall go first.' The little man was quite delighted, and beamed with satisfaction at the prospect. Little touches like this show up in a flash the various characteristics of different races.[14]

Younghusband then distributed presents to the assembled multitude, giving the Kirghiz leader Turdi Kol a turban, nine hundred rupees and a revolver.

A combination of absolute power and a belief in racial superiority (perhaps assisted by the thin air) had combined to give Younghusband a dramatic sense of self-importance. Before leaving Simla he had refused the offer of another British officer to accompany him. He relished the role of the lone white sahib, imposing his will on fractious peoples. 'It was most impressive,' he wrote after his performance in front of the Kirghiz, 'to see these rough nomads bowing there before me.'[15] But his skill at high altitude theatre was not matched by political nous. The Kirghiz lived too far from India to come under effective British protection. 'His temporary adoption of the Kirghiz of the Kun Lun had typically disastrous consequences,' wrote Keay. 'The Kashmiri soldiers were in due course withdrawn; the Hunza raiders relieved the Kirghiz of the rupees . . . and three years later the Kirghiz leader, with whom Younghusband had hit it off so well, was paying for his pro-British sympathies in a Chinese prison.'[16]

Having sent Jan Mohamed Khan to Yarkand to arrange more supplies, Younghusband set off to find the raiders. Turdi Kol had agreed to accompany him and to reveal the hidden Shimshal Pass into Hunza. Several mounted Kirghiz came too, accompanied by a flock of sheep and goats to be eaten en route. In the middle of October the party reached Chong Jangal, a grass valley on the edge of Hunza. During the journey Younghusband had explored another secret pass called the Saltoro which was rumoured to lead to Baltistan. Four days' climbing a glacier (which Younghusband subsequently named the Urdok Glacier 'because I saw a duck on it, and "urdok" is the Turki for a duck') had been followed by an avalanche. 'But we could not run, for we were on an ice-slope, so we crouched in an agony of fear. And just as it seemed to be crashing right upon the top of us the avalanche rushed past us just ahead in the very ravine we were about to enter.'[17]

By the time they rejoined the escort Younghusband's appearance 'was not becoming, for my eyes were bloodshot and inflamed from partial snow-blindness, and my nose, ears and lips blistered from the bitter wind . . . my knuckles cracked from the cold.'[18] At Chong Jangal they waited until Turdi Kol and his men arrived with fresh flour, rice and ghee. They were carrying a letter from the Resident in Kashmir, Colonel Parry Nisbet, warning of danger in Hunza. The Foreign Secretary's brother, Colonel Algernon 'Algy' Durand, had been sent from Gilgit to confront the Mir of Hunza and received a hostile reception. Younghusband was warned to tread carefully. He wrote a spidery reply, apologizing for not being able to seal the letter correctly. 'My signet ring has fallen off through my finger having become thin from the cold and is lost, so do not be surprised at the seal to this letter having Persian characters to it.'[19]

He was in a state of high spiritual ferment, earnestly studying Monier Williams's *Buddhism* in the chill air. Dangerously thin and increasingly impulsive, his mind was journeying into the realms of mysticism. Like wandering soldiers from 'Chinese' Gordon to Orde Wingate and Lawrence of Arabia, his travels in remote places acted as a spur to his religious tendencies. Later he wrote that his real task in these places had been 'an exploration of the very heart and soul of things, the discovery of the real Power, the inner Being, of which the outward features of Mother Earth's face, the plants and animals and we men, are but the expression'.[20]

Crossing a frozen stream at the base of a narrow valley they reached Darwaza, the 'Gate of Hunza'. High above them sat the object of the expedition, the raiders' lair – a stone fort perched on the edge of a sheer cliff. Younghusband reconnoitred the position with his field-glasses: 'the exciting moment had now arrived when we should have to beard these raiders in their very den.'[21] With rash audacity, he set off up the zigzag path with two interpreters and a Gurkha soldier. The rest of the party were left behind to provide covering fire if necessary. The four men steadily climbed up the precipitous edge of the ravine, aware that an artfully rolled boulder could annihilate them at any moment.

When they reached the fort it seemed to be deserted. But as Younghusband approached the open doors they slammed shut in his face, and in an instant 'the whole wall was lined with the wildest-looking men, shouting loudly and pointing their matchlocks at us from only fifty feet above us, and in a twinkling it looked as if the worst was going to happen.'[22] Captain Younghusband kept his nerve, shouting up in Turki that one man should be sent down to parley. Gradually the clamour ceased, and two Kanjutis came out of the fort. Younghusband announced that he was heading for Hunza to see the Mir. After delicate negotiations, and a careful assessment of his military escort, the Kanjutis agreed to allow them inside the fort. The Gurkhas and Turdi Kol's Kirghiz followers climbed up the slope to join the advance party. Then as they made their way through the gates of the fort, one of 'these wild Hunza men' lunged forward and grabbed the bridle of Younghusband's pony.

A double row of Kanjutis with matchlocks stood behind him, and I thought for a moment there was treachery. But the man sprang aside again with a laugh, and seeing it was intended for a joke I laughed too. It might have cost the gentleman dear though, if he had kept it up a moment longer, for he would certainly have had a bullet through his head from my Gurkhas . . . if not from my revolver. It was very cold and the Kanjutis lit a large fire round which we all stood – Kanjutis, Kirghiz, Gurkhas, Ladakhis, a Balti, a Pathan, and one Englishman, in the heart of the Himalayas, where no European had ever before penetrated.[23]

Younghusband was in his element, ensconced in the robbers' den telling them 'the Queen of England was naturally very angry at her subjects being raided, and had sent me to see their chief'. His patriotism had convinced him that his success 'was mainly due to the fact that I was an Englishman, that I stood for the British Empire and . . . the good name which England during long centuries had established.'[24] The Kanjutis were uncertain how to treat him, and seemed surprised by his high moral tone. They did not raid the Kirghiz out of choice, they assured him, but because they were ordered to do so by their ruler. Younghusband told them that he intended to travel across the Shimshal Pass into Hunza proper, but that his Kirghiz friends would now return home. The Kanjutis agreed reluctantly, for they had been ordered to send the Kirghiz to meet the Mir.

They were particularly keen to identify Turdi Kol, since he had shot and killed one of their party during the raid the previous year. The Mir of Hunza, whose skills as a slave trader were said to be esteemed throughout Central Asia, had decreed that the Kirghiz leader should have his head removed from his shoulders once he was captured. Throughout the meeting in the fort Turdi Kol was therefore in mortal danger should his identity be discovered. When asked the names of all his escort, Younghusband pretended that Turdi Kol was a lowly herdsman called Sattiwali. But a moment of acute anxiety came when they were leaving the fort and one of the Gurkhas carelessly called Turdi Kol by his real name. Luckily the Gurkha instantly covered the mistake by 'correcting himself and going off into a loud laugh'. One more crisis had passed off safely, but Younghusband's nerves were left on edge. 'Gurkhas are brave, cheery little men,' he concluded, 'but they have not the wits of a hog.'[25]

In the journal that was written during the expedition itself, it is not a Gurkha who lacks the wits of a hog, but an Englishman. Younghusband's original version of the events in the fort reads as follows:

> As he left, Turdi Kol salaamed to me, and, in an unguarded moment, I said 'Salaam Turdi Kol' instead of 'Salaam Satti-wali'. Fortunately the Kanjutis were squabbling amongst themselves, and did not notice it, and Shahzad Mir instantly covered my mistake by shouting in a loud tone to our remaining Kirghiz, Sari Kol, which name somewhat resembles Turdi Kol.[26]

I was brought up short by this adjustment, and left wondering about other possible discrepancies. *The Heart of a Continent* is Younghusband's most celebrated book, going into four reprints in its year of publication alone (1896), and into a modern edition as recently as 1984. But as John Murray wrote in a 'Notice' to the first edition, 'inasmuch as many of the incidents described are known to the author alone, the process of verification, when any uncertainty arose, was in some instances impossible'. Was Younghusband a reliable witness? If he blamed a slip of the tongue on a Gurkha soldier, what other blunders might he have omitted from the text?

The most obvious omissions relate to events which might have made him look foolish. His mistake over Turdi Kol's name is a good example, as is the episode in Manchuria when he stuck a pair of scissors in his foot. He had a fear of ever seeming to be weak, which meant that the implications of his behaviour were left unwritten. The crossing of the Mustagh Pass is presented as an act of logical bravado, but its impact on others is discounted. He glosses over the fact that the party of Balti villagers he ordered back up the Mustagh to rescue Liu San and Drogpa were placed in extreme danger, three of them being severely injured. His activities in Shahidula were similarly disruptive. Even in his later books he portrays himself as the saviour of the Kirghiz, when he knew that in fact his whimsical promises of British protection had landed Turdi Kol in a Chinese dungeon.

In *The Heart of a Continent* Younghusband is anxious to appear as the level-headed frontier officer, dutifully fulfilling the orders of his superiors. In fact he was impetuous and emotional, his actions often bearing little resemblance to his instructions from Simla. Whenever he found himself in Himalayan isolation, his personal agenda would take over from the official one. He would make lengthy notes, often on spiritual matters or on questions of evolution or philosophy. At the same time he would push his remarkable physical stamina to its furthest limits, usually climbing a new peak 'for interest' at the end of a day's march. But his emotions are ruthlessly excluded from *The Heart of a Continent*, as are the internal impulses which provoked his ceaseless exploration of new peaks and passes. He was on a permanent quest, always anxious to be 'the first white man' to see an unknown part of Central Asia.

After comparing the various versions of his travels, I felt that Younghusband was usually accurate as a factual witness. There is generally a high degree of corroboration between the published and unpublished accounts, although the intricacies of the Great Game are removed from public scrutiny along with the emotion and the slips of the tongue. He had a definite wish to present his own actions in a favourable light, but there is no evidence he was a fantasist. *The Heart of a Continent* is reliable by the standards of the Victorian travel narrative. There was at the time a vogue for wild tales of journeys to distant countries, such as Henry Savage Landor's *In the Forbidden Land* – an account of his supposed exploits in Tibet ('A white man going into that country had no chance of coming back alive') which is so overblown as to be ridiculous. Younghusband was following the conventions of the time by presenting himself as a flawless hero. The episode concerning the man with fewer wits than a hog suited his intentions; and besides, all good travel books are works of fiction.

Francis Younghusband and his Gurkha escort set off in search of the raiders' ruler: the Mir of Hunza. On the way he searched for unexplored passes, returning to Chong Jangal. Four days later a message reached him from his superiors in Simla warning that Russians were in the area. As he was heading for the Taghdumbash Pamir, a level plain on the edge of the Kun Lun range, another courier galloped up with a letter. It was from Colonel Grombtchevski: Great Gamer extraordinaire and 'the rising explorer of the Russian Geographical' – Captain Younghusband's alter ego. Would the British officer care to visit his camp at Khaian Aksai?

'Colonel Gromchevsky is a thorough gentleman to start with,' wrote Younghusband to Parry Nisbet.[27] The celebrated Colonel turned out to be a great bear of a man 'with a pleasant, genial manner' and a thick black beard, who promptly invited Younghusband to dine with him. Although he was Polish by birth, Grombtchevski had 'the ear of the Tsar' and was on a special expedition from Ferghana on his behalf, supposedly with the intention of establishing closer links with the Mir of Hunza. With him was a German naturalist called Conrad, and an escort of Cossacks whom Younghusband found to be 'very dirty and clothed in khaki jackets, tight pantaloons, and high boots reaching above the knee'.[28] The Russian and the Englishman sat down to 'a very substantial repast of soup and stews, washed down with a plentiful supply of vodka'.[29]

Grombtchevski gained a favourable impression of his rival, reporting to the Imperial Russian Geographical Society that Younghusband was 'a young man who had made his name with a brave journey from Peking to Kashmir across the whole of China. He was accompanied by a small escort of Bengali soldiers, some Pundits and countless servants. Our encounter was most friendly.'[30] The similarity of their interests gave the two men an instant rapport. Younghusband had been expecting a tense confrontation with a hostile rival; instead he experienced a home-coming. Here in the barren isolation of no man's land he found a fellow traveller, another person who loved bleak wilderness more than human society.

With French as their only common tongue, they fell into an intense discussion: the conversation was a mixture of mutual admiration and cut-and-thrust diplomacy, Grombtchevski insisting that nearly half a million Russian troops were ready to march south at the drop of a hat. He called some of the Cossacks over to the door of the tent and received 'a rousing cheer' when he asked them if they would like to invade India. 'We are both playing at a big game,' wrote Younghusband, 'and we should not be one jot better off for trying to conceal the fact.' Although Younghusband was a supporter of the 'forward policy', he saw that Grombtchevski was being unrealistic. When asked how they planned to provision troops marching across mountains and deserts, the Russian laughingly replied that his men went wherever they were told and did not worry about trivial matters like supplies. The discussion continued long into the night, Younghusband broaching his solitary bottle of brandy as 'the bitter winds of these high lands' buffeted the small tent.

In the morning they turned out their respective forces, Grombtchevski being 'much taken with the appearance of the Gurkhas, and with the precision and smartness of the few drill exercises they went through'.[31] The Gurkhas, meanwhile, were dismissive of the Cossacks, regarding them as slack and ill-equipped. Afterwards Grombtchevski took a picture of the combined parties with his box camera, a remarkable photograph which still survives today. Keay describes it as 'the most representative and memorable vignette in the whole of the Great Game . . . as a remarkable record of a celebrated and desolate encounter it can scarcely be equalled; imagine the excitement if a photograph of Stanley's meeting with Livingstone ever came to light.'

The two explorers pose at the centre of the picture while Gurkhas, Cossacks, Andajanis, Ladakhis, Baltis, Kanjutis, Pathans and Kirghiz stand ranged behind them. Younghusband, who was nearly a foot shorter than Grombtchevski, has taken the trouble to clamber onto an ammunition box in an effort to appear taller: a pile of wood has been placed in the foreground of the photograph to hide his prop. 'Instead of the conventional studio portrait, here we see the explorer in action. Bearded and in a battered bush hat, with one hand on hip and the other on his gun, Younghusband at last looks convincing.'[32] It was the first time that rival Great Gamers had met on the frontier, and both men must have been conscious that they were making history.

The following day Younghusband struck camp. Before leaving he ordered the Gurkhas to present arms, and the Cossacks responded by 'carrying swords'. Grombtchevski was impressed, 'saying to me that he hoped we might meet again, either in peace at St Petersburg or in war on the Indian frontier; in either case I might be sure of a warm welcome.'[33] Younghusband headed off towards the Pamirs, knowing that his rival had plans to try to enter British-controlled territory in Ladakh. He decided to counter this move by sending Grombtchevski on the ultimate adventure – a short-cut from nothing to nothing. By ensuring that the Russian travelled to Ladakh by an impossible route, he could be fairly certain that he would not complete the journey. Younghusband persuaded the Kirghiz to show Grombtchevski the direct course from Shahidula to Polu. In a letter to Parry-Nisbet he describes it as 'a route of absolutely no importance, leading from nowhere to nowhere, and passing over very elevated plateaux and mountains without grass or fuel, and to cross which in winter will cause him extreme hardships and loss to his party.'[34] Younghusband's credentials as a serious Great Gamer were firmly established.

And so the Cossacks caught frostbite, the ponies died, and nearly a year later Grombtchevski was still on crutches. Younghusband carefully excluded any mention of his scheming from published material. In *The Heart of a Continent* he ignores his own role in the debacle, blithely writing: 'When I recall how inadequately he and his party were supplied with camp equipage, and how roughly altogether they were travelling, I cannot help admiring the stolid perseverance of this Russian explorer in ever attempting the task he did.'[35] Given Younghusband's character, it is unlikely that he ever intended to send Grombtchevski and his escort to their death. But what is characteristic is the way in which he tried to suppress his own responsibility for their suffering. It is only in the Political and Secret files of the India Office Library that his secret is exposed.

The Taghdumbash Pamir is a wide, grey, desolate valley, nearly 15,000 feet above sea level, caught between two mountain ranges. A bitter wind blows over the grass night and day. Francis Younghusband found the people to be 'mostly bad characters' – Sarikoli and Kirghiz pasturists who had been cast out of their own communities. He engaged some of them to carry his loads. In Tashkurgan he met up with a pair of British officers who were on a related mission: 'The pleasure of meeting Englishmen again, and being able to talk in my own language, may well be imagined.'[36]

After surveying the head of the Khunjerab Pass he travelled south towards Hunza. The time had come to beard the Mir. It was now early November, and the weather was deteriorating fast. Younghusband was physically debilitated and still very thin, frantically drawing maps and making jottings in his notebooks. The influence of Clifton had not deserted him. Although the temperature regularly fell to minus 20° centigrade, each morning he would dutifully perform the traditional ritual which formed the bed-rock of the British Empire: 'I still kept up the custom of a cold bath, and there was a coating of ice on the bath almost immediately the water was poured out.'[37]

At Mintaka Aksai Younghusband was greeted by a pair of Kashgari officials. They had been sent by the Chinese Taotai to investigate frontier matters, and wanted to know what a British officer was doing in Chinese territory. With the help of a commanding voice, several cups of tea and the discreet presence of six Gurkha soldiers, Younghusband was able to persuade them that his intentions were respectable. He was on his way to see the Mir of Hunza, he said, and had just happened to cross the edge of the Taghdumbash Pamir. The Kashgaris withdrew, apparently satisfied.

That afternoon Younghusband paid off his Kirghiz porters, giving each of them a sum of money and some cloth. One of them, Juma Bai, was rash enough ('impertinent enough', in Younghusband's words) to ask for more. 'I immediately sent my interpreter to throw away the tea and cloth, etc., which I had given him, before his eyes, to turn the sheep loose in the valley, and to express my extreme displeasure at being insulted in this way.' 'This had a marvellous effect,' considered Younghusband, 'for all the rest of the Kirghiz proceeded to turn upon the wretched Juma Bai and soundly beat him.' On their way back to Shahidula the booty-laden Kirghiz were nearly set upon by the Hunza raiders, only being dissuaded by the influence of Colonel Grombtchevski.[38]

Having descended the Mintaka Pass into Hunza, Younghusband and the Gurkhas found 'the marrow-freezing blasts of wind were left behind'. The Chief Minister of Hunza, Wazir Dadu, was waiting at the fort with the Mir's half-brother, Mohammed Nazim Khan. 'The Wazir is a handsome-looking man, with good features and a very fine beard . . . a clever, shrewd man,' thought Younghusband, and 'a keen sportsman and a good shot.'[39] The state officials accompanied them along the course of the Hunza river. Younghusband was nervous, for the Mir of Hunza was notoriously unstable and brutal: 'He had poisoned his father and thrown two brothers over precipices, and I had to be on my guard.'[40]

As they approached the village of Gulmit a thirteen-gun salute was fired and the roar of drums could be heard in the distance, 'dozens of them all being beaten with might and main by frenzied drummers. On the hillside hundreds of people were collected, and as I neared the chief's tent ... I found a double row of wild, hard-looking men, armed with matchlocks and swords.'[41] Captain Francis Younghusband, representative of the Government of India and envoy of Her Majesty the Queen Empress, was being summoned to the august presence of Raja Safder Ali Khan, Mir of Hunza, Chief of Mintaka and Ruler of all Kanjut.

Younghusband was bedizened in his 'scarlet full-dress King's Dragoon Guards uniform', while the Gurkhas were clad in dark green rifle dress. As he thrust his way proudly into the Mir's tent (which had been stolen from Captain Durand), Younghusband was astonished to find himself 'in the presence of a man with a complexion of almost European fairness, and with reddish hair. His features, too, were of an entirely European cast, and, dressed in European clothes, he might anywhere have been taken for a Greek or Italian.'[42] Safder Ali was supposed to be playing the role of the standard Oriental despot, but he did not look the part. Rows of Hunzamen were kneeling inside the huge tent 'with solemn, upturned faces', watching the British officer's every move. Noticing that there was only one throne amidst the carpets and brocade, Younghusband swiftly sent for his canvas camp chair whilst simultaneously keeping up 'a string of complimentary questions about the health of the various relatives of the chief'. A Gurkha placed the chair squarely beside the seat of the Mir, and the two men sat down.

Safder Ali ('Young Saffy') 'was under the impression that the Empress of India, the Czar of Russia, and the Emperor of China were chiefs of neighbouring tribes'. When asked if he had ever travelled to India, 'he said that "great kings" like himself and Alexander [the Great] never left their own country!' Hunza, he said, was a harsh country, 'nothing but stones and ice', and if the British wanted him to stop raiding the trade route they would have to pay compensation. Younghusband was not amused. 'I said the Queen was not in the habit of paying blackmail, that I had left soldiers for the protection of the trade route, and he might try for himself how much revenue he would get now from a raid. Much to my astonishment, he burst into a roar of laughter.'

Captain Younghusband decided that a show of military strength might shake 'such a man as this'. The Gurkhas went through their drill 'very smartly' before firing volleys at rocks on the other side of the valley. The Mir was 'mightily impressed' and asked the

Gurkhas to fire at a man walking on the opposite bank. Young-husband refused, saying that the Gurkhas 'were so accurate they would certainly hit him. "What does it matter if they do?" said Safder Ali; "he belongs to me." Though so nervous about his own life he was utterly callous of other people's.'[43]

Over the next few days they held more meetings. Younghusband pointed out that Hunza was allied to India through Kashmir, and that its ruler therefore should have no dealings with Russians such as Grombtchevski. His diplomacy had little effect. Safder Ali was more interested in acquiring his guest's mule-trunks, and 'a few tablets of soap wrapped up in "silver" paper for his wives. He seemed utterly without shame.'[44] It was only on the day of Young-husband's departure that he tried to make amends, coming down on foot and apologizing 'for any annoyance'. But Younghusband drew himself up to his full height: he would not be trifled with by a mere Mir. 'I knew that he was a cur at heart, and I have no doubt he was impressed by my bearing.'[45]

In the end the Mir of Hunza was not sufficiently impressed by Younghusband's bearing to change his ways. Two years later he sent a letter to the Political Officer in Gilgit, declaring that any British officer setting foot in Hunza territory would have his head chopped off and served up on a platter. The result was the Hunza Expedition: the fortress at Nilt was blown apart, and Hunza fighters defeated on their own ground. The Mir, realizing that Grombtch-evski's promises of Russian help had come to nothing, fled to exile in Sinkiang and his half-brother was installed as a puppet ruler. When the British troops reached the Mir's palace they found a portrait of the Tsar, and a collection of Younghusband's letters to the Indian Government which had been intercepted by 'these wild Hunza men'.

SIX

That Sinkiang Feeling:
Outwitted in High Asia

Down in Calcutta Francis Younghusband was feeling unusually buoyant. He dashed from dinner to dance and back again, 'going it very strong'. A telegram had been handed to him as he entered India at the end of December: 'Please tell Younghusband', it read, 'that his Excellency the Viceroy has heard with much satisfaction of his return and congratulates him upon the successful issue of his expedition.'[1] The Foreign Office of the Government of India was impressed by the range of his achievements and the new maps he had drawn; they listened keenly when he suggested the only way to tame the Mir was by invading Hunza and dictating terms to him.

The Himalayan journey and the experience of power had given Younghusband a renewed sense of confidence. May Ewart had drifted from his mind, temporarily at least, and his sister Emmie had re-emerged as his confidante. He had been introduced to the Prince of Wales in Calcutta, he told her, who 'made some ordinary remarks about it being very interesting and asked me a few questions not very much to the point'. The following day he wrote to Emmie again:

> The Foreign Office seem keen ... they say the Viceroy thinks very well of me ... I see every prospect of doing some brilliant service before many years are out as a magnificent chance (unknown to outsiders) is gradually coming on for military politicals – and they will be only too glad to employ me as they have every confidence in me after my last journey.[2]

Uplifted by his sudden advance in status and the opportunity to bypass the imperial bureaucracy, he sacrificed the sensible option of returning to regimental life in favour of possible adventures on the frontier. There was no certainty that the 'magnificent chance' he was being offered as a 'military political' would lead to a stable career in the future. Characteristically he was able to convince key

81

decision-makers to let him fulfil his ambition: to take the most dramatic route, one which would never have been available to him had he followed the conventional line.

For the first four months of 1890 he remained in Calcutta, writing a long report on his exploits. He then put forward a proposal that a mission be sent to the Pamirs to investigate the gap between Afghanistan and the Chinese Empire. There was a stretch of land, known as the Wakhan Corridor, which the Russians were in danger of claiming. Under the terms of the 1873 Granville–Gortchakov agreement the area appeared to be Chinese, although Afghanistan also insisted it had a claim to the land. Younghusband suggested that he might be sent to survey it, and then travel on to Kashgar in Sinkiang to resolve the matter with Chinese officials. The power of the Ch'ing dynasty was fading, which made it possible that the western fringes of the Chinese Empire might be gobbled up by Russia.

While Younghusband was waiting for a reaction from the Foreign Office he went pig-sticking with his regiment at Muttra. Shortly after his twenty-seventh birthday a coded message came through saying that the mission could go ahead. With Lord Lansdowne as Viceroy the authorities in Calcutta were becoming increasingly hawkish. Younghusband was in a state of discreet ecstasy. Two months earlier he had been awarded the Founder's Medal of the Royal Geographical Society (the Patron's Medal for that year having gone to Emin Pasha) and now he was being given another opportunity to consolidate his reputation as an explorer. He set off for Leh and Yarkand, little realising that he would shortly bring Britain to the brink of war with Russia.

Pony and baggage men were engaged under the supervision of his old travelling companions Shukar Ali and Mahmood Isa (formerly known as Drogpa). Younghusband also took on a young Ladakhi called Ghulam Rassul Galwan, who later wrote a remarkable auto-biography cum travel book called *Servant of Sahibs*. Rassul records this exchange at Yarkand with his employer:

'Sir, all servants got clothes from you. Please give me some.'

'Boy, I have heard you not doing any work. For that, I don't want you any more. I will let you go from here.'

'Sir, I have done very good work. In the camp I have cooked for the men and looked the ponies. You do not know.'

'I don't want you, you lazy boy.'

'Sir, it is my bad luck. If you not want me, cannot help.'

On returning to camp, Rassul realized that Shukar Ali had instigated the conflict, and challenged him: 'It is back biting to sahib you have done . . . My God will help me and God will punish them who make lie matter about me.' Rassul then approached a Chinese secretary whom he knew and asked him to intervene with Younghusband. This resolved the matter, for the next day he was summoned: 'Big Sahib [Younghusband] said to me: "Boy, you are a good working boy. I do not know. The doctor sahib and Chinese munshi and the other sahibs told good things about you. I am sorry. I have made one bandobast [package] for sending the post to Leh."' Rassul was then given the job of postal runner and his future was assured.[3]

Pushing on over the frontier, Younghusband wrote a letter to Emmie: 'I have a good tent and plenty of good tinned provisions and a cook whom I pay Rs. 40 a month to look after me . . . Macartney is not exactly the sort of chap one would choose as a particular pal in civilisation – but he does not bother one and he takes a good deal of interest in things so that we get along very comfortably – going our separate ways during most of the day and meeting at meals.'[4] George Macartney was an interpreter from the Political Department. He was a little younger than Younghusband and, most unusually among the officials of the British Raj, half-Chinese.

In the racially hierarchical world of British India, Macartney's origins were dealt with by being politely glossed over. Official documents always stress his 'good knowledge of Chinese customs', while ignoring his mixed parentage. Younghusband hints at it in *The Heart of a Continent* by describing him as 'a son' of Sir Halliday Macartney rather than 'the son'. Only in private letters was candour possible, Younghusband complaining that his interpreter tended to approach diplomatic problems from a Chinese point of view: 'Macartney is a good enough fellow in his way but he is not English.'[5] Macartney himself was reticent and withdrawn as a result of his enforced double identity. During his childhood in Nanking, his Chinese mother had never associated with his father's European friends. But in his teens, George was sent to an English public school to become a sahib. According to his son, Macartney maintained a 'silence about his mother throughout his life, even to his own children'.[6]

Younghusband and Macartney travelled from Leh to Yarkand. They dined with the principal merchants ('a very sumptuous repast'), were photographed with the Amban, and met the convalescing Grombtchevski. Any fear that Younghusband might have had was soon allayed: it is clear that the Russian did not suspect this English gentleman of having sent him close to death. In his report on his travels Grombtchevski simply wrote that 'Captain Younghusband . . . was able to repay me for the hospitality I had shown him some months before.'[7] Before heading off to Tashkurgan they explored and mapped the Alichur Pamir, encountering small groups of nomadic Kirghiz and the skulls of Marco Polo sheep with horns five feet long. Some nights the temperature fell to minus 30° centigrade. At Lake Yeshil near Somatash, Younghusband came across an ancient inscription, detailing the expulsion of the Khojas. This persuaded him that he was at the western boundary of the Chinese Empire.

The two men and a handful of servants travelled on towards Rangkul. Younghusband was keen to investigate the legendary 'Lamp Rock' on the edge of Lake Rangkul which, according to Kirghiz histories, was inhabited by a dragon. 'On coming up to this rock I asked to be shown the light, and there, sure enough, was a cave, in the roof of which was a faint white light, which had the appearance of being caused by some phosphorescent substance.' To the horror of the local people, Younghusband climbed the rock 'in cat-like fashion, without boots' until he reached the back of it. Much to his disappointment he found that light entered the cave through a hidden hole in the bottom. 'This, then, was the secret of the Cave of Perpetual Light.'

After a brief excursion to Lake Karakul, in the region that is now Tadzhikstan, the party turned east towards Kashgaria. Winter was setting in as they moved swiftly over the wind-swept pass called the Kizil Jek. Soon they were on the plains of Turkestan approaching Kashgar, reaching it at the beginning of November. A house had been requisitioned for them on the edge of the city by the Chinese Taotai. It was called Chini Bagh or 'Chinese Garden', a secluded wooden building with a view over the Tien Shan mountains.

Younghusband was in a positive frame of mind. He was looking forward to seeing Petrovski, the Russian consul whom he had met on his way back from the Gobi Desert, 'and it was a comfort to think that during the winter we should not be thrown entirely upon our own resources, but would have the advantage of intercourse with other Europeans'.[8]

The fertile oasis city of Kashgar was at this time the focus of a power struggle. Just over a decade earlier Yakub Beg had fallen and the Chinese central government had reconquered Eastern Turkestan, naming it Sinkiang or 'The New Dominion'. A Taotai or Governor was appointed, but otherwise life continued much as it always had done, the indigenous Turkis growing their exotic fruits and haggling at the weekly horse fair. In 1882 the Russians had gained permission to station a consul in Kashgar, and the indomitable Petrovski appeared, temperamental, charming and immensely capable. With an escort of forty-five Cossacks and a network of informers, it did not take him long to become the 'virtual ruler' of Kashgar. The Taotai was an elderly diplomat in the Confucian mould, who paraded frequently in a sedan chair but exercised little power. Like many Chinese he was racially exclusive, dismissing the people he ruled as 'turban heads'. Petrovski manipulated him skilfully, even managing to gain access to his official communications.[9]

During the 1880s the British had tried unsuccessfully to station a representative in Kashgar. Ney Elias went to Yarkand to negotiate but was sent back with a flea in his ear. The Chinese government was still smarting over Britain's dealings with the rebellious Yakub Beg. Given the Chinese preoccupation with 'face' and ancestry, Francis Younghusband's status as an envoy to Kashgar can hardly have been enhanced by the fact that his uncle was Robert Shaw, the man who had first negotiated with Yakub Beg in the 1860s. Younghusband's position was weakened further by his initial dealings with the Taotai, who had complained of Afghan troops expelling Chinese citizens from the Pamirs. The Afghans would withdraw from the area, Younghusband assured him, and the British would guard the frontier on China's behalf. When the Emir of Afghanistan heard this news he complained angrily to Simla, and Younghusband's promises were promptly disowned. The Taotai was not impressed.

By the end of the year little progress had been made, but Captain Younghusband realized he would have to bide his time. He was kept occupied by a colourful cast of players in the closed world of

Kashgar, the city which is further from the sea than any other on the planet. There was Petrovski and his wife, the Taotai's secretary ('a thorough scamp'), Father Hendricks (a defrocked Dutch missionary who lived on scraps of vegetable), a corpulent Chinese general named Wang and a host of itinerants. They all sat down for 'a good sized dinner party' on Christmas day, including 'a wonderful tinned plum-pudding, which went off with an explosion when it was opened.'[10] Sven Hedin had to decline an invitation, sending his visiting card with a note pencilled on the back: 'My dear Mr. Younghusband, I thanks you very heartily of your friendly and hospitable invitation to Christmas day but I am very sorrow not to be able to come, because I have already sent my baggages early to day and must myself follow now.'[11]

This was the first occasion that Younghusband had met Hedin, a short, bookish Swedish explorer who was on a journey through Sinkiang. The two men were to remain in regular contact for life, a competitive friendship and great mutual respect being tempered by profoundly different ideological views. During the next decade Hedin was to discover the lost cities of the Taklamakan desert and spend several death-defying years in southern Tibet, producing a comprehensive scientific and geographical survey that has yet to be superseded.

Younghusband's relationship with the Russian consul became strained in the early months of 1891. At first Petrovski had been hospitable, inviting Younghusband and Macartney for discussions at the Russian consulate, an elegant building in the centre of Kashgar. He had talked freely about Kashgaria and Chinese weakness in an effort to draw out the British officers, even hinting that a revolution might be brewing among the Kirghiz. But he became increasingly awkward. His aim was to destabilize Younghusband, and make him feel his grasp of Central Asian politics was superficial. Petrovski succeeded in this ambition, Younghusband writing in a private letter that he felt isolated and uncertain: 'The prestige of England is in my hands and at the same time I am almost entirely cut off from seeking advice from Govt. for it takes four months to get an answer.'[12]

Younghusband was way out of his depth. Although he could scarcely be matched on the passes of High Asia, in the confines of Kashgar he was continually wrong-footed. Behind his urbane diplomatic exterior, Petrovski was manipulating the Englishman with great cunning. Russian agents had trailed Younghusband and Macartney across the Pamirs, and now their letters to Simla were being intercepted. Younghusband seems to have been gloriously unaware of the fact, even writing in *The Heart of a Continent* that he felt indebted to the Consul 'for many civilities during my stay in Kashgar. He had been most obliging in forwarding our letters through his couriers to Russian Turkestan.'[13] Petrovski was also aware of the substance of Younghusband's dealings with the Taotai, with the result that every move the British made could be pre-empted.

As the months went by Younghusband came to realize that Petrovski was winning the Game. No progress was being made with the Chinese over the Wakhan question, while the Taotai was becoming ever more disturbed (thanks to the rumour-mongering of the Russian Consul) about British activity in Hunza. Younghusband tried to convince himself that all would be well, since Petrovski had '40 soldiers and not a single Chinaman, whereas I have a Chinese munshi, a Chinese cook . . . and I gave the Governor a regular Chinese dinner. This I believe they appreciate.' Moreover Petrovski had 'no sense of honour': he and his fellow Russians 'have all the cunning and unscrupulousness of an Asiatic and yet expect to be treated on a European footing'.[14]

The truth was that Younghusband felt confused and depressed. His religious faith was in turmoil. After the trip to the Mir of Hunza his conviction about the spiritual power of mountains was reinforced: 'That there is a Power at work in the whole making for higher and forcing good out of evil is the true secret of the Himalaya.' But around the same time his belief in a Christian God began to falter. He became irritated by Emmie's emphasis on Jesus and his teaching, writing to her, 'I believe I have got as much if not more good from having intercourse with real good-hearted fellows who never go to church than from all the sermons I ever heard in church.'[15] Here in Kashgar his mind and soul remained troubled, scientific books offering no convincing answers to the doctrinal and spiritual questions which dogged him. His journey from painfully self-assured Evangelical Christianity to equally convinced Eastern mystic was underway. Younghusband became increasingly eccentric, refusing to live in Chini Bagh. He had a large Kirghiz yurt erected in the garden which he lived in through the winter, taking cold baths whenever the tension became too much for him.

At the end of February a letter arrived from India via Rassul the postal runner. It was from Mrs Ewart, announcing that her daughter May was getting married to a Mr Kane. Younghusband was crushed by the news. He had put May out of his mind and tried to forget his love for her. But now the knowledge that she was to be married to another man left him distraught. He attempted draft after draft of a letter, trying hopelessly to offer his 'warm congratulations' to May and her family. In desperation he gave up and wrote to his mother about his heartbreak: 'My love seems to be quite deadened and gone out of me.'[16] But before his letter was five days' march out of Kashgar, more mail arrived through the Russian postal system. There was a letter from his father in England: his mother was dead. 'Oh my poor mother that I wasn't there to comfort her in her last moments and to comfort you too my poor old father,' Francis wrote. 'She did know I loved her didn't she? But if there is anything I have ever done to grieve her do you forgive me?'[17] 'Dear old chap,' he told his brother George, 'I know you will be with them as much as you can and try to make up for the many sacrifices they have made for us boys.'[18]

Francis had no shoulder to cry on, as he waited in the desert isolation of Kashgar. He hid his desperate grief from Macartney. The letters from home made him feel guilty about his sadness. 'The Governor and Emmie and Ethel are wonderfully plucky over it,' wrote his younger brother Leslie, ending with a typically vacuous Victorian injunction: 'Goodbye old boy – you know how much I feel for you being alone to hear the sad news, but it is selfish to grieve too much.'[19] Francis felt an overpowering shame at his failure to have shown love to his pious, elusive mother when she was alive. This repression of emotion is reflected in *The Heart of a Continent*, where the whole episode is dismissed in one sentence. 'At this time my life was saddened by two of the hardest blows which can befall a man.'[20] Only Emmie could feel his hurt, writing in an anguished letter, 'I know that you loved her and what it will be to you . . . Dear Old Frank, if you only knew how intensely now I long for you.'[21]

The nine months in Kashgar were one of the low points of Frank Younghusband's life. His spiritual certainties were drifting away and his inner confidence was fading: at the same time his feelings were being suppressed and his awkward formality grew more intense. I found a fascinating letter in the India Office Library that he had written to Emmie in May 1891. It gives a vivid picture of the Englishman abroad, stiffly determined to keep foreign customs at arm's length:

> I feel very unfit for active diplomatic work just now as I still am very shaken and can't keep up sufficient assurance to do my part properly ... The Russians are not bad privately – about a fortnight ago was their Easter and they asked Macartney and me over to supper on Easter Eve. Towards midnight the Cossacks sang some hymns and a chant ... I was utterly flabbergasted at seeing the [Russian] Secretary go up and kiss the Consul three times on both cheeks and then see the Consul go up to Macartney and kiss him likewise! He then advanced on me but much as I like him I draw the line at kissing him, so I extended my hand well in front of me to keep him at a respectable distance while I wished him Happy Easter.[22]

The letters Francis wrote to Emmie represent the most important record of his early thoughts and development. For the first thirty years of his life she was almost the only person to whom he could open up his heart. For all the mutual anguish that was caused by their bizarre relationship, it did at least give Francis some form of emotional security. Their protracted correspondence was one of the most important discoveries I made in the India Office archives, at least as far as Francis's psychology was concerned. After his death the letters between them appear to have been hidden away by his daughter Eileen. It is possible that George Seaver read some of them when writing the first biography of Younghusband, but if so he was unable to cope with their ardour. Emmie receives occasional mentions in his book, but the nearest he comes to detailing sibling intimacy is in the sententious: 'A perusal of her diary during this period leaves the reader with the feeling that her love for her brother, though very deep and true, was nevertheless of the possessive kind.'[23]

The India Office Library also threw up an undiscovered photograph taken in 1891. I was leafing through a thick file headed 'Unidentified Persons': men on horses, men with guns, officers in plumed helmets, a lithe young man in shorts holding a pair of dumb-bells, an actress with a feather, a badly torn photograph of men in thick coats. I was about to toss it to one side when suddenly I noticed a pair of familiar, solemn, labrador eyes staring up at me.

They belonged to a hunched man in an embroidered coat, with a black astrakhan hat and a thick, dark beard. He looked like a Russian merchant; but the eyes were unmistakably those of Francis Younghusband.

While the other inhabitants of the library tapped at their lap-top computers or dozed in the gentle winter sunlight, I sat in a fever of excitement. The crumpled photograph was stuck to a battered piece of blue card, but as I turned it over bits of ancient Sellotape began to flake away. Aware that I was breaking every regulation in the library rule book, I gently peeled the card off until I had the photograph in my hand. Nobody seemed to be watching. On the back I could discern Younghusband's handwriting in faint pencil. With the aid of a magnifying glass I read:

> Group at Kashg   1891
> Ma   tney (now Sir George)
>   nard (S   Henry)
> F.E.Y.
> R   Beec (ince dead)

Which on consideration must have referred to Macartney, Lennard, Younghusband and Beech. I remembered Lennard and Beech from *The Heart of a Continent*. They had popped up briefly in Kashgar, supposedly 'for sporting purposes': judging by Lennard's subsequent role in the Hunza Expedition it is certain that he at least was an agent of the Indian Government. This was one of the few photographs to show Great Gamers in action, and the only one of Younghusband at Kashgar. The four men sit on trunks or boxes on a patterned carpet, a crouching bulldog at their feet. Macartney looks more Chinese than in any other picture, Lennard smokes the stub of a cigar and folds his arms over his British Warm, Younghusband has a perplexed and faintly demented air, while the gargantuan Beech sports an unlit cigarette, Bolshevik hat, knee-length leather boots and long sheepskin coat.

Quite what Lennard and Beech were up to in Kashgar and the Pamirs we may never know. I slipped the photograph carefully back into its folder and returned to the interminable files. The dichotomy often struck me between the easy serenity of the India Office Library and the events which were described in its documents. Every battle, durbar, migration and massacre in the modern history of the Indian subcontinent is chronicled within its quiet walls. I used to sit in a warm, soft chair, escaping temporarily from the desert and the mountains, holding the very journal that Younghusband had scribbled in at a height of 16,000 feet and a temperature of minus 30°. Matching the range of the archive material was a bizarre international collection of writers and library addicts. During February 1991 I made a list of some of the sights I saw there, including:

A demure Bhutanese princess; a Canadian researcher with hair extensions and a Hunza cap; a retired Tibetan cabinet minister with a concave chest; a colonel writing a monograph on Skinner's Horse; an English academic with a shell suit and a look of post-colonial guilt.

Six Orthodox Jews at a table meant for one. All wearing black frock coats, hats, curls and identical glasses, poring over a map of Tamil Nadu and gesticulating frantically.

An enthusiastic Indian student who is writing a Ph. D. on anti-British Agitation in the Hill States (1938–39). As we leave the library one evening he wheezes, 'Oh my goodness – I feel as if I had just made fifty runs.' I mention that I have found an unpublished account of the invasion of Tibet. He says: 'What you must realize, Patrick, is that there is no such thing as a neutral historical archive. Every text contains its own ideological strategy.' I promise to bear this in mind.

Observed in the canteen during lunch: a tiny Japanese man with horn-rimmed spectacles and a bad leg, eating a cheese salad roll with the aid of a knife, fork and spoon. The roll is still wrapped in cling film.

A retired Bengali civil servant in a tie and tweed jacket. We fall into conversation when he opens the door of the Reading Room with courtly style. He says he has read all of Sir Francis Younghusband's books, 'particularly the Everest'. When I ask him why he is here he replies: 'Actually I have come primarily for information. You see, even old men need intellectual food.'

All these people came to the India Office Library that winter, exactly a century after the bearded Captain Frank Younghusband was photographed at Kashgar. I returned to my papers, conscious that three centuries of history – the bizarre tale of the British in Asia –

had been telescoped down and installed in a concrete office block
in south London.

Younghusband rode out of the city at the end of July 1891. His
spirits were buoyed somewhat by the award of a CIE (Companion
of the Order of the Indian Empire) in recognition of his exploits
with the Mir of Hunza. The Foreign Office had decided that nothing
further was to be gained by his trying to negotiate with the Chinese
Taotai. Together with a handful of servants and a young lieutenant
called Davison, Younghusband crossed the hot plains of Kashgaria
and passed the foot of the Mustagh Ata mountain on the edge of
the Great Pamir. Davison had appeared in Kashgar a month earlier.
While on leave he had tried – hopelessly – to emulate Younghusband's feat of crossing the Mustagh Pass, only to end up half-
starved on the fringes of Sinkiang. Perplexed but flattered by the
young subaltern's adulation, Younghusband had adopted him as a
trainee Great Gamer. When they reached Lake Bulunkul, Davison
was sent west to Somatash while Younghusband continued towards
the Pamirs.

George Macartney, meanwhile, was left behind as the sole and
unofficial representative of British India's interests in Central Asia.
Macartney was to remain in the obscure listening-post of Kashgar
until 1918, returning briefly to Britain to marry a teenage Scottish
bride. Younghusband had found him 'even-tempered, and willing
to give and take' – an essential characteristic in dealing with the
irascible Russian consul. Before leaving Kashgar, Younghusband
had gone to see Petrovski only to be denied entry on the grounds
that calls were not to be made in the afternoon. Younghusband
apologized at once, while pointing out that he had frequently
visited Russian diplomats at that time of day when he was in Peking.
'But M. Petrovsky replied that he was only concerned with Kashgar,
and that at Kashgar the custom was to call in the middle of the
day.' As the years went by Petrovski was to become ever more
truculent, jumping at every possible and impossible opportunity to
take offence. After one perceived slight by Macartney in 1899, the
Russian broke off all relations. Locked in the desert isolation of

Kashgar, the two men did not exchange a single word for nearly three years.[24]

As Younghusband continued south he became aware there were Cossacks in the area. 'All this time reports kept coming in that a small Russian force had entered the Pamirs, and proclaimed them Russian territory, and at the head of the Tagh-dum-bash Pamir I found several families of Kirghiz who had fled before the Russians.' Some reports even said that Russians had annexed sections of Afghan-controlled land. Younghusband trailed the Cossacks across the Little Pamir, pausing briefly to write a note to his father: 'The Russians have done a good many barefaced things in their time but by Jove this one takes the cake.'[25]

On 10 August he reached Bozai Gumbaz and found a small encampment of Cossacks. By this stage he thought the problem had been exaggerated, writing in a private letter the next day, 'I am inclined to think the whole thing is a piece of brag and that the Russians will return [home] in the winter.'[26] But then a larger party arrived with a Russian flag. Younghusband decided on a direct approach, and 'sent out a servant with my card and invitation to the officers to come in and have some refreshments'. A 'quiet-mannered' man called Yanov appeared, wearing 'a white enamel Maltese cross, which I recognized as the Cross of St. George, the most coveted Russian decoration, and I at once congratulated him upon holding so distinguished an order'.[27]

Over a glass of Russian wine, Yanov confirmed that his government was laying claim to the Pamirs. He produced a map with the relevant region shaded in green. 'They are opening their mouths pretty wide,' Younghusband told his father. 'Even this place, which is distinctly Afghan, they claim, and what is more almost down to the Baroghil Pass and right up to the Hindu Kush.'[28] But he avoided discussing the implications of the Russian move with Yanov, and in the evening the rivals settled down to dinner together. 'Russians always seem to be able to produce soups and stews of a good wholesome, satisfying nature,' recorded Younghusband, 'such as native servants from India never seem able to imitate. The Russians had vegetables, too – a luxury to me – and sauces and relishes, and, besides vodka, two different kinds of wine and brandy.' At the end of the meal Yanov and Younghusband drank the health of the Tsar of Russia and the Queen of England, crouched in a small tent on the fringes of High Asia.

The next morning Yanov and his men headed north 'with many protestations of friendship' while Younghusband settled down to wait for Davison. 'But three nights later, as I was getting into bed, I heard the clatter of horses' hoofs on the stones outside my tent, and, on looking out, saw, in the bright moonlight, about thirty mounted Cossacks drawn up in line, with the Russian flag in the centre. I hastily put on a great-coat.'[29] Colonel Yanov dismounted and came over to Younghusband's tent. He 'courteously and civilly, and with many apologies' informed the British officer that he had been ordered by his superiors to escort him out of Russian territory.

'But I am not in Russian territory,' declared the indignant Captain Younghusband. Yanov replied that he considered it Russian, and that he would have to remove him by force if he refused to leave. 'Well,' said Younghusband, puffing out his chest, 'you have thirty Cossacks, and I am alone, so I must do as you wish. But I act under protest and shall report all the circumstances to my Government.' With characteristic imperial politeness he added that he felt no personal grudge against Yanov, and 'begged the Colonel and the rest of the officers to stay and have some supper'.[30] Quivering with emotion, the Russian hugged Younghusband to his breast and apologized for having to behave like a 'police official'. He then drew up a document, in French, which stipulated that his rival would proceed to Chinese territory and not return to India by any one of twenty-one named passes. This would avoid the embarrassment of his having to escort Younghusband from the Pamirs: rather he would rely on the Britisher's sense of honour. After the instrument had been copied and countersigned, they sat down to a 'rough supper' together.

In the morning Younghusband and his servants gathered up their belongings. Yanov came to bid farewell, bearing a haunch of venison and begging to be forgiven for the course of action that had been forced upon him. Younghusband accepted his apology (and the venison) with gracious dignity and rode proudly from the camp. Before he headed for the Chinese frontier he sent a runner down to Gilgit with a full account of his encounter with Yanov at Bozai Gumbaz.

When the news reached Simla the Indian government sprang into action. These Russians, said senior voices, had over-stepped the mark. They needed to be taught a lesson. An escort of Gurkhas under the command of Lieutenant 'Curly' Stewart (an old Cliftonian) was despatched to search for Younghusband. The Commander-in-Chief ordered the Quetta Division to mobilize, and announced that he was 'quite prepared to go ahead'. Calcutta telegraphed to London for instructions. 'Where is Buzai Gambaz?' came the desperate reply from the Foreign Office.[31]

Back in London Lord Rosebery rode the wave of popular Russophobia. Bozai Gumbaz, he declared, was 'the Gibraltar of the Hindu Kush'. Something must be done to assuage the insult to the celebrated young explorer. The British Ambassador to St Petersburg requested an instant retraction and an apology for the treatment of Younghusband: his demand was so forceful 'that de Giers, the Russian Foreign Minister, thought we meant immediate war'.[32] Meanwhile stories were circulating in the Indian press and the bazaars of the Himalayas. A British officer had been killed by Cossacks on the frontier, it was said. At the end of September *The Times* of London ran a carefully worded report: 'In spite of repeated contradictions, it is persistently rumoured that Captain Younghusband has been killed by the Russians in the Pamir country.'[33]

But Captain Younghusband was very much alive, eating venison on the edge of the Wakhijrui Pass.

SEVEN

Loving a Splendid Colonel and Seeking God's Kingdom

Holed up in a bleak, grey valley on the edge of the Pamirs, in the company of a handful of Pathan servants, Francis Younghusband sat and waited. His camp was opposite the opening to the Kilik Pass into Hunza, a vantage point from which he was able to watch the activities in the region.

After a fortnight Lieutenant Stewart and his military escort arrived from Gilgit, the fulcrum of Asia, with news that a flurry of diplomatic telegrams were racing between London, Calcutta and St Petersburg. Rather than return to India, Younghusband took the opportunity to set up an elaborate spy network in the area around his camp. He was determined the Russians should not get away with their acts of 'lawless violence', and he did not want to leave the Himalayas until he heard what had happened to Lieutenant Davison.

'Two officers each with a party of troops have been placed under my orders and I am now responsible for the frontier from Kanjut to the Baroghil Pass,' he wrote privately. 'I have got men out all over the Pamirs to give me instant news of any Russians.' The note also gives a rare insight into the practical workings of the Great Game. His agents, most of whom were inconspicuous hillmen, encoded messages using a strange alphabet as a cipher: 'Our correspondence is carried on in Hindustani written with English letters – the notes are wrapped very small and stored away in the lining of a man's hat or his boot and stitched into the wadding of his coat – all sorts of dodges.'[1]

During September 1891 Younghusband heard that Davison had been 'carried off as a prisoner', but otherwise there was little news of Russian activity. Yanov's troops appeared to have withdrawn from Bozai Gumbaz, rather than consolidating their hold on the area. As the days passed, Younghusband's thoughts turned to May Ewart and his memories of her presence. 'On these long lonely evenings I often sit dreaming of my love, and I think I would like to sit down and write all about it.' In a thick black notebook he detailed their meeting and hopeless courtship, and his feelings of desolation when he discovered she was to marry another man. Many years later he discovered the black notebook and wrote a footnote in the back, dated April 1928: 'Again on reading this through I see how very stupidly I behaved.' Forty years on he still felt a powerful love for May, 'right deep down the same devotion still stirs as something very, very sacred within me'. He added that 'even now' he would find it painful to have to see her again.[2]

In early October Davison appeared. 'He had been treated in an even more cavalier manner by the Russians than I had, and had been marched off back with them to Turkestan from the Alichur Pamir.' After being released at the Chinese frontier, Davison had made his way through Kashgar down to Younghusband's hide-out by the Kilik Pass. While 'Curly' Stewart and his escort of Gurkhas returned south, Younghusband and Davison made plans to head for India by an indirect route. When he had been expelled from Bozai Gumbaz by Colonel Yanov, Younghusband had signed a document saying that he would not cross any one of twenty-one named passes into India. Although there was no possible way that Yanov would discover whether or not he had kept his word, Younghusband was determined not to leave the region by a named pass. Under the rather bizarre code of honour by which the Great Game operated, he felt it would be 'ungentlemanly' to pursue any other course of conduct.

After climbing up the side of a nearby glacier, Younghusband, Davison, a few servants and a couple of yaks managed to reach the Pamir-i-Wakhan. The ground was covered in snow, and they had to burn their tent pegs for fuel. Through detailed questioning of a group of Wakhi shepherds, they discovered there was an unfrequented gap in the mountain range further down the valley. Following an early start, they climbed for twelve hours along an ice-covered glacier until they reached the crest of the pass. 'I never experienced such an icy blast as that which met us as we reached the summit,' wrote Younghusband. 'It came concentrating down upon us with terrific force, and sharp as a knife.' Their faces were badly slashed during the crossing; but Captain Younghusband knew he had kept to the terms of his agreement with Colonel Yanov.

Three weeks of trekking brought them to the Kashmir valley, and soon they reached the luxuriousness of Srinagar. Younghusband was glad to be back and in buoyant spirits, having been away from India for nearly a year and a half. He said goodbye fondly to Davison, but it was the last the two men were to see of each other. Following Younghusband's recommendation, Davison was employed in reconnaissance work; two years later he died of enteric fever on the Gilgit frontier. 'He had all the makings of a great explorer,' wrote Younghusband, 'he had unsurpassable energy, what one might almost call blind pluck, for nothing to him was dangerous . . . and his loss must be deplored by all who can admire true manliness and resolution.'[3]

The storm over the Bozai Gumbaz expulsion was still blowing, so Younghusband was in great demand in Srinagar. The rumours of his death, the machinations in Kashgar and the behaviour of the Russians combined to make him a focal point of social activity. Although he was naturally reticent, he enjoyed the glamour of his position. He was able to report home to his father that the Commander-in-Chief, 'Bobs' Roberts had 'squeezed my arm in that way he had'. Roberts reassured him that his conduct had been admirable, while the Viceroy, Lord Lansdowne, said 'he wanted to hear all I had to say on the subject . . . We talked a good deal at dinner and after the other guests had left he asked me into his private study, took an arm-chair by the fire and had a long talk.'[4]

Younghusband always maintained that his actions at Bozai Gumbaz were vindicated by subsequent events. 'After much correspondence and fencing,' he wrote in his memoirs, 'the Russian Ambassador in London apologised to Lord Salisbury. The Russians had to admit that Bozai Gumbaz, the place where I was arrested, was Afghan territory.'[5] Yet the truth was more complicated. Although the Viceroy said kind words and the Chief squeezed his arm, Younghusband found his Great Gaming career was badly dented by the affair. The last thing the British Government wanted was that their frontier agents should become involved in skirmishes over remote borders. Relations with Russia were difficult enough without 'incidents' in the Himalayas.

Although it was true that the Russian Ambassador did 'apologise' to the British Prime Minister, Lord Salisbury, he did so in the context of a climb-down by Britain. There was no mood in the Foreign Office in London for military action to avenge the humiliation at Bozai Gumbaz. Lord Salisbury was explicit in his rejection of Younghusband's requests for a re-appraisal of frontier policy and retaliation against the Russians, writing that it would be better to 'ignore' the precise nature of Yanov's offence. St Petersburg responded by officially repudiating Yanov's actions and describing him, absurdly, as a headstrong young officer on a shooting expedition. The upshot was the establishment of a Boundary Commission – precisely the result that Younghusband had sought to avoid. It meant there would be years of proposals, counter-proposals, negotiations and diplomatic horse-trading. Any hawkish hopes of British Indian expansion would have to be postponed.

After four years the Commission concluded that the territory was Afghan; a victory of sorts for Younghusband, but one that came too late to be of any use to him. Poor communication and the limited scope of his political vision had lain behind the crisis. In Younghusband's eyes the presence of Russian troops in the no man's land around the Wakhan Corridor was of great significance. His isolation in the Pamirs made him feel obliged to maintain and represent the prestige of the British Empire with great vigour. Where a more cautious officer might have under-played an encounter with Colonel Yanov, Younghusband milked it for all it was worth, in the hope that he might stimulate Calcutta into a more aggressive frontier strategy. Although he had important supporters within the Indian administration and army, their power was not enough to shift official policy.

Back in Whitehall, Younghusband's aggressive telegrams were seen as a source of trouble. From the perspective of the British Foreign Office, scuffles in Central Asia merely interfered with Anglo-Russian trade and diplomacy. They could neither spell nor pronounce Buzai Gambad; the Pamirs were a barren irrelevance in the context of pan-European politics. As far as they were concerned India's northern edges should remain quiet but undefined, with buffer zones to prevent direct conflict with foreign powers. Younghusband was quite unable to appreciate this wider perspective: for him the Himalayas were the centre of the world. His determination to play the 'lone agent' meant that he became progressively more awkward in his dealings with Calcutta and Whitehall. In a sense Younghusband was too good at his job. He went to absurd lengths to defend imperial interests on the frontier. As a result, sections of the administration came to perceive him as a loose cannon rather than a wise diplomatist. It was this naive, determined, occasionally unstable method of operation which would lead to the collapse of his professional career.

The beginning of 1892 found Francis Younghusband back in Britain on leave, staying with the remains of his family in Southsea, frequenting the Junior Conservative Club and lecturing at the RGS. He was summoned to see the head of the Intelligence Department, General Chapman, and the Secretary of State for India, Lord Cross. Cross took a 'perfunctory' interest in Younghusband's travels, inquiring after the weather in the Pamirs. But his deputy began an animated discussion about the Russian threat to the frontier. 'He knew the whole subject well,' recorded Younghusband, 'and was keenly interested in it. No one else I had met – not even in India – was so well informed and so enthusiastic. And he was young and fresh and very alert and able. His name was George Curzon; and this was his first appointment.'

The meeting marked the beginning of what was to be the most significant professional friendship of his career. Curzon, with his pink cheeks, sleek hair, curved spine and superior demeanour had been keeping track of Younghusband and his adventures for some years. He had great admiration for explorers, even going to the extent of describing himself as one in the epitaph above his tomb at Kedleston. Younghusband in turn was flattered by the attentions of an up-and-coming Member of Parliament. Although they were contemporaries, Curzon's aristocratic connections and political success represented a world of which Younghusband had little personal knowledge. 'We were mutually attracted to one another,' he wrote. 'Except for my own father, no man ever did anything like so much for me as Lord Curzon. Staunchness in friendship was a marked trait in his character.'[6] Two years later they would meet again on the Indian frontier.

During his leave Younghusband also had time to make a lasting acquaintance with the mountaineer Martin Conway. Conway had decided to make his name as a Karakoram explorer, and was constructing a huge expedition modelled on Whymper's voyage to the Andes. Younghusband gave him information about flower presses and altitude barometers and the temperament of the Baltis. 'My dear Conway,' he advised, 'mere climbing of peaks just for the sake of saying one has been up them I don't much care about, but what I shall look forward to with special interest are yr. observations on these glaciers and their actions and any comparison you may make between them and the glaciers of European mountains.'[7] After a brief excursion to Northumberland, Captain Younghusband returned to Southsea before fleeing to the Himalayas in late March.

He found himself in Hunza again, acting as Political Officer. The recalcitrant Mir had been deposed the previous winter during the Hunza Expedition, and replaced by his half-brother Mohammed Nazim Khan. Younghusband's brief was to represent British interests discreetly, ensuring that the new Mir stayed on good terms with neighbouring territories. From late August until the end of December Younghusband lived in a tent in an orchard of apricot trees, 'and from it we looked out over orchards and terraced fields to the great Rakapushi Peak filling up to the end of the valley with a wall of snow.'[8] Guarding him was a detachment of a hundred Kashmiri troops under the command of another British officer. There was little to do except play polo and make preparations for the winter by building simple stone huts. The landscape was stunning, but Younghusband was in low spirits; he wondered whether he might not do better leaving government service altogether. His gloom was only alleviated by an earnest correspondence with a plump middle-aged woman he had met in Srinagar, by the name of Nellie Douglas.

Nellie Douglas took the place of May Ewart and Emmie Younghusband. Trapped in a marriage to an ineffectual army officer called 'Boy', she spent much of her time away from her husband. Like many British women in India by this time, she was able to lead a relatively independent life within the strictures of station life. In his autobiographical novel *But In Our Lives*, Younghusband characterizes her as 'Lady Meara' and describes their exchanges about mystical experiences. 'My poor body seemed too utterly frail for so stupendous a power to force its way through,' declares Lady Meara about a visit from the divine spirit. 'I was filled to the very brim, and could contain no more. But oh! the rapture of joy, the holy ecstasy!' Evan Lee (Younghusband) and Lady Meara engage in chaste spiritual union. Nevertheless he is careful to emphasize that she was the sort of woman who 'might be trusted not by one single word or sign, by glance of the eye or touch of the hand or tone of the voice, to inflame him unworthily'.[9]

Within days of leaving Kashmir for Hunza Younghusband had begun writing emotional letters to Mrs Douglas. 'You don't know how much you are to me and it is so hard having to go away from all that is dear to me to that hard frontier life again – still it is noble work . . . Oh! Mrs Douglas it will be a terrible wrench going away from you my dear, dear friend.' A fortnight later he admitted, 'I struggle against depression but I do need your sympathy badly . . . strength seems to fail me.' But by early September his mood had lifted as he exulted, 'Oh you are the dearest best friend that any man did have . . . I do appreciate so much your wishing to call me by my Christian name and letting me call you by yours.' Never before had he been permitted such a liberty: 'Do call me Frank and I will call you Nellie . . . Oh Nellie Nellie you are so kind and good.'

Frank convinced himself that the relationship was perfectly proper. She was his 'dear friend' and confidante but not his paramour. 'I could not bear to think that people might go talking about you,' he wrote, 'and that yr. husband and brother wd. be hurt at having you talked about.' At times his letters are disingenuous on the subject of the 'purity' of their friendship, but it is clear that sexual desire was never Younghusband's motivating force. He needed love and support, and a friend who would listen to his fears. In the physical and emotional isolation of the Himalayas he found little sympathy, and dared not express his emotion to anybody. Although he had powerful feelings for Nellie Douglas, she was closer to a therapist than a lover.

Since only two of Nellie's letters to 'dear Frank' survive, it is hard to know what she thought of him. From the frequency of his correspondence it would appear that she relished his attention, but often there is a sense that she was startled by his ardour. At the end of October he confided in her about his relationship with Emmie, and the depression she was suffering. 'She never used to make many friends and . . . she sometimes tells me she just wishes to die. I do all I can to encourage her to mix with people and make friends but somehow it does not seem in her to do so.'[10]

During the late autumn of 1892 Captain Younghusband idled away his days in Hunza. Belatedly, he sent the Foreign Department of the Indian government his expense claims from the previous winter: 'Sir, I have the honor to forward a statement showing details of my expenditure on Secret Service to Chinese Turkestan,' including 'the services of a Chinese writer', presents for village headmen and 'a gift for the Beg of Kashgar'.[11] But shortly before Christmas a messenger brought news of the death of the Mehtar of Chitral, and within hours Younghusband was galloping off into the distance once again.

On New Year's Day 1893 a small expedition departed for Chitral. It was commanded by Surgeon-Major George Robertson, an army doctor turned political official, and consisted of Francis Younghusband, fifty Sikh soldiers, 'twenty coolie loads of presents' and a bullish young lieutenant from the 5th Gurkhas by the name of the Hon. Charlie 'Bruiser' Bruce. They headed west towards the

Afghan frontier, crossing the Shandur Pass despite the deep snow and the bitter cold. Several men caught frostbite.

During the journey Younghusband fantasized about going to Tibet. His idea captured Robertson's imagination, and shortly before they reached Chitral a proposal was made. 'About a week ago,' Younghusband told Nellie Douglas excitedly, 'Mr Robertson asked me in confidence whether I would care to accompany him on a journey to Lhassa with Mr Macartney of Kashgar and Mr Bruce . . . Mr Macartney would go as a Chinaman in charge of a caravan of merchandise. Mr Robertson would go as his secretary and Mr Bruce and myself as servants and camel men.'[12] It was not the only plan that the three men dreamt up. Lieutenant Bruce, who had been on Conway's expedition to the Karakoram, proposed as they sauntered across the polo ground at Chitral that they might explore the foothills of Mount Everest with a view to making an ascent. Many years later Bruce and Younghusband would come together to organize the early Everest expeditions.[13]

The situation in Chitral, a mountainous kingdom on the north-western fringes of British influence, proved to be calmer than antici-pated. The death of the old Mehtar (King) had led to a scramble for power among his relations. After the assassination of several pretenders the Mehtar's eldest son, Nizam ul Mulk, had ascended the throne. One of his first moves had been to request military support from Colonel 'Algy' Durand at Gilgit. Although he realized this would weaken his popularity internally, the new Mehtar felt the threat of British force would be the most effective method of silencing unrest. The Indian administration jumped at this opportu-nity to extend the boundaries of their power. Younghusband, Robertson and Bruce spent some nervous months in the capital, also called Chitral. There were frequent scares of looming insurrec-tion, but as the British became more entrenched, 'these ugly rumours grew less frequent, and the disposition of the people more favourable'.[14]

Once a week Younghusband would hand the postal runner the stack of letters he had written in his cramped, dusty hut. 'It has no window,' he told Nellie, 'and no chimney – you simply light a fire in the middle of the room . . . I have put a cloth dado round, have nailed some maps on the wall and covered them with pictures from the illustrated Harper's Magazine.' Some days Younghusband made 'little excursions' up nearby mountains with Bruce, and was greatly taken by his 'ice-axes and Alpine appliances'. Although he was glad to be among mountains, 'breaking upwards in crests of white snow', the truth was that Younghusband felt severely depressed. He disliked Robertson, while Bruce was affable but insensitive: inevitably Nellie Douglas was flooded with his worries.

'I don't quite know what is the matter with me,' he wrote on 22 February, 'an oppressive sort of feeling on me which I can't shake off and which puts me in a very nervous state.' Then a few days later: 'Another of those fits of nervousness have come over me and it is very unpleasant . . . Talking with anyone puts me in a regular nervous state.' Some days he forced himself to play polo with the Chitralis, but he lacked enthusiasm and became absurdly irritated by their inaccurate line-calls. A 'doleful letter' from his sister Emmie plunged him further into gloom. Her depression seemed to mirror his own. 'Poor girl,' he confided to his 'dearest Nellie', 'she says she has asked God for help again and again and she seems to get none, till she almost feels as if God has forsaken her.'[15]

Although Younghusband is far too discreet ever to mention his bodily functions, his writings at this time indicate that he may have been suffering from diarrhoea or dysentery. The exhaustion, apathy, insomnia and melancholia that plagued him are all symptoms of a physical debility of this kind. He lived off the same poor diet he had eaten during previous trips to the Himalayas, but lacked the sense of purpose that had kept him going in the past. He suspected that the bureaucrats in Calcutta had taken against him – the proposed trip to Tibet had been blocked, and they were insisting that he take Political Service examinations.

His glamorous but erratic career had meant that, technically at least, he was low down the official hierarchy. Although he could see no real purpose in doing so, he forced himself to learn the details of the Penal Code, Criminal Procedure, Urdu and political economy. Younghusband felt his life was losing its meaning. His job was tedious, while he could see no possibility of being sent on another special mission. At the end of May both Robertson and Bruce were sent back to Gilgit, abandoning him to the tenuous post of Acting British Political Officer in Chitral. Almost alone, Francis Younghusband celebrated his thirtieth birthday.

The isolation gave him a certain exhilaration. Although he felt worried and nervous, Younghusband enjoyed the power and prestige of his position. He was able to travel around Chitral with the Mehtar, a hawk on his arm, accompanied throughout by an escort of Sikh soldiers. They discussed railways, religion, the manufacture of ice and methods for the artificial incubation of eggs. 'The King and I are getting on capitally,' he wrote to his sister Ethel in June. 'He has called on me three times this week and we play polo together . . . I get a glow in me sometimes little Ethel, which makes me feel as if I could carry these people along anywhere and lead them as I like.'[16]

He fell to imagining himself as the saviour of Chitral, the sahib who would raise his adopted people to magnificent heights. Riding past bowing Chitralis, through the vales of willows, poplars, 'the orchards of apricots, peaches, pear and apple trees', it was not hard for Younghusband to picture himself as a Kiplingesque Himalayan king, a parent and guide to the 'child race' in his charge.[17] In his novel *But In Our Lives*, the hero Evan Lee finds himself in the same situation in a frontier state called Chitas. His thoughts are an exact encapsulation of the philosophy of High Imperialism.

> The Chitasis are children. But the people who treat children best are English nurses . . . They exercise a patience which never tires; and they are quick and firm to check the first incipient sign of naughtiness. But in the bottom of their hearts they love their little charges . . . Some of the children we shall have to deal with will be quite sensible, and we can treat them well. Others will be rough and unruly, and they will deserve a good sound spanking. But always we can remember the English nurse. These people will know quite well when they deserve a smacking, and if it is given with no ill-feeling behind it they will, like children, take it in good part and respect us for it.[18]

But Younghusband's fantasies were soon brought down to earth by the machinations of Surgeon-Major Robertson. Since leaving Chitral, Robertson had advised caution and pressed the authorities in Calcutta to order a British withdrawal from the territory. With a Gladstonian government back in office, his views had received a sympathetic hearing. Younghusband, as ever, had urged imperial expansion and the establishment of a permanent presence throughout Chitral. But his junior rank and reputation as a hothead meant that Robertson's view predominated, so at the end of August he was told to retire to Mastuj, a village on the frontier between Gilgit and Chitral. 'As I predicted the row has come on between Robertson and myself,' he wrote to his father. 'My blood is up now and nothing shall prevent me carrying things before me. What Govt. likes is to be served by clever fools.'[19] Many years later his irritation over the forced move from Chitral rankled. In March 1940 he made a note in the margin of an old letter: 'The withdrawal to Mastuj was the silliest possible move as it left me without the chance of influencing the Mehtar. It was all due to the way in which Robertson had frightened Government.'

Francis Younghusband rode through the lush valleys that fell between the dark brown faces of mountain rock, crossing the narrow rope bridges slung across the Yarkhun river on his way to the tiny settlement at Mastuj. A scattering of huts became his home. In frustration he fired off wild letters to Nellie Douglas: 'Oh I long to be by you when I cannot restrain myself from pouring out all that is in my heart . . . I want to explore the interior of Chinese Turkestan and Tibet and finish up in South West China . . . I am not going under Govt. I want to be free.'[20] He also wrote a letter to his one firm ally, the former Under Secretary of State for India, who replied enthusiastically via Younghusband's father.

> My dear Sir,
>   Many thanks to you for so kindly forwarding me the letter from your son. I was delighted to hear from him and get his views about Chitral. It is a pleasure to cooperate with so brilliant an explorer & so great an authority on matters of such transcendent importance as Indian Frontier Defence.
>   Yours faithfully, George Curzon[21]

Their views on the Great Game coincided exactly; both men feared Russian expansion and felt they had a moral duty to retain Chitral. A letter from Curzon was delivered to Younghusband's hut in Mastuj, hoping that he did not 'feel very lonely away in Chitral. Anyhow it is all good work which will fit into the great scheme. All luck to you.'[22]

In late October the Mehtar invited the Political Officer on a tour of his people. Younghusband made an earnest study of his methods of administration, comparing the Mehtar's benign dictatorship favourably with 'the elephantine British Government' and its 'useless correspondence'. He was able to assure Nellie Douglas that 'The King has the most charming manners . . . they are a very bright, cheery people.' Each day their progress would be greeted by dancers and banquets. 'It was really very impressive altogether – the king and myself surrounded by these wild, free hill men in the midst of their mountains out in the open with the snowy peaks towering above,' he wrote one evening. 'It was quite a unique occasion and all the ceremonial was free and characteristic of the people – none of that stiffness and supernatural solemnity which we indulge in.'[23]

On Christmas day 1893 his isolation at Mastuj was tempered by the arrival of provisions. After skating and football with his military escort, he wrote to his sister Emmie: 'At lunch we had mince pies and now at dinner we are going to have the two plum puddings, champagne which Gordon sent me up from Gilgit, and a sirloin of beef – this last mind you is a great luxury.'[24] But as the freezing winter drew in he lapsed into depression. More Political Service exams were looming, and he found his insomnia had returned with a vengeance. 'What the minimum is at night I don't know. My thermometer only marks down to zero [Fahrenheit] and it went down to that long ago.' Instead of reading textbooks Younghusband concentrated on philosophy, and even toyed with the idea of emigrating to Canada to establish a dairy farm.

The world of officialdom sent him a memorandum in February outlining a proposal to withdraw representation from Chitral altogether. 'One feels inclined to go up to these people who invent such timid counsels,' he spluttered to Nellie, 'and just shake them up and tell them to for God's sake remember they are Englishmen.' In a curious prophecy of the events of the following year, he wrote: 'We are deliberately incurring the risk of having on some future occasion to regain our position by bloodshed and force of arms . . . Pitting our civilisation against these poor mountain people is what I loathe above everything.'[25] Another letter was fired off to his new friend at the House of Commons. 'I am writing to Lord Lansdowne [the Viceroy] – of course mentioning no names and not even suggesting the source of the rumour,' came Curzon's 'Confidential' reply.[26]

In May Younghusband moved to Gilgit to take his exams, but found it difficult to deal with his fellow officers. 'The nervousness is a great trial to me,' he recorded in his diary, 'for I find it very hard to face any strangers and though I long not to be serious I cannot be anything but extremely grave, and feel that I am keeping others so.'[27] His battle with the Government continued, the Foreign Department blocking his attempt to organize the military training of selected Chitralis. They were anxious not to enter into any further commitments. Informal training would be allowed, 'provided that it is understood that . . . no scheme of military organisation, such as that sketched by Captain Younghusband, is attempted'.[28] His frustration grew.

During his spare days in Gilgit Younghusband escaped from the limited society of Bruce and Robertson. He explored a pass above Hunza: 'no living man had ever been across it before,' he assured his beloved confidante Nellie Douglas. They had now been corresponding weekly for over two years, their long-distance relationship sustained by Francis Younghusband's desperate need for intangible companionship. She had become the only person with whom he could communicate, now that Emmie's unhappiness had made him fearful of communicating with her. 'You always turn out so smart and look so well,' he remembered, adding that he longed for her photograph. When it arrived by postal runner Francis racked his brains for an appropriate statement of appreciation. 'You would make a splendid Colonel of a Cavalry Regiment if you were a man,' he wrote.[29] What greater compliment could a woman be paid?

The sheer boredom and loneliness of life out on the frontier was pushing him to the edge. While others sought relief in alcohol, shooting or sex, Younghusband directed his troubled energies towards mountains, spirituality and the remote spectre of Nellie. As John Masters wrote in *Bugles and a Tiger*: 'In India there was always an unnatural tension, and every man who pursued the physical aim of sexual relief was in danger of developing a cynical hardness . . . Of those who tried sublimation, some chased polo balls and some chased partridge, some buried themselves in their work, and all became unmitigated nuisances through the narrowness of their conversation.'[30] Younghusband had reached a point beyond this; he felt too nervous even to engage in conversation.

On his way back to Chitrali territory in August, he made a detour via Chizr, where he came across a 'sulky and exclusive' tribe who puzzled him greatly. 'They belong to a people who seem to be independent of every body. They are not Pathans and are not connected with the Chitralis . . . In appearance they are very like Italians – quite as fair and with very much the same look.' Probably they were the Kafirs of the Hindu Kush (now usually known as the Kalash), a people rumoured by romantics to be descended from the stragglers of Alexander the Great's army. Younghusband's anthropological interest soon gave way to colonialist musings. 'I have thought over this question of dealing with thoroughly exclusive and hostile-minded tribes and . . . my present impression is that a good hammering is by far the best thing in every way.'[31]

Yet within days his attitude towards violence, money and his fellow humans had altered. For several weeks his spiritual fervour had been increasing. Just before leaving Gilgit he had written in his diary, 'I think I have had from time to time the feeling that I was born to recognise the divine spark within me . . . I shall through my life be carrying out God's Divine message to mankind.'[32] A day or two after arriving in Mastuj he was thrown from his horse. He lay unconscious for fourteen hours, and as he came round began to read Leo Tolstoy's *The Kingdom of God Is Within You*. The book seemed to lift a veil from his eyes. For months he had been reading the works of Darwin, T. H. Huxley and Ruskin, wrestling with ideas about economics and society. The evolutionary philosopher Herbert Spencer, who coined the phrase 'the survival of the fittest', had influenced him powerfully. Spencer's dry, scientific emphasis on the continuous adaptation of the human race offered a justification for the development of the British Empire, and a rational solution to specific spiritual problems. But although Younghusband was almost convinced by him, he was not inspired. It was Tolstoy who made his heart leap.

On the last night of August 1894 he wrote in his diary:

> It has influenced me profoundly . . . I now thoroughly see the truth of Tolstoi's argument that Government, capital and private property are evils. We ought to devote ourselves to carrying out Christ's saying, to love one another (not engage in wars and preparations for wars) and not resist evil with evil.
>
> Tolstoi does not say how society can exist without Govt, capital and private property but he says the few great ones, like Colombus, must plunge into the unknown and discover the way. And this is what I mean to do. To set the example first of all by giving up Govt service and all my private property except what is absolutely necessary for supporting life.[33]

'I have determined to leave the service for good and to devote my whole life to God,' Frank told Nellie. 'I shall lead the most absolutely simple life.'[34] On 4 September he took the plunge and sent a formal letter to the Government declaring his intentions. 'Partly on account of my wandering life, partly on account of the opportunity for reading and thinking which, away from civilisation, I have had leisure for, I have acquired an insatiable desire for greater freedom than I can obtain in the public service.'[35] He would buy a plot of land, he informed his father, and cultivate it either alone or as part of a commune. 'I should try to get this land within 20 or 30 miles of London – or close to Oxford or Cambridge – my object being to keep close in touch with the leading men of the day.'[36] His life was to be transformed and simplified; leaving him free to preach God's message and follow Tolstoy's path.

Then the news came through that the Hon. George Curzon was on his way to Chitral.

EIGHT

Clubland: Travels with a Most Superior Person

On the third day [Curzon] emerged into more open country and rode down grassy slopes towards Mastuj, where he was to meet his friend Francis Younghusband and march with him to Chitral. In the distance he saw a solitary horseman approaching him, and knew that this must be the native servant despatched by his host to guide him to camp. But it was no ordinary servant who now greeted him with a salaam. Curzon, parched and exhausted, uttered one word: 'Beer.' Without a moment's hesitation the bearer put his hand into the fold of his tunic and drew out a bottle of Bass. The traveller was once more within the comforting embrace of Pax Britannica.

KENNETH ROSE, *Curzon: A Most Superior Person*[1]

Within hours of Curzon's arrival Younghusband fell to interrogating him about theological and philosophical matters, but was soon disappointed by his indifference. 'I gather that he believes in a deity,' he told his diary, 'but not in the divinity of Christ, his resurrection, ascension, virgin birth and miracles.' Curzon had 'no interest' in scientific or evolutionary questions, seeming 'to think more than anything else of power and worldly success'. George Curzon, meanwhile, milked his host for information. 'I did not discover till later,' Younghusband exclaimed, 'that he was writing a series of letters to *The Times*, and that he was all the time forcing my views out of me.' So the two men sat round the camp fire at Mastuj, their thoughts and conversation veering off in different directions.

Curzon's duties as a Member of Parliament were tempered by an industrious fascination with the East. His departure from ministerial office on the fall of Lord Salisbury's government had done nothing to diminish his interest in Asian affairs. He had already written *Russia in Central Asia*, *Problems of the Far East* and the monumental *Persia and the Persian Question*. Following a series of skirmishes with the Viceroy he had gained permission to travel to the Himalayas.

111

Accompanied by the elusive Great Gamer Henry Lennard (a friend from his days at Eton), Curzon rode up through Hunza and the Pamir-i-Wakhan, questioning everybody he met and jotting down multifarious notes. Captain Younghusband was to be the perfect source of information about the defence of India's northern frontier.

'Curzon did have an argumentative turn of mind,' his host wrote years later. 'I suppose it was the House of Commons debating habit . . . His manner grated on us on the frontier, as all through his life it grated on the British public.' Privately he was 'disappointed' by the itinerant statesman. 'He is smart and clever and wonderfully clear headed and direct and strong too, but there seems so little real depth and so little sympathy . . . He will though undoubtedly rise to great eminence because he has indomitable energy and industry – and these alone are great qualities.'[2]

It took them two days to reach Chitral, Curzon's horse spitting blood and dying during the strenuous journey. By this stage Younghusband's mind was in a state of whirling confusion. His every thought was of Tolstoy's message, yet he was obliged to play the courteous frontier officer and answer the parliamentarian's trail of enquiries about Great Gaming strategy. He confessed to Colonel Nellie Douglas that he was 'fearfully hustled running Mr Curzon . . . I had a regular dose of travelling all day long with him and then having meals with him and talking "shop" hard all the time. My head got into a regular fuzz and I have to take large doses of sulphonal to get myself to sleep.'[3]

The Mehtar of Chitral greeted them with a salute from his two brass cannons. A ceremonial game of polo was played and they ate a banquet beneath a picture of Curzon's friend Margot Tennant, which the monarch chanced to have torn from the pages of an illustrated magazine. Curzon was intrigued by the indolent Mehtar, and unruffled by his manifest bisexuality: for 'although of weak character and debauched habits, he never in any situation looked anything but a gentleman'. In Younghusband's writings there are rare and oblique references to the Mehtar's practice of keeping catamites; Curzon's attitude was less discreet and most amused. 'At Chitral I fraternised with fratricides, parricides, murderers, adulterers and sodomites,' he wrote to his friend Wilfred Scawen Blunt. 'I start tomorrow for Kabul, where a female donkey is the object of favourite solicitude.'[4]

Having questioned the Mehtar carefully, and taken note of his wish to have a more precise definition of imperial policy on Chitral,

Curzon careered back towards India. A night was spent at Mastuj, where he managed to offend his host once more. 'Curzon, glancing at the philosophical books, said, in his decided way, that I would not get much out of them,' recorded Younghusband dolefully.[5] They rode east along the banks of the swirling Yassin river, the temperature falling as each day passed. Late in October the two travellers reached Gilgit, the Member of Parliament (sporting a pair of large golden epaulettes) peeling off towards Afghanistan to meet the Emir while the retiring frontier officer (dosed heavily with a crystalline hypnotic) hastened fretfully towards Rawal Pindi.

Racked by insomnia, possible malnutrition, unspecified 'nervousness' and spiritual turmoil, Captain Younghusband did all he could to avoid encountering his colleagues. After two and a half years out on the frontier he was shocked by the quality of people's clothes and the size of their stomachs. On 17 November 1894 he was summoned to see the dour new Viceroy, Lord Elgin: 'He is a very insignificant man in appearance, but a few minutes conversation showed me that he has more in him than most people give him the credit for.' By the end of the month he was sailing out of Bombay towards England, trying his hardest to avoid the lure of the 'clever and pretty' Mrs Beddy. 'If I lost my control for just a moment,' Francis wrote in his diary, 'I might be carried away for she can be fascinating, and she admires me I know.'[6]

After a fortnight's convalescence on the south coast Younghusband found his gloom had disappeared, as had many of his moral resolutions. The radical plans to divest himself of all material possessions were shelved as he scuttled about London seeing 'the best men' of the day. 'Bobs' Roberts, anxious for the latest information about India, invited him to stay for Christmas, while John Murray of Albemarle Street agreed to publish an account of his journeys. Younghusband visited the writer Leslie Stephen (Virginia Woolf's father) to discuss spirituality and mountaineering, reporting to Nellie that Stephen was 'the sort of man you can talk to, and he is evidently a big minded man'.

Although his depression had lifted, Younghusband remained uncertain about his future. His father advised a return to government service, while others urged him to try journalism or business. For the first weeks of the New Year he stayed at Kensington Court Gardens in London and put together an outline of the book that would become *The Heart of a Continent*. In the evenings he went to lectures or quiet dinners, even bumping into the enigmatic Ney Elias at the Royal Geographical Society. Then on 13 January the shocking news came through that the Mehtar of Chitral was dead. He had been shot in the back by his 'sullen and repulsive' half-brother while out hawking. 'Poor fellow,' Francis wrote to Nellie, 'he was always saying to me he had to expect to be murdered. But he always mentioned this very brother who has committed the act as his successor and had never suspected that he would be the very man to murder him.'[7]

Over the next two months, events in Chitral grew ever more disturbing. The usurping sibling asked Younghusband's successor as Political Officer, Lieutenant Gurdon, to recognize him as the new Mehtar. Gurdon played for time while Surgeon-Major Robertson moved from Gilgit to Chitral with a small escort and installed the assassinated Mehtar's youngest brother as a puppet ruler. Around the same time yet another brother, accompanied by a tribal leader from neighbouring territory, began to march on Chitral with an army of 3,000 Pathan warriors. The Chitralis saw that this offered an opportunity to free themselves from British rule.

By the beginning of March Robertson, together with his troops and a hundred or so civilians, had withdrawn to the Mehtar's fort where they were quickly surrounded by a hostile force. The besieged garrison soon caught the imagination of the press and public back home. As Hopkirk wrote in *The Great Game*: 'The vision of a handful of British officers, with their loyal native troops, holding out against overwhelming odds in a remote and picturesque fortress, brought to mind the recent tragedy in the Sudan. "It is Khartoum all over again," declared *The Graphic*.'[8]

These events left Younghusband in an influential position. His repeated warnings about the danger of instability in Chitral had been proved accurate. He was able to claim, with apparent justification, that the debacle would not have occurred had his strategic views been followed. Although Curzon was 'fearfully busy' he found time to meet privately and plan a line of attack in the Commons. The crisis in Chitral offered a useful stick with which to beat the Liberal government, and an opportunity to revive the threat of a Russian take-over of India's northern territories.

An alternative frontier policy sprung up, loosely oriented around Curzon, and supported by influential voices at both *The Times* and the Royal Geographical Society. Younghusband, with his inside knowledge of Chitral, became a convincing mouthpiece for the hawks. To the irritation of the India Office he made several speeches which contained implicit political criticism. Since he was owed two years of furlough (leave of absence) Younghusband was technically still a member of the Political Service, but this did not deter him. He remained convinced that the Government would quit Chitral altogether if they were given the chance.

On 12 March he spoke at the Royal Colonial Institute under the title 'On the Kashmir Frontier'. After a dissertation on the benefits of colonialism (under British rule 'not only their country but their character will be developed'), Younghusband moved carefully on to the subject of the Great Game. 'In Asia we cannot stay still,' he declared. 'Another power on the North is advancing steadily step by step towards us, and we have been compelled to throw forward outposts.' Those faint-hearts who advocated a withdrawal from Chitrali territory were soon dealt with. 'There are some Englishmen, however, who ask what is the use of our pushing out into all these remote parts, and interfering at all with these wild tribes.' They should realize that 'men who have studied the question most deeply' were sure 'that in order to guarantee quiet in the plains of India we must have a control over the mountains bordering on them'.[9]

After the lecture Younghusband was in great demand for his views on the defence of India, and the text of his speech was printed up and distributed. The celebrated adventurer Henry Morton Stanley invited him to dinner at his house. 'He is a pleasanter man to meet than I had expected,' Nellie was told in her weekly letter, 'a hard, determined sort of man who would stick to the thing he had in hand' although 'not troubled with any very high principles'. Meanwhile another speech was arranged for 25 March. The subject was explicit: 'Chitral, Hunza and the Hindu Kush'; the location was apt: the Royal Geographical Society, home of the hawks.

On 23 March the political temperature rose at the news that a small relieving force on its way to Chitral had been 'cut to pieces'. Younghusband felt betrayed by his former subjects, 'all those people whom I have lived amongst and done my best for gone wild, clean carried away by a want of feeling'. By the time he stood up to speak at the RGS two days later the atmosphere was electric: a force of 15,000 men had just been mobilized in Peshawar under Major-General Sir Robert Low, and there was a public mood for vengeance. The lecture theatre was packed with eminent figures such as Curzon, Stanley, Sir Clements Markham and Lord 'Bobs' Roberts of Kandahar, the former Commander-in-Chief in India.

The following day *The Times* reported the sections of Younghusband's speech relating to Chitral verbatim, and he was able to tell Nellie that 'the reception altogether was very enthusiastic'.[10] His robust defence of a 'forward' frontier policy was 'warmly applauded', and he was formally praised by both Roberts and Curzon, who insisted 'that Captain Younghusband is eminently gifted to win and to retain the confidence of the native peoples and their Chiefs'.[11] Younghusband was glad to record that Curzon 'said in public that if I had been [in Chitral] and left to myself, I could have kept the place steady'.[12] The next morning he was asked by *The Times* to return to Chitral as their Special Correspondent. He agreed at once, while pointing out that the Government was unlikely to allow him to accept such a position. But after string-pulling by the Manager of *The Times*, Charles Moberly Bell, the Viceroy gave permission on the understanding that Younghusband could not expect to be employed again on the frontier. So on 29 March he sailed for India, in the company of the terrified Mrs Robertson, wife of his old enemy the Surgeon-Major.

On the same day the inhabitants of the besieged fort raised 'a Union Jack, made up from the red cloth of the sepoy's turbans and other material', and from then on 'their luck began to turn'. Night attacks were repulsed, and an attempt by Chitralis and Pathans to tunnel into the fort was foiled by Robertson's diligence. 'Light balls made up of chips of wood and resinous pine, and soaked in kerosene oil, were lighted and thrown over the walls' at their attackers.[13] General Low's army was moving ponderously up from India, and a smaller force under Colonel Kelly was heading west from Gilgit. The British public was entranced by the race across the Himalayas, and Younghusband was anxious to be there first. 'We are all very keen upon getting up there sharp & we ought to arrive in time for the relief of Chitral certainly,' he wrote to his friend Martin Conway, who had lent him the latest mountain tent for the journey.[14] Their ship raced across the Indian Ocean, and by 21 April Francis Younghusband was riding into Chitrali territory.

On the way he had managed to file several stories to *The Times*, his reports contending with the trials of Oscar Wilde for the public's attention. During the previous fortnight General Low's force (which included Sikh, Scottish, English and Kashmiri soldiers) had fought several gruesome battles with the Pathans, but had still managed to advance a substantial distance. Younghusband even managed to scoop the story of the capture of Munda fort. 'I galloped back hard with the information to the nearest telegraph station (a telegraph line accompanies the force march by march) and got my telegram in first of any,' he told his beloved Nellie. That night they had camped at Munda, and 'one of the sentries over the General's camp was shot within twenty yards of the General's tent'.[15]

During the march north Younghusband spent much of his time with Major 'Roddy' Owen, who was reporting for the Lucknow *Pioneer*. A glamorous adventurer, and 'the best gentleman-rider of his day' who had won the Grand National three years earlier, Owen was a paragon in Younghusband's eyes. In *But In Our Lives* he is depicted as the roguish but profoundly spiritual Ronnie Mostyn. 'They were all good fellows – Bunty Bing, Harty Pingfield, and the rest – but Ronnie was the pick of the bunch.'[16] As General Low's force advanced, Younghusband and Owen decided to head towards the besieged fort alone. In contravention of military regulations they slipped past the Sikh sentries at dawn on 27 April.

At Drosh Fort 'I sent a Chitrali in to say that Younghusband Sahib was outside and wished to speak to [the Governor]. He came out mild as a lamb, and gave us ponies and a guide for Chitral. By dusk we reached the besieged garrison without mishap.'[17] Counting on his knowledge of the country, Younghusband had calculated that the Chitralis, aware of the approaching army, would not attempt to resist him. In the event he was lucky to be proved right. They were 'worn, trembling and utterly cowed . . . I could not greet them in the friendly way I should like to have done. It was wretched and I hated it.'[18] Younghusband took their fight for freedom as a personal betrayal, an ungrateful response to all he had done on their behalf. 'When I asked them why they had been so foolish as to fight us, they wrung their hands and said, "Why were we?"' On reaching the fort the galloping reporters found the Pathans had fled; Colonel Kelly's small force had reached the town a week earlier and broken the siege.

Robertson and the inmates of the fort resembled 'walking skeletons', and were still fearful of a renewed Pathan onslaught. They knew they would not be truly safe until General Low's force reached them. 'We found the officers just sitting down to dinner,' wrote Captain Younghusband, 'in the very house in which I had lived for many months, and in which Mr Curzon and I on the previous October had entertained the late Mehtar at dinner.'[19] The recapture of Chitral was of limited strategic importance – except to those who believed a Russian take-over was probable in the absence of British representation – but it was an impressive military operation which excited the public. A flurry of decorations were awarded, Surgeon-Major Robertson being summoned home for a knighthood by the grateful Queen Victoria.

After filing reports on the brave defenders of the frontier fort, Younghusband travelled swiftly down to Simla, saying fond good-byes to 'Roddy' Owen. He seems to have fallen in love with Owen in a cautious sort of way, and for the rest of his life held him up as a figure of great reverence. This may have been aided by Owen's death on the Nile a few years later: Younghusband had spent a stimulating month in his company, and there were no drab recollections to dull his memories. In his memoirs, *The Light of Experience*, he praises 'Roddy' with touching candour:

> He was just about perfect in body and spirit. Beautifully built, tall and slim, slick and supple, and erect . . . a forceful compelling charm — one which came after you and seized you. He was quite irresistible. You simply could not help doing what he wanted.[20]

At Simla the Viceroy, the Commander-in-Chief, the Military Member of the Viceroy's Council and the Foreign Secretary all interviewed Younghusband. He was irritated to find that more weight was given to his opinions as *Times* correspondent than had been when he was a serving official.

By the beginning of June he was back in London, staying at the Cannon Street Hotel. His account of his travels through Manchuria and the Gobi desert was almost complete, so he began 'a regular course of study in biology at the College of Science, South Kensington' in order to develop his understanding of evolution.[21] The recent exploits in Chitral had given him access to a new world, and he found for the first time that he gained pleasure from society. Some evenings he would go to dances with his friend Charlie Townshend, a siege veteran who strummed the banjo and told lewd jokes in French. One day he even had the emotional jolt of bumping into his old flame May Ewart at a party.

'I came up to town for a dinner Mr Curzon had got up for Chitral and Gilgit officers,' he was able to tell Nellie Douglas on 30 July, after which he went to the Savoy with Curzon 'to meet Arthur Roberts (the Music Hall man) and General Kitchener from Egypt. So we had rather an evening of it altogether.'[22] The next day found him dining at the Athenæum with Kitchener, Frederick Lugard and Reginald Wingate, staying up late into the night. During this period he gave a number of lectures on Chitral, including one at the Imperial Institute, and began to write a book about the siege with his brother George, who had served in Low's relieving force as a Captain in the Corps of Guides.

Younghusband continued to correspond keenly with the recently married George Curzon. There were hints that the Government was thinking of abandoning Chitral once more, Curzon wrote. 'I have already seen Lords Salisbury, Lansdowne and Roberts about it and we are prepared to make it just as hot for them as we care. It will be a monstrous scandal.'[23] But the scandal never materialized: a month later the Conservatives were back in office and Curzon was appointed Under Secretary of State for Foreign Affairs. Chitral was to remain firmly under British influence.

Frank Younghusband presents a puzzling spectacle at this stage of his career. Profoundly moved by the writings of Leo Tolstoy, he has quit government service in order to devote his life to God. Instead he falls into a job as a journalist and public speaker, anxiously defending a 'forward' policy in the Great Game. The summer of 1895 finds him living with his old father in Southsea, aged thirty-two, with little money, thinning hair, few definite prospects and a vague wish to find 'that form of religion which is best adapted to the men of the present day and which would form the religion of the future'.[24] At the same time he has recovered a certain social confidence.

His actions during the mid 1890s seem to have stemmed from a fear of stagnation. Stuck out on the Chitrali frontier he found that he could not influence official policy, and was unable to develop his ambitions as an explorer. The hostility of men like Robertson conspired with the monstrous bureaucracy of the Indian government to drain his life of stimulation. It was the futility and loneliness of his job that made him look for new spheres of activity. Like many British colonials in isolated outposts, he found his mind wandering up eccentric avenues; one of the signs, according to contemporary wisdom, of a man about to 'go bush'.

Philosophical speculation became his chief occupation, culminating in his dramatic conversion to Tolstoyan idealism at Mastuj. When he retired to London and reverted to activities more typical of a British officer, it was not because he had abandoned all thought of a life of religious simplicity. Rather he realized the enormity of the practical leap he would have to make in order to implement Tolstoy's teachings, and lacked the certainty to make it. Before long he was distracted by the sheer excitement of the social possibilities that were opening up to him. His flit to Chitral as a *Times* reporter followed the same pattern: he spotted a fresh opportunity and could not resist taking it.

Younghusband was always sincere in his spiritual aspirations. 1894 and 1895 were years of transition during which his ideas bounced off in many directions, leaving him uncertain whether he should try to pursue a religious life. His underlying devotion remained intact, but he could see no practical outlet for his personal version of God. Religion had a primarily social function in military and upper-middle-class Britain, while the pietism and dogma of the established church held no appeal for a man of his mystical nature. It was not until nearly twenty years later that Younghusband finally felt able to bare his soul.

Running parallel to his religious quest was an increasingly close relationship with Nellie Douglas. At the end of 1894 he had visited her in Cairo on his way back from India; their first face-to-face encounter for two and a half years. She was still married to Major 'Boy' Douglas, although by this point the union appears to have been little more than a formality. Through the summer of 1895 'dearest Frank' and 'sweet Nellie' met frequently in London, and exchanged gold rings. During September they spent a fortnight together. Their friendship was still sufficiently respectable for their hosts to be Nellie's parents, and for Frank to write to his sisters telling them where he was staying. Nellie's father was a wealthy Mancunian industrialist, who enjoyed showing off the acclaimed Himalayan explorer to his acquaintances. His views on his married daughter's intimacy with his guest are uncertain, but there is no indication that Frank's stay was anything but a social success.[25]

The correspondence that passed between them at the end of September shows this visit was the culmination of their protracted epistolary romance. 'You see dear Nellie,' Frank wrote the day after leaving, 'for years I have had to keep all my affection to myself and I have never been with anyone soul to soul as with you.' During his fortnight in Manchester he had been able to unburden himself of the pirouette of emotions which filled his heart. A week later he felt sure that their closeness would endure: 'Our friendship seems to be entering on a new and still more sacred stage . . . You trust me Nellie. I will be true to you and I don't think anything on earth will ever part us now.'[26] Nellie had been elevated from confidante to lover.

While reading through the Frank–Nellie correspondence in the India Office Library one morning, I realized that a chunk of their letters was missing. The period following the visit to Nellie's parents was not covered in the appropriate file. I filled in a requisition slip, only to have it returned an hour later marked 'Closed to Public Access'. A protracted argument followed, during which I tried to persuade several impassive archivists to release the letters, or at least to describe their contents to me. But my appeals to the need for biographical accuracy, my exhortations to Truth and Reason, to the fact that almost a century had elapsed since Nellie's paramour put pen to paper, had no effect. Under the terms of Dame Eileen Younghusband's bequest (or rather the interpretation put upon it by her executors) intimate letters of this kind were to remain confidential.

There was a temptation to speculate wildly about their contents. I wondered if the vaults of the building held page upon page of the most sensuous and exotic simpering, ancient testaments of illicit love. But there is nothing in Younghusband's disposition at this stage of his life to imply that he was motivated primarily by carnal desire. It is easy to cast him as a standard product of the age of Victorian prudery, as a newspaper article portrayed him in 1991: 'Empires, like revolutions, often consume their creators. Francis Younghusband, like Gordon, Lawrence and Wingate, was a doomed fanatic, driven by a combustible mixture of religion, militarism and sexual repression.'[27]

Given his severe Evangelical upbringing, his awkward reticence in social situations, his natural Puritanism and the physical isolation of his time on the frontier of India, he would have been hard pressed not to have become in some sense a victim of sexual repression. But he was not driven by a psychological compulsion to repress or express his sexuality. On the rare occasions that Younghusband mentions sex in his private writings, it is always in the context of a spiritual bond. Nellie's importance was that she enabled him to let out trapped feelings; I could find no sign that physical lust ruled his actions.

Much of his life was devoted to a quest for 'soul-union', to a search for the human and divine love that ultimately he found only in the last three years of his life. He had a need for the closest unity with other people, but found it difficult to know how to express or fulfil that need. As his daughter wrote, 'one of the clues to his personality' was a 'warm-heartedness which never quite hit the mark'.[28] During the first half of his life Younghusband found he could hide this longing within the bluff fraternity of an exclusively male world. The regiment, the club and the frontier outpost were places where emotions could be concealed with relative ease. Although, like many of his fellow Victorians, Younghusband had a great admiration for clean-limbed youths and the male physique, there is no evidence that he was homosexual. Rather he tried to find camaraderie among men. He did not seek friendship so much as protection within a cocoon of maleness.

The feminist writer Elaine Showalter wrote that 'the construction of masculinity' within 1890s Britain depended upon 'the institution of "Clubland", the network of men's clubs which served all social classes and provided alternatives and substitutes for domestic life. Clubland reinforced the spatial as well as the social boundaries separating men and women.'[29] The Great Game was an extension of 'Clubland', in that it was a solely male world where women were physically excluded and men's ideas and preconceptions reinforced. It also offered many opportunities for subterfuge and disguise, that essential ingredient in Victorian life and fiction, from Conan Doyle and Buchan to Kipling and Stevenson. The terrain of the Great Game, the harsh, unreceptive plains and mountains of the Karakoram and the Himalaya, was an unknown territory which only men could penetrate. High Asia's no man's land was certainly no woman's land.

Travel beyond the frontier offered an opportunity to escape from the normal codes of society. Each day involved serious physical challenges, and every success reinforced the imperial system for which Younghusband was fighting. The Game offered an opportunity for a male unity with the other players, whether they were British like Davison or Russian like Grombtchevski. Despite his racial prejudice, Younghusband clearly felt a close fraternal bond with Shukar Ali following the crossing of the Mustagh Pass, and with the Mehtar during his time in Chitral. All his journeys, from the trip across the Gobi Desert to the invasion of Tibet, were steadfastly masculine. He travelled vast distances across the mountains and plains of Asia supported by a cast of men, his servants and soldiers. For as Kim observes towards the end of *Kim*, becoming more sahib-like as the book progresses, 'How can a man follow the Way or the Great Game when he is so-always pestered by women?'[30]

Women had no role in the Great Game. The political structures of the time meant they had no direct influence on official policy, and could take no part in the diplomatic machinations between British India and Tsarist Russia. Younghusband's use of language reflects the masculinity of the environment in which he worked: 'any man knows', 'he would understand', 'men who have studied the subject'; while his ultimate compliment to Nellie Douglas was the news that she would make a splendid Colonel *if she were a man*. Officers serving on the frontier were expected to be unmarried; their intended brides stayed in the hill stations to be flirted with at convenient times. Some women such as Annie Taylor and Alexandra David-Neel travelled to unknown parts of the Himalayas, but never as part of 'the Game'.

The only woman to feature significantly was Queen Victoria. For nearly three-quarters of a century her squat image loomed over the antics of her minions. Throughout the British Empire, the Queen Empress was immortalized in the name of countless states, railway stations, cities, medals, lakes, hotels and waterfalls. Younghusband would invoke her name when dealing with recalcitrant rulers such as the Mir of Hunza, or drink a toast to her high in the Pamirs while dining with Colonel Yanov. The abstract conception of the mythological mother – She, the Great White Queen – was easier to cope with than real live women. This short, plain, solemn widow presided over the Great Game, its symbol and its purpose.

NINE

'Not Only a Fiasco': African Intrigue

It was not long before Captain Younghusband was entangled once more in the world of intrigue and intelligencing. His new mentor was Charles Moberly Bell, a huge, sharp, resourceful man whose title of 'Manager' of *The Times* of London concealed an influence which extended well into the corridors of Whitehall. He used his newspaper as a weapon with which to bludgeon his way to political power. As the *Dictionary of National Biography* decorously puts it, 'Bell's overflowing energies prompted him to utilise the resources of *The Times* for many enterprises that were strictly beyond the bounds of journalism.' During the Chitral campaign Bell had spotted Younghusband's potential as a reporter cum undercover agent, realizing that he combined adequate literary ability and an inquisitive approach to current affairs with the natural daring of a freelance adventurer.

On the evening of 15 November 1895, Younghusband dined with Bell and Flora Shaw, the Colonial Correspondent of *The Times*. His brief was to act as the link-man or 'Messenger' between *The Times* and a group of colonial conspirators. 'My only qualification for the work,' Younghusband wrote candidly some years later, 'must have been that I knew absolutely nothing about it.'[1] Within the week he had been appointed Special Correspondent and entrusted with a secret code to use when communicating with his newspaper. 'All I can say,' he told Nellie Douglas as he sailed out of the docks at Southampton, 'is that it is even more interesting and far more important than my last trip.'[2]

His destination was South Africa. The conspiracy was the Jameson Raid.

Of all the adventures in which Younghusband became involved, the Jameson Raid was the most unlikely. It was an interlude which bore little relation to his previous or subsequent career, except perhaps in its foolhardy glamour. He had no experience of Africa, and no obvious motive for supporting Jameson and Cecil Rhodes. Yet an undefined impulse to be at the heart of the action made him take up the offer. In the inquiry following the Raid, Young-husband's involvement was suppressed so as to protect the reputation of *The Times*, while in his private papers he deals with the subject cursorily. But it is certain that he knew what Jameson was doing. As Elizabeth Longford wrote in her book *Jameson's Raid*: 'That Younghusband's considerable part in the affair escaped all notice is one of the many remarkable facts in the Raid story. Moberly Bell's activities also escaped attention, but they were confined to London. Younghusband operated at the very heart of the conspiracy.'[3]

The scramble for land, power and gold in southern Africa was reaching its climax towards the end of the nineteenth century. Hordes of British, Irish, German, Portuguese and American speculators were trying to make their fortune, the most dramatically successful being the son of a Hertfordshire vicar, Cecil Rhodes. The scope of Rhodes's power by the 1890s was phenomenal, and would have been impossible in any other part of the British Empire. He owned a host of gold mines, ninety per cent of the world's diamond production, and had effective control (through the charter of his British South Africa Company) over what is now Zimbabwe (Rhodesia), Botswana, Malawi and Zambia. In addition he was Prime Minister of Cape Colony, with fervent ambitions to unify all South Africa's whites within a British federation.

Impeding his imperial vision was the resolute independence of the Boers, the descendants of early Dutch settlers. Their territory, the Transvaal Republic, was close to being encircled by British and Portuguese colonies, leaving them determined to resist any further encroachment. The discovery of huge mineral deposits – gold, in particular – had sent a flood of brash Uitlanders ('foreigners') into the Transvaal, so that by 1895 the Boers were outnumbered. Yet they retained political power, under their rugged, Bible-quoting President, Paulus Kruger. There were angry mutterings from the British about 'Boer despotism', and leading Uitlanders began to plan a rebellion against Kruger's government.

Failure is an orphan, which is perhaps why it is so hard to establish precisely the parentage of the Jameson Raid. Owners of mining concessions in the Transvaal, ambitious Johannesburg entrepreneurs, elements in the Colonial Office in London (including the Colonial Secretary Joseph Chamberlain), *The Times* newspaper, Cecil Rhodes and his henchman Doctor Jameson were all in some way responsible. Had the Raid succeeded there is little doubt that Jameson would have been hailed as a hero. Younghusband's initial involvement left him in no doubt about the virtues of the rebellion. 'They are perfectly right in striking a blow for their emancipation,' he wrote in a private letter.[4] Like most of the British public, he saw the Boers as an obstacle to the expansion of imperial power.

After landing at Cape Town, Younghusband went straight to Cecil Rhodes's house to pass on information from Charles Moberly Bell of *The Times*. Ever the newspaperman, Bell was adamant that his scoop should not be jeopardized by the excitement beginning on a Saturday. 'I want to impress upon Rhodes', he told Younghusband, 'that we hope the *New Company* will not *commence business* on a Saturday. PS. Because of Sunday papers.'[5] Younghusband found Rhodes difficult: he 'disliked being shown deference – being addressed as 'Sir' for example – and the more I showed of it the ruder he became.'[6] Over the question of the proposed uprising, he suggested that Younghusband travel to Johannesburg to see his brother Colonel Frank Rhodes.

Up in the City of Gold, Francis Younghusband was soon taken into the conspirators' confidence. Towards the end of December Doctor Starr Jameson (the administrator of Rhodesia) would lead a mounted force across the border from the British Protectorate of Bechuanaland and march on Johannesburg. His pretext would be a 'letter of invitation' from five prominent citizens claiming that 'men, women and children of our race' were in danger of being massacred by Boers. Simultaneously an Uitlander uprising would begin in Johannesburg, while an armed band would ride out to meet Jameson and his posse. Kruger's government would either have to make severe concessions or face being overthrown.

As the plot creaked awkwardly into life, its foundations were continually shaken by doubts over timing and the likely level of support. Jameson and the plotters telegraphed back and forth between Johannesburg, Cape Town, Kimberley and Bulawayo, cancelling and adjusting their plans. Meanwhile a haphazard collection of young English aristocrats and adventurers were gathering at the border, waiting for the order to march into the Transvaal. On 20 December the conspirators sent the man from *The Times* down to

Cape Town. During the journey Younghusband wrote a letter to his father, saying that at first he had not been 'altogether satisfied about the rights of the thing', but now was:

> What is going to take place is a revolution against the Boers. The leaders of the movement have taken me into their confidence and have asked me to go down to see Cecil Rhodes about final arrangements. As a matter of fact I knew the general idea before I left England and that is why I came . . .But they must not quaver about it, and turn the whole thing into not only a fiasco but a disaster.[7]

When – over thirty years later – Younghusband publicly mentioned his involvement in the Jameson Raid, he was disingenuous about the information he gave Rhodes. He paints himself as a neutral player who tried to stop the uprising, while Rhodes is portrayed as a dreamer who talked 'dreadful rubbish'. He quotes this conversation which supposedly took place beside a hydrangea bush in Rhodes's garden:

> I told him the Johannesburgers were not for it and wanted Jameson stopped. He said, 'What! do you mean to say that there is not a man in Johannesburg who will get up and lead a revolution and not mind if he's shot?' 'Apparently there isn't,' I said. 'Would you do it yourself?' he asked. 'Certainly not,' I replied. 'I don't want to lead revolutions in Johannesburg.' He gave his customary grunt as if he thought the whole crowd, including myself, were a white-livered lot.[8]

The lack of documentary evidence about Younghusband's involvement makes it hard to know which version is closer to the truth. Certainly the letters he wrote in late December 1895 ('they must not quaver') indicate that he was in favour of Jameson and his rag-tag army advancing over the border. It is only after Jameson is defeated that he sees the folly of an attempted revolution, writing to Nellie, 'I never saw more clearly in my life the evil of going crooked.'[9] It would become apparent to him later that the plotters had brought him in as a naive but intrepid outsider who could be used for specific underhand tasks.

Leaving the grunting Cecil Rhodes to his hydrangeas, Younghusband took a train back to Johannesburg. The atmosphere was tense when he arrived there on Christmas Day. On 28 December he cabled Bell at *The Times* asking whether he should continue to

support a possible uprising; but it was too late, for the next day
Jameson made his move. With a force of a few hundred men –
many singing 'God Save the Queen' and drinking champagne – he
crossed the border and marched into the Transvaal. But, after a
few feeble skirmishes, he and his men were soon surrounded by
Boer commandos. The Uitlander uprising in Johannesburg had
failed to happen.

Younghusband was the first journalist to arrive on the scene. He
rode out through the lines into the thick of the action, just as he
had done at Chitral. Despite an encounter with a hostile Boer patrol
he managed to reach the site of the final showdown near Doornkop,
where he saw Jameson and his men taken prisoner. He galloped
back to Johannesburg, fired off a telegram to *The Times* and went
to break the news of Jameson's surrender to the failed plotters.

Before long Jameson and the conspirators were in prison. Five of
them were handed down the death penalty by the Boer authorities,
although the sentence was later commuted to a heavy fine. Younghusband managed to visit Jameson in his cell, but 'he seemed
utterly broken and crushed, and all the officers at that time were
labouring under a sense of having been deserted by the Johannes-
burgers'.[10] In the aftermath, the wily President Kruger was able to
present himself to the world as an injured innocent – the victim of
wanton British aggression. Boer farmers began to arm themselves
with Maxims and field guns, and the scene was now set for what
was to become, four years on, the Boer War. Under pressure from
Parliament the British government established a Committee of
Inquiry to investigate the affair. Proceedings dragged on into the
summer of 1897, until an insipid report was produced: the work
of 'The Worshipful Company of White-Washers', according to one
journalist.

Francis Younghusband's role in the debacle was carefully
obscured. His second cousin, Flora Shaw, took the witness stand at
the Inquiry on behalf of *The Times*. Tall and beautiful, with an
impeccable grasp of international politics and economics, she had
been given the job of the newspaper's Chief Colonial Correspondent
on the curious grounds that she had 'the reasoning capacity of a
man'. By means of skilful casuistry and judicious lying, Miss Shaw
denied her advance knowledge of the Raid. Questions about 'the
Messenger' – Younghusband – were dodged on the grounds that
his life might be put at risk were his identity revealed. Her interroga-
tors' fear of appearing ungentlemanly in their questioning of a lady
in a 'seasonable' hat enabled her and her paper to slip gracefully

through the net. The final report effectively exonerated *The Times* and its staff.

Shaw was a vigorous imperialist who wanted British control over the Transvaal. Throughout the period leading up to the Raid, she had direct access to the Colonial Secretary, 'Pushful Joe' Chamberlain. Like him, she gave her tacit support to Jameson, but escaped blame when the putsch failed. The 'Messenger' was shocked to discover some years later quite how far Flora Shaw's policy (and hence his own actions as her subordinate) had been determined by Rhodes's views. Younghusband's correspondence after the failure of the Raid shows that he regretted his own role in it. He came to realize the way in which Stock Exchange speculators in Johannesburg had manipulated political events for their own ends, and was shocked when he realized the mercenary motives of most of the Raid's supporters. Their principal objection to the Boer government was the tax on labour and dynamite; visions of the Union Jack flying over the Transvaal were of secondary importance. By January 1896 he was telling Nellie that his sympathy lay with the Boer farmers:

> There is far more grit and manliness in them than in the Johannesburg crew, and as to Jameson's raid that was I may tell you in confidence a deep political move of the most criminal type. The whole business has been utterly unworthy of Englishmen and it is a relief to my mind to find that right has conquered.

Younghusband had been caught up in something bigger, more complex and more corrupt, than he had anticipated. Always an idealistic imperialist rather than a gold-grabbing dicer, he found he was out of his depth in the world of South African intrigue. After the event he avoided writing a full account of his own involvement in the Jameson Raid, and appears to have destroyed many relevant papers. Probably he felt he had been duped by the Johannesburg conspirators, and did not wish to dwell on the matter. 'In India we fight for the honor of the country,' he declared to Nellie. 'Here it was for nothing but political schemes.'[11]

The Relief of Chitral was launched to an excited public by Macmillan and Company in November 1895. The authors were 'Captain G. J. Younghusband Queen's Own Corps of Guides, author of "Eighteen Hundred Miles on a Burmese Tat"; "Frays and Forays"; "The Queen's Commission", etc, etc. And Captain Frank E. Younghusband, C.I.E. Indian Staff Corps (late Political Officer in Chitral)'. Like most instant books it is badly written, as Frank acknowledged to Nellie: 'I was far too hurried and as you know did it nearly all with a short hand writer.' The quality of the prose did not affect the book's sales: the reading public fell on this eye-witness account of the recent events in Chitral. 'My book is going off capitally. Two editions of 1500 each have already been sold through, and so my brother and I have accordingly made more than £300 each off it in this first fortnight.'[12] Given that a junior government minister at this time earned £1500 a year, the royalties amounted to a fair sum.

Much of the material was cobbled together from the articles Frank had written for *The Times*, while George's contribution concentrated on the military side. The decision to write a joint book seems to have been the result of circumstance rather than fraternal intimacy: Frank knew the background to the crisis in Chitral while George knew the details of the campaign. George (Jack) was a hearty, soldierly character, with a scornful view of his brother's philosophizing. In his memoirs he berates Curzon for being concerned (when Viceroy of India) about the 'accidental' murder of a 'punkah coolie' by soldiers of the 9th Lancers. Even by the standards of the time, his racial prejudice is particularly crass:

> The low physique and stamina of the class of Indians which supplies menial servants, is phenomenal. A box on the ear, such as a school-master often gave us at our private schools, might kill him straight away. So might a kick, of only half the value which every English schoolboy gets at football, or in the course of his career as a fag . . . the British soldier is the kindest-hearted and most easy-going person imaginable, especially in his dealings with the natives.[13]

The Thunderer endorsed *The Relief of Chitral*'s drum-beating style: 'British fortitude and native devotion have never been more splendidly displayed; and seldom have these fine qualities and heroic deeds found worthier record, vivid and inspiring, and yet modest and temperate withal, than in the pages of the brothers Younghusband.'[14] Their achievement even excited the admiration of the young Winston Churchill, serving on the North West Frontier of India with the Hussars. Captain Younghusband, he informed his mother, had made 'a large sum of money' writing about the Chitral Campaign. Why not write about his own experiences? 'I do not see why I should not make an account of the much more severe fighting we experienced equally interesting.'[15] *The Story of the Malakand Field Force* was the result.

Three months after the appearance of *The Relief of Chitral*, John Murray published what would come to be seen as Francis Younghusband's most significant book. *The Heart of a Continent* gives a full account of the journey through Manchuria and the Gobi Desert, the descent of the Mustagh Pass, both trips to the Pamirs and the winter in Kashgar, before ending with a brief report on his time in Chitral and Hunza. During 1896 alone the book went into four reprints, and established Younghusband's reputation as an explorer in the world beyond the Intelligence Department and the RGS. The veracity and discreet style of *The Heart of a Continent* have been examined in previous chapters, as have the events the book describes. Most of the text avoids personal insight; only in the last few pages does Younghusband veer off towards his own philosophy. For the first time he gives some public indication of the themes that intrigued him.

Still fearful of appearing outlandish, Younghusband is careful not to shock his readers with revolutionary spiritual notions. Some Christian missionaries perform great works, he insists. However, Christianity is not 'so far superior to the Buddhist or Mohammedan religion', since all faiths aspire to a similar goal. He touches on the idea of a 'Universal Spirit', a concept he was to develop in subsequent books. People of all religions sensed 'that there was some Great Spirit or Influence guiding and ruling all things, and that in some indefinable way they were dependent on this Spirit'. This idea is tenuously linked to the possibility of life existing on other planets: 'There may be more perfect beings than ourselves. There may be beings with the senses more highly developed, who could see, for instance, with the power of telescopes and microscopes . . . may we not conceive of societies as superior to our own as ours is to the savage tribes about us?'

This hierarchical vision is taken up a few pages later in the context of human evolution. Younghusband concocts a neat theory to justify racial distinction and hence colonial rule. Although in 'mere brain-power and intellectual capacity there seems no great difference between the civilized European and, say, the rough hill-tribesman of the Himalayas . . . the European may feel his moral superiority.' Proof of this, he claims, is Indian willingness to finance British rule in India. 'Every English officer and soldier receives his pay from revenue drawn from the natives of India; so the English-man does not pay the natives to fight for him, but they actually pay him to control them!' There is no mention of the fact that Indians have no choice in the matter.

By 1896, Younghusband's theoretical imperialism was well developed. Like Chamberlain, he believed that the British Empire amounted to more than the sum of its constituent parts: from New Zealand to Ireland, there was a unifying bond. Colonial rule could be justified on grounds of 'character'. By the turn of the century, this supposed ethical superiority was a vital component of British rule in India. Younghusband believed that 'higher moral develop-ment' enabled the British to triumph over races 'who fail in the struggle because they have not the same "grit" or resolution'. It is for this reason, he wrote, 'that in spite of the Englishman's cold, "stand-offish" exterior, he has the interests of the natives under his charge very deeply at heart.'[16]

The mood of the late Victorian era, when imperial brain-washing was at its height, is caught perfectly in *The Heart of a Continent*; the adventure, the absurdity, the conviction.

After the collapse of Jameson's ambitions Frank Younghusband stayed in Johannesburg for a couple of months, wrote a few reports for *The Times*, learnt bicycling ('it is a good business') and then returned to England. Acclaim for his two books awaited him, as well as a silver cigarette box 'as a little memento of the pleasant time we had together in Chitral' from George Curzon. 'You may perhaps remember that as we rode together I more than once pledged to you my word that Chitral could be saved for the Indian Empire. I rejoice to have proved a true prophet, and, in conse-quence of the experience that I acquired in your company, to have played some part in bringing about the desired result.'[17] For the first time Younghusband found he was relatively rich. Both the Chitral and the travel book were selling well, while invitations had begun to appear to literary dinners. He set himself up at the Royal Palace Hotel in Kensington and fell into London society.

Intense wooing of Mrs Douglas began again: 'Yes, dear Nellie, you may trust me. Nobody will take the place you hold in my affections. I get very fond of other people but nothing in the same way as with you . . .' A few days later he confessed, 'I don't think I have ever felt towards you as I do now.' Then in May he went to stay at her parents' house near Manchester, writing afterwards, 'Nobody is the same to me as you are and it was such a happiness to have that sweet quiet intercourse with you. It soothes and softens me like nothing else does.'[18]

Yet Africa was still in his thoughts; he made tentative plans to mount a 'scientific expedition' into 'the interior'. Then Charles Moberly Bell (wanting him out of the country during the official Inquiry into the Jameson Raid) asked him to write a series of articles on the situation in South Africa. During the voyage back to Cape Town the itinerant writer played football on deck and struck up transient friendships with some other passengers. On 19 July 1896 he reached the Transvaal, finding the atmosphere considerably calmer than five months before. He visited coal mines, offices and farms, and in October interviewed President Kruger in Pretoria, who 'wore an old frock coat', banged the table a good deal and assured Younghusband 'most emphatically that I might tell people in England that unless attacked he would never attack us'.[19]

Younghusband's new-found friend Harry Cust accompanied him on this occasion, and painted a vivid portrait of the incongruous Boer President in a letter to George Curzon: 'The old man dresses in a broad-cloth sleeping bag and swaddles a shocking bad topper in hat-bands of crepe. He dwells in a cloud of foul smoke and spits like a Maxim gun. We've had some quite bad rows but discovered that our birthdays are on the same day and wept and are going to exchange pipes.'[20] Cust was a gentleman journalist, amateur MP, putative lover of numerous society women and probable father of Lady Diana Cooper. His frivolity had just got him sacked from the editorship of the *Pall Mall Gazette*. Younghusband had known him slightly in London, and the two men agreed to travel up to Rhodesia together.

Crossing the hot, rough terrain of the veldt, Younghusband felt feverish and depressed. Cust was as ebullient as ever, sparkling and fizgigging as they headed north towards Salisbury. 'My dear Francisco,' he would write eight years later when the invasion of Tibet was in full swing, 'I shouldn't at all mind a young monk lama properly trained to wait at table.'[21] By the middle of November they were settled in Cecil Rhodes's house, although Younghusband was still uncertain about his host's qualities. 'I am not sure,' Younghusband noted privately, 'whether Rhodes is really a big statesman or only a big businessman. He suits the temper of the colonials though who are not blessed with too many principles.' By now Rhodes had been forced to resign the Prime Ministership of Cape Colony on account of his involvement with Jameson. Younghusband thought 'adversity has done a lot for him', although Rhodes continued to surround himself with a 'court of very inferior men' and even 'scoundrels'. Only the future Chief Scout escaped censure: 'Baden Powell I like and he is quite the best they have out here.'

Cust and Younghusband set off around the country in a haphazard two-wheeler pulled by eight scraggy mules. Little gold had been discovered in Rhodesia, leaving no obvious future for the colonial settlers other than farming. The wars against the indigenous peoples of Mashonaland and Matabeleland, and in particular the recent massacre of the Ndebele following an uprising, had left the territory tense and dangerous. Younghusband was not hopeful: 'The worst of it is the whites are now so wild at the treatment of their comrades they want to kill every black man they see. But blacks and whites have to live here and how is the matter to end?'[22] The two men spent December in Bulawayo, travelling down to the comparative comfort of Cape Town in early 1897.

Younghusband wandered off alone across the Cape Colony towards Natal, collecting information for newspaper articles and making an outline of a new book on South Africa, provisionally entitled 'Impressions of an Imperialist'. In Durban he met Mohandas Gandhi, who at this stage of his life was a practising barrister campaigning for the rights of Indians in Natal. Gandhi's manifest ability and resolution in the face of British intransigence and hostility impressed Younghusband. In a letter to his sister Emmie he described their meeting:

> I saw a good many of the leading Indian merchants and also their spokesman Mr Gandhi. They asked me to dinner and I found about thirty of them seated in two rows of ˙ chairs ... They presented me with a bouquet of flowers and sprinkled me with rose water ... Mr Gandhi had been three years in London studying for law exams. He was a moderate unassuming man with excellent manners. He is

a good-plucked fellow too. Personally I much prefer some of these better class Indians to the rough style of colonial one frequently meets with out here.[23]

By early March Frank Younghusband was at sea again, heading back to Southampton. He was approaching his mid-thirties and his resolve was beginning to droop. His fondness for Nellie remained strong; but she was married and their long-distance relationship was going nowhere. *The Times* had paid him nearly £1000 plus expenses for his articles on South Africa, yet he could see no long-term future in journalism. Perhaps he should write a book about the importance of religion. Alternatively he might try for a political career in England, although Harry Cust insisted his future lay in India.

He sailed on, gloomily contemplating his future.

On April 26, Younghusband had to write an awkward letter:

Yes dearest Nellie, that is it, I have fallen in love and I have wanted to tell you but feared it would hurt you . . . It came about on boardship coming home . . . My poor little sister [Emmie] is almost heartbroken at this thought of my marrying at all. She has been so looking forward to keeping house for me in India.

I can tell you that she is above everything a lady. That she is very bright, very clever and very musical, that her people once had one of the finest houses in London and the most beautiful place in the country but suddenly lost all their money and then she had trouble after trouble . . .[24]

Quite what made Francis Younghusband fall in love with Miss Helen Magniac is hard to fathom. She was fatter, taller and older than he was; had a doughy face and no interest in Asia or mountains or mysticism; was intensely snobbish, severely depressed and terrified by the thought of intimacy. 'Dearest of Captains,' she told her suitor, 'why, when there are so many charming girls about you should have quite accidentally met a woman who hates the very thought of marrying – alas! passes my comprehension.' Married life was an impossibility: she could not face 'the vulgarity of it'.

The Dearest of Captains could only reply that he had 'never been in such harmony with anyone before and there seems nothing but brightness to look forward to'. 'I could not have found anyone so absolutely suited to me as you are . . . Let my love surround you always.'

But Miss Magniac did not want to be surrounded by his love. She could not sleep at night; her family wanted her to marry a man with money; she would never marry anybody; felt unwell; was destined for unhappiness; had disappointed the memory of her late father; could not bear the thought of being seen 'in any form of dishabile'.

Captain Younghusband tried his utmost to calm her fears. He understood her worries; after all, had they not both experienced desperate 'trials and struggles'? As for her thoughts on being seen 'in dishabile', he would not wish to be seen naked himself, 'and you may trust to my delicacy of feeling not to look at any time when unnecessary . . . We need never sleep all night in the same bed, for if there were only one bed available I cd. always sleep on a sofa or somewhere, for I am accustomed to sleep in every sort of place . . . whether I may lie with you in bed – and whether I may consummate the marriage are all minor points.'

Miss Magniac was placated a little, although fearful her ardent wooer might have other lovers up his sleeve. Well, he admitted, there were women he had been friendly with, 'but with not one of these have I gone so far as embracing'. On the subject of Nellie Douglas he was disingenuous. 'We were thrown a great deal together in very exceptional circumstances', and even 'called each other by our Christian names'. But Mrs Douglas now understood the situation ('her husband is a Major in the 2nd Dragoon Guards'), and was glad to hear he had fallen in love with Miss Magniac.

A month later the Captain confessed to more definite activities, while insisting he now repented his actions. 'Darling, when you are constantly with men who talk so much on that subject – who are constantly intimate with low women – and when the passion comes very strong . . .' While out on the frontier (or perhaps on return to Rawal Pindi) he had succumbed: 'So when I was away so long from all refined society this sexual craving overcame me and I degraded myself.' Miss Magniac was not unduly distressed by the news; her primary worry was that the Captain's 'sexual craving' might be pointed in her direction. Yet her resolve was weakening.

In the middle of June, three months after their first meeting on board the Cape Town-to-Southampton liner, Helen Magniac consented to marry Francis Younghusband. The condition was a no-sex-before-death pact. 'That is settled then, darling,' Francis wrote. 'I believe that we shall have a happier union if all that "perfectly natural but lower" part is eliminated from it.'[25]

Helen's worries and depression – her 'trouble after trouble' – appear to have acted as a powerful lure. Francis felt that her troubles matched his own: his spiritual and philosophical struggles, the protracted conflict with the authorities over frontier policy and his present uncertainty about the future. He thought he had found a soul mate who would understand his worries and share his problems. Shortly after their engagement he wrote a private memorandum 'now that there is possibility of marrying':

> I shall be helped by marriage. I have been finding of late that my faculties were being warped and dried by having no adequate outlet for the sympathetic and emotional part . . . The gaining of her love stimulates all the energies of my nature.

Francis was reasonable in thinking that the mutual support and companionship of marriage would help him relax into life, although misguided in seeing Helen as a suitable partner. She was in the right place at the right time, but she was the wrong person. By constructing a mental picture of her as the ideal companion, he was able to convince himself that the relationship would work. His desperate fantasy even made him willing to contemplate chastity within wedlock. For the first few years the marriage was happy enough, but it never gave either of them true satisfaction. As the years went by Helen's excursions into 'illness' would grow more frequent, while Francis wandered off into the realms of the spirit.

His personal ambition was also a factor in his choice of bride: marriage to Helen would help him 'to get and keep in touch with the very best people of the time'.[26] While the Younghusbands were staunchly middle class, the Magniac family had social links extending to the aristocracy and the Palace. Despite Helen's great regard for her own position in society, these connections were largely the consequence of money rather than birth. Her grandfather, Hollingsworth Magniac, was the unscrupulous son of a Kensington clockmaker, who had gone east to make his fortune. By masquerading as the Danish consul he had gained access to opium trading concessions in southern China, and as his business prospered he entered into partnership with a young Scot, William Jardine. Some years later Magniac sold his share, and the company became the legendary trading house Jardine, Matheson and Co. Back in England Magniac used his vast fortune to buy Colworth in Bedfordshire and Chesterfield House in London, illuminated manuscripts, Renaissance paintings and a fine collection of French eighteenth-century furniture.

Hollingsworth's son Charles became a gentleman and a Member of Parliament. According to his obituary, Charles Magniac was a 'Robust Radical' who 'held the respect and affection of the "classes", not only through his birth and breeding – Eton, Trinity and foreign travel had given him both distinction and polish of manner – but because he was one of the straightest riders to hounds in the neighbourhood.'[27] He married a young widow, the Hon. Augusta Dawson, daughter of Lord Castletown of Upper Ossory. She already had two sons, but soon produced seven more children, of whom Helen was probably the eldest.

Helen Magniac's childhood and teenage years were spent in a haze of wealth and social glamour, attending balls and house parties. Governesses gave her a desultory education. 'Many thanks for your letter,' she wrote to a correspondent, 'the above is my address; and should you mislay it, a glance at the work you mention, "Burke", or "Who's Who" will reveal it . . . My education was entirely carried out in French and German; English grammar and spelling were of no importance.'[28] Yet the demands of such a life, and the pressure to find a 'suitable' (preferably titled) husband made Helen ill; she was sent to Scotland, Switzerland and Italy in search of 'bracing air' and a cure.

In the 1880s Charles Magniac speculated heavily on the stock market, leaving massive debts on his death in 1891. His family were forced to sell Chesterfield House and auction its magnificent contents. 'Sic Transit Gloria Mundi,' wrote Helen in a firm hand across the sale catalogue, and promptly went into a decline. She began to overspend what was left of her inheritance, found she was badly in debt and took out a secret loan, regarding it as 'beneath her dignity' to mention the matter to her family. In 1896 she escaped to South Africa for a 'rest', writing in her diary: 'For the last three years I have found existence . . . a damned horrid grind.'[29] It was in this inauspicious frame of mind that she met her future husband.

Their formal engagement was announced on 22 July 1897, with the date of the marriage set for 11 August. Quick weddings were common in Victorian times, but during the period of preparation the atmosphere was fraught with foreboding. Helen caught a bad cold and suffered from headaches and depression. 'Things down again,' Francis noted, '– almost despairing in one way.' The Hon. Mrs Magniac wrote a curt letter to her future son-in-law inquiring into his financial affairs. 'In regard to business matters,' Francis was forced to confess, 'I have, I am sorry to say, nothing but what I can make – now about £800 a year. As much as I can possibly spare of that shall be spent for your daughter's comfort.' He also made a tentative grab at the remains of the Magniac fortune. 'Could I meet one of your sons early next week to see what arrangement most satisfactory in her interests we can come to?'[30]

As the day approached both Helen and Francis had second thoughts, but convinced themselves all would be well once the wedding was over. Extravagant presents of china, glass and silver began to appear. Mr and Mrs John Murray gave a pair of toast racks, the Duchess of Devonshire a set of plated candlesticks, while an embossed and chased tea caddy was presented by George Curzon. A few days before the wedding the couple had to attend a social event at which May (Margaret) Ewart was present. Afterwards Helen wrote a melodramatic description of the encounter in her journal:

> His pale face is paler still as he masters who it is who is even now coming towards him – the girl who . . . would for six years have been his <u>wife</u> his wife. She is a woman now this "rare pale Margaret". She and her companion have stopped. They are contemplating a picture hung high over the door . . . and as he looks he gnaws his long heavy moustache.[31]

Francis and Helen were married at Datchet Church near Windsor, retiring to Mrs Magniac's large, white-washed house for a 'garden party'. An unsourced newspaper cutting called it a 'Fashionable Marriage' between 'the famous Pamirs traveller' and 'the eldest daughter of the late member for Bedfordshire. Mr Magniac was at one time extremely wealthy, but he lost heavily at speculation.'[32] According to the same press report, none of the bridegroom's family was present. This was not unusual at the time, so it may not be significant. But given that the wedding was a large and sociable one, it does seem odd that Francis's father and his sister Emmie

did not travel the sixty miles from Southsea to Datchet. Although
there is no clear evidence either way, the circumstances of the
wedding and the lack of letters of congratulation give an impression
that the Younghusband family did not approve of the match.

At thirty-four, Francis Younghusband was not a young husband,
but neither was he an old one by Victorian standards. What was
unusual was the comparative antiquity of his bride. Helen was of
an uncertain age (probably thirty-eight) although in the staged
photographs at the garden party she looks older. Stolid and uncertain, she sits on a chair while Francis stands awkwardly by her side,
his pointed ears jutting out from the side of his head and his watery
blue eyes gazing glumly at the camera. In another picture he loiters
on the lawn surrounded by six of his new brothers-in-law. They
look cheerful in a clubbable sort of way; Francis looks as if he is
drowning.

A month's honeymoon was spent in Paris. They borrowed a
house in the Avenue de Bois de Boulogne from Helen's half-
brother, Douglas Dawson, who was the Military Attaché at the
British Embassy. Frank's letters from Paris reveal no sense of excitement about married life. 'Both of us are ever so much better for
the complete rest we are taking,' Nellie Douglas was informed.[33]
'We just wander down to the Louvre or some such place or stroll
in the Bois,' he told Emmie, before diverting to the climate: 'The
weather is quite mild with slight rain every day.'[34] Whether the
no-sex agreement survived the honeymoon is not known; Helen
was pregnant by the end of the year.

PART TWO

TEN

An Interlude in Rajputana

Those with a fond vision of the days when the sun never set on the Empire often forget the limits to British power in India. Even at the height of imperial glory in 1897, little more than half of 'British India', or what is now India, Pakistan and Bangladesh, was under the Viceroy's direct control. There were Dutch and Danish trading posts along the coast; Pondicherry, Karaikal and Mahe were French colonies; Goa and the enclaves of Daman and Diu remained under Portuguese colonial rule. Most of Rajputana (now Rajasthan) and swathes of central and northern India consisted of independent kingdoms known as 'Native States', administered by indigenous rulers. Each Native State had entered into its own treaty with the British, permitting a degree of outside interference. The British never ruled all India.

Doctrinaire anti-colonialists make the corresponding mistake of viewing British India as the straightforward product of conquest. Unlike the colonial take-over of parts of Africa, or the 1950 Chinese annexation of Tibet, it was in fact obtained largely through guile rather than military force. The process began as a series of legitimate trading agreements between the British East India Company and individual rulers. As the years went by and power shifted, princes and nawabs often found their personal interests were best secured by entering into treaties with the British. Political structures in states and villages across the subcontinent began to alter. The gaining of India was a gradual, insidious process, not a sudden invasion.

It was only in the last fifty years of the British presence that the pomp and vulgarity of 'the Raj' – the Jewel in the Crown of current legend – became the face of India. 'I have done the one *unforgiveable* thing by not bringing a dinner jacket and am obliged to have dinner in my room as a result,' wrote the travel writer Robert Byron to his mother from Karachi in 1929. 'The whole of India is one enormous conspiracy to make one imagine one is in Balham or Eastbourne.' Strict segregation only came into its own in the latter part of British rule: 'We lunched with a minor Indian prince, to the fury of all the

Europeans in the restaurant . . . One can't be seen with natives.'[1] It was around the turn of the century that British administrators in India first became seriously concerned with the theory of racial difference, and the intellectual justifications for colonial rule.

Younghusband's interest in such matters grew during the months after his marriage. 'I wish in a quiet way to guide the policy of the nation in its rule of subject races,' he noted privately. 'I wish to aid in the development of native races to higher standards.'[2] Having succumbed to pressure to begin a steady career befitting his status as a married man, he arrived hopefully in Bombay with the intention of rejoining the Government of India's Political Department. But the bureaucratic hierarchy took a dim view of his qualifications: Great Gaming adventures beyond the frontier counted less than the official examinations he had failed to pass. In the absence of high-level string-pullers to plead his case, the conqueror of the Mustagh Pass, the tamer of the Mir of Hunza, the celebrated author, journalist and explorer, Captain F. E. Younghusband CIE was posted to an obscure hill station in Rajputana to be Third Assistant to the Political Agent.

By 1897 the power of the given ruler of a Native State depended, in practice, on the extent to which he was willing to cooperate with the Viceroy's representative. If a Raja or Maharajah was nationalistically minded or incompetent (which tended to come to the same thing in the eyes of officialdom) his administration would be virtually taken over by the British Political Agent. In some cases a constitutional coup would be engineered, and the ruler's brother or son or nephew installed on the throne. Mount Abu, where Younghusband was sent, was a minor outpost of the territory of Maharajah Ganga Singh of Bikaner. An imposing and intelligent seventeen-year-old, he was to become one of the country's most esteemed princes, combining sharp pragmatism with an ability to gain support from both British and Indians. Each summer he went to his palace in Mount Abu, high above the blazing plains of Rajputana.

Abu was a political and diplomatic backwater. Sitting in a poky office with the rain drizzling on the corrugated-iron roof, Younghusband found himself shuffling paperwork backwards and forwards. He tried to decide where the boundary line between two villages should be drawn; which tents should be used for an official journey to nearby Gaumukh; whether a new road should follow this route or that. Often his recommendations were turned down by his superior, the Political Agent's Second Assistant. The decline in his career was matched by a drop in income: his pay was now a measly 600 rupees a month, or little more than £500 a year. 'The work of course is rather unexciting after what I have been accustomed to,' he admitted to Nellie Douglas, before trying to convince her and himself that the job 'gives me the experience I much needed in ordinary office routine and regular administration . . . We live in rather a small bungalow.'³ His letters to Nellie were becoming increasingly formal and awkward: in February 1898 their correspondence petered out altogether.

A visit in May from Francis's younger brother Leslie and his wife Kathleen offered some respite. Leslie, who was now in the army serving in India, managed to boost their spirits with his relentless frivolity. One day the two couples went for a drive down to Chipaberi, only to find the road blocked by a collection of immobile bullocks. Nothing would make them move, Francis told Emmie in a letter, 'although the men set to work hammering at them and shouting at the top of their voices. Leslie explains to Helen. "It's all done by kindness – kindness and conversation – mostly conversation!" He is an amusing young bounder.'

The pregnant Helen Younghusband entered into a desultory acquaintance with the other British wives, despite a conviction that they were her social inferiors. Much of each day was spent reading tomes on French history. With the money from her marriage settlement an English maid by the name of Miss Woolford was engaged, and plans made for the welfare of the new baby. Helen was nervous about the birth; the fate of one of her friends in Mount Abu was not encouraging. Mrs Tobin 'was wildly delirious, screaming incessantly and struggling so much she had to be tied down. This went on all day and night and even with sleeping draughts she had only an hour or two of sleep. She would eat or drink nothing and gradually sank and died.' The newly married pair attended her funeral in the small Christian graveyard: Francis found it 'the most pathetic thing I have ever seen'.⁴

In August he wrote a letter to Emmie. Their new baby, a boy called Charles, had been born and lovingly swaddled and ceremonially photographed and installed in a beautiful wooden crib. But after a few days the little child had died. 'This has been a very sad time, and I could never have believed the loss of one so young and tiny could have affected us so much. Poor Helen is inconsolable. But to me there is something very sweet in the memory of our little one so soon taken from us. He was wonderfully intelligent looking for a baby.' Francis tried his hardest to encourage Helen to keep a stiff upper lip, but a month later she was still too distraught to leave the house. 'She can't get rid of her grief and feels it every hour of the day.'[5]

The trail to Mount Abu was nearly incandescent, bleak sunlight hitting the rusted ground of the Indian desert. I was travelling into Rajasthan on the Chetak Express, a string of dark red carriages trailing a straining, hooting engine. The hills that passed us were lumpy and yellowy brown. Sharp miniature mountains stood beside them, shimmering up from the parched earth, littered with multi-armed cacti and forlorn grey plants. After many years as a decidedly single man, Younghusband was setting off in a new direction, shifting towards family life and apparent stability. Letters and diaries could feed me information, but never the sense of immediacy and closeness that I sometimes felt when chasing his shadow, knowing that I was standing on the spot where a crucial moment of his life had taken place.

Grinding up the slope from the railhead at Abu Road in a DE LUXE! bus I could see the vegetation turning green where tiny streams were flowing down from Mount Abu. Higher up huge misshapen black rocks covered the landscape, threaded with holes where the wind and rain had scooped out ears and noses from them. It was as if the Scottish borders had merged with a dark moonscape. When the clouds parted to reveal the town it proved to be singularly ugly, with shops and scrappy buildings sprawling hopelessly along a ridge. On the far side was a wooded drive which led to the Maharajah of Bikaner's old palace, now a stately hotel.

I took a room and spent several frightening hours deciphering the hot water geysers which erupted around the exquisite green-tiled bathroom. As it got dark I began to ramble through the endless corridors, wondering which ones Younghusband had walked down. There were animal heads and Victorian sporting prints, and ancient retainers who appeared suddenly from doorways with polite salutations. At the bottom of flights of cold stone steps I came across a huge billiard room with an empty bar in the corner. There were no other guests at dinner, except a rather plain Dutch woman and her beautiful daughter who were travelling the subcontinent together in the Victorian fashion. The mother smoked thin cheroots and ordered gin-and-limes at impressive speed. Before long I noticed I was playing outlandish parlour games and it was two o'clock in the morning.

The next day I set off into the town. There was no Christian graveyard in Mount Abu, a keen young clerk assured me, although there were Christians on the hill behind the market place. An hour later I reached some buildings and found Father F, a whisky-priest from County Wicklow who seemed to have escaped from a Graham Greene novel. It turned out that he was one of a number of Christian Brothers who ran a boys' boarding school for the sons of Bombay businessmen.

Father F wore a plastic dog collar, an embroidered black shirt and a filthy grey suit which was buttoned too tightly at the stomach. On his feet were a pair of corduroy pumps. I explained to him why I was in Mount Abu. He cocked his head to one side and began to smile.

'Well, *that's* all right then. When I first set eyes on you I thought you must be one of them Brahma Kumaris. Seeing you wearing that kurta pajama and all.'

'A Brahma what?'

'A Brahma Kumari – from their great place down in Abu. There's a whole set of them from Australia and Spain and everywhere thinking they'll find the secrets of the world out here. They're a kind of Hindu off-shoot. What did you say your name was?'

He sent an Indian woman to fetch Brother M, who knew about history. As she walked off he whispered, 'She's a good woman, a Christian. Did you know it was Ash Wednesday today? There are Protest-ants nearby too, or what we call here the Anglicans. There's only twelve Christians left in Abu now except for the Sisters. Things have changed since all those settlers came up from the plains.'

Brother M appeared, huge, ancient and wheezing with a blotched red face. On the strength of my vague kinship with Percy French, he invited me in. '"Are You Right There, Michael" and "Abdul Abulbul" and that other one about Ballyjamesduff? Oh, God love you! He wrote the finest songs of any man in Ireland.' We sat down at a long wooden table. Around the priests' room were pictures of the Blessed Virgin and the Holy Father, crucifixes and pious books. We might easily have been in Killorglin, or Krakow, or Liverpool. Tea and peppered rusks were brought by a beaming Tamil in a hat, but Brother M advised against the rusks. He still stuck to European food after many years out of Europe.

'The Indian food it doesn't agree with me. I find it's by way of being spicy. But we can't get hold of beef. The cow you see it's that sacred; it's *that* sacred in Abu.'

When I explained my purpose he produced a gigantic crumbling brown ledger. It made depressing reading. 'In sacred memory of No. 7329 PTE. George Booth "H" Coy. 1st Battalion Lincolnshire Regiment who died at Mount Aboo aged 26 years . . . aged 28 years . . . wife of . . . aged 23 years . . . Pedro Luis Baez (Goanese butler) . . . at the age of nineteen . . . of a fever aged 22 years, erected by his brother officers.' Almost all were astonishingly young, in their twenties or early thirties, while the causes of death tended to be similar: of a fever, malaria, dysentery, typhoid, endemic fever, peritonitis, diarrhoea caused by disorders of dentation, fever and more fever. Each one was listed by denomination: Methodist, Roman Catholic, even the occasional Orthodox.

Finally we found the record of Francis and Helen's child. Beside the entry in the register it read, 'Class of Monument: Marble Column. Endowed 1934. Repaired 1927. Repaired December 1953.' This implied that Francis, or more probably Helen, had chosen to pay specially for the upkeep of the grave nearly forty years after the baby's death. Her devotion to the memory of her dead son appears to have lived on keenly throughout her life. Having overcome her fears about sex and marriage, it must have been a desperate blow for the product of the union to be taken away so quickly. Her natural grief was compounded by the circumstances of their marriage and her physical isolation.

When their only other child, Eileen, was born four years later Francis wrote to his mother-in-law: 'The baby is a strong sturdy little thing. But poor dear Helen was so grieved at first it was a girl. She cried bitterly when I saw her and said it only made her long still more for her sweet little lost one.' A woman who knew Helen during the 1920s said she used to treasure a photograph of the dead infant carefully, and show it to people from time to time as 'a very great privilege'.[6] I had a feeling that Helen never recovered from the death of her baby boy.

'It's mainly us Catholics on the left-hand side of the graveyard. You'll probably find him up in the top corner,' said Brother M. We walked slowly out into the sunlight. 'When I came here there was hardly a building in Abu – only the old British ones. I used to ride up from the railhead in a tonga, and we'd swap horses at Chipaberi.

But now they use the motor veh-i-cles. You'll find the place has changed since your man Younghusband's time.'

As I was about to set off down the hill I asked Brother M when he had arrived in Mount Abu. 'Well,' he said, shading his eyes with his hand, 'I first came to India in the 1920s and I got here a year or two after Partition, 1952 it was.'

'Do you ever want to go home to Ireland?'

'Well, I went there in the 1970s to take a look. It turned out the Brothers didn't know I was still alive.'

'What do you mean?'

'You see, they'd lost me off their books and had forgotten we were still out in Abu. But never mind that – this is my home now.'

I left him on the crumbling wooden verandah humming 'The Mountains of Mourne'; a fantastic figure in a grubby, billowing cassock.

On the way to the town there were cricket pitches and school-uniformed children who doffed their caps with a 'Good morning, sir'. I found this oddly touching. A rickshaw driver directed me to the Christian cemetery. 'Follow yourself straight to the end of the road, then turn up backside,' he insisted. The gate was padlocked so I made a biographer's leap over the railings. There was a little hut with grave-digging equipment and a length of rope. At the far end a family had set up home under a tree with some wooden slats and plastic sheeting.

I wandered through the zigzag of stones, through all these people who had died serving an Empire which had now dissolved into history. It was a strange ecumenicism, representatives of every branch of Christianity gathered together in one plot of land in a Hindu country. Next to a failing tree I found it; a small grave surrounded by rusted ornamental railings. At one end was a cracked marble pillar with a neat rose carved on the top, covered in bird droppings. The stone read:

FRANCIS CHARLES DELAVAL
DARLING CHILD OF
CAPTAIN AND M^{RS} FRANCIS YOUNGHUSBAND
DIED AT MOUNT ABU 6TH AUGUST 1898
AGED TEN DAYS

I wondered what the baby had died from, and tried to picture the day of the burial. The first-born child of the rather old newly married couple; tragic, awkward, broken-down Helen, maybe still too weak to attend the funeral, and the proud, reserved, overcome father with the dead son in the miniature coffin.

After a while I walked back into Mount Abu to find some flowers, but there were none to pick and the stall-holders did not sell them. In the end I decided to make a Buddhist food offering. Back in the cemetery it was getting dark as I knelt down and laid a cauliflower and some eggs at the foot of the little grave. Then I stood up and walked through the scrubby grass and the pieces of broken marble, out of the Christian graveyard.

Six months later I happened to pick up a leaflet in Bath. It advertised a Year of Inter-Religious Understanding and Cooperation, involving a 'Sarva-Dharma-Sammelana'. A retreat was to be held 'by invitation of the Brahma Kumaris at their World Spiritual University in Mt Abu in North India. This event is sponsored by the World Congress of Faiths, which was founded in 1936 by the British diplomat and mystic Sir Francis Younghusband.' I investigated; the decision to hold it in Mount Abu was pure coincidence. But I had a sense that the trail was leading in strange directions, following strange patterns, circling in on itself.

The years 1898–1902 were a time of stagnation for Francis Younghusband. His life and career took no unexpected turns; his philosophical speculations found no significant new paths to go down. Caught in the tight mesh of the Indian government's bureaucracy, his interests became increasingly parochial. He drew up elaborate plans for a definitive book on the administration of India's Native States. He wrote chapter outlines and devoured quantities of relevant books, but the plan never developed, and his attention shifted to a projected work on British policy in Asia. Again jottings were made, only to be discarded. From time to time he produced articles for the London monthly *The Nineteenth Century* on subjects relating to the Empire.

Lured by the dubious glamour of administrative power, Younghusband had begun to develop an increasingly pompous and authoritarian streak. In October 1898 he was relocated, after representations to the Foreign Department, from Abu to a more senior position in Deoli covering the nearby states of Bundi (or Haraoti) and Tonk. For his first meeting with the Nawab of Tonk he 'was carried down in a chair to the foot of the hill'. Helen was too weak to make the journey, but was kept informed of events by letter. 'All the way through the city the people turned out and salaamed profusely' while 'a guard of honor presented arms and saluted'. A few days later Younghusband travelled to Bundi and engaged in a similar performance. The state officials stood outside the royal palace while the Raja's band struck up 'God Save the Queen', but 'I would not get down from the carriage until it had finished . . . In spite of a lot that is comical about it all, it does make one proud of oneself.'[7]

This emphasis on ceremony was complemented by a sudden concern for material status. 'There is a fine large house at Deoli – all the reception rooms of wh. are furnished by Govt. and Govt. have just sanctioned the expenditure of Rs. 2500 on new furniture,' he told his sister Emmie, 'so we ought to do ourselves very well.' A month later he added, 'I have four clerks, five chaprassies [messengers], several minor Govt. servants, an elephant, six camels, three carriages, four mounted orderlies and I have just under Rs 3000 worth of new tents.' The absolute justice he was able to dispense gave him satisfaction. 'I have . . . 40 villages directly under my supervision inhabited by a criminal tribe called Meenas whom we are in the course of pacifying . . . All this afternoon I have been engaged in trying a case of dacoity [gang robbery] . . . I caught twelve dacoits and have just sentenced them to seven years' imprisonment each.'[8]

At the end of the year Helen moved from Mount Abu to the isolation of Deoli. She was frequently left alone, since her husband would go off on horseback for days at a time visiting outlying villages. His work involved a continual promotion of British interests; while taking care to preserve the balance of power between Calcutta and the relevant prince. One means of doing this was through the distribution of largesse and career opportunities to aspiring Indians. Each day Younghusband would be greeted with a plethora of carefully wrought petitions, such as: 'To His Excellency the Agent Sir – I beg most respectfully to inform you that I wish to learn the art of doctoring, considering this state my benefactor . . .'

There were frequent official banquets which the Agent Sahib and his wife were obliged to wade through. The menu for a dinner given in Younghusband's honour by the Nawab of Tonk in January 1899 has been preserved. It included:

First Dose
clear Brun saley soap
Fish morness (cold)
Pegeon, Potridges sides
chiken rone nice
joint dish
Duck rossed
Saddle mutton rossed
Beef sarlain rossed with Yishapodin [Yorkshire pudding]

Second Dose
Seori rosed patris
Do: unchobi potridges
Morr's cherries tod
Plump butter potui bail[9]

By April Helen was physically and mentally exhausted with India. Younghusband took three months' leave and they sailed for England, staying at Claridges and making a few excursions into society. Younghusband lunched with Lord Kitchener, who had recently gained glory at Khartoum, but afterwards denounced him to Emmie as 'a coarse blob of a man. He said he had just been having a fight with Cecil Rhodes who had told him that he never wanted to see his face again.' In the same letter Younghusband confided that he had been to visit the eminent physician Sir William Broadbent to seek a cure for his worsening insomnia. 'He said the remedy was to take a glass of hot water with salvotile the last thing at night and not to drink cold phizzy water of any description after dinner. This is a good tip.'

Early August found him back in Tonk while Helen remained with her family at Datchet. 'No one to talk to,' he admitted to Emmie, 'except a pleasant enough but somewhat narrow minded Scotch Presbyterian Missionary.' The Boer War was about to break out, provoking a resigned response from Younghusband. In his dry, factual book *South Africa of Today*, which had come out the previous autumn to limited acclaim, he had predicted such an outcome if the British did not defuse the crisis. 'One thing I am beginning to be slowly convinced of is that we are the most consummate humbugs,' he went on. 'I fear it will be a terrible [war] for the Boers fight as roughly as all Europeans fought three centuries ago.'

His pessimistic percipience about South Africa was soon overtaken by events in Rajputana. In 1899 the monsoon failed and crops started to wither. By the end of September nearly 20,000 people in Bundi and Tonk were in need of relief, but the states had stockpiled only enough food to feed one thousand.

For the rest of the year Younghusband galloped around the territory organizing famine relief. Hospitals and poor houses were set up and grain was shifted to needy villages. He managed to extract 171,000 rupees from the British authorities, and also set up a Deoli Bazar Relief Fund and a Bundi Medical Assistance Fund. Back in England Emmie, Helen and Helen's mother launched an appeal, raising nearly £500.

At the end of 1899 his wife returned to run the orphanage in Deoli. By January the famine was 'too awful for words', he told Emmie. 'You can't go out without meeting human corpses by the road side – often half devoured by dogs and vultures.' The scale of the problem was too great for effective action. 'The hospital is nothing more than a long shed and the poor wretches lie there in rows – miserable human skeletons moaning and writhing and dying one by one even as you stand looking at them.' In his memoirs Younghusband wrote that starving Indians resorted to eating roots and leaves: 'I even saw men seizing burnt remains from the funeral pires and gnawing at them. Scorching winds blew across the parched-up plains. The sun was pitiless.'[10]

Through the desperate heat of the early summer no rain fell on Rajputana. During May there was an outbreak of cholera in the relief camps and hundreds of people died each day. Finally in the second week of July the monsoon broke and the rivers began to flow once more. Convinced that lack of infrastructure had been partially to blame for the famine, the Agent set about building a railway line into Bundi. He scampered tirelessly to and fro setting up the project, but by September 1900 was on the verge of collapse. Then an invitation arrived from George Curzon to come and stay in Simla, the summer capital of British India.

ELEVEN

'A Really Magnificent Business'

Lord Curzon took over as Viceroy of India at the beginning of 1899. Aged only thirty-nine, he gained the position he had been coveting since boyhood. Yet during the seven years of his Viceroyalty, his energy and wit would give way to irritation and arrogance. The monumental demands of the job coupled with his obsessive attention to detail, debilitating working habits and crippling back pain were to leave Curzon truculent and exhausted. Surrounded by the pressures of office, he seems to have seen Younghusband's visit to Simla as a welcome reminder of their carefree days together on the wild frontier at Chitral.

'I nearly shed tears when I think how much you would have loved all this,' Helen wrote to her mother, conscious of her husband's lowly official status compared to the other guests at Viceregal Lodge. 'As you may imagine F. is the embodiment of dignity, & much admired by all: tho' alas all his toil at D[eoli] has had the inev.e. result of making him very silent.'[1] Each evening before the formal dinner Helen had 'an attack of nerves'; but she would not have missed the glamour and the pageantry for the world. During the visit Curzon awarded Younghusband the Kaiser-i-Hind Gold Medal for his work during the famine, and appointed him to a more congenial posting in the comparatively wealthy Native State of Indore. On return to Rajputana Younghusband wrote a letter:

> My dear Lord Curzon . . . We were just at our lowest ebb when we got yr. invitation to Simla and we have come back here so freshened up . . . It was indeed a privilege to visit you as we did and to be made to feel so unmistakeably that you still regarded me 'as an old friend and fellow-traveller'. A friend I hope I shall always remain . . . I have not been favoured with the same initial advantages with wh. you started – great natural abilities and an assured position. But I can at least try to imitate yr. strength of purpose and yr. wonderful industry.[2]

This is the first indication that Younghusband's feelings for Curzon had changed from respectful friendship to friendly adoration: he had chosen Curzon as his mentor. A year earlier he had been ambivalent: 'At present I am engaged in trying to put off George Curzon,' he had told Helen. 'Why on earth he wants to come wandering around Rajputana in the midst of a famine I can't say.'[3] But the compliment of being chosen by the Governor of 300 million souls as a special friend captured Younghusband. The sweep of the Viceroy's ambitions for India and the grandiloquence of his actions impressed him; the similarity of the two men's imperial vision bound them together.

Over the next two years Curzon was kept briefed on Younghusband's research into colonial theory. Younghusband wrote to him about the social theorist John Beattie Crozier, with whom he was 'in constant correspondence':

He knocks down the theory of the equality of man and shows that all men are not equal and even becoming more and more unequal. And he declares that it is not only our interest but our duty and privilege to take over the government of the inferior races and to administer, discipline and protect them . . . it is our special part in the World's history to rule and guide these Asiatics and Africans who cannot govern themselves.[4]

Younghusband had appointed himself as the Viceroy's personal racial philosopher. 'Lord Curzon will one day be Foreign Secretary or Prime Minister,' Emmie was informed by her excitable brother. 'But the man who will guide the nation in its policy will be Frank Younghusband and he will do it by getting at the real heart and . . . kindling the religious feeling without which no nation is good for anything.'[5]

Fresh ambitions started to form in Frank Younghusband's head as he sailed towards Europe for a year's leave. 'General Outline of Life's Work', he wrote: 'Seek to know the best men possible – leaders in religion, politics, learning . . . Obtain instruction in elocution and in writing . . . Attract young men whom I could assist in training and who could assist me in collecting details of information.' But his capacity to attract young men was severely hampered by his renewed social incompetence. 'I shall endeavour', he noted, 'to make the acquaintance of as many people as possible in order to accustom myself to intercourse and to overcome the nervousness which is partly innate in me and partly the result of the secluded life I have led.'[6] He was worried by the Government's indifference to imperial matters, and decided his best plan was to become a Member of Parliament.

Captain and Mrs Younghusband spent the New Year of 1901 in France, staying with Helen's aunt in Nice. Towards the end of January Younghusband thrust his way to Britain in search of a new career. 'I believe our position in the world will depend upon how we lead & attach to us these weaker races of Asia & Africa who have fallen and will fall within our control,' he wrote to Henry Newbolt, whose reputation as a poet had leapt into life a couple of years earlier with the publication of *Drake's Drum* and *Vitai Lampada*. With his breathless enthusiasm for 'Playing the Game', Newbolt no doubt applauded his old school friend's sentiments. 'I have the greatest possible faith in our race & in its high destiny,' Younghusband continued, implying that the spread of British colonialism was divinely ordained. 'The Empire must grow: we can't help it.'[7]

One idea was the formation of a learned society devoted to Central Asia. The original proposal came from Alfred Cotterell Tupp, a member of the Indian Civil Service who had travelled in the regions around the Nepalese border. Knowing that Younghusband shared his belief in the existence of a Russian threat, he proposed a group for 'the consideration of Central Asian questions from their political as well as geographical, commercial, or scientific aspect'.[8] Younghusband enlisted Algy Durand, Colonel Bell, John Murray and Evan James to the cause, as well as gaining unofficial support from the Viceroy. The Society was soon assembled, becoming a haven for both active and armchair Great Gamers. Younghusband even toyed with leaving the dullness of the Political Service to become its honorary secretary.

As an organization, the Central Asian Society was firmly in favour of an aggressive policy in the empty spaces between the Indian and Russian empires. Cotterell Tupp subsequently told Younghusband that he was 'very much disgusted with Macartney of Kashgar' for admitting in a lecture that a British retreat would be inevitable if the Russians invaded Sinkiang.[9] Over the years Younghusband made speeches to the Society on Tibet and India, as well as giving a more arcane discourse on 'The Patriotism of Humanity', needling the bureaucrats with his opinions on foreign policy. His credentials as a proponent of the Great Game remained intact long after his views on India had begun to change.[10]

In the spring of 1901 he took a train to Wales to stay with his sister Ethel, who was now married to a clergyman, before travelling to Southsea to see his old father and Emmie. While visiting Clifton College Frank learned that Helen was pregnant once more. He rushed back to France and worried about their future, before returning to London to discuss parliamentary prospects with acquaintances. No political openings were forthcoming, so he wrote a handful of articles on Expansion in Asia for Newbolt's *Monthly Review*. By the autumn he was restless, and departed on a tour of Scotland, staying in North Berwick and stalking stags in Argyllshire before being invited to stay at Glamis Castle by another Old Cliftonian, Bobby Blackburn.

Blackburn's father-in-law was Lord Strathmore, whose one-year-old granddaughter would grow up to marry George VI. Even by Younghusband's standards the family were patently eccentric. Lady Constance, Blackburn's wife, 'was extraordinarily shy and nervous', he wrote to Helen. 'She looked like a person who had shut herself up by herself for a long time, and that is what I think she must have done,' while her mother 'was very quiet and kept quite apart talking very little'. At dinner on the first night none of the family appeared, only to materialize in a flurry at the end of the first course. One evening they all went reeling at a nearby castle. 'These Highlanders are almost as great peacocks as the Sikhs,' Younghusband told Emmie. 'They love getting up in their kit and being admired.' For nearly a week he wandered around entertaining himself, since the whole family were so aloof. 'Blackburn seems to do everything . . . but the family merely look on in a shy sort of way while the guests amuse themselves.' One morning no hot water was provided for shaving, and 'Poor old Lord Strathmore apologised in the most sincere and dignified way for the want of attention to me by the servants.'[11]

Shortly after Christmas Emmie Younghusband decided to kill herself. There had been a tentative proposal of marriage from a local vicar, the Rev. A. L. Keith; but she was now forty-four while the vicar was not yet thirty, and the prospect seemed quite impossible. She could see nothing to live for. Her one wish was to be forever close to her darling brother, her dear Frank, the man whose letters and presence she had come to live and die for. But she knew he was soon to be leaving London for India with his wife and the nascent baby. Depressed beyond measure, Emmie felt she could bear it no longer.

> This letter you will only get when I have passed away –
> Thank you oh so much sweet little Frank for all your love
> and goodness. This box contains my dear relics of you and
> all your letters . . . I feel I shall be very near you and shall
> still be looming and watching and praying for you.[12]

Frank received the letter on 31 December. The following day his wife gave birth to a nameless girl in a nursing home off Grosvenor Square, spiralling into a frenzy of longing for the baby boy who had died in Mount Abu. How Emmie was saved from a bungled suicide attempt is unclear – what is certain is that Frank scooped her up and carried her away to India, accompanied by his mother-in-law and a maid, while Helen and the new-born baby remained in London.

On the voyage back he tried to straighten out his life, making earnest entries in his notebook. 'Take trouble to find out ways of doing personal kindnesses to those about me, no matter who they are . . . In all dealings with natives avoid assuming tone or air of superiority. Remember their good points – the excellence of their manners, their patience, their spirituality, their intelligence.'[13] A guilt-ridden letter was sent to Helen: 'I really have been most ungrateful to you . . . for all that you have gone through for me.' Frank insisted that she should engage a first-rate nurse for the new baby, since 'we are quite three times as well off now as we were when we landed in India 4 years ago'.[14] In March Helen sailed out to join him, accompanied by their new daughter, whom they had decided to name Eileen Louise Clara Nina.

As British Resident in Indore, Younghusband was given 'a great large dull looking house'. It was a comfortable posting in central India: the problem came with the Maharajah, 'an enormously big man with a clean shaved face dressed in tight trousers and a light cashmere coat'.[15] Maharajah Holkar of Indore was a mercurial character, well informed and widely travelled. But he was dangerously unpredictable, and 'undoubtedly subject to fits of madness . . . One day he harnessed the Indore bankers into the state coach and, getting on the box himself, drove them round the city.'[16] To Younghusband's consternation, the Maharajah announced that he hated the British, despite a deep personal attachment to the recently deceased Queen Victoria. 'He said that some people spoke of her as an ugly old woman but [that he] saw she had the light of God in her. To be in her presence was like being in a temple.'

In April Younghusband was summoned to Delhi to see Curzon, taking Emmie with him for the journey. The infrastructure was being prepared for the Coronation Durbar, a monumental celebration to mark the ascension of Edward VII to the King-Emperorship of India. Younghusband visited the main audience hall, which was being knocked down and rebuilt on Curzon's orders. 'The Viceroy, my dear,' he told Helen, 'proposes to sit in that high marble throne sort of place with a canopy on the top where the old Mughal Emperor used to sit . . . It seems to me just a little too much.'[17] But the old magic soon began to work, for at luncheon the next day he was placed next to the Viceroy, who talked to him 'literally the whole time' about the frontier and the state of Indore and the newly founded Central Asian Society.

There was a certain tension in the Younghusband household. Emmie returned sadly to Britain; the Hon. Mrs Magniac remained at Indore; Helen grew a little more cheerful; the baby Eileen thrived. Francis became increasingly exasperated. At first he had 'tried to see the good' in Maharajah Holkar, but 'I am now determined to smash him'. '(Confidentially between you and me),' he told Henry Newbolt, 'Holkar is going to retire into private life and F.E.Y. is for all intents & purposes going to rule in his stead.'[18] In December the Maharajah and his British Resident had to take a special train together to Delhi. Preparations were now in full swing for the Coronation Durbar; or the Curzonation as it had been dubbed. 'I am perfectly certain the Chiefs [Princes] will absolutely hate all their part,' Younghusband told Emmie.[19]

Protocol began to crumble when the King-Emperor's brother, the Duke of Connaught, arrived at Delhi railway station on the first day of the Durbar. All the princes of India were lined up in strict order of precedence to greet him. As the Duke alighted, Holkar shot forward to shake his hand, only to have his tails grabbed from behind by the diminutive Resident, aghast at this breach of orders. 'The coat tails were of the most gorgeous silk;' Younghusband wrote, 'but they held, and the situation was saved. By such resourcefulness do British officers keep the Empire together!'[20]

In James (Jan) Morris's *Farewell the Trumpets* the bloated opulence of the Curzonation is caught vividly: the city of tents, the telegraph wires, the trussed-up Maharajahs, the intricate timetables, the bewigged high-court judges, the armies of trumpeters, caparisoned elephants, blind veterans of the Mutiny, 40,000 parading soldiers – and at its centre, the Lat Sahib:

> ... upon his slender-pillared dais stood the Viceroy of India, the Crown's embodiment, George Nathaniel Curzon of Eton and Balliol, forty-three years old, half-crippled with pain in his back, an accomplished inventor of comic verse, a well-known eastern traveller, dressed in the flamboyant accoutrements of his office.[21]

The Great Durbar represents the symbolic climax of British rule in India. It was the moment before the bubble burst, an absurd, magnificent, gargantuan crescendo at the end of Victoria's reign. Only the most ardent imperialist could fail to see that the whole stunning edifice was beginning to crumble, its foundations torn apart by Indian dissent, ground down by its own stifling bureaucracy, toppling under the weight of overwhelming pomposity and grandeur. The Curzonation was the perfect prelude to the most remarkable and the most pointless of British India's military adventures – the Younghusband Expedition.

Frank Younghusband returned to Indore in the first week of 1903 and deposed the Maharajah Holkar, installing the ruler's son upon the throne. The Chief Minister, Nanak Chand, was made Regent. Younghusband considered him 'one of the ablest Indians I have met', and was content to leave much of the day-to-day running of the administration in his hands. Influenced by an elderly swami, Younghusband's thoughts turned increasingly to religion. A year earlier he had been dismissive of Hinduism, referring to it in a letter as 'a second rate religion'. But now he began careful study of 'the Bhagavatgita with a fine old Brahmin, he reading it in Sanskrit and I following him in an English translation. I also read books on Vedantism.'[22] His musings were interrupted at the end of February by the death of Helen's mother at Indore, and then by 'a mysterious letter' which arrived in early May.

'I have been put into a state of agitation,' he told his father, by a letter from a colleague in the Foreign Department 'asking me to take him with me on my journey'. Mystified, Younghusband wrote back inquiring what journey he was referring to, only to receive an urgent wire instructing him not to mention a word, and by the same post a letter from the Viceroy summoning him to Simla. On 20 May 1903, during a lively gymkhana at the Annandale racecourse, all was revealed.

Perched on a camp chair beneath the looming deodar trees, the ponies cantering up and down in front of them, Lord Curzon told Younghusband that he would like him to go to Tibet, 'and said there was no man in the whole of India who could do it better than me'. After all, the Tibetans had been 'troublesome neighbours' of late, were not keeping to the terms of a treaty which China had made on their behalf, and were now trying to have secret dealings with the Russians. 'My dear Father,' wrote Younghusband excitedly. 'This is a really magnificent business that I have dropped in for.'

> Lord Curzon's original idea of sending an imposing Mission
> – like Malcolm's to Persia and Burnes' to Kabul in old days
> – to Lhasa itself has not been sanctioned: and I am not to
> go to Lhasa itself as far as is present settled, but only just
> inside Tibet.[23]

The Viceroy left him with an abiding impression that an advance to the heart of Tibet was his ultimate strategic ambition. But the needs of diplomacy and political caution meant that a tentative advance to the border was all that could be sanctioned – for the moment.

On the day of his fortieth birthday Younghusband travelled quietly east across the plains of India to Calcutta, telling his friends that he had business in Darjeeling. For nearly a week he trailed around departmental offices in the sweltering heat making arrangements for the expedition, trying to extract money and equipment from the Government of India's tangled bureaucracy. The Accounts Department told him all withdrawals would have to be made in instalments. 'I replied, well I want at the present moment an instalment of Rs. 10,000 in ten notes of Rs. 1,000 each. This quite flumaxxed them: but they had to give it; I walked off with it in Mr Mutter's waistcoat pocket!'

Mr Mitter, an Indian clerk from Indore who was accompanying Younghusband, was soon joined by a natural history collector, a photographer, a collection of fine tents and the indomitable Mahmood Isa. Under the impression that the whole adventure was going to be a sophisticated re-run of the Taming of the Mir of Hunza, with the Dalai Lama playing the title role, Younghusband also put in a request for the services of the Pathan surveyor Shahzad Mir, but he turned out to be unavailable. Armed with an array of staff and a new revolver, the Tibet Frontier Commissioner took a train to Siliguri, and next day wound his way up through the clouds on 'a most ridiculous little railway' to Darjeeling.

'This is a funny quiet sleepy little place', Helen learnt on 13 June, 'full of mist at present and no view of Kangchenjunga yet visible. The air is certainly better than Simla – softer and less extreme.'[24] When he did catch a glimpse of Kangchendzonga, the third highest mountain in the world, Younghusband was deeply moved. It became his favourite mountain, a sort of bench-mark of Himalayan beauty against which other peaks could be measured. 'Through the rent in the fleecy veil,' he declaimed in The Heart of Nature, one of his 1920s works of mystical philosophy, the traveller can see from Darjeeling 'clear and clean against the intense blue sky the snowy summit of Kinchinjunga, the culminating peak of lesser heights converging upward to it and all ethereal as spirit, white and pure in the sunshine . . . We are uplifted.'[25]

For several days he stayed in the misty hill station, the Bengal administration's summer capital, making practical arrangements for his departure to Tibetan territory. He met up with his interpreter, a tall Irish officer called Frederick O'Connor, one of the only Tibetan speakers in the British army. At the same time Younghusband tried to gain information about the workings of the Tibetan government and the political background to his adventure. At this stage he was acutely aware that, despite his fame as a Great Game player a decade earlier, he had little knowledge of Tibetan affairs, or of the events that had given rise to Curzon's wish to arrange an invasion. Rather to his surprise, the Darjeeling authorities (who had not been consulted about the virtues of the operation) did all they could to help him and ensure his comfort.

On the morning of 19 June 1903 he rose early and dressed in 'Marching Order': breeches, gaiters, brown boots, flannel shirt, khaki coat and forage cap. A small crowd had assembled outside the Rockville Hotel to wave farewell to his party. Swathed in dark oilskins, the horses snorting in the damp air, the Commissioner made a final check on his luggage and equipment before riding off into the distance to an anonymous shout of 'Good luck'. 'The monsoon was just bursting, the rain was coming down in cataracts, and all was shrouded in the densest mist.'[26] The first stage of the Younghusband Expedition had begun.

Despite the pouring rain, he made frequent pencil notes as he rode north into Sikkim, the launching pad for his advance into Tibetan territory. Historically Sikkim had been an independent Buddhist kingdom with strong links to Tibet, but in 1861 the British had annexed some of its southern territory, including Darjeeling. By 1903 Sikkim had 'special status' under international law. Theoretically it was a sovereign country (the ruler was not obliged to swear loyalty to the British Crown), but in practice it was administered in much the same way as any other Native State within the remit of British India. Its people were culturally and ethnically closer to Tibetans than Indians: 'lacking in vigour but evidently possessing a certain amount of hardihood,' according to Younghusband's jottings, 'polite, no caste, very Mongolian type. Women go about just as the man & instead of hiding their faces as they did in India look straight at you just as a man wd.'

In his 'Rough Notes Passing Through Sikkim on my Mission to Tibet 1903', there are as many references to nature as to politics. 'Ride through forest. Ferns 10–12 ft. Bracken, bananas wild. Beautifully fresh . . . Shoots of wild asparagus 6 or 7 ft. Cross Teesta by Suspension. River in places like the Tweed at Kelso. Deep valley. Long rope like creepers dangling down 50 ft. Haunting suspicion of fever.' That night he stayed in a dak bungalow near the village of Rangpo, setting off next morning through the thick leech-infested forest that covers the slopes of the Eastern Himalayas. 'Torrential rain during night,' he scribbled. 'At Sinkam cross river by picturesque cantilever bridge . . . Most beautiful orchids in a long cluster.' He tangled his way through bamboos and elephant creepers, catching sight of Kangchendzonga for a few seconds as the mist lifted. Late in the evening he reached Gangtok, the capital of Sikkim.

His host was John Claude White, the British Political Officer, who until then had held official responsibility for Tibetan frontier affairs. An arrogant, opinionated character, with the customary walrus moustache, White had gradually turned Sikkim into his private fiefdom. By manipulating Maharajah Thutob Namgyal, the hereditary monarch, and even imprisoning him in his palace at one point with no food or water, White had gained a degree of control way beyond that of most Political Officers. He had begun to settle Nepalese workers in southern Sikkim, on the grounds that the indigenous inhabitants were 'too lazy'. His natural pomposity was compounded by an understandable irritation at Younghusband's presence on his territory. Although he had been appointed Joint Commissioner for Tibet Frontier Affairs, he knew that Younghusband was the Viceroy's nominee. White was effectively in thrall to a junior political official from Central India with no experience of Tibet. The prospects were not auspicious.

On 24 June the King of Sikkim – known as the Chogyal by the Sikkimese but as the Maharajah by the British – paid them a visit. 'Dressed in Chinese clothes,' Younghusband noted. 'Never been further than Darjiling. Not particularly intelligent but self-composed.' The Chogyal cut an uncertain figure. On succeeding his step-brother in 1874 he had strengthened his country's links with Tibet, only to have the ground cut from under him when a British force invaded Sikkim in 1888, and ransacked his palace on the edge of the Chumbi valley. The following year Claude White materialized: the Buddhist king and his family fled over the border to Tibet, only to be captured and put under palace arrest. Over the next decade the unfortunate, hare-lipped Chogyal shrank into himself. For some time he refused even to speak in the presence of the malignant Political Officer.

His second wife, Yeshe Dolma, was a more commanding figure. She made a great impression on the Princess of Wales and the Vicereine in 1905 when she met them in Calcutta. Strong-willed and politically astute, she was a substantial scholar in her own right. With the aid of Kazi Dawa Samdup (the first translator of the *Bardo Thotrol*, otherwise known as *The Tibetan Book of the Dead*) she compiled a partial but impressive History of Sikkim. At dinner at the Political Officer's spacious bungalow on 26 June, Younghusband was most impressed by her. He had never seen, let alone spoken to, the wives of the other rulers he had encountered on his journeys. In Tonk his conversations with the Nawab's wife had been conducted through a purdah curtain. But the Gyalmo of Sikkim was something altogether different.

'She is v. self possessed. I took her in to dinner arm in arm . . . she looked straight ahead at everybody and talked away as any English lady wd.' Aware that she came from a Tibetan noble family, Younghusband tried to convince her of the benefits of contact with the British. 'I sat on a sofa with her and had a talk with her about Tibet as I knew she wd. report to Tibet everything I said.' He also had a long conversation with Sidkeong Tulku, the Chogyal's son by his first wife: 'a nice youth . . . simple and unaffected in manner with plenty of intelligence' who had written a journal about his travels to Burma and Ceylon, and longed to go to Oxford to take a degree.

As he lay in bed the following evening writing his diary, Frank Younghusband could not get the Chogyal's compelling consort out of his mind:

> She sipped a little champagne and port after dinner when the King's health was drunk . . . In fact she is an uncommonly slim little thing & she looked very picturesque in her peculiar high head dress of pearls & coral . . . After dinner I asked her if she wd. give me a photo of herself and she promised to send it to me the next morning – which she did![27]

The spell was soon broken as Younghusband packed up and set off again, inspecting his military escort as he left Gangtok. He had 500 sepoys from the 32nd Sikh Pioneers, commanded by a British officer, and knew that more soldiers could be summoned if necessary. The monsoon was bursting all around him, rain streaming down his oilskins as he rode cheerfully north towards the Tibetan border.

At the beginning of 1903 Younghusband had been disillusioned, his life and career drifting nowhere. Indore was an adequate posting, but he was almost forty and there were few openings in the distance. I had not realized quite how desperate the situation had become until I began to look at files in the National Archives of India, a huge red brick building in the centre of New Delhi. It contains some material that is duplicated in the India Office Library in London, but also a monumental stock of papers that the British left behind when India gained independence. A protracted battle with the Director of Archives had concluded with permission being granted to enter its labyrinthine book stacks.

It turned out that from 1898 onwards, Younghusband had been dispatching petulant requests for promotion. However justifiable his irritation was at his stagnant career – and it is true that the brakes seem to have been put on it ever since the debacle at Bozai Gumbaz – allowing anger to escape into his official correspondence can only have had a detrimental effect. There was one distinctly tetchy letter to Louis Dane, the Foreign Secretary to the Government of India, in which Younghusband threatens to resign unless he is promoted from Indore, and makes a whining reference to his personal friendship with Curzon. Those in authority should remember, he insists, that he had 'acquired a reputation which extended beyond the British Empire', as well as writing three books 'which according to such reviews as the "Spectator" largely added to my reputation'.

Although self-advertisement of this kind was not unusual at the time, Younghusband's peevishness can only have weakened his case. The internal notes in the margins of the file are not favourable towards him. After being shifted around the Foreign Department, his letter was eventually referred to the Viceroy himself. 'Why answer at all,' came the reply, 'until we have settled the question of his employment on special business elsewhere? C.'[28] An earlier memo in the same block of papers shows that this intervention made no positive difference to his prospects: Curzon had already marked him out at the end of 1902 as the ideal leader of any mission to Tibet.

Younghusband's anger at his incarceration in Indore was certainly understandable. I sometimes wondered how on earth the officials of British India, trussed up in their stiff uniforms, had ever managed to do anything at all in the blinding heat of the Indian plains. Judging by the sheer volume of documents in the hot, dusty gloom of the State Archives, they must have lived in an interminable cocoon of paper. It was not the best of times, attempting to work in the Archives in mid-summer. The Reading Room was a building site, replete with buckets, ropes, liquid cement, bamboo ladders and yelping workmen in thin cloth turbans and lungis. It was desperately hot, so stifling that some afternoons I could do nothing but sit very still and dream of endless icy water and sleet and snow.

Beetles, silverfish and white ants had eaten their way through the official papers: crucial sentences were missing, the firm trace of Curzon's handwriting consumed by an insect's jaws. Some files were lost, some destroyed, some forbidden. The rules were bizarre: I was not allowed to see a map Younghusband had drawn in Manchuria in 1886 on the grounds that it might be prejudicial to National Security. One afternoon there was a power surge and the ceiling fan above my desk revolved faster and faster. An elderly ledger started to disintegrate, flakes of yellow paper spiralling upwards about my head like a cloud of locusts. I decided it was time to move on, to escape from the dry history of reports and telegrams. I took an auto-rickshaw to Lok Nayak Bhawan to get a travel permit for Sikkim.

TWELVE

The Sikkim Adventure

Miss Goswami of the Ministry of Home Affairs had all the trappings of a middle-ranking Indian bureaucrat: a dingy private office, locked filing cabinet, huge telephone, cloth screen, giant stapler, damp towel, desk fan, personal tea boy and lurking sweeper. The regulations for visiting Sikkim were in the process of being changed, and nobody had the first idea what was happening. It was only after the intervention of 'HB', a well-manicured Sikh with ironed moustaches and a baby-blue turban, that I had found my way to Miss Goswami's lair. Her purpose in life was to stamp and initial permits for north-eastern frontier areas. It was a job of limited significance, but one that gave her absolute bureaucratic power over potential travellers. She held all the cards; and she knew it.

I filled in my third set of forms. Miss Goswami sat smugly behind her plastic desk while a massive over-wrought Dane tried to bribe her with a gold pen. She ignored the pen and told him to come back in six weeks. Then it was the turn of a Frenchman with a lisp. He didn't stand a chance.

'Namaste, madam. I wish to visit Atham.'

'Assam – only *group*. No individual.'

'I am in a group, madam.'

'Come back Thursday, 2 p.m.'

'Madam, on Thursday I must take a flight for Madrath. May I come please in the morning?'

'*Morning!* Morning I cannot entertain.'

She recognized me from an earlier visit. I had tried everything from flattery, explanation, reasoning and enthusiasm to desperate pleading, base cajolery and exquisite politeness – but it was no use. I was not going to get anywhere near the Tibetan border. Nothing would overcome Miss Goswami's impassive joy at being able to stop me.

'Sikkim contains sensitive frontier. I will give permission for Gangtok and Pemayangtse, but north and eastern Sikkim *strictly off limits*.'

She was an ardent conspiracy theorist. In her updated version of the Great Game there were Pakistani, Chinese or CIA agents lurking under every stone.

'Is there any chance I might go up to Singhik or Chunthang?'

'That I cannot allow. Don't forget before now we have had nuclear-powered listening devices planted in the Himalaya.'

'Do I look like a spy?'

'*We must protect our India.* You are saying that you are a student following the route of the British invasion. That I cannot know. It is possible you may be an agent travelling in the garb of an aficionado.'

Giving up, I went forward to take the Gangtok permit.

'Oh no,' said Miss Goswami sweetly. 'You cannot collect the permit today. *Issue* is Tuesday, 4 p.m.'

The early morning express to Siliguri was overflowing with people and baggages of every shape and size. On the outskirts of Delhi the train decided to stop indefinitely. The sweet pungence of blazing railway food, *aloo chole* and tamarind water made me retch as we waited and waited in the heat of the risen sun. Oily drinking water, miniature flower-pots of *chai*, beggars' stumps and streaming bottles of Thums Up and Limca were thrust through the bars of the window. I was wedged next to an excitable engineer from Chandigarh, who questioned me at length about the relative prices of consumer durables in India and Britain.

My original idea had been to follow the entire route of the 1903 invasion of Tibet, but I quickly realized this would be impossible. Apart from a handful of Tibetan refugees, nobody had crossed the Sikkim–Tibet border since the 1962 Sino–Indian border war. Now the frontier was a web of mines and barbed wire, Indian and Chinese soldiers facing each other grimly across the mountain passes. But I was still anxious to reach Sikkim. This tiny, isolated, mountain kingdom had the hopeless glamour of a truly lost cause. Trapped between the competing demands of Nepal, India and Chinese-occupied Tibet, it was swept into history in 1975 when that arch-democrat Indira Gandhi sent in troops to depose the last Chogyal. Since then Sikkim has been the twenty-second state of the Indian Union, a forgotten victim of Superpower politics.

It took two days and two nights of travelling before I reached the cool green of the Tista valley. Our jeep was crammed with kerosene cans, cloth-wrapped parcels and an assortment of people: Sikkimese Bhutias (whose forebears had migrated from Tibet centuries earlier), Sikkimese Lepchas (the indigenous people of

Sikkim), Sikkimese-Nepalese (settled by the British), Bengali tourists, hitch-hiking villagers and occasional straggle-haired urchins. At Rangpo they all waited patiently while I was taken into the Jawan's Tea Hut to have my rucksack searched by a young soldier. Shortly afterwards we crossed a stark military bridge outside Singtam (Younghusband's Sinkam) and reached another road block: the searching and the permit stamping began again.

Rising up through the hills we passed trails of lush foliage and elegant swathes of green bamboo swaying on the banks of the Tista. I could catch diagonal views of the wide, muddy, rushing river every few miles as we carefully crossed sagging wooden bridges. On the side of the road were grazing goats and dark monkeys, and Lepcha women with babies in baskets on their backs who stopped and stared as we drove past. Finally towards nightfall we reached Gangtok, as small a capital city as you are likely to find, perched on a strip of land overlooking a misty valley. I found a bed in the basement of Hotel Tibet, ate some noodles and went to sleep.

On my third day in Gangtok things leapt into life when I chanced to meet a man called Mr Wingrove at an exhibition of rare Sikkimese orchids. Mervyn Rhys Wingrove was a professional amateur of the old school – photographer, biplane pilot, traveller and botanist. In the days when 'profession' was still listed on your passport, his would undoubtedly have read simply 'Gentleman'. He seemed to live in Scotland and New York; had contacts in the Gangtok hierarchy; had travelled across the western Himalayas and played snooker in São Paolo with Geoff Crowther. Through his influence I had some remarkable meetings.

Kesang Tenzin was a versatile Sikkimese politician with plump earlobes and twinkling eyes. Although he had been Private Secretary to the late Chogyal (and director of his fledgling intelligence service) he had now metamorphosed, Talleyrand-like, into a distinguished elder statesman in the new administration. We sat in his book-lined study on the hill above Gangtok. I was drinking hot *chang* from a bamboo pot; he was drinking whisky.

'There was a kind of passive resistance to the British, but nothing

Above The first photograph of Francis Younghusband, taken in Bath shortly after his fifth birthday.

Painted Indian miniatures of Clara Younghusband with a servant, holding her daughter Emmie, and John Younghusband on horseback.

Francis Younghusband's uncle Robert Shaw in Yarkandi costume, 1869.

Above The Church of St John in the Wilderness in the foothills of the Indian Himalayas.

A Lahauli mother and son beyond the Rhotang Pass, spring 1990.

The exquisite May Ewart, shortly after her rejection of Frank Younghusband.

The 'kind and good' Nellie Douglas, who would have made 'a splendid Colonel of a Cavalry Regiment' had she been a man.

'Play Up!' Henry Newbolt in his days as a Clifton College cadet – his only excursion into uniform.

The legendary pony-man Mahmood Isa, who accompanied Younghusband through Tibet and Central Asia.

Left An imperious Captain Younghusband with George Macartney and the Amban of Yarkand, setting off to solve the Turkestan Question in 1890.

Below Bearded and exhausted eight months later in Kashgar, with Macartney and the mysterious Great Gamers Lennard and Beech.

Above The extraordinary
meeting between
Younghusband and his
Russian rival Colonel
Grombtchevski,
high in the Pamirs.

Right Chitrali horse-
men go wild on the
world's highest polo
ground, near Mastuj.

Right The young Maharajah of Indore, who usurped his father's throne after a plot by Younghusband and Curzon.

Far right The Maharajah of Bikaner, a commanding personality who spent his summers at Mount Abu.

Below Helen Magniac and Francis Younghusband on the day of their 'fashionable wedding'.

A studio portrait of Colonel Francis Younghusband, taken at Darjeeling a few days before he set off to invade Tibet.

Below A fictionalized view of the Colonel and his Mission from a contemporary French cartoon strip.

Above Younghusband and his 67 shirts holed up in the compound at Gyantse, guarded by a sentry and Lieutenant Hadow's Maxim Gun.

The Staff in Tibet. Freddie O'Connor stands with hands in pockets, 'Hatter' Bailey to his right with a light cane, Younghusband sits squarely in a greatcoat with General 'Retiring Mac' Macdonald to his left.

more than that. What could we do? One story I remember hearing is that some men diverted Younghusband's escort into fields of aconite – wolf's bane, I think you call it. Many of the mules and pack ponies ate it and died.

'You see, what could we Sikkimese *do*? We realized what was going to happen to the Tibetans if the British did invade – we knew from our own experience: "It will be like an egg being smashed against a rock," that was what the Chogyal warned the Tibetan General at Chumi Shengo. But Tibet couldn't understand how serious things were.'

'So what happened to Sikkim at the end of the Younghusband Expedition?'

'Well, Claude White stayed on for a bit longer cracking the whip. Then the old King died and was succeeded by his son Sidkeong Tulku – an incarnate lama, very scholarly, very strong-willed, Oxford-returned, Pembroke College.'

'Yes,' I said, remembering. 'Younghusband met him and mentioned he was bright.'

'Ha! Too intelligent for the British.' Kesang Tenzin leapt out of his chair and scampered across the room like a dancing bear. 'Let me read you this from our State History: "In December 1914 while Sidkeong was somewhat indisposed a British physician from Bengal administered a heavy transfusion of brandy and put him under a number of blankets; at the same time a fire was kept beneath the bed. Death came in the hour. Thus ended prematurely a promising career in most suspicious circumstances." His spirit was too strong, you see. The British liked their rulers to be compliant.'

At supper that evening we were joined by several of Kesang's relations, the fleeting Mr Wingrove and the headmistress of the Paljor Namgyal School for Girls. By some odd twist of history she came from Scotland – a tradition dating back to the school's establishment.

'Of course Sidkeong Tulku wasn't murdered,' said Miss Ritchie firmly. 'He died from an illness. I wouldn't have my girls being told anything different.'

'Well,' said our host in conciliatory tones. 'At St Joseph's Darjeeling they never did mention the brandy.'

The next day Kesang told me a story his father had told him:

'When Basil Gould, or Charles Bell maybe, was Political Officer – some time in the 1930s or 40s – he invited all the Kazis – aristocrat landlord class – not my father, he counted as a commoner – to afternoon tea. They put on their brocade *khos* and arrived at his residence on the morning of the appropriate day. The PO didn't know what to do! So the next time he decided to have a function in the morning, but all the Kazis stayed sitting on his lawn until evening, chattering away to each other. Gould said they were ill-mannered, but they thought Gould was rude for stopping hospitality at a certain time of day. In Sikkim it was not the custom for a party to stop and start like that.

'After the party several of the Kazis went home with the cutlery Gould had given them to eat their meal with. We use our hands for eating, you see, and they thought he was presenting a gift. The PO was *furious!*' Kesang's shoulders were heaving with laughter. 'Our outlook was so different, you see. Gould thought we were just ignorant savages stealing his silver knives and forks. But how were we to know the manners of English gentlemen?' Kesang Tenzin spread his hands wide enough to carry a young goat. 'How were we to know such things?'

One morning Miss Ritchie took me on a tour of her school. She carried an air of relaxed discipline wherever she went, striding along smartly in her tweed skirt. When we passed the pig-tailed uniformed Sikkimese school girls they dipped their heads, smiling shyly, chorusing: 'Good morning, Miss Sahib.' 'Good morning, Dolma, Rinzin, Pema,' came the firm reply.

'Well, no,' said Miss Ritchie a little later, 'I have never felt inclined to become a Buddhist.'

'Not even when you went to ceremonies at Rumtek monastery – weren't you impressed by the Karmapa?' I asked foolishly.

'I don't think one attends a religious service in order to be impressed,' she said in her crisp Dunfermline accent. 'One goes there to worship.'

In the New Year's honours lists of 1975 Miss Ritchie was awarded two medals by different monarchs. She flew to Buckingham Palace and the Queen hooked an MBE upon her breast. When she got back to Sikkim the ceremony for the Conferment of Orders had been postponed. The medals had arrived from Spink's but the

Chogyal was too busy: his country was about to be invaded by Indian troops. Miss Ritchie never got the second medal.

The school bell rang. Walking up the path towards Gangtok I could see her through the window, standing serenely by a blackboard, held in time and space, a Miss Jean Brodie of the Himalayan foothills.

When the last Chogyal died of throat cancer in 1982 he left four children. There had been five, but the vibrant Crown Prince Tenzin (an old Harrovian) was killed some years earlier on a hair-pin bend, to the great convenience of New Delhi.

The Chogyal really died of a broken heart. He had lost his country, both his wives, his eldest son, everything. They took his passport, kept him short of money, harassed him when he journeyed to Calcutta; even his personal car number-plates were removed. His name was stripped from public buildings. But if you go up the hill out of Gangtok you will still meet the Claude White Memorial Hall.

It was a rag-tag and bob-tail court by the end: visiting Americans, an Irish-Indian airman, a misplaced central European, an Australian teacher, some inconsequential Indian hangers-on, international flotsam and jetsam. The Chogyal took to drinking and playing mah jong, knowing that things were falling apart. He had responsibility without power, the prerogative of the deposed monarch throughout the ages.

After his Tibetan wife died, the Chogyal had married a young American called Hope Cooke. The newspapers described her as a fashionable debutante; the Kazis treated her with cool disdain. She was nervous and lonely. The Sikkimese would not accept her as their Gyalmo, not truly. The Indians and the agitators (led by Kazini Ethel Maud Dorji Khangsapa of Chakung, herself scarcely of Sikkimese origin) said Hope Cooke was a CIA stooge, a Himalayan Marie Antionette. But she was just a young American girl dressed up in a *chuba*, whispering in kitchen Sikkimese.

Hope Cooke and the Chogyal had two children: Palden and Hope Leezum. They swept into the spangled ballroom of Hotel Tashi

Dalek one evening, over from America on a visit, followed by a trail of hangers-on. Mr Wingrove leaped up in a flurry of good manners to greet his old friend the Prince. 'Pempa-la, Pempa-la,' said the hotel management, pushing and pulling at chairs, hovering assiduously. Princess Hope Leezum was helped to a seat. Previously lackadaisical waiters came running with trays of drinks and bowls of roasted cashews.

The Prince had the insecure, endlessly assessing eyes of a man who has been caught unhappily in the limelight. It was late in the evening. There were distractions and interruptions, people talking at cross purposes, too many drinks and cigarettes. Monarchists popped in and out, bowing, touching the floor with politeness, glad to see the Chogyal's son, their young Pempa-la back from America.

We talked about Sikkimese history, carefully avoiding the recent past. He was intrigued to hear that Francis Younghusband had considered his great-grandmother 'an uncommonly slim little thing'. But Prince Palden could not concentrate on the conversation; he had to watch the room, checking that all was well. He was wary that I knew too much about his family from reading books, and slipped the discussion on to neutral territory.

There was a cluster of affable American bankers, the Prince's colleagues from Wall Street. 'I knew Paul was something special in his country,' one of them told me in hushed tones, 'but I never realized he was royalty.'

He was Prince Palden Namgyal of Sikkim; he was an American merchant banker called Paul. So history turns. Out in the sleeping bazaar damp clouds were enveloping the buildings.

Kesang Tenzin had set to work on the bureaucracy. In the government offices we were served tea by a bowing man. Officials bustled up and down the corridor. Outside the monsoon was breaking, rain tumbling on to bobbing black umbrellas. 'No, today,' insisted Kesang into a telephone. 'Not next month.'

Some moments later paper started to erupt from a giant telex machine. I tried to look casual, squinting. 'TO: CHIEF SECRETARY GOS,' it read. 'FM: MISS PREM GOSWAMI DOCUMENTATION OFFICER.'

Victory of a sort. The telex paused and then coughed again: 'INNERLINE PERMIT CLEARANCE IS TRANSMITTED AS FOLLOWS: SUBJECT: GRANT OF RESTRICTED AREA PERMIT FOR SIKKIM. NAME OF THE FOREIGNER: MR. PATRICK FRENCH...'

I was on my way to the border.

Francis Younghusband rode up through Sikkim, writing notes in the saddle, just as he had when crossing the Gobi Desert on camelback sixteen years before. 'It amused me to see the way the natives treat [Claude White]. Whenever we met the natives they wd. take off hats and prostrate themselves with heads on the ground but come up again with a broad grin. They seems a simple cheery pleasant lot, and what astonishes me is the way they stand in the rain. They get drenched to the skin.' He passed the night at Raiotdong where there was a long Coolie Shed for his baggage carriers.

The next day Younghusband and his escort reached a small settlement at Singhik, passing huge waterfalls. 'Exceedingly picturesque suspension bridge over deep gorge of the Runchu. Steep cliffs, gorge filled with foliage – foaming torrent beneath,' he noted. 'The summit of the mountains today is hid in clouds, but here and there patches of snow can be seen ... We are putting up at Singhik in a Lepcha house. The roof is strips of bamboo laid over one another and said to be quite watertight. The walls are of stripped bamboo interlaced and plastered in places. There is an altar with a holy book on it elaborately tied up. 5 saucers filled with holy water and a sort of candlestick.'[1]

Before leaving Gangtok, he had been sent a cipher telegram from Simla ordering him not to advance into Tibetan territory until he knew that Tibetan delegates were waiting over the frontier at Khamba Dzong. Feeling that this might indicate a lack of aggressive purpose in his Mission, he decided – characteristically – to turn a blind eye to official instructions. By sending troops on ahead, he knew his own status would be enhanced when he did deign to cross the border. 'I am taking these orders as personal to myself,' he wrote to his father from Camp Singhik on the evening of 28

June 1903, 'that is to say I am going to read the "you" in the telegram as meaning F.E.Y. only: and I am going to send on the escort and O'Connor and probably White too to Khamba Jong.'[2] Confident of the Viceroy's underlying ambitions regarding Tibet, the Commissioner could afford to take a risk.

They pressed on into northern Sikkim, along slippery mule tracks and fearful suspension bridges of plaited twigs and creepers. A night was spent on the top floor of a Buddhist monastery at Chung Thang before Younghusband advanced to Langteng. There he met Mr Harrison, the Paymaster-General of Bengal, who was analysing the Expedition's financial requirements. 'He is great impressed with the grandeur of the mountain scenery in Sikkim and thinks it more striking than Kashmir . . . He had marched up with the escort and said they had a very trying march . . . The coolies broke down – the men were exhausted – the main body cut off from the advance guard by a river. Coolies transport is always trying and I must make some arrangement to have mules instead.'

Finally on the last day of June, after a long day's ride up a valley of walnut trees and rhododendron bushes, Younghusband reached Tangu. It was a rough, wet, flower-covered plain about fifteen miles from the Tibetan border. 'Cold damp morning,' he wrote on 1 July. 'Heavy clouds, drizzling rain. Khaki-clad sepoys wading about in mud. Dripping mud-covered mules standing about with drooping heads.'[3] By now the whole of the Tista valley was strung out with coolies, soldiers and mule trains; advance parties, escorts and back-up support; cooks, medical staff, transport officers, engineers, road-workers, clerks, gallopers and dak runners; rations, stores, rifles, ammunition, bedding, entrenching tools, fodder, telegraph wire, winter clothing and signalling equipment: all the paraphernalia needed to maintain the supply lines of a military force.

A few days later two hundred sepoys from the Sikh Pioneers reached Tangu, under the command of young Captain Bethune. They were soon joined by a further three hundred, sixty of whom were suffering from severe exposure. Younghusband sent an urgent order for more clothing, and within the month each sepoy was issued with a poshteen (sheep-skin coat), a blanket, a thick pajama, a pair of puttees, some boots and a cardigan jacket. On 4 July Younghusband sent White, O'Connor, and the bulk of the troops over the Kangra La, the 17,000-foot pass which led into Tibet. There was a small scuffle between Sikh soldiers and Tibetan officials at the frontier, but three days later the invading force was encamped at Khamba Dzong. A message was sent back across the frontier by dak runner to say that Tibetan and Chinese officials were awaiting the arrival of the Senior Commissioner.

But Francis Younghusband remained on the Tangu plain, examining the primulas and orchids, reading Tennyson, biding his time.

Obtaining a permit for northern Sikkim was one thing: getting there was quite another. Buses did not exist, military trucks would not carry passengers, private jeeps were too expensive and lacked the required authorization. In the end I had to attach myself to a Sikkimese tour group who were going as far as Yumtang, and then hope for the best. We set off from the Gangtok bazaar early one morning in a glorified mini-bus: eight Nepalese youths, singing what sounded like rugby songs, a small family of semi-Sikkimese Sikhs, a dozing Marwari cloth merchant, a Bhutia-Lepcha driver, four scrawny chickens to be strangled en route and the ubiquitous Mr Wingrove.

It was pouring with rain as we drove up the Tista valley, the road snaking round corner after corner as it rose through the terraced rice fields. Younghusband's bamboo forests were giving way to undulating ridges and valleys, dipping up and down as we edged forward, Kangchendzonga's white edges rising in the distance. Every five miles we were halted by soldiers at a road block. The documents of the other inhabitants of the mini-bus received a cursory inspection; Mr Wingrove and I had our Restricted Area Permits and passports scrutinized minutely, military radios squawking like parrots in consternation.

Outside Singhik we stopped to look at a religious shrine. It consisted of a fresh-water spring emerging from a large rock, in which there was a series of strange indentations. Beside the rock were prayer flags and a Buddhist *stupa*; behind it a small Sikh *gurdwar*, 'erected by 5th Sikh Rifles' according to a painted sign.

'This', announced Ram Bhim, a Sikkimese-Nepalese Hindu, 'is the footstep of our saint Padmasambhava.'

'No, sir,' responded a Sikh soldier, 'it is the footprint of Guru Nanak Sahib, founder of our faith.'

'Padmasambhava, I must tell you, is a Buddhist master – not Hindu,' said the Bhutia-Lepcha bus driver. 'Guru Rimpoche we call him. He made this footstep when on his way to Tibet to give teachings.'

'I am sorry, sir,' insisted the Sikh, 'but you must stand corrected. It is historical fact that our Guru Nanak Sahib placed his foot on this sacred rock while making pilgrimage to the Himalaya.'

'Padmasambhava . . .' cut in Ram Bhim.

Back in the mini-bus Mr Wingrove was adjusting his camera equipment. 'Did it occur to you,' he asked, stroking his protruding chin in a mysterious fashion, 'that it might just be the footprint of Sir Francis Younghusband?'

Then we were off again, rattling along, the mini-bus vibrating to the noise of a Hindi film song. As the day wore on we reached Chuntang, the vegetation dissolving outward into stretches of rock. The air was becoming thin and cold, the rain turning to patchy mist, the ground too high for the monsoon to reach. Every few miles hooting jeeps, four-tonners and truck-loads of soldiers would pass us, grinding their way along the narrow road. Through the forest there were gaps and twisted roots where they had taken trees carelessly for building and fuel, scarring the hillside. We crossed the Tista river and its tributaries on layers of dark green military metal, rigid Bailey bridges replacing plaited twigs and creepers.

On the side of the Lachung Chu were gargantuan vertical water-falls, sheets of just-liquid ice clattering down onto the boulders. Younghusband mentioned them in his diary: never before had he witnessed waterfalls of such height and length and volume. Coming through a valley below Lachung I could see high above me two trails of flying water colliding continuously in mid air, merging and melding into one colossal stream which bounced and twisted its way down the face of the mountain. At the foot of the waterfall was a squat concrete lump. On it was painted proudly, in foot-high garish yellow: PUBLIC LATRINE CONSTRUCT BY 7/42C. GOORKHA RIFLES. ACN.937714D–7.

We stayed in a small bungalow that night, clustered around a wood-burning stove. The Sikkimese-Nepalese youths sang and drank beer until it was late, then called out to each other in falsetto voices, snorting, belching, whooping and giggling in the darkness. When it started to grow light I got out of my sleeping bag, dressed quickly in layers of thermal clothing and went outside. Beneath me I could see the Tista valley stretching down towards India. The family of Sikhs were crouched over a bucket of water, cleaning their teeth. 'Good morning,' said Mr Singh, straightening up. 'Please excuse the behaviour of those rowdies last night – they just aren't used to drinking liquor.' He had not yet had time to wind up his turban, so for decorum's sake his head was covered with a beige anorak hood, tied neatly beneath his chin.

In the lee of a rock Mr Wingrove was fiddling with his high-pressure reflective hurricane stove. The idea of a night in the bungalow had not appealed to him, so his mountain tent was pitched beneath a solitary pine.

'Fine specimens,' he said as I approached. 'Wonderful primroses, *Primula sikkimensis*, slipper orchids, lousewort.'

'Where?'

'About half a mile along that ridge. Saw a Himalayan blue pheasant up there. Rare thing. No snow pigeon though.'

Down at the bungalow the rowdies were emerging, clutching their heads and groaning plaintively. Rain was starting to drizzle through the mist. Before long I could see them opening bottles of beer and wandering over in our direction.

'Peculiar blue, the Himalayan blue,' said Mr Wingrove, turning the pages of a huge Royal Horticultural Society tome. 'Same sort of glistening turquoise blue as the Tibetan lakes; and Bailey's poppy, for that matter.'

Soon his camping spot was swarming with Ram Bhim and his colleagues, who pulled and poked at the array of gadgets and instruments. 'This is London,' announced the short-wave radio as it came alive in Ram's inquisitive hands. 'Very good model,' came the response. 'How much this cost in your country?' The miniature water-filtration pump was inserted into a puddle; the magnesium block scraped and ignited; the electronic compass pointed in every direction; the halogen lamp switched on and off again at great speed. Flattered but alarmed by their technical interest, Mr Wingrove raced up and down, simultaneously demonstrating the workings of a given object while trying to put it back in its place. Things came to a head when he caught sight of Ram, who had inserted a length of flexible metal tubing into his ear while his friend Lal Bahadur manipulated its end expertly.

'I am thinking this is a device to assist with your personal hygiene?' said a beaming Ram Bhim.

'No, it damn well isn't,' snapped Mr Wingrove. 'It's a percussive cable release for my box camera and I won't have you fiddling around with it.'

The hooded Mr Singh, who had assumed a paternal role over the group, sent the rowdies back to the bungalow.

'They are young boys actually,' he said. 'They come here only to have a jolly, for drinking purposes. We come to view the beauty of the hills, but for them the scenery has no interest.'

'Why on earth don't they stay and drink in Gangtok?' asked Mr Wingrove.

'Oh no, that would not be permitted. Take Ram Bhim – he is of good family. His father and uncle are selling cloth in Gangtok, early Nepalese settlers from the British time, quite wealthy. But they are *strict* authorized Hindus. They would not allow their children to be taking alcohol. So they come here – out of sight, out of mind, as you say.'

So this is what the mountains of Sikkim have become, I thought; a speakeasy and an army proving ground.

The subsequent days were most frustrating. I wandered the slopes of the primula-covered valley, climbing the wet scree, but whenever I neared the road a military patrol would soon appear, turning me back towards Yumtang. I was still a good forty miles from the Tibetan border, and knew my only hope of advancing further along Younghusband's trail was if I went with the rest of the tour group. This was clearly impossible: Mr Wingrove chased orchids, Mr Singh and his family went for walks, but Ram Bhim and his friends did nothing but sit drinking (they had progressed to a foul concoction called 'sharp rum') in the poky bungalow.

My breakthrough came one evening when Mr Wingrove was being pestered for his maps. He had two magnificent specimens: a US air force map which showed elevations and contour markings, covered in dire warnings about the dangers of unlisted radio emission, and a fine-scale Austrian one which depicted villages, glaciers and peaks in intricate detail. Spotting a Shiva temple marked near Yume Samdong, Ram Bhim showed an interest. Seizing my chance, I did my best to whip up enthusiasm for a sight-seeing visit, ardently praising the architecture of northern Sikkim's Shiva temples.

We set off early in the morning, crammed together in the mini-bus, mud and rain spattering on the windows. Mr Singh and his daughter sat in the front with the reluctant driver, overseeing pro- ceedings; Mr Wingrove had his head in Joseph Hooker's guide to the plants of Sikkim; the rowdies were working themselves up into a state of religious fervour, chanting prayers and mantras. For all their frivolity, they turned out to have a surprisingly keen attach- ment to their faith. At the first road-block Mr Singh chatted us through easily, while at the second he pleaded the importance of our pilgrimage with an uncertain boy soldier. The sight of Ram Bhim, moaning and writhing, his forehead smeared with deep red paste, was enough. After that it was plain sailing. We were far enough into the militarized zone not to be bothered by checkpoints.

The road was like a raw wound now, a gash in the landscape, its edges ragged and torn. It had been cut through impossible terrain by Tibetan refugees, hacking their way forward through rock and frozen earth on the army's behalf. As we rose beyond the tree line it grew colder and the air took on a thin, dry sharpness which seared our lungs. Puzzled yaks, their shaggy black coats knitted with ferns and bracken, watched us as we drove past. The road petered out at a huge army base, which spread across a sandy grey valley. Huts and hangars stretched into the distance, overseen by a metalled heli-pad with bright markings.

The Samdong Shiva Munder turned out to be a tiny corrugated- iron shed, constructed by a Hindu regiment which had served at the base some years earlier. I expected the rowdies to be furious, incensed that I had brought them on a wild goose chase to what looked like a rusty latrine. But they were utterly unfazed, treating the shed with the greatest reverence, ringing the devotional bell politely to alert Lord Shiva to their presence. There were only a handful of soldiers about, surprised but rather pleased to find visi- tors to their remote 'non-family-posting'.

'Long guns,' Ram Bhim told me pointing at an extended hangar across the parade ground. 'Bofors guns, purchase of Mr Rajiv Gandhi.'

'Bofors guns!' It was the scandal over the purchase of these weapons which had lost Gandhi the 1989 election.

'Forty K range – China *bang whoosh!* – acha, okay – no problem,' declared a cheerful Lal Bahadur.

'Do you think China might fight a war with India?'

'No,' he said dolefully.

I set off towards the northern border, scrabbling up the side of the Changme Kangku, a long, gravelly moraine coming down off

the mountain range. I had six hours before the bus returned to
Yumtang. Below me lay the army base, tiny vehicles driving to and
fro. My boots kept slipping off the cold boulders as I climbed the
slope, every footstep throwing up a thin cloud of grey dust. Around
me sounds and smells were multiplied by the lightness of the air,
all my senses heightened by the strange texture of the atmosphere.
But my limbs had no energy, no power to run. I pulled myself on
to a ridge of ice and rock and stood there excitedly, looking towards
Tibet.

The snow-covered mountain tops beckoned me towards them,
tipping forward, swaying, luring me higher, then pushing me away,
indifferent, scornful of humans. According to the map I was seventeen thousand feet above sea level. About five miles to my left, on
the far side of the first mountain range, was the Tangu plain where
Younghusband had sat and waited, biding his time before crossing
the frontier. Ten miles to my right, I calculated, was Tibet itself.
Ahead of me, shrouded in strands of soft white cloud, was the
Kangra La, the pass which led over the border to Khamba Dzong.

When I stared again the snow peaks were still and serene, monu-
ments, giving nothing away, no indication of movement or feeling,
like a wild beast which feigns sleep to confuse its prey.[4]

THIRTEEN

Sixty-seven Shirts, a Bath and an Army

Escorted by a posse of armed horsemen, Francis Younghusband crossed into Tibetan territory on 18 July 1903. The time was right, he considered, for a triumphal appearance at Khamba Dzong. Riding across the barren plain, he could see the British camp ensconced at the foot of the *dzong*, the huge hill fort cum administrative centre which was home to the *Dzongpon* (District Officer) of the Khamba region. Trenches and barbed wire surrounded the neat rows of British tents. But it was not long before he realized his fellow Commissioner, John Claude White, had offended the Tibetan and Chinese delegates by his high-handed behaviour. 'He has never been out of Sikkim,' Younghusband wrote home on 19 July. 'He is a little god there, but he is absolutely useless and worse than useless in dealing with high officials of an independent nation.'[1]

Younghusband tried to rectify the situation by calling a conference, to take place the following day in his camp. The political and spiritual leader of Tibet, His Holiness the Thirteenth Dalai Lama, was represented by Lobsang Trinley, his *Trungche* (Chief Secretary) and a senior *Depon* (General) called Tsarong Wangchuk Gyalpo, whose father had been responsible for demarcating the Tibet–Sikkim border fifteen years earlier.[2] These two officials were escorted by an impromptu battalion of levies, raised by the local Dzongpon. There was also a Chinese official present by the name of Ho Kuang Hsi, who was the Chinese representative at Shigatse, Tibet's second largest city.

With the help of his interpreter, Captain O'Connor, Younghusband made a formal speech in which he listed the Indian Government's grievances against Tibet. He pointed out that the Viceroy's letters to the Dalai Lama had been returned unread, Sikkim's boundaries not respected, Indian trade with Tibet restricted, and the Conventions of 1890 and 1893 largely ignored. Uncertain as to who would bear responsibility for making the decisions, Younghusband presented the delegates with a written version of his peroration. 'But they could not have got rid of a viper with greater haste,' he wrote, 'than they got rid of that paper.'

The Tibetan officials refused to discuss anything further until the British had crossed back over the border into Sikkim, and to Younghusband's great consternation, retired to the *dzong* without him. 'These so-called delegates never came near us again at Khamba Jong, but shut themselves up in the fort and sulked.'[3] Ho Kuang Hsi returned to Shigatse, citing ill health as the reason for his departure. Letters from Sidkeong Tulku of Sikkim to the Tibetan Government produced no discernible effect. With no delegates to negotiate with, all Younghusband could do was wander the freezing, arid plains of Khamba Dzong, racking his brains for new ideas. In his irritation he even committed the cardinal sin of forgetting his anniversary. 'My own precious darling,' he wrote on 14 August, 'I cannot tell you how grieved and vexed I am that I should have let our wedding day go by without noticing it.'[4]

His only consolation was the fact that his pay had risen to 2579 rupees a month, plus a 'sumptuary' allowance for clothing and accessories of 1000 rupees a month. This was almost six times what he had been earning at Mount Abu, and gave him some relief from his worries about Helen and the baby. Some mornings he would get up early and climb the surrounding mountains, gazing hopefully towards Mount Everest. According to W. D. Shakabpa (the former Finance Minister to the Fourteenth Dalai Lama) the British took to shooting birds and gazelles, and 'passed their time carrying out impressive military exercises, taking photographs, hiking in the hills, mapping the surrounding country, botanizing, and geologizing.'[5]

By this stage the British Mission had been joined by Ernest Wilton of the China Consular Service and Captain Randall Parr of the Chinese Customs Service. Wilton, a keen Sinologist who had been summoned from Shanghai, was to remain with the Mission as Younghusband's special adviser. In his view, nothing could be achieved until new delegates arrived, since neither the Tibetan nor the Chinese representatives were of sufficient rank to negotiate. Parr was a rather different quantity. Officially he was in the employ of the crumbling Chinese Government (like many European adventurers at this time) but in practice his loyalties lay with the British. Younghusband found him useful but irritating: 'a terrible talker and rather a low class kind of man,' Helen learned, 'but full of information. Among other things he says the Russians are moving on Lhasa and at any rate the Tibetans count on their support.'[6]

Although Parr was meant to be acting both as a Chinese Commissioner and diplomatic go-between, he found to his regret that the Tibetan delegates took no notice of him.

There was a glimmer of hope on 21 August when the Abbot of Tashilhunpo Monastery and his retinue arrived for discussions. Tashilhunpo was the seat of His Serenity the Panchen Lama, Tibet's second spiritual leader after the Dalai Lama, and a figure of substantial political authority at certain points in the country's history. Younghusband was hopeful that the Panchen Lama's court might put pressure on the Lhasa administration to begin proper negotiations. But the Abbot, while affable and keen to engage in metaphysical debate (he insisted the earth was not only flat but triangular, shaped like a shoulder of mutton), could offer no practical suggestions beyond a British withdrawal followed by the prospect of talks.

Younghusband became increasingly frustrated by the lack of progress. He sent frequent reports to the Foreign Department, some of which verge on the fantastical, listing every conceivable reason why the mission should advance deeper into Tibet. In one letter to Louis Dane he quotes Annie Taylor, a missionary based at nearby Yatung: 'The Tibetans are to attack India from Khamba Jong . . . and twenty thousand Russians are said to be on their way to help the Tibetans.'[7] A private letter from Lord Curzon on 14 September confirmed his opinion that an 'incident' would have to be manufactured if things were to proceed. 'The Home Govt. just at present is not in a very potent condition,' wrote the Viceroy. An advance into the Chumbi valley would be the most they were likely to sanction, 'and that only upon some definite provocation.'[8]

Curzon had been exercised by the question of Tibet since the start of his Viceroyalty. He saw that its geographical location, caught between China, India and Russia, gave it a unique strategic significance in Central Asia. As early as May 1899 he was writing letters to Lord George Hamilton, the Secretary of State for India in London, about the need for direct contact with the Dalai Lama and an end to Tibet's diplomatic isolation. Unlike his predecessors, Curzon saw it was pointless to try to negotiate with Tibet through China. After commissioning a variety of reports, including one from O'Connor and several from the legendary Pundit Sarat Chandra Das (who had gone deep into Tibet on Great Game business), Curzon had sent a letter to the Dalai Lama via a Bhutanese emissary called Ugyen Kazi. Some months later it was returned unopened, the relevant Tibetan officials having declined to accept it. During 1901 and 1902 similar methods of communication were employed, unsuccessfully.

To a person of Curzon's disposition, stonewall diplomacy of this kind was supremely galling. It was the most extraordinary anachronism of the twentieth century, he wrote elegantly to Hamilton, 'that there should exist within less than three hundred miles of the borders of British India a State and a Government, with whom political relations do not so much as exist, and with whom it is impossible even to exchange a written communication'.[9] The Viceroy's anger was kept on the boil by the weekly Darjeeling Frontier Report, a compendium of intelligence, gossip and speculation on affairs relating to Tibet. It tended to confirm his hawkish suspicions about Russian intrigue.

Imperial paranoia had been thriving since the appearance of an article in the *Journal de Saint Petersburg* in June 1901, which stated that an envoy of the Dalai Lama of Tibet had recently been received by the Tsar. The following summer the same envoy, a certain 'Dorzhievy' or 'Dorjiew', was reported to be on a similar journey (having travelled through India) with an ambition to conclude a secret treaty between Russia and Tibet. Over the next two years rumour after rumour about Agvan Dorzhiev would materialize, until by late 1903 he was elevated to the position of Evil Genius at the Court of the Dalai Lama, two parts Rasputin to one part Macavity the Mystery Cat. 'Even the Dalai Lama himself, influenced by the insinuating Dorjieff . . . has gone to an extreme length in writing autograph letters to the Czar,' Younghusband wrote in an official report, although he had not a shred of firm evidence on which to base his allegation.[10]

Any understanding of Dorzhiev's role depends upon knowledge of his origins. He was born in 1854 near Verkhneudinsk (now Ulan Ude), three and a half thousand miles east of Moscow. As a Buryiat, he was culturally and religiously closer to the Dalai Lama than to his ostensible ruler the Tsar; there is evidence that he did not even speak Russian. Dorzhiev first went to Lhasa in 1873 to study with Buddhist masters, rather as a Roman Catholic priest might visit Rome. In time he fell into a position of great influence over the teenage Dalai Lama, becoming his tutor and 'debating partner'.

Early in 1898 Agvan Dorzhiev travelled to St Petersburg. There was at this time in Russian high society a vogue for Eastern mysticism, and the Buryiat monk was taken up by Prince Esper Ukhtomsky, gentleman of the bedchamber to the Russian Emperor. Some said the White Tsar was the White Tara, the deity prophesied in

Buddhist scripture. After being presented to the thoughtful but feckless Russian ruler, Dorzhiev travelled to Paris, and possibly even to London before returning to Lhasa. His remarkable journey, unparalleled within Tibetan society, aroused suspicion from members of the young Dalai Lama's court. In other quarters there was support for him, and respect for his understanding of international affairs. Dorzhiev proposed that Tibet should seek closer links with Russia, a notion which was anathema to ecclesiastical traditionalists.

In 1901 the incomparable Dorzhiev set off for Russia again, accompanied by three Tibetan officials, and in August had another meeting with Tsar Nicholas II. According to the Russian diplomat I. Y. Korostovets, a reasonably reliable source, 'Dorzhiev spoke with marked authority and expertise, and mightily pleased the Tsar . . . [Dorzhiev] had orders to put out feelers and try to direct the attention of the Russian government to Tibet, and particularly to gain diplomatic support against China and Britain.'[11] This meeting was reported in the Russian and the foreign press.

The Russians seem to have been reluctant to take up Dorzhiev's challenge, aware that it would carry substantial risk while creating little tangible benefit. There were elements within the administration who supported Dorzhiev's concept of pan-Buddhist unity between the people of Tibet and those of the Tsar's eastern Empire, but they were not in the ascendant. There are, however, indications that the Tsar personally encouraged Great Gaming in Tibet. For instance in January 1904 he was visited by two Kalmyks who were heading there on a secret mission. They wanted to observe the activities of Younghusband and his army, but the Tsar encouraged them also 'to incite the Tibetans there against the English'.[12] Significantly, he made sure that his Foreign Minister, Count Lamsdorff, was not told of this expedition. So when Lamsdorff made his repeated assurances to the British that his government was not engaging in clandestine adventures in Tibet, he was in all probability being sincere. It was the random meddling of the Tsar and his army officers that fuelled Lord Curzon's paranoia.

Some modern accounts of the Younghusband Expedition have implied that its origins were rooted in invention, and that suspicions about Russian activity in Tibet were made up by Curzon and his allies as an excuse for a shameless act of imperialism. If anything, the reverse was true: their genuine fear of Russian expansion made them invent flimsy pretexts for sending Younghusband's Mission across the border. It is clear from private papers, as well as official correspondence, that by 1903 both Curzon and Younghusband had a firm but misguided conviction that Russia and Tibet had signed secret treaties which threatened British India's security. The focus of their fear was a short, square-jawed Buddhist monk from the eastern fringes of the Tsar's Empire by the name of Khambo Agvan Dorzhiev.

While he waited for a response from the Tibetan delegates, Younghusband could do nothing but sit tight in the cold winds of Khamba Dzong. An assortment of 'specialists' had arrived to take advantage of the access to Tibetan territory: Mr Hayden the fossil hunter, Captain Walton the bird man and Colonel Prain the plant collector. 'I have an idea that Khamba Jong has become a sort of scientific playground,' wrote Curzon to Younghusband, 'with botanists, geologists, mineralogists etc sticking their heads out behind every rock.' But his correspondent was in no mood to be amused. 'We have merely to burst that bloated bubble of monkish power,' he fumed in his reply to the Viceroy, 'and we shall have the people with us, and be able to oust that Russian influence which has already done us so much damage.' He especially resented the lack of reverence for his Mission among the inhabitants of Khamba Dzong. 'There is not a native of this border . . . who does not think the Tibetans will beat us here; and all of them think the two Lhasa delegates are infinitely bigger men than I am.'[13]

Doubts about his official stature were exacerbated by a running battle with Claude White over seniority. According to a letter from Helen (who was now staying at the Darjeeling Sanatorium, apparently suffering from general debilitation) the two men were believed to be in joint command of the Mission. Mrs White had managed to get a report into the Darjeeling newspapers which implied that her husband was equal in rank to the Senior Commissioner. Frank told his wife not to worry, since 'officially without being conceited I may say that he is whole streets below me, and the Viceroy knows that very well'.[14] But Mrs Younghusband was greatly exercised by questions of status, and began a running battle with Mrs White.

The stalemate at Khamba Dzong was the product of an assortment of misunderstandings. Younghusband's actions were constrained by the orders of the Indian government, which in turn was restricted by the policy emanating from Whitehall. His decisions were also circumscribed by the varying advice given by Wilton and White, both of whom had more intricate diplomatic knowledge than he did. Things were complicated further by uncertainty over the structure of the Tibetan government. In a way which is almost incomprehensible today, the whole country was, literally, uncharted territory, politically and geographically. China was officially regarded as having suzerain power over Tibet. But, as was clear from the problems with the 1890 Tibet–Sikkim border agreement (which had been signed by China on Tibet's behalf), the Tibetans were not inclined to respect Chinese authority. As the writer Sunanda Datta-Ray has put it: 'As far as Tibet and Sikkim were concerned, the self-styled Kaiser-i-Hind (as Queen Victoria was proclaimed) and the tottering Son of Heaven might as well have agreed between themselves that Germany had no right to the moon.'[15]

During previous centuries, Chinese control over Tibet had relaxed and tightened according to fluctuations in the political situation. By 1903 there was a Chinese *Amban* (Resident) in Lhasa, and representatives such as Ho Kuang Hsi elsewhere, but their power had become largely ceremonial. Lord Curzon even described China's claim to suzerainty as a 'constitutional fiction', and wrote privately to Younghusband: 'I do not myself believe that a hundred Ambans will induce the Tibetans really to come to business.'[16] The internal problems of the Manchu Government prevented firm action being taken to bring the Tibetans into line. Tibet was simply too large, and its people too disparate, for Peking to exercise genuine authority. Parr and Ho found themselves in a difficult position at Khamba Dzong, obliged to represent the Emperor's interests yet unable to influence the Tibetans.

The Tibetan delegates, in turn, were uncertain how they should proceed. Their initial instructions had been to employ delaying tactics against the British, but these were later followed up by firm orders to prevent any advance into Tibetan territory. Tibet's National Assembly, the Tsongdu, had convened to declare that the British were enemies of the teachings of the Buddha, and that Tibetan troops would expel any invading soldiers. Other elements within the Lhasa Government, in particular those lay officials who had been to India and witnessed British power, counselled against this policy, suggesting it would lead to disaster. But the Tsongdu, most of whom were ignorant of life outside their own borders, resolved to expel Younghusband and his mission.

According to Peter Fleming in *Bayonets to Lhasa*, the Tibetan decision not to negotiate at Khamba Dzong 'was based four-square on infantile obstinacy'.[17] This ethnocentric judgment fails to appreciate the position in which Tsarong and Lobsang Trinley found themselves. They had been ordered to avoid dialogue with Younghusband until the British Mission retired over the border. Yet without military backing, they could do nothing to enforce this command. Both men knew that their personal prospects depended upon not being held responsible for whatever might go wrong. Their best strategy was to procrastinate and wait for winter, refusing to accept any diplomatic communications and hoping the problem would disappear.

This is precisely what did happen on the seventeenth day of the ninth month of the Year of the Water-Hare, when the British Mission retreated back into Sikkim. Under the impression that their strategy had succeeded, Depon Tsarong and Lobsang Trinley headed for Lhasa. But it was a false dawn for Tibet. What had begun as a small diplomatic mission to Khamba Dzong was about to turn into a full-scale British advance into their country. As the *Pall Mall Gazette* observed, 'The shyness of the LAMA's subjects cannot be allowed to exempt them from the ordinary penalties attached to twisting the Lion's tail in those latitudes.'[18]

Back at the mini-bus Mr Wingrove was in a state of great excitement, flicking through his reference books.

'Ah, yes, here we are . . . exotic trumpet-shaped flowers . . . dry stony terrain . . . strong stems . . . brilliant rose pink . . . Yes, I think that must be it.' He pointed at a drawing. '*Incarvillea younghusbandii.*'

'What Younghusbandy?'

'Incarvillea. Known as Younghusband's lily. Erroneous really, given the genus. But still, here it is – all around you.' He waved his arms. 'All over Sikkim.'

After less than a mile the mini-bus was halted by two army

trucks, slewed across the road. Mr Wingrove swallowed the piece of paper he had just been writing on. A pack of soldiers moved forward, headed by an officer with blank eyes and a Saddam Hussein moustache. Mr Singh got out, apologetic and professional, showing his papers. For some minutes they talked, the officer gesticulating towards the army base while Mr Singh looked contrite. Then the driver was ordered off the bus. He gazed at the soldiers and their rifles in quiet fear, answering questions in a monotone.

The officer was tapping his fingers on the bonnet, deciding how to proceed. Then he turned, glanced into the mini-bus and saw us both for the first time.

'Foreigners – off the bus.' We got out and stood on the cold earth.

'Passport. Permit.' The officer flicked through the documents, expressionless.

'This is a permit for Restricted Area. You are now in a Military Zone.' I shrugged my shoulders, feigning surprise, innocence, contrition.

'English, wait by the truck.'

Having received a summons from the Viceroy on 10 October, Younghusband galloped as fast as he possibly could down through Sikkim, reaching Gangtok in only four days. The distraught Helen met him at Darjeeling, and together they travelled by train to Simla and took a suite of rooms at the Grand. Younghusband wrote an instant 'Note on the Present Situation in Tibet', concluding: 'I have no hesitation in recommending that the power of the monks should be so far broken as to prevent them any longer selfishly obstructing the prosperity both of Tibet and of the neighbouring British districts.'[19] Some days later he was ushered into the presence of Lord Curzon, who was lying irascibly in bed having been kicked by a horse. Curzon proceeded to denigrate each of Younghusband's proposals, only to endorse them keenly at a meeting of his Council the following day.

Curzon was at this time at the height of his unpopularity among British Indian society, and Younghusband noted his overbearing stiffness in social situations. In a letter to his father, Younghusband tells a revealing story about the personal trust which the Viceroy seems to have placed in him, probably as a result of the unusual origins and longevity of their friendship. After one official dinner Helen had spoken to Curzon about the difficulties of his position, assuring him of her husband's support. 'And Lord Curzon at once replied with great emotion, "Yes, I would never doubt Younghusband's loyalty and devotion to me." I am I believe one of the very few out here that he unbends to.'

The Viceroy's Council (officially known as the Executive Council) was intended as a constitutional check on Viceregal power, but with Curzon at the helm there was little opportunity to express dissent. 'He does not so much invite discussion,' Younghusband told his father, 'as lay down the law and almost defiantly ask if anyone has any objection. If anyone has he is promptly squashed.'[20] With Younghusband sitting by his side, Curzon proposed that the Mission should advance into the Chumbi valley in Tibet, and even as far as Gyantse if necessary. Extra troops would have to be provided to ensure its safe passage. As had become customary, the Council agreed to all of the Viceroy's suggestions.

For the preceding two months, Curzon had been persuading the Government back in London of the virtues of a substantial military advance. Ably assisted by Younghusband, he had dredged up every possible excuse to justify his proposals. Two Sikkimese subjects, who were in fact untrained spies in the employ of Captain O'Connor, had been arrested and imprisoned by the Tibetans. Younghusband promptly arranged for their families to present humble petitions asking for firm action against Tibet, which were forwarded to Simla. Curzon then raised the subject specifically in a telegram to the Secretary of State for India, citing the disappearance of the Sikkimese men as an example of the Tibetan Government's 'contemptuous disregard for the usages of civilisation'. Were not the spies (or traders, as Curzon preferred to call them) entitled, like Don Pacifico, to the protection of Pax Britannica?

The Viceroy's representations on matters of commerce were similarly disingenuous. Although there were certainly restrictions on Indian merchants travelling to Tibet, there was far more cross-border traffic than he cared to admit. During the period 1898–1903 there was a declared two-way trade between Tibet and Bengal of nine million rupees, or about £670,000, a substantial although not excessive amount.[21] Yet throughout the events of 1903–04, the need for access to Tibet's supposedly lucrative markets was a continual theme of the British case. In a *Punch* cartoon of November 1903,

Younghusband was depicted as the British Lion holding a tray of goods and a pair of revolvers, saying: 'I'VE COME TO BRING YOU THE BLESSINGS OF FREE TRADE,' to which the Dalai Lama (represented as the South American quadruped the llama) replies: 'I'M A PROTEC-TIONIST. DON'T WANT 'EM.' 'WELL, YOU'VE GOT TO HAVE 'EM!' responds the Lion.

Lord Curzon's finest piece of diplomatic casuistry takes the form of a despatch which relates not to trade, or spies, or people, but rather to the bovine inhabitants of High Asia. '4 November 1903: Tibet,' wrote the Viceroy. 'We now learn that Tibetan troops attacked Nepalese yaks on the frontier and carried many of them off. This is an overt act of hostility.'[22] The fact that the Viceroy of India was sending telegrams about the fate of frontier livestock to the Secretary of State (and hence the Cabinet) shows the flimsiness of the justifications he was putting forward for invading Tibet. To describe yak-rustling as 'an overt act of hostility' by a foreign power is plainly absurd. It shows the way Curzon was willing to use almost any excuse to obtain sanction for a further advance into Tibet, so certain was he that the Russian Bear needed to be checked.

At the beginning of 1904 in a private letter to Younghusband, he makes his views on Russian influence explicit, while reminding him that they should not be stated openly: 'Remember that in the eyes of HMG [His Majesty's Government] we are advancing not because of Dorjieff . . . or the Russian rifles in Lhasa – but because of our Convention shamelessly violated, our frontier trespassed upon, our subjects arrested, our mission flouted, our represen-tations ignored.'[23] Curzon was well aware that the British Govern-ment regarded Younghusband's Expedition with grave suspicion; their political position at home was weak, and the last thing they needed was to become entangled in an unpopular military adven-ture in a distant land.

Mr Balfour's Government never wanted to invade Tibet. Rather the advance to Lhasa was the result of manipulation, indecision and chance circumstance, of reaction rather than action. The tall, languid, cynical Arthur James Balfour and his ministers mistrusted the Russophobia of Curzon and Younghusband. Whitehall's foreign policy had to be based on wider considerations than the demands of India's northern frontier. While Balfour could accept his Viceroy's hawkish views on the Persian Gulf, he believed that Tibet lacked a similar strategic importance. He had imperial and European factors to contend with, as well as the need to remain on good terms with the Tsar's ministers; for Curzon and Younghusband, India and its putative needs lay at the centre of the diplomatic universe. As Balfour once observed, if George Curzon were to get his way, India would be elevated to the status of a foreign and not always friendly power.

The invasion can with hindsight be seen as an inevitable product of the Mission's original existence. Once the advance to Khamba Dzong had taken place, the troops could not retire without achieving something of substance. Curzon was able to take this fact, embellish it with tales of imprisoned merchants and stolen yaks, and use it to twist the arm of his arbiters in London. As long as the Tibetans refused to negotiate, he observed, quite reasonably, a further advance into Tibet was the only possible course of action if the British were not to lose face.

The new Secretary of State for India – St John Brodrick, an old friend of Curzon's lately turned adversary – was well aware of the potential for imperial adventure, and tried to control the development of events by permitting an invasion only on strictly controlled terms. In a telegram written on 6 November, he wrote that the Cabinet would sanction an advance to Gyantse, but 'for the sole purpose of obtaining satisfaction'. This nebulous phrase was to work against him, for it enabled Younghusband to interpret the telegram in various ways. Who was to judge what 'satisfaction' might mean, and how best should it be obtained? Brodrick's instruction might relate to any one (or all) of the discrete gripes that the administration had against the Tibetans.

Once permission had been given for an advance to Gyantse, discussions began between Younghusband and the recently appointed Commander-in-Chief in India, Lord Kitchener. The famously bad-tempered Kitchener was more amenable than at their previous meeting five years earlier, and readily agreed to Younghusband's request to send 'white faces' to accompany the Indian troops. The expedition was to be supported by a Royal Artillery Mountain Battery with two ten-pounder screw guns, a Maxim Gun detachment from 1st battalion the Norfolk Regiment, a half-company of 2nd Sappers, eight companies of 23rd Sikh Pioneers and six companies of 8th Gurkhas. In addition there were to be field hospitals, medical staff, military police, telegraph and postal officers, specialist engineers, surveyors, road-builders and scores of coolies. Six camels, 3000 ponies, 5000 yaks and buffaloes, 5000 bullocks and over 7000 mules were pressed into service; the majority of which were to die during the journey.

Francis and Helen caught another few days together in Calcutta, where they were joined by little Eileen and her nurse. The looming separation drew them together, although Helen was nervous and depressed about the coming months. It was hard to know what she should do. Their home at Indore was now occupied by the new Resident, leaving hotels and rented houses the only possibility. Darjeeling was close to Tibet, but accurate information about her husband's Mission might better be obtained in Simla or Calcutta. Leaving her in a flurry of doubt, Francis travelled up to Darjeeling on 18 November to make final arrangements for his departure.

Some skilful internal diplomacy followed, as a result of which the Foreign Department agreed to restructure the Mission. Younghusband was appointed Commissioner for Tibetan Frontier Matters, with John Claude White and Ernest Wilton as his Assistants. White was furious at Younghusband's manoeuvring – he would lose his special allowances for one thing – and began telegraphing in every direction, even to Curzon and Kitchener, asking to have the order rescinded. Younghusband reprimanded him for this 'act of gross insubordination', and was backed up by his masters in Simla. Late in November the British Commissioner played his trump card: White would remain in the leech-infested forests of Sikkim to organize mule and coolie traffic into Tibet.

By 5 December 1903 Colonel Younghusband – he had been promoted to boost his status as a negotiator – was ready for action. His departure point was once again the Rockville Hotel, which had become the Mission Headquarters. With Mrs Wakefield, the Manageress, keenly waving a Union Jack at the head of a crowd of patriotic well-wishers he mounted his horse. Helen 'became like one distracted' as she watched her husband riding up Rockville Road towards Chowrasta, towards Rangli, towards the high passes, towards Tibet itself. She ran to her room and scribbled him a pencil note. 'My own beloved it is not ten minutes since you rode away – I meant to have kissed yr. little face all over – eyes, nose, mouth – I was so dazed I can't remember what I said or did. I only know it was like having myself cut in.'[24] 'I left poor Helen in great distress at Darjiling,' he told his father a day or two later, 'and not at all well.'[25]

Younghusband felt apprehensive but in good spirits, buoyed by a recent editorial in his old friend *The Times* of London. An advance to Gyantse, even to Lhasa, was to be welcomed said the newspaper, since the Tibetans had been deeply insulting towards his Mission, and 'from unpunished insults Orientals readily proceed to violence'. Other papers were less supportive, the *Spectator* referring to it as a 'disagreeable expedition', and the *Westminster Gazette* saying it was about time 'that the Government should tell us what they are doing in Tibet and why they are doing it'.[26] Initially, the British press was lukewarm in its support for the adventure in Tibet. There were flattering profiles of Younghusband and long, excited accounts of life on the Roof of the World; but nobody seemed to be quite certain what the Mission was doing there in the first place.

For several days Younghusband lingered at Gnatong while military equipment was assembled. The troops were commanded by Brigadier-General James Macdonald of the Royal Engineers (recently promoted from Colonel), who had spent the previous four months supervising road-building in Sikkim. His role was purely military, leaving Younghusband in command of the diplomatic mission and its immediate escort. At this stage, Younghusband had no reason to suspect that his relations with the General would be anything less than commendable, referring to him in a letter as 'an excellent sound solid fellow . . . I have told Macdonald that from now till I reach Gyantse he must regard me simply as a precious parcel of goods to be carted from one place to another, and taken the greatest possible care of on the way.'[27]

There is a head-and-shoulders photograph of Francis Younghusband in uniform taken around this time. It is an official studio portrait, the work of Thomas Paar of Darjeeling. The British Commissioner has a stern, important air, demonstrating that he has a substantial job ahead of him. His expression is almost supercilious, although his shoulders are sloping and his chest looks thin. The eyes are careful to display no hint of emotion. His soft mouth and upper lip are hidden from public view by the bristling soup-strainer moustache, armed to repel intruders. He looks like a Man with a Mission, which is precisely what he was.

On the morning of Sunday, 13 December, Younghusband stood on the snowy crest of the Dzelap La, the valley below him dropping away into Tibet. Behind him came a straggling column of soldiers, headed by a single mounted orderly bearing the Union Jack.

We escaped from our temporary arrest in the mountains of Sikkim after many hours of tedious questioning and frightening uncertainty. Army radios crackled between Yume Samdong and Lachung, then signals flew between Lachung and North-East Command, until the order came back to release us with a stern warning. The fear lifted from the pit of my stomach, and I returned to Gangtok. As for Mr Wingrove, he flew to Pakistan to stay with the present Mir of Hunza's cousin, with whom he was acquainted.

My next ambition was to travel up to the Dzelap (Jelap) La, the main pass leading from Sikkim into Tibet. The General dealing with my request passed the buck to the Chief of Police, a hugely fat man with bulging eyes and a tumbler of whisky. I had a semi-social interview during which I tried to persuade him to give me permission. His English was slurred and confusing ('J. K. Galbraith' and 'Hendon Police College' were the only words I could decipher with any certainty) so his brother-in-law spoke on his behalf.

'You should count your blessings. You have been further up into Sikkim than any civilian since the 1950s. What will you see at Dzelap La? Barbed wire, trenches, military post. Maybe one Chinese soldier,' said the brother-in-law. He was an inverse replica of the Chief of Police, small and thin with a face like a chipmunk. 'That is not worth an outing. Why not travel to Madras or to Rajasthan? Have you seen our beautiful Taj Mahal in Agra?' The Chief of Police nodded vigorously and the interview was terminated.

I went in the end to Darjeeling where life was cold, damp and romantically old-fashioned. It was not hard to visualize Young-husband striding up the Mall, past the Planter's Club on his way to the Rockville Hotel. The town was a strange one, dangling off the side of a promontory below a swathe of snow mountains. Robert Byron described it in *First Russia, Then Tibet* as 'Margate, Filey and Bognor Regis wholly roofed in red corrugated iron'. I found it was the hill station which seemed to have maintained the most distinctive taint of British India. Effete white planters marched around in pocketed safari suits. Uniformed public schoolboys sauntered up and down Nehru Road (otherwise known as The Mall) with furled umbrellas, treating one another with exquisite courtesy, miles away from the affected loutishness of their British counterparts. At Keventer's unimaginable bacon sandwiches were on the menu. 'Oh yes,' said the waiter, 'it is tip-top quality ham. Cut from one blighty pig.'

Younghusband remained fond of Darjeeling, although he never

went there after 1904. In a vain mood, he once wrote that he wanted a memorial to be built to himself outside the town. 'I should like it to take the form of a portico, like Sir Dighton Probyn's at the Norman Tower garden Windsor Castle. From this shelter the snowy range could be viewed, and to this spot [will] come men from all over the world. Inside it would be inscribed:

Francis Younghusband
who
Strove for the Highest
Sought the Farthest
Loved the Purest

It should be built of solid stone to last for ever.'[28]

I did have a brief look for this doubtful stone edifice on Tiger Hill and other likely spots, but clearly no disciple had yet thought fit to erect it. Nor was there any sign of the Rockville Hotel, although I did find Helen's sanatorium. It was in a hollow below a row of trees, and had become an extended concrete lump, a cross between a derelict factory and a grain silo, surrounded by balls of wire and heaps of old metal. In the dusty yard outside, two small boys were throwing stones at a yelping, mangy dog.

Helen had unhappy memories of Darjeeling. While her husband was in Tibet she experienced feelings of great agitation, journeying between the Rockville Hotel and the sanatorium while a nurse looked after young Eileen. It appears that she was suffering from no specific illness, but perhaps from an Edwardian combination of stress, worry, loneliness and exhaustion. She wanted to do something to help Francis, yet knew she could do nothing but sit tight; and hope. Fiercely proud of her husband's new-found importance, but desperately anxious about his fate, she swung between moods of excitement and deep depression.

When the fancy took her, Helen would send off a great flurry of letters: to Mr Mitter and Frederick O'Connor, requesting information about her husband's health; to the military authorities in Simla, berating them for supplying ineffective cough medicine to the troops; or to James Dunlop-Smith, asking for advice on questions of official procedure. She even travelled down to Calcutta and tried, unsuccessfully, to arrange a meeting with the Viceroy. In a state of high dudgeon she returned to Darjeeling and took to writing intricate notes on her favourite subject – the life of Marie Antoinette.[29]

The Place of the Thunderbolt (Dorje Ling) had an atmosphere of dislocation, as if it existed accidentally. It did in a way, the British having turned a forested settlement with no adequate water supply into the thriving home of schooling, tea and summer recreation. During the 1940s and 50s this frontier town had been a haven for international misfits – Tibetan subversives, East European refugees, fleeing White Russians and displaced monarchs like the Emir of Afghanistan (still collecting his pension from the British Government). There had been nests of spies of every persuasion, some working for the British, some against the British, others for the Japanese, for the Kuomintang or for Bose's INA.

I found the place still had an alluring atmosphere of discontinuity, even of invention, with different cultures all jumbled up together. There were traders from Rajasthan, ponymen from Sikkim, Sherpa jeep-drivers, Nepalese tea-pickers, Czech shopkeepers and Bhutanese gem sellers; Anglicized Indians, Indianized Anglicans, Canadian Jesuits, Tibetan Buddhist monks, Hindu holy men and smiling Christian nuns from Mizoram; Goorkaland separatists, lost American hippies, unreconstructed Naxalites and Bengali poets, all jostling along the narrow zigzag streets which covered the tumbling hill. In the afternoons I would sit on the verandah at the Planter's Club, reading books and watching things happen in the streets below. There was one particular document which provided continual entertainment. It was a 'Kit List' that I had copied from Younghusband's pale brown notebooks in the India Office Library in Blackfriars, marked: 'December 1903, Darjeeling.'

This extraordinary creation seemed to encapsulate the spirit and the style of the Younghusband Expedition to Tibet. Set out in the manner of a boy's prep-school clothes list and written in Francis Younghusband's careful hand, it details the garments and objects that he took with him over the Dzelap La, all carefully supervised by the caravan leader Mahmood Isa. It does not include his official paraphernalia or that of his colleagues, but merely the clothing and accessories that he personally thought necessary in order to maintain his status as Commissioner. Younghusband was not especially attached to material possessions: these were simply the props he needed when acting as the representative of British India on a diplomatic mission. To me the list symbolized the epic grandeur of the Empire at its zenith, absurdly theatrical in its overblown Edwardian magnificence. Younghusband's collection included:

White Shirts (15)
Flannel shirts (12)
Twill shirts (19)
Silk Shirts (1)
Coloured stiff shirts (12)
Coloured smooth shirts (8)
Full dress coat and trousers
Morning coat and grey trousers
Mess coat and waistcoat
Assam silk coat and waistcoat
White evening waistcoat
Light grey suit Flannel suit
Norfolk breeches

An assortment of coats was also thought useful; although he had to make sure that there was an appropriate one for each and every occasion, including an old ulster, two jaeger coats, two khaki coats, a great coat, a long covert coat, a Chesterfield coat, a poshteen long coat, a fur coat, a Chinese fur coat and a waterproof coat. His head, meanwhile, had to be kept covered. So there was a shikar hat, a thin solar topi, a thick solar topi, a khaki helmet, two forage caps, a brown felt hat, a white helmet and a white panama.

I found the Kit List became a source of endless speculation. It certainly gave a whole new meaning to the idea of a 'laundry list' biography. Why did Younghusband decide on sixty-seven shirts? Would sixty-six have been too few? Did he ever find an occasion to wear the Assam silk coat, or was the weather too cold? When should a shikar hat be worn? (Answer: when shooting partridges in the Chumbi valley.) There were two particular items on the list which never ceased to excite me: a cocked hat and a campaign bath. Did the cocked hat survive the journey? (Yes, I later found a photograph of Younghusband wearing it in Lhasa.) How often did he find time to use the bath? These were the questions that I puzzled over in Darjeeling.

In his book *Persia and the Persian Question*, George Curzon insisted that a British traveller in outlandish parts should never be without 'a suit of dress clothes . . . I am convinced that I should find them equally useful were I to meet in audience either the King of the Negroes or the Dalai Llama [sic] of Tibet.' His disciple clearly took this sartorial advice to heart, expecting as he was to meet the Thirteenth Dalai Lama. He brought a Camp Suit, a Camp Dinner Suit (white shirt, dress trousers and smoking coat), a Cold Weather

Marching Suit, a Warm Weather Marching Suit and a set of Ceremonial Plain Clothes, consisting of: great coat, homburg hat, morning tail coat, grey trousers, town black boots, white shirt, collar, tie, vest, drawers, socks and studs.

In addition Younghusband managed to find space for:

Drawers (28)
Vests (10)
Socks (28)
Collars (32)
Boots and shoes (18)
Shoe trees (2)[30]

Now in order for a squad of coolies to carry his vestments, Younghusband needed an assortment of trunks, cases and boxes in which to put them. There were twenty-nine containers in all, including two large steel trunks, a hat box, a despatch box and a tea basket. And while resting at camp he had need of several tents, a camp bed, folding tables, a camp chair, a deck chair, an umbrella, a pair of field glasses, a stick, a box of Mannlicher ammunition, three rifles and two swords.

Over ten thousand coolies accompanied the invasion, carrying boxes, trunks, baths and cocked hats up and down the mountain passes, through forests and icy rivers, over dry plains where your eyeballs could freeze in the sockets. Eighty-eight coolies died, mainly of frostbite and exhaustion. They staggered forward under the weight of British India's last great military excursion, carrying Colonel Younghusband to Shangri La.

FOURTEEN

'The Empire Cannot Be Run like a Tea Party'

The land called Tibet has a symbolic value in the Western mind which extends way beyond any experiential reality. Although *Lost Horizon* was not published until thirty years after Francis Young-husband set foot in Tibet, the mystical romanticism the book embodies had been around since the reports of Jesuit missionaries appeared in the seventeenth century. Younghusband's obituary in the *New York Times* fittingly merged the man who led the British invasion with the Hollywood myth: 'If as James Hilton strongly suggests in *Lost Horizon*, Shangri La is somewhere in Tibet rather than merely somewhere – anywhere . . .then Sir Francis Young-husband probably came closer than anyone else to being Robert Conway.'[1]

Tibet's diplomatic isolation and physical inaccessibility helped the legend to develop. Here on the borders of British India was a huge country – the size of Western Europe – which was closed to the representatives of the King Emperor. Fantastic tales abounded among Younghusband's contemporaries of flying yogis, peculiar tortures, polyandrous practices, lecherous lamas, rare jewels, strange reincarnations, excrement pills, astral projection and even (myth of all myths) no wheels – except the prayer wheel of course. Unconquered kingdoms always hold a special excitement for great empires: at the turn of the century Tibet represented the ultimate in pure, virgin territory.

One of the few public figures to acknowledge Tibet's symbolic lure was the Liberal politician Sir Henry Cotton. In an interview with the *Daily News* in December 1903 he stirred up a hornet's nest of imperial outrage by questioning the motives for the forthcoming invasion. When he had been in India, he said, there were countless young men 'to whom the glamour of the Forbidden City was irre-sistible, to whom the romance attaching to the unknown formed the great temptation of their lives, and whose curiosity to trample out the secrets of the Grand Lama's palace was only one degree less burdensome to them than their desire to go simply for the fun

of knocking the stiff-necked old exclusivit off his perch and hum-
bling him before their "march of civilisation" merely because he
just chose to be exclusive.'

Cotton went on to claim that Curzon himself had fallen for the
glamour of the myth, and was 'now seeking the glory and world-
wide fame of being "the Viceroy of India who opened Tibet and
carried the British flag into Lhassa". Ah! That would be renown,
eh?'[2] The letters pages throbbed with denunciations of Cotton's
opinions, but he had undeniably touched a raw nerve. There was
indeed a 'romance attaching to the unknown' which had caught
the public's attention. In the rash of publications which followed
the invasion, the authors did their utmost to capture the 'magic
and mystery' of Tibet. Austiné Waddell's *Lhasa and its Mysteries* was
matched by Sir Thomas Holdich's *Tibet, the Mysterious*, while the
Daily Mail correspondent Edmund Candler published *The Unveiling
of Lhasa*.

But far from 'unveiling' and thereby destroying the mystery of
Tibet, the British invasion served to heighten it by stimulating
world-wide interest. In his book *The Last Secrets*, John Buchan
wrote: 'It was impossible for the least sentimental to avoid a certain
regret for the drawing back of that curtain which had meant so
much to the imagination of mankind . . . With the unveiling of
Lhasa fell the last stronghold of the older romance.'[3] His disappointment was short-lived: the myth has flourished into the late twentieth century. Over the decades after Younghusband's Expedition,
countless travelling writers have continued ostensibly to uncover,
discover and unveil this island in the sky.

Novelists in particular were able to use Tibet to epitomize inexplicable mystery. Such a distant country could mean whatever you
wanted it to mean. In the work of Kipling and Rider Haggard it
becomes the fount of arcane Eastern mysticism; H. G. Wells's Mr
Polly fantasizes about going there; Sherlock Holmes does go to Tibet
(in disguise of course) after apparently tumbling to his death from
the Reichenbach Falls. A 1948 boys' adventure story called *On the
World's Roof* has Adolf Hitler and a gang of renegade Nazis launching
a nuclear war from Tibet. Spiritual writers such as Georgei Gurdjieff,
Alexandra David-Neel and Madame Blavatsky could use their supposed experiences in Tibet as justification for their more extravagant claims. At least one Tibet-inspired mystical work has proved
to be fraudulent: the clairvoyant Tibetan lama Lobsang Rampa,
author of the highly successful *The Third Eye*, turns out to have
been a Cornish plumber called Cyril Hoskins.[4]

In the 1960s the spiritual mysteriousness of Tibet took another step forward. All self-respecting flower children had a copy of the mis-named *Tibetan Book of the Dead* sitting happily beside Chairman Mao's *Little Red Book* — at the very moment that Mao's Red Guards were busy destroying Tibet's six thousand monasteries and temples. A cult group was founded in California called the Sacred Order of Tibet, based on a loose mixture of Buddhist teaching and psychedelic ufology. This gave way to a spate of films and comic books, such as *The Golden Child*, *Little Buddha* and *Le Lama Blanc*, usually combining tales of reincarnation with martial arts and occult power.

The supposed transformative powers of Tibet have even been credited with changing Younghusband's own religious views and converting him to a belief in non-violence. Although it is true that one of the two profound spiritual experiences of his life did occur in Tibet, he had strong mystical tendencies long before he led the invasion. There is even a surprisingly widespread misapprehension, especially among admirers of Younghusband's later religious work, that the vibrations of Tibet somehow converted his Mission into a peaceful one. In a BBC radio interview the League of Nations enthusiast and Classical scholar Gilbert Murray said that his friend Francis Younghusband 'wanted to penetrate Tibet because he so liked the Tibetans . . . he wanted to get into their country and talk with the lamas and to see if they had some real sympathy about religion.'[5] Murray was admittedly almost ninety years old at the time, but he was not alone in his confusion.

Rom Landau, a Polish-American sculptor and mystical writer, suggested in a memoir of 'Tibet Younghusband', as he liked to call him, that one particular event on the road to Lhasa was 'the outstanding one of his life'.

> That event took place toward the end of his mission [when] it was uncertain whether the small contingent of troops that he was leading would have to fight the Tibetans facing them. During one harrowing moment of uncertainty he suddenly 'saw' that God's will was not conquest by arms but friendship through mutual understanding . . . He entered Lhasa without having to fire a shot and signed there a convention with the regent. When soon afterwards he had to leave Lhasa, he did so as a friend.[6]

This extraordinary manipulation of the facts is typical of the way that Younghusband's identity has been colonized by his various chroniclers. Either he was a *Boy's Own* swashbuckling imperialist, or he was a peaceful, luminous mystic; or alternatively, he had a split personality.

The reality, as I came to perceive it, was both more complex and more human. Younghusband's experiences in Tibet were a formative part of an extraordinary journey of personal discovery and development. His rare, quirky, almost child-like view of life enabled him to go through an enormous range of apparently contradictory experiences, and encompass them all. As Jan Morris wrote in *The Spectacle of Empire*, Younghusband 'most nearly filled the part of Everyman' in the great imperial drama.[7] He never stood still, never stopped changing.

On the far side of the Dzelap La, one officer so forgot himself as he bedded down for his first night in Tibet that 'he put his teeth into a tumbler of water. In the morning he reached for the tumbler and found it frozen solid, his dentures in the midst like a quail in aspic.'[8] Indian and British troops were settling into the Chumbi valley, soon to be joined by the escort which had been based at Khamba Dzong. The force was still just within the tree line, so wood could be burned in an effort to keep warm. Supplies continued to slip and slide their way over the frozen pass. There was an atmosphere of gloom: droves of Bhutanese and Nepalese coolies and mule drivers were deserting, while the pack bullocks had caught foot-and-mouth disease.

Colonel Younghusband met his first significant obstacle as he rode into the small village of Yatung. Waiting for him in front of a stone arch was the legendary Miss Annie Taylor, an invincible Presbyterian missionary – and 'intolerable nuisance', according to Captain Parr – who resided there. Ten years earlier she had made a reckless attempt to reach Lhasa with a view to converting its inhabitants to Christianity. 'She came up dressed in Tibetan style without any hat shouting "Is this Colonel Younghusband? Is this Colonel Younghusband?"' Having confessed to his identity, Younghusband was questioned closely about his religious beliefs before being allowed to proceed into Yatung. After an inconsequential meeting with local Tibetan officials, during which he was exhorted fruitlessly to return over the border to Sikkim, Younghusband proceeded to 'Camp Chumbi' which had been set up on the banks of the Ammo river.

While an advance party reconnoitred over the next mountain range, a base was established for the troops. For three weeks the Mission waited restlessly, celebrating a desultory Christmas and New Year with the help of some well-chilled champagne. While the other officers entertained themselves shooting snow pheasants, the Commissioner entered a renewed bout of spiritual inquiry. The stimulus was a work by the Theosophist and political campaigner Annie Besant, whom he had met at Indore, concerning the power of mystical intuition. 'I have also been reading another most beautiful book,' he told Helen, 'on Cosmic Consciousness which I will explain to you some time and which gives a most intensely beautiful and peaceful idea of the Universe.'

On 7 January 1904 they began to move out of the Chumbi valley, past the dzong at Phari, which was now held by two companies of Gurkhas, and up on to the snow-covered plains of Tibet. At temperatures of minus 30° Centigrade and an altitude of more than three miles above sea level, a column of troops and equipment, preceded by mounted infantry, trailed over the Tang La. When they reached a small settlement at Tuna, numerous cases of frostbite had developed. 'We moved in y'day to the village turning out the unfortunate inhabitants of half the village and occupying the other half,' Younghusband told Helen.[9] Leaving him at Tuna with a garrison of Sikh Pioneers, Sappers and the Maxim Guns, Brigadier-General Macdonald and his 'flying column' returned to the Chumbi valley to consolidate their supply lines.

In the desperate cold at Tuna the soldiers did their best to invent entertainment. 'I have arranged to get some shooting up here,' wrote Lieutenant Arthur Hadow, the twenty-two-year-old Maxim Gun Commander, in a letter to his father. 'So far I have got 7 Tibetan gazelle and three burrell, though one of the heads of the latter is small, and not worth keeping. I hope to see them hanging up in the hall of the Vicarage some day!' But it was hard work making his guns work in such weather. Hadow replaced the water in their cooling system with a mixture of kerosene and rum: 'I have to take the locks to bed with me to prevent them getting frozen.'[10]

Even at this early stage of the expedition, Younghusband's

relationship with General Macdonald was dangerously unsatisfactory. Macdonald's role was deemed to be a purely military one, but once the border of Tibet had been crossed the distinction between military and diplomatic decisions began to blur. Younghusband was responsible for deciding how the Mission should proceed, but once he had made up his mind to move to a given place the practicalities of the advance were in the hands of Macdonald. Tension was heightened by the competing ambitions of India's civil and military authorities. In time the conflict even came to mirror the struggle between Curzon and Kitchener, the Viceroy and the Commander-in-Chief each backing their own 'man on the spot'. Nor was it helped by Macdonald's sensitivity over his own status, which manifested itself in endless petty skirmishes. He insisted, for instance, on always pitching his camp to the right of Younghusband's – the senior position.

Colonel James Macdonald had originally been sent to Sikkim to supervise road building. A plodding Royal Engineer, his previous military career had been undistinguished. While serving in Uganda in the 1890s he gained a reputation for being difficult to work with following a protracted conflict with Frederick Lugard, the soldier and administrator who later married Flora Shaw (of Jameson Raid fame). His most recent appointment had been the career backwater of Director of Balloons in Peking. When the Tibet Mission was converted into a large-scale advance at the end of 1903, he found himself almost accidentally falling into the position of its military commander. A naturally cautious man, who had never been near high-altitude territory before, found himself having to perform an exceptionally difficult task in co-operation with an impulsive Himalayan veteran.

Their first dispute concerned the *dzong* (fort) at Phari, which Younghusband had assured Tibetan officials would not be occupied: Macdonald promptly sent troops in on the grounds that it would be strategic folly to leave such an important position unsecured. Younghusband was furious, feeling that it would impugn his honour with the Tibetan negotiators. On reaching Tuna another incident occurred which put an end to any hope of reconciliation. Within hours of the dramatic advance over the Tang La, wrote Younghusband in a letter, 'Macdonald came up to me and said we could not stay here and would have to retire the next day as there was no fuel and grass and the men would not be able to stand the cold. I told him I would . . . consider it abounding in fuel and grass compared with the Pamirs and that . . . I would absolutely refuse to move.'[11] After a ferocious argument, Macdonald backed down and the Mission remained at Tuna.

It may have been an emotional urge to challenge what he saw as Macdonald's pusillanimity that made Younghusband commit an act of extraordinary foolhardiness four days later. Like the hero Evan Lee in his autobiographical novel *But In Our Lives*, Younghusband decided to ride unheralded, unescorted and unarmed into the heart of the enemy camp. To do so was an act of remarkable bravery, but it was also a foolish and quite unnecessary risk which put the future of the whole Mission in jeopardy. But as Evan Lee observes: 'Fellows take risks hunting and racing and big game shooting, and we must take risks in this frontier work . . . The Empire cannot be run like a tea party.'[12]

Accompanied by Captain O'Connor the interpreter and a young lieutenant called Sawyer, Younghusband slipped out through the British lines as day broke on 13 January. Ernest Wilton had done his utmost to dissuade him from this course of action, but the Commissioner's large, pointed ears were closed to advice. As O'Connor wrote in his autobiography: 'His decisions were deliberately made, but once made they were absolute, and his "yes" or "no" were more convincing and reassuring than half a dozen speeches from a more voluble man.'[13] The three men rode across the wind-swept plain towards the Tibetan camp at Guru and, as groups of Tibetan soldiers looked on incredulously, made their way to the principal house. With O'Connor's assistance their intention was made clear, and a 'courteous and well-mannered' Tibetan General ushered them into a long, gloomy room. Here they were joined by three more high-ranking officers and three monk-officials.

The proceedings began ceremoniously with Younghusband and his two supporters being offered cushions and tea. His purpose, he said, was to have an informal discussion which might lead to a peaceful resolution of their dispute. The Tibetan General responded by saying his country was closed to foreigners, and that negotiations could only take place at Yatung. Younghusband reacted by bringing up his favourite topic. Why did the Tibetans have dealings with the Russians while refusing to answer the Viceroy of India's letters? This produced an angry response, particularly from the monk-officials, who roundly denied being in contact with Russia. At this point Younghusband digressed to matters of religion, pointing out that the British had never interfered with the faiths of the people of India. What threat could his Mission possibly pose to Tibetan Buddhism?

Soon the discussion was degenerating into a futile wrangle, and when Younghusband announced that he must be returning to his camp at Tuna, 'the monks, looking as black as devils, shouted out: "No you won't; you'll stop here." One of the Generals said, quite politely, that we had broken the rule of the road by coming into their country, and we were nothing but thieves and brigands in occupying Phari Fort . . . The atmosphere became electric.'[14]

Colonel Younghusband takes up the story in a talk he gave some years later to the boys of Eton College:

> I was in a nasty fix. Soldiers closed round behind me. Trumpets were blown outside and there was a sense of frightful suppressed excitement. I was really in mortal fear but I kept as cool as I could.[15]

When Depon (General) Tsarong Wangchuk Gyalpo and Trungche (Chief Secretary) Lobsang Trinley returned to Lhasa from Khamba Dzong late in 1903, they were probably under the impression that they had achieved a victory of sorts. Winter was setting in, and there were as yet no signs of a further British advance. There are no extant records of what they reported to the Tibetan Government: all we know is the reaction that their return provoked within the hierarchy. The Kashag (Cabinet) decided that serious negotiations with the British should begin, while the Tsongdu (National Assembly) insisted that no concessions could be made.

Tibet was at this time making administrative reforms, and taking advantage of China's weakness. Since the death of the 'Great Fifth' Dalai Lama in 1682 the country had lurched through periods of instability, the reincarnations of successive Dalai Lamas dying in mysterious circumstances. When the Thirteenth Dalai Lama, Thubten Gyatso, reached the age of eighteen in 1894 a system was set up whereby the Kashag would consist of one monk minister (the Kalon Lama) and three lay ministers (Kalon or Shape), who would be able to exercise substantial power. In September 1903 the Kashag stressed that armed resistance to Younghusband's Mission would be futile. Two of its ministers had only recently been appointed to senior positions, and it would appear that a Kalon named Shatra was the chief proponent of this policy of negotiation.

A sharp operator in his mid forties, Shatra Paljor Dorje was by Tibetan standards a cosmopolitan figure. In 1890 he had made his name by expelling from Tibet an expedition led by two Russian travellers. In fact they were the French explorers Gabriel Bonvalot and Prince Henri d'Orleans, but at that time 'Roos' (Russians) and 'Inji' (English) were the only Europeans of whom the Tibetans had knowledge. After being appointed a deputy Kalon in 1892, Shatra was sent to Darjeeling to negotiate the forthcoming trade agreement. But British India was at this time convinced that China had full control of Tibetan affairs, and refused to allow Shatra to take part in the discussions. The 'Regulations Regarding Trade, Communication and Pasturage' were signed on Tibet's behalf in 1893 by two Chinese officials, with the result that the Tibetans took little notice of them.

Shatra remained in Darjeeling for nearly a year. According to Tibetan oral history, he had the ignominious experience of being thrown into a drinking trough by a group of British soldiers. Unaware of the intricacies of imperial protocol, he had failed to make way for a Memsahib who was taking an afternoon promenade down the Mall, thereby incurring the wrath of the soldiers.[16] This experience must have been profoundly humiliating to a senior Tibetan official and aristocrat, and it is said to have given him a life-long hatred of the British. He returned to Lhasa with a selection of manufactured goods (including a 'magic lantern' projector with views of the Tower of London) and an understanding of British methods of operation. He saw that an ostrich-like policy of splendid isolation would be futile for Tibet.

But Shatra's policy of constructive engagement provoked allegations of treachery from the Tsongdu, whose monastic members had little or no knowledge of the scope of British power. They had no way of comprehending quite how seriously their country was being threatened. According to one Tibetan account: 'Not only was suspicion and discord aroused in the Tsongdu, but for a time Kalons Shatra, Sholkhang, Changkhyim and Horkhang were held captive. While in a state of fear and depression, Horkhang drowned himself and furthermore because Shatra when previously in Darjeeling had sent a message to the Government on the desirability of a peace treaty with the British, the Tsongdu wondered if he had taken the British side and an inquiry was initiated.'[17]

Unlike the timid Horkhang, Shatra refused to go down without a fight. He presented a dossier to his investigators stating that all the reports he had made were truthful, being based on his own knowledge of British power in India, and that his accusers would do well to study his advice. Although Kalon Sholkhang and the Kalon Lama Changkhyim endorsed their colleague's policy, saying that it had been made with their full support, no decision was reached by their inquisitors. As was common in times of crisis, guidance was requested from the Nechung Oracle: but the Oracle's trance did not last long enough to make any revelations. In the end a public trial was held outside the Dalai Lama's summer palace, the Norbulingka, where the Kalons were being held.

Shatra's adopted son, Shenkhawa Gyurme Tobgyal, attended this event. He was aged seven at the time, and in later life himself became a senior government official, fleeing into exile in India with the Fourteenth Dalai Lama in 1959. In his autobiography *The Unadulterated Copper of My History*, he describes this memory of his childhood:

> We were all happiest when we did not have to go to school and could stay with our father. We used to sit, without making a sound, in two small spaces by the wall of the Norbulingka's yellow park. One night father gave a show called 'machik labtun' [magic lantern] on a white cloth lit by butter lamps. Not long after this Kalons Shatra, Sholkang, Changkhyim and Horkhang were examined by the Tsongdu in a tent set up at the centre of the Norbulingka's arena. After that father had to go away to [internal exile in] Kongbo.[18]

The other ministers were treated in a similar way and a new Kashag was appointed. Shatra's policy of negotiation was of course vindicated by subsequent events; in 1907 he was appointed 'Lonchen' or 'Great Minister' by the Dalai Lama. But for the moment the Government of Tibet was in the hands of four men who believed that confrontation with the British could be successful – a belief that the Dalai Lama himself seems to have shared.

The new Kashag contained a Kalon Lama called Chamba Tenzin, an experienced monk-official who had visited India. His lay colleagues were Serchung, an ineffectual aristocrat, Yutok Phuntsog Palden, a descendant of the Tenth Dalai Lama, and Tsarong, the General who had refused to have discussions with Younghusband at Khamba Dzong. It seems strange that Tsarong failed to appreciate the seriousness of the foreign threat: perhaps his experiences had convinced him the British were hesitant about advancing further into Tibet. When the Kashag heard that Younghusband's army had reached the Chumbi valley, preparations were made to mobilize troops. Plans were drawn up to intercept the enemy at Guru, a village about five days' march south of Gyantse.

Towards the end of 1903 between two and three thousand Tibetans travelled to Dochen and Guru. China's central government ordered the Manchu Amban to go there to oversee proceedings, but the Tibetans refused to provide him with horses so he was forced to remain in Lhasa. Representatives from Tibet's three great monasteries, Ganden, Drepung and Sera, reached Guru in January 1904 with a force of 'dob dob' or warrior monks. With them came Trungche Lobsang Trinley, the Chief Secretary who had been at Khamba Dzong with Tsarong. A local militia had been raised from the Phari region to complement the soldiers and horsemen who were arriving from the east. It was commanded by Kyibuk, the *Dzongpon* (District Officer) of Phari.[19]

In freezing weather they began to build fortifications, including a long wall across the barren plain below Guru. The majority of the Tibetans were irregular soldiers carrying simple weapons, with no knowledge of what they were likely to face from the British. As the author of *The Annals of the All-Revealing Mirror* puts it: 'Soldiers of Tibet armed with matchlock guns, swords, spears and slingshots with undaunted heroism fought the invaders who carried modern weapons such as cannon and machine gun rifles. They sacrificed their lives to protect their country and secure their ancestral borders.'[20] This informal army was under the command of Depon Lhading, a tall, striking figure from Lhasa, who turns out to have been the brother (or possibly the half-brother) of Yeshe Dolma, Queen of Sikkim.

Lhading must have been the 'courteous and well-mannered' General who received Colonel Younghusband into the Tibetan camp on 13 January 1904.

Hemmed in by armed guards, Younghusband was doing his best to keep his voice 'studiously calm'. One of the monks shouted that he would not be permitted to leave their camp until he had agreed to withdraw from Tibet. Realizing that a careful climb-down was his only option, Younghusband said that he could not give that assurance himself, but would have to refer the question to his Government, adding 'that I would be only too glad to go back to India tomorrow, for Tibet was a deadly cold and inhospitable country, and I had left a wife and little girl behind in India'.[21] 'This eased matters a little,' he wrote. 'But the monks continued to clamour for me to name a date for withdrawal, and the situation was only relieved when a General suggested that a messenger should return with me to Tuna to receive there the answer from the Viceroy.'

The British officers were escorted outside by the General, where they mounted their ponies and galloped hard for their own camp. 'It had been a close shave,' Younghusband wrote later, 'but it was worth it.' He regarded his foray as a pre-destined obligation. In one account he mentions that he 'had wakened in the night with the strong conviction' that he must visit the Tibetans.[22] Despite the dangers involved he could not resist following his intuition. This was a time when his mystical faith was at its most intense, and he believed it was his special destiny to take the risk.

A sanitized account of his reckless excursion was sent to his father and Helen, while Curzon was told only its barest outline. Although he seems not to have realized just how close Younghusband came to being taken hostage, Curzon responded with a polite reprimand. In reply Younghusband wrote an extraordinary letter of justification, in which he suggests that he deliberately offered himself as a sacrificial lamb in order to vindicate his mentor's policy:

> If the Tibetans had seized me, it would have been the most signal proof Your Excellency's policy of coming to a settlement with them was justified . . . There is nothing I would not do for you; and if you asked me to eat dirt before the Tibetans for the next six years . . . I would do it, knowing full well that it could only be for the best.[23]

Younghusband's increasingly obsessive devotion to Curzon was matched by other signs of instability which began to manifest themselves around this time. Compelled to inaction by General Macdonald's languid advance, his thoughts were turning to spiritual matters. In a revealing private note written some years later, he admits that meditation on Walt Whitman's *Leaves of Grass* occupied much of his attention: 'Important as was the task upon which I was engaged, I all the time thought it of very minor consequence in comparison with the great main deeper interest of my life in which I was now absorbed.'[24]

His spiritual ponderings found their way into a book which he began to write – in pencil, since ink froze in the pen at Tuna. Provisionally titled *The Religion of a Traveller*, it allowed his visionary abilities their fullest rein: 'This subliminal self can affect others at a distance. It can as it were get away from the body.' After mentioning the range of religions he has encountered on his travels, Younghusband speculates on the likelihood that on other planets there are 'beings more highly developed than ourselves – not necessarily with bodies like our own but with increased powers of telepathy; with that power which the Yogis possess of transferring their consciousness to a distance.'[25] His exhilaration convinced him that his fellow humans would appreciate and understand his message.

The combination of cold, hunger, mountains, adulation and power had sent Younghusband into a state of intoxication. Although press reports in Britain were generally cautious about the advantages of invading Tibet, Helen sent him several complimentary profiles of the leader of the Mission. 'Colonel Younghusband is just the man who would gladly give years of his life to look once upon Lhasa,' wrote the *Daily Mail*. 'Beneath the mask of his genial manner, behind the reserve of his quiet voice, there lies an active, eager brain without a single cobweb or a grain of dust upon it . . . There you have the elements that go to make the ideal administrator in the ancient and changeless East.'[26]

Praise of this kind was complemented by the reverential support he received from his staff. Ever since news of the foray into the Tibetan camp had leaked out, his reputation among his own men had soared. To those around him his mystical rumination manifested itself simply as quiet self-reliance. Accounts by those who took part in the Mission tend to be remarkably flattering about Younghusband; not in the superficial way that military memoirs often are, but with a real depth of admiration. His wide experience and astonishing physical resilience (at an average temperature of minus 30°) impressed them, as did his inscrutable, imperious impassivity when dealing with Tibetan officials.

Frederick O'Connor, who had himself spent much time in mountain territory, wrote that Younghusband seemed to be impervious to his physical surroundings:

I remember so well seeing him sally forth nearly every morning in the bitter wind after our so-called breakfast, clad in his British warm with a book under his arm. He would ensconce himself under the lee of some rock and remain for hours reading or writing and return for lunch perfectly contented and cheerful.[27]

Another officer who had been on the Mission wrote a reminiscence in 1929 which invested Younghusband with legendary qualities of heroism. He claimed it was 'doubtful whether any expedition had as leader a man of the forceful character of ours'. 'The unhalting success of the biggest shot in the dark, of our frontier history, I ascribe to the personality of one man,' he wrote. 'His head a little bent, his eyes a little sunken under beetling brows; and the faintest lilt in his walk . . . Do you understand me when I say that man's smallest wish, unexpressed or half-divined, was both law and stimulus to the least of us?'[28]

Although this eulogy is written in the exaggerated style of the period, it does capture the public face that Younghusband presented. His spiritual adventure was strictly private, but the luminous glow it gave him made him an inspiring leader. The very qualities of daring and intuition that were beginning to worry the Indian administration were the ones that so attracted those around him. To be the ruler of an isolated force, high in the forbidden land of the Himalayas, was for him a dream come true. It was the culmination of Francis Younghusband's fantasies.

For nearly three months they waited in the frozen desolation of Tuna while supplies and reinforcements were brought laboriously over the passes from Sikkim. There was a constant drip of rumours predicting a Tibetan attack. Gun bolts froze in the breech; dried yak dung was the only available form of fuel. When a dozen Sikh Pioneers died of pneumonia, firewood had to be dragged from the Chumbi valley for their cremation. Younghusband, who was anxious to advance to Gyantse as soon as possible, found himself in a state of perpetual frustration at the General's caution. 'Macdonald is a regular stick,' he informed his friend James Dunlop-Smith, an official back in India. 'He sucks in every rumour and lays out his plan as if the Tibetans were commanded by a Napoleon and were the most bloodthirsty people in the world.'[29]

Aggressive despatches to the Indian Government urging a rapid advance were stymied by the competing advice of Kitchener's minions, while the demands of Whitehall blocked any chance of rash decisions. 'Home Govt. have to be treated like a pack of children,' Younghusband wrote in a letter to his father, 'and as I have said my diplomacy has to be exerted much more in the direction of the Home Govt. than of the Tibetans.'[30] Personal appeals to the Viceroy were not yielding fruit: having just been reappointed for a second term in office, Curzon was working even more frantically than usual in advance of a six-month break in England.

By mid March Younghusband began to suspect that General Macdonald was procrastinating deliberately down in the Chumbi valley, and told him as much in a series of letters. Stuck out in the cold at Tuna, he did not appreciate the practical problems of moving an entire army over the Himalayas. The ratio between combatant troops and the logistic tail was as high as one to eight: in other words each Sikh Pioneer needed a backup of eight coolies. On his previous adventures, Younghusband had been accompanied by a small, experienced, lightly equipped escort; Macdonald was having to organize well over ten thousand men, many of whom had as little experience as he did of the terrain. Younghusband was also incensed when the General threatened Colonel Hogge, the commander of his personal escort, with court martial for using regimental mules to transport personal belongings. 'Old Macdonald himself is as rigid and stolid as a donkey,' Helen was informed.[31]

There was a brief moment of respite when Younghusband had discussions with Ugyen Kazi, the Bhutanese merchant who had tried to deliver Curzon's first letter to the Dalai Lama some years before. He was now acting as a representative of the Tongsa Penlop Ugyen Wangchuk, who was, effectively, the ruler of Bhutan. Realizing that the British advance offered the chance to boost his own political status, the Tongsa Penlop proffered his services as a mediator. This was an important coup for Younghusband. A crucial neighbouring state with intimate cultural and religious links to Tibet had become a potential ally. Ugyen Kazi agreed that the Tongsa Penlop would send a letter to the Tibetan Government encouraging them to negotiate. According to the Bhutanese state history *Druk Karpo*, he also 'agreed to be the witness that the British would not commit any atrocities to Tibetans on their way to Gyantse.'[32]

It was not until the very end of March that the main advance was ready to continue. Then the bombshell dropped. On Kitchener's orders, General Macdonald was to assume command until they reached Gyantse, on the grounds that fighting could be expected. Not for the last time, Younghusband reached for his pen and threatened to resign. If the order was not rescinded, he wrote,

'I would ask to be relieved of such a delicate political matter as the conduct of our relations with Tibet.'[33] On 30 March the decision was amended by Louis Dane: Macdonald would only take control if fighting was about to begin. Younghusband was satisfied with this ruling, and the following day the force began to move.

First came the Mounted Infantry, skirting along the edge of the gravelly plain, then the thrusting Colonel and his laggardly General, riding together for form's sake, pursued closely by the dozen men from the Norfolk Regiment with their deadly pair of Maxim Guns; next a handful of British soldiers from 7th Mountain Battery (armed with two dismantled ten-pounder screw-guns), followed by nearly a thousand Gurkhas and Sikh Pioneers, marching along with their freezing Lee Metford rifles and two elderly seven-pounders known as Bubble and Squeak. Ninety per cent of the fighting force was made up of 'native troops' or sepoys. Under the carefully orchestrated policy of divide and rule, it was a British voice that called the order, an Indian finger that would squeeze the trigger.

Into the distance trailed the army of supporters: the Coolie Corps (including several hundred Sikkimese women) with their enormous loads balanced on their shoulders, dodging past the six British military doctors (nicknamed The Troglodytes for their habit of putting up in caves rather than tents), the four newspaper correspondents, anxious for a story, and then the frost-bitten messengers and postal runners, clerks and writers, cooks and bearers, baggage guards and military policemen, the Native Field Hospital Staff, telegraph operators and mess-tent porters, all supported by a trail of bleeding-hoofed bullocks, yaks and mules.

When the Younghusband Expedition halted a little way below the village of Guru, the Tibetan army could be seen camped behind a long, low wall between a salt lake and some hot springs. Depon Lhading, wearing full ceremonial dress, rode out across the plain to attempt one, last, desperate parley with his opposite number. He would be dead within the hour.

FIFTEEN

'Bolting like Rabbits': Blood in the Land of Snows

Major Sobta (Retd.) was tall with tired eyes. As Secretary of the Planter's Club (Darjeeling) he felt it was his duty to maintain standards.

He approached me one morning in the club library as I was reading a smudged Indian edition of Younghusband's *Wonders of the Himalaya*. The works of Francis Younghusband seemed to be undergoing a revival in India: there was also a 1986 reprint of *The Epic of Mount Everest*, with an incomparable blurb on the dust wrapper. 'Man with his instinct of attaining the unattainable must be graplling with it. And just how the idea of climbing the Mount Everest was put into execution is the content of the book aptly titled "The Everest". The book addresses itself to distinct high adventrue phases. The first reconnaissance phase – of prospecting the mountain carefully. The second – first-actual attempt to reach summit . . .'

'Ahem,' coughed Major Sobta. 'Might I mention, er, that we usually wear ties after six p.m. I noticed that last night you were, er, well, incorrectly attired.'

He marched off with his hands behind his back, pausing only to straighten a book and mutter, 'Hmmm – Dornford Yates – excellent,' as he clicked the door shut.

The next morning I moved on, knowing it was time to step off Younghusband's trail for a while and return to written records. I took the 'ridiculous little railway' down through Darjeeling's clouds and deep green tea plantations to the blaze of the Indian plains, and endured a hot, slow train journey across Bihar and Uttar Pradesh. Back in Delhi I spent a few days with Mr Dal Ram Pul, an eminent explorer, famous for discovering an important historical site that nobody had realized was missing. After a week of luxuriousness, his cook having plied me with bulging samosas and dripping gulub jamuns, I set off by clanking bus to Dharamsala. It had been my first destination, the starting point for the twenty-year-old Frank Younghusband's foray over the Rhotang Pass.

Although it was in Tibet itself that I had the inspiration to write about the Younghusband Expedition, I knew there was little point in returning there to do research. Many of the Tibetan Government's records were destroyed during or after the Chinese invasion of 1950, and anything that remains in the Lhasa archives is out of bounds to inquisitive foreigners. My only hope of finding Tibetan primary sources was among the exiles in northern India. A library had been established at Dharamsala during the 1970s in an attempt to collect together any books, scriptures or documents that had been taken out of Tibet by fleeing refugees.

When I had begun researching the events of 1903–04, I found that a patronizing attitude towards Tibet seemed to infest almost every historical account. 'In 1903 the position of Britain and Tibet was like that of a big boy at school who is tormented by an impertinent youngster. He bears it for some time, but at last is compelled to administer chastisement,' wrote John Buchan.[1] To Younghusband and his fellow travellers the Tibetans were 'not a fit people to be left to themselves' – a collection of scheming monks and deluded tribesmen who needed to learn respect for authority. Chinese Communist propaganda presents a brave but hopeless confrontation between the noble savages of Tibet's 'local government' (a sort of glorified County Council) and blood-thirsty imperialists. More recent Western versions tend to represent the 1903 Mission as a foretaste of the Chinese invasion of 1950 – a doomed encounter between a ferocious modern army and peace-loving innocents.

All these views assume a degree of prelapsarian ignorance within Tibet itself. It is an endearing notion, but one that has the effect of politically castrating the Tibetan people by turning them into the helpless victims of (depending on your ideological view) monkish oppression or external aggression. This left me anxious to find out what Tibetan chroniclers had thought of the British. The diplomatic background to the invasion had already been documented in great detail. There could be no doubt as to who wrote what in which India Office despatch, to whom, and on what date. Peter Fleming's *Bayonets to Lhasa* gave a readable and occasionally accurate account of the military practicalities of the invasion, as well as revealing the conflict between Younghusband and Macdonald. But what no writer had done – with the exception of W. D. Shakabpa in half a chapter of his *Tibet: A Political History* – was to attempt to seek a Tibetan angle on this crucial period in that country's past.

I took a room at Tse Chok Ling, a small Buddhist monastery on the hill between McLeod Ganj and the Library of Tibetan Works and Archives. Each morning I would walk up the steep ridge to some houses, past a tethered sheep named Father Benet, through a buzzing wood and down to the library. After several weeks I began to find Tibetan writings on the period 1903–04, in many different scripts and styles. Some were the memoirs of retired officials, some were excuses to rehearse the case for Tibetan independence, while others were propaganda treatises published by the Chinese. But they all succeeded in casting new light on what Younghusband and his Mission had been up to in Tibet.

One unusual book was the *Annals of the All-Revealing Mirror*, which was written by a Tibetan but published under Chinese control in 1987. Although its conclusions are suspect, the style being a flowery blend of mythology and Socialist Realism, it is clear the author must have had access to original sources. According to this account, General Lhading, having consulted the prophecies of the legendary King Yeshe O, went forward from his own lines to engage in peace talks with the British. Younghusband and Macdonald told him that his soldiers should extinguish the fuses for their matchlock guns as a guarantee of good faith. Once this had been done the weapons were effectively inoperable, since it takes several minutes to light a new fuse from a flint:

> When the Tibetan soldiers had extinguished their fuses, the British soldiers opened fire with machine guns from the surrounding area. It was as if the heroic Tibetan soldiers had had their hands disabled, and they fell on the wasteland. The British invaders, having disabled the Tibetan soldiers, then savagely massacred them.[2]

A similar account was written by Namseling Paljor Jigme, a descendant of the Shigatse general who acted as Lhading's deputy during the confrontation. His autobiography, which was published following his death in 1973, reads as follows:

> Father at that time was a Depon stationed at Phari. He took his army about fifteen miles from Phari to a place called

Chumi Shengo [Hot Springs] . . . During the battle some of the Tibetans had a gun for which you light a fuse and put one bullet [matchlocks] and the rest had swords and spears. The British had some guns where you could put seven or eight bullets at one time, and two types of cannon . . . All of a sudden the British fired and many Tibetan soldiers were killed.[3]

Namseling goes on to give an indication of the effect the battle had on the household: his father and all but one of eighteen family servants were killed.

A survivor of the events at Chumi Shengo, Tseten Wangchuk, wrote an eye-witness report. He was in command of a *dingshok*, roughly equivalent in British military terms to a platoon: 'While we were waiting at the wall during the discussions, a hail of bullets came down on us from the surrounding hills. We had no time to draw our swords. I lay down beside a dead body and pretended I had been killed. The sound of firing continued for the length of time it would take six successive cups of hot tea to cool.'[4]

As the light began to fade at the end of the day, and the weather grew even colder, predators appeared: 'In the evening when the British had stopped firing at the Tibetans the Inji Coolie [English Coolies], the men who carry luggage and the wounded, searched the injured Tibetan soldiers and found earrings and jewels . . . All their weapons and clothes and bedding were taken away by the British soldiers.'[5] The *Annals* recounts an even more chilling story, which relates to General Lhading:

Depon Lhading-se was also wounded and feigned death among the corpses. That night the British army's porters came to pick things up from among the corpses. A Sikkimese woman saw Depon Lhading-se's gold ring and drew a small knife and was about to cut off his finger. Lhading-se again and again repeated, "I will give you that gold ring, but please don't give me away to the British." She took the gold ring, then told the British that there was a Tibetan officer feigning death, and the British came to take him.[6]

Although these accounts lack the verifiable details which would make them incontestably convincing, they do produce a consistent impression. It is clear the Tibetans thought the British had been guilty of a massacre – and that it had been achieved through treachery, by persuading them to put out their gun fuses. *The Times* of

London took a rather different view. 'The whole affair was brought upon the Tibetans entirely by themselves,' wired their special correspondent, 'as both Colonel Younghusband and Brigadier-General Macdonald and the troops exercised the greatest possible forebearance and patience.'[7]

Younghusband's version of events went as follows. The previous evening he had argued with Macdonald about the virtues of a surprise attack. 'If General Macdonald had had a perfectly free hand, and had been allowed to think only of military considerations, he would have attacked the Tibetans by surprise in their camp, without giving them any warning at all.' Having persuaded the General to hold the attack, the troops set out for the village of Guru. As they approached the Tibetans' defensive wall, General Lhading rode out across the plain. An impromptu conference took place in the bitter wind, Younghusband, Macdonald, O'Connor and Lhading sitting on sheepskins beneath a snapping Union Jack. For some time they debated fruitlessly, both sides insisting their ambitions were peaceful. The conclave ended indecisively, Younghusband announcing that the Tibetans had a quarter of an hour in which to surrender.

When the minutes had ticked away, General Macdonald twice requested permission to start firing. Younghusband refused, and the Indian troops were ordered to approach the Tibetan positions, guns at the ready. Within a few minutes the Tibetans were surrounded. The mounted infantry had wheeled round behind them; the Gurkhas crouched on the rocky slope to their right; Sikh Pioneers stood to their left; the Maxim Guns faced them from the front. General Lhading sat forlornly in front of the low stone wall, muttering to himself. Colonel Younghusband had won.

While the British officers began to take photographs of the defeated Tibetan troops, Younghusband scribbled a telegram to his masters in India and handed it to an orderly. Then something happened which turned a bloodless victory into a vicious bloodbath. According to subsequent British accounts, it was General Lhading who began the battle. Younghusband, Candler and Fleming all claim that as his troops were disarmed, Lhading jumped on to his pony, shouting hysterically: 'He threw himself upon a sepoy, drew a revolver, and shot the sepoy in the jaw.'[8] This, supposedly, was the match which lit the powder keg and made the British response unavoidable.

It is interesting that there is no mention of this event in the reports written immediately after the confrontation. According to a telegram Younghusband sent later that day, 'order was then given by General Macdonald to actually commence disarming Tibetans. This they resisted, attacking the troops with swords and firing. Firing on our side then commenced.'[9] General Macdonald's own despatch of the same evening reads: 'Pioneers began to disarm Tibetan troops . . . At this point without any previous warning the Tibetans behind the wall opened a hot fire point blank at our men 15 or 20 yards off which they maintained for some minutes, several men also rushing out with swords.'[10] Although it is possible that Depon Lhading did shoot a sepoy through the jaw, there is no convincing evidence to suggest that this precipitated the massacre. It seems more likely that it was the attempts by Sikh Pioneers to disarm the Tibetans of their family matchlocks that triggered the opening shot, and that the scenario of the wild General with the revolver was a myth which grew up later.

Once the shooting began the Tibetans were helpless. Guns were firing at them from every direction, shells bursting on their line of retreat. The Maxims chattered away remorselessly in the thin air, scorning the protective amulets of the huddled Buddhist army. 'I got so sick of the slaughter that I ceased fire, though the General's order was to make as big a bag as possible,' wrote Lieutenant Hadow, the Commander of the Maxim Gun detachment, in a letter to his father. 'I hope I shall never have to shoot down men walking away again.'[11] Some Tibetans tried to escape towards the village of Guru, but were cut down in their tracks by the mounted infantry who chased them as they fled. Many just stayed where they were, crouching behind the grey stone wall, or wandered hopelessly away.

'Why, in the name of all their Bodhisats and Munis, did they not run?' asked Candler of the *Daily Mail*. 'They were bewildered . . . They walked with bowed heads, as if they had been disillusioned in their gods.'[12] Before long the firing ceased of its own accord, but a few minutes had been enough to decimate the entire Tibetan force. While the mounted infantry charged off to capture Guru, the Indian soldiers and British officers walked over the battlefield they had created. There were half-eaten meals and half-finished games of chance lying in the Tibetan camp, which gave some of the victors the uneasy feeling that the enemy may never have intended to fight at all. Rather to their surprise, wounded Tibetans found they were whisked off to the military field hospital.

Tseten Wangchuk, the Tibetan platoon commander, managed to reach the nearby village of Dochen where he met up with his cousin who 'had been informed that the British army was such, that if it lost one hundred soldiers today, it could replace them with one thousand tomorrow, and that Kushab Sahib [Chief Sahib – Younghusband, in this case] possessed glasses through which he could see great distances.'[13] Tibetan surprise at being treated by doctors was matched by British admiration for their enemy's stoicism during the battle. Several British officers engaged Tibetan survivors as personal batmen or valets, impressed by such exemplary fortitude under fire. 'I hope I shall not be considered a pro-Tibetan,' wrote Candler, 'when I say that I admire their gallantry and dash.'[14]

Colonel Younghusband – and it should be remembered that despite his military rank he had never before seen war at close quarters – was left shocked and horrified. Who was to blame for this massacre? 'I have had an absolutely miserable day,' he wrote to Helen. 'It was a horrible sight, but I feel I did every single thing I could to prevent this, and it was only the silliness and ignorance of these Tibetans that caused it.'[15] 'It was nothing but pure butchery,' he told his father in another letter. 'The poor things were penned up in a hollow within a few yards and even feet of our rifles.' It had been 'a pure massacre – brought on by the crass stupidity and childishness of the Tibetan general'.[16] In a letter to Dunlop-Smith the blame shifted a little further: 'The Dalai Lama . . . is at the bottom of all the trouble and deserves to be well kicked.'[17]

In a confidential despatch to Curzon the next morning, General Macdonald assessed the score. His men had used 50 shrapnel shells, 1400 machine gun rounds and 14,351 rounds of rifle ammunition. Their casualties were: six lightly wounded, six badly wounded, none killed. Most of the injuries were the result of sword blows or sling shots. On the Tibetan side, Macdonald estimated that 2000 men had been present, of whom about half were 'regular troops'. 222 were wounded and 628 were killed, including the Lhasa General (Lhading), the Shigatse General (Namseling), the Phari Headman (Kyibuk) and two monk-officials. A grand total of three Russian-made rifles were found on the battlefield.[18]

I came to see the massacre at Chumi Shengo as the symbolic pivot of the Younghusband Expedition. Once blood had been shed on so lavish a scale, there was no turning back for either side. Curious foreigners from over the mountains had become treacherous killers; a jaunty excursion to the Roof of the World had become a bloody invasion. From now on there was no room for compromise or reconciliation. The Tibetans understood the military might they were facing, and did all they could to oppose it, while the British became determined to follow up their advantage by pressing on quickly.

Chumi Shengo was the turning point in the meeting of two civilizations. A Western perception of territory, diplomacy and political necessity hit an Eastern one head on: the result was a bloodbath. Had the mutual comprehension between these two island races been greater, the outcome might so easily have been different. But they were operating on different planes, basing their ideas and assumptions on contradictory foundations. Lhading could see no reason why his country should not be left to itself; Younghusband could see no reason why a neighbouring state should not enter into treaty relations with British India. Tibet's isolation had given it no mechanism with which to challenge the relentless internal logic of High Imperialism.

When I spoke to the Tibetan academic Dawa Norbu, he described the Thirteenth Dalai Lama's refusal to open Lord Curzon's letters as a deliberate strategy. 'I think it represented a moral refusal to communicate,' he said. Lhading's behaviour at Guru was a similar act of refusal: he would not fight, but he would not surrender. The fuses for the matchlock guns were symbolically extinguished. The low stone wall the Tibetans built across the barren plain – which Lhading sat squarely *in front of* during the battle – was the physical embodiment of their diplomatic policy. As one British officer wrote: 'It was their equivalent for "full stop".'[19] The Tibetan Government had seen the fate of India, Sikkim and Ladakh, and had no wish to come into contact with the British. Stonewalling seemed a fair way of expressing their policy of non-cooperation.

To Younghusband and Macdonald, the principles of passive resistance would have been less than apparent. After numerous warnings, the Tibetan General had remained recalcitrant. In a sense the Tibetans were lucky to have lasted as long as they did. Under General Macdonald's Rules of Engagement, they might easily have been slaughtered as they slept. Yet to those Tibetans who did survive, it must have seemed incomprehensible that the British chose to shoot them so shamelessly, and then bandage them up again inside a green canvas tent.

I felt that misunderstanding and mutual incomprehension were the essence of the conflict. This may go some way to explaining why the two sides had such dramatically different versions and interpretations of the same event. Younghusband was exceptionally patient; he was cunningly duplicitous. It was a necessary battle; it was a treacherous massacre. For historical myths and perceptions are more potent than any factual record. History is what people believe it to be.

So they charged on to Gyantse, trailing the telegraph line in their wake. (Inquisitive Tibetans were told the wire was to lead the troops back to India.) Beyond a salt lake called Kala Tso more Tibetans were spotted defending a high, narrow ravine, which was soon named Red Idol Gorge. On 10 April there was a battle, but muskets, sling shots and leather cannons (known as *jingals*) were no match for Maxims and ten pounders: the Tibetans fled leaving two hundred dead. Although he was genuinely shocked by the bloodshed, Younghusband responded with an air of apparent oblivion. He was experiencing a reaction which is common in war: the sight of gore and killing produces an exhilaration which carries the soldier forward, blocking out feelings of remorse. Rather than being moved to a quest for peace, he finds the enemy has been objectified and dehumanized. 'Kangma. Tenth,' Younghusband telegraphed to Helen. 'Tibetans bolting like rabbits.'[20]

Another skirmish took place at Nenying, an important Buddhist shrine beyond Kangma. Troops approached the settlement in a pincer movement, the Nenying monks having installed themselves in a nearby nunnery with some weapons. Many of the monks were killed in the ensuing battle, and there was substantial damage to the ancient Indo-Nepalese paintings and statues inside the *gompa* (temple). According to the author of the *Annals*: 'It was as if the courtyard of Nenying Gompa was a lake of blood. Even today you can see traces of the blood of the malevolent invaders.'[21]

Back home the press, public and politicians had responded to the

Chumi Shengo Massacre (or 'the scrap at the Hot Springs', as one writer described it) with varying degrees of concern. In Parliament the Government looked as if it would have a hard time of a debate on the subject, but in the event their enabling motion to finance the Mission was carried despite strong Liberal opposition. Winston Churchill, at that time a young MP on the Conservative benches, wrote in a private letter that it 'must be an evil portent' to find such an event greeted 'with a howl of ferocious triumph by Press & Party'.[22] In fact the howl was less than triumphant, most newspapers endorsing the action with cautious reserve. It was the British Indian papers which were the keenest, the *Overland Mail* declaring that 'a thrashing or a drastic beating operates as a wholesome lesson and earns respect, which is a necessary foundation to the establishing of lasting friendly relations'.[23]

As Younghusband advanced, letters of support arrived. The Viceroy assured him of 'the implicit support and backing of the Govt. of India and myself', while regretting the necessary bloodshed. 'When I leave here [for England] I will get them to send you a case of champagne as a little present to drink my health in with your comrades at Gyantse.'[24] 'You gave me an account of the fighting at Guru and of your victory, and I was exceedingly rejoiced,' wrote the Tongsa Penlop of Bhutan, who knew on which side his bread was buttered.[25] Another indigenous ruler also took the opportunity to improve his standing, and sent a telegram to the Foreign Department: 'H. EX. maharajah of indore desires that his respectful congratulations may be conveyed to his majesty's government for victory over tibetans.'[26]

Gyantse was reached on 12 April. It was Tibet's third largest town, overlooked by an ancient *dzong* (fort) perched on a huge outcrop of grey brown rock. Beside it was a monastery housing several thousand monks, and below it a market place. Most of the defenders having fled, the Gyantse *dzongpon* had little choice but to let the British occupy his *dzong*. But Macdonald and Younghusband thought it might prove difficult to defend, so after raising the Union Jack on its roof, installed themselves a mile due south at Changlo, an aristocrat's compound by the Nyang river.

The negotiation of a new trade and border treaty with Tibet was the British Commissioner's apparent task now that he had reached his destination. But with nobody to negotiate with except the ubiquitous Captain Parr, who was still trying feebly to represent the Chinese Government, Younghusband sought alternative activities. Spring was in the air, and the climate was a great improvement on

Tuna. 'Landon the Times Correspondent lives in our mess now,' he wrote to his sister Emmie. 'Reuter's is not a bad fellow personally but he does write the most appalling balderdash.'[27] Everybody was enjoying themselves, Helen learned, except General Macdonald who smoked forty cigarettes a day and had caught a bout of fever. After a week Macdonald and his troops retired to the Chumbi valley to consolidate supply lines, leaving Younghusband with a force of around five hundred men.

Some afternoons the British officers went off on shooting and fishing expeditions, or engaged in casual robbery. 'From the top of the Jong [Dzong] we discovered that the huge monastery behind appeared to be deserted, so we decided to go and investigate and do a bit of looting on our own,' wrote Hadow years later in his regimental magazine.[28] In a letter home to his mother at the time he gave a more immediate account: 'After I had inspected the Jong I went down to do a little looting . . . I had one of my own men & 2 lamas with me. It was great fun! All the doors were locked, but we found a sledge hammer, and then not a single door withstood me.'[29]

The question of looting has always been a hotly disputed aspect of the Younghusband Expedition. Chinese Communist history has made much of it, devoting a whole section of the *Compiled History of the Tibetan People's Struggle* to a detailed inventory of what was taken, down to the last sheep. British books published at the time gave assurances that everything had been paid for; assurances that some writers take at face value even today. It is true there was no widespread looting of ordinary people. Potatoes, livestock, turnips, buckwheat and grain were purchased from local farmers at a reasonable price. In Lhasa itself there was minimal looting, following a stern warning from the Viceroy.

The lure of the invaders' foreign currency even gave rise to a Lhasa street song:

> First they were called Enemies of the Faith,
> And then we labelled them Outsiders.
> But when their rupees appeared in our land,
> They became known as Honourable Sahibs.[30]

However there was substantial theft from 'hostile' villages, temples and monasteries, particularly during the central stage of the Expedition. This gave rise to an opposing verse, which was sung in the Gyantse region:

Gyantse the turquoise valley,
Is filled with marauding outsiders.
Oh! When I see such things happen,
I wonder what the use is of gathering riches.[31]

Monasteries were a particular focus of interest, the British believing they might contain stocks of Tibet's legendary gold and precious stones. Painted clay images of the Buddha were smashed open, but to the disappointment of the marauders there was nothing inside them but block-printed mantras. The officers were also motivated by prejudice against the monks, whom they regarded – with justification in some cases – as despotic oppressors of the populace and stirrers of anti-British feeling.

Religious antagonism played its part. Thigh-bone trumpets, skull cups and colourful paintings of wrathful deities were taken as evidence of 'degeneration' and devil worship. With no real understanding of the subject, the British decided the Tibetans had corrupted the teachings of the Buddha. The outward trappings of Tibetan Buddhism have always disturbed Protestants; Roman Catholics are said to find the images and the incense a little easier to tolerate.[32] Younghusband had surprisingly few qualms about the looting, writing blithely to Helen: 'There has been a committee today distributing brass images and things found in the fort. I have been allotted twelve things.'[33] Over the months bronze statues, silver charm boxes, carpets, *thangkas*, ceremonial robes, trumpets, lamellar armour and a host of trinkets found their way back to India. Every soldier wanted to complement his campaign medal with a memento.

The unfastened power that Younghusband enjoyed at Gyantse brought out an unpleasant and disturbing side of his character. 'I have been engaged today in keeping monks in order,' he wrote to Emmie:

> A more cringing lot I never came across. They are not worth powder and shot. I have them in great awe of me though. All the head men of the monastery here came to me today to beg me to let them off the fine [thirty-six tons of barley] I had imposed on them . . . I silently motion them to seats and ask what they want. They rise to their feet but not presuming to stand upright before me or look me in the face remain bending low and with eyes cast down. I rebuke them sternly for fighting against us. They say that those who presumed to have been well beaten with sticks . . .

I tell them it is too serious a matter to be passed by unnoticed and unless the fine is paid within the next five days troops will occupy their monastery. They make regular whinnies of pain and say they are all as poor as church mice; but knowing that they are as rich as many Croesuses and are really laughing in their sleeves at my moderation I remain obdurate: and they retire still bowing profoundly and stepping backwards like we do before the King . . . It is great sport. Love to the Father.

Yr. affect. brother Frank.[34]

Knowing that Emmie doted on every word he said or wrote, Frank was able to show off his feelings of power and importance without shame, embarrassment or the fashionable false modesty of the era.

Yet keeping monks in order was no substitute for action. Until Tibetan negotiators deigned to appear at Gyantse, the Commissioner and his followers could do little. The manufacture of another 'incident' was one possibility: fortunately an ideal opportunity presented itself at the beginning of May. Several thousand well-armed enemy soldiers had dug themselves in at the Karo La, a 16,600-foot pass on the road to Lhasa. Although they presented no discernible threat to the riverside camp at Changlo, both Younghusband and the military commander, Colonel Brander, were keen to fight. Brander had been with the Mission since Khamba Dzong, and shared the Commissioner's love of risks. Leaving just over a hundred Indian soldiers (many of whom were unwell) to guard Younghusband at Changlo, Brander set off for the Karo La on 3 May with the rest of the force.

The feverish General – lately nicknamed 'Retiring Mac' by the Gyantse officers – was informed tardily by telegram, and responded with alarm and consternation over the telegraph wire: 'From Gen. Macdonald, Chumbi. To Lt. Col. Brander, Gyantse. CLEAR THE LINE. The Moveable Column should not have gone as far as the Karo La without reference to me. If you are not committed return at once to Gyantse.' Having been an admirer of Admiral Nelson since his schooldays, Younghusband turned a blind eye to the order. He spent some time finding a messenger, and added a covering letter for Brander saying the man's pony was slow. 'I need hardly assure you that we are perfectly safe here . . . On political grounds I would have the strongest objection to your returning . . .'[35]

For all Younghusband's assurances, the remnants of his Mission were most unsafe at Changlo. Before sunrise on 5 May, hundreds of armed Tibetans took the opportunity presented by weak defences and 'yelping like hyenas' tried to storm the compound. Enemy muskets blasted through loopholes while the waking Sikhs grabbed for their Lee Metfords, quickly realizing that the camp was surrounded. Wearing nothing but a pair of pyjamas, Colonel Younghusband sheltered in a reinforced section of the building. At first the Tibetans seemed to have the advantage, but before long the modern weapons of the British proved more effective, killing at least two hundred Tibetans.

Younghusband was left badly shaken, gazing at the dead bodies which lay around his post. He knew full well that with greater stealth and better planning the Tibetans might easily have been victorious. But as he wrote privately to Curzon, his opponents had played into his hands. What better proof could there be that the Tibetans were treacherous and violent? Surely the Prime Minister's permission for an advance to Lhasa could not be far off. That night he slept nervously, shocked by the news that Tibetan collaborators in Gyantse had been killed and mutilated. He had a disturbing dream, in which it was revealed to him that Lady Curzon had given birth to no fewer than twelve children before marrying her husband. What might this signify, he wondered?

Late in the day on 7 May he heard the sound of hooves as Brander and a handful of mounted infantry rode exhausted into camp. They had fought a battle at the Karo Pass, despite receiving General Macdonald's order to return. Four of their men had been killed, including Captain Bethune, and thirteen badly wounded. At first the confrontation had looked hopeless, the Tibetans outnumbering them heavily. As the British troops advanced towards the mouth of the gorge they were fired on by enemy emplacements, known as *sangars*, built high into the rock. Most of the Tibetan troops were hidden behind an impregnable stone wall stretching between the two sheer cliff faces. Superior weaponry proved useless against this ideal defensive position.

Colonel Brander saw their only hope lay in outflanking the Tibetans by climbing above them, if that were possible. With a bitter wind blowing, Gurkha Riflemen and Sikh Pioneers scrambled perilously up the frozen cliffs, their rifles webbed over their shoulders, guided by some shepherds. After three hours the soldiers reached a point where they were able to fire on and then storm the *sangars*. The Tibetan defenders fled, many being shot as they scrambled over the rocks and snow, some losing their footing and tumbling over the sheer precipice. From their commanding position the Sikhs were able to shoot into the gully below. Before long the Tibetans took fright, and started to retreat from the defensive wall. Having gone into combat at a height of at least 18,500 feet, the soldiers had fought the highest skirmish in military history.

Down in the ravine the mounted infantry had breached the wall, and were chasing the hapless Tibetans across the windswept plain, shooting the stragglers, capturing ponies and burning camps. From a military point of view, the versatility of the mounted troops in reconnaissance and pursuit was essential for success in Tibet. They played a vital role which was never to be repeated, for by 1914 their unique capability was becoming obsolete. Yet many British newspapers were less than impressed by events at the Karo La, A. R. Orage's journal *The New Age* even asking, 'Who ordered this bloody butchery? Who is responsible for the fact that British soldiers rode for twelve miles on the flanks of these wretched Thibetans shooting them down from the saddle?'[36]

Younghusband reported the victory to Lord Ampthill, who had taken over from Curzon as acting Viceroy. Brander had been most successful in 'removing threats to our line of communication', he wrote, adding that it was now time to 'shove soft words aside and stiffen ourselves a bit'.[37] Being in possession of a map of Tibet, it did not take the new Viceroy long to establish that the Karo La was nearly fifty miles due east of Gyantse, and had therefore been of no conceivable threat to Younghusband's Mission. It was also apparent that the adventure had allowed the base at Changlo to be attacked. Kitchener's representative on the Viceroy's Council made it clear that Younghusband's behaviour was unacceptable. Previous fears about his headstrong impetuosity and poor judgment were exacerbated. 'He is evidently a man of very highly strung temperament,' Ampthill noted, 'who has his ups and downs.'[38]

These worries were crowned a few days later by the news that Changlo was now under siege. Tibetan troops had gained control of surrounding villages, and taken to firing miniature lead and copper cannon-balls into the compound from Gyantse Dzong. Maxim Guns and a pair of ancient seven-pounders could do little against this barrage. To Younghusband's fury, he was put under the long-distance control of Retiring Mac until 'military consider-ations' had been resolved. Although the siege was not total, there was little he could do until reinforcements arrived, despite the min-istrations of the faithful Mahmood Isa. With frayed nerves, inadequate food and his beloved George Curzon away in England, Francis Edward Younghusband felt he had been abandoned. It was exactly a year since he had been summoned from Indore to take on this gruelling task.

'I am in despair about the Home Govt. They are behaving most disgracefully,' he told Emmie in a flustered letter on 16 May. 'So just at the critical moment when I ought to feel I am supported by my country I am left in the lurch. It is the old old story – Sir Bartle Frere and General Gordon over again . . .'[39] He was at the end of his tether. After all, there were reports that the infamous Agvan Dorzhiev was in charge of the Lhasa arsenal, while some rumours even had him ensconced in Gyantse Dzong directing military operations.

Foolishly, Younghusband sought to stampede the new Viceroy into action. With masonry tumbling on to his head and lice crawling into his scratchy beard, he fired off a telegram:

> Gyantse 20th May:
> Evident Lhasa monks are raising whole country against us; and are relying on, and probably receiving, outside support. I consider advance to Lhasa shd. be something more than for purpose of taking Mission to negotiate. No result will be obtained till power of Lhasa monks is thoroughly broken . . .[40]

Lord Ampthill was most disturbed, knowing full well the British Government would never sanction action of this kind, and that Kitchener and the military authorities would use the telegram as further ammunition against the unstable Commissioner. Younghusband's suggestion matched the tone of another of his letters a fortnight earlier, which insisted they should 'smash those selfish filthy lecherous Lamas'. With nervous fingers, Ampthill removed the offending documents from the official file.

The thruster had overreached himself. He must have known the telegram would infuriate the desk-bound government servants who controlled his Mission; yet he sent it. 'Another thing I want to strive against is a sort of way I have of doing exactly the opposite to everybody else,' he had written to his sister Emmie when he was sixteen years old. 'I don't mean to do it but I can't help it coming out.'[41] It was a tendency he never eradicated: an impetuous self-certainty which guaranteed the mistrust of cautious policy makers.

'This telegram is distinctly petulant in tone,' noted the Viceroy with a headmasterly air. 'The prolonged strain, the disappointment and the trying climate are telling on Colonel Younghusband's nerves . . . He is going off the rails.'[42]

SIXTEEN

'Helpless as if the Sky Had Hit the Earth'

Following a flurry of telegrams between Simla, London and Darjeel-ing, Younghusband was granted permission to advance to Lhasa. The condition was that the Tibetans should first be told they had a month in which to come to Gyantse to negotiate. Any idea of annexing territory or smashing lamas should be forgotten. Although he saw this policy as an inadequate and impractical compromise, the Commissioner duly prepared an official ultimatum.

With the assistance of Frederick O'Connor the terms were drawn up on a large sheet of parchment informing the Dalai Lama in both English and Tibetan that he had until 25 June 1904 to send 'competent negotiators' to Gyantse. The document was inserted into a cream-coloured envelope, the ends of which were duly looped with papal-purple ribbon, covered with huge gobbets of red sealing wax and stamped 'Tibet Frontier Commission'. A Tibetan prisoner was entrusted with the delivery of the ultimatum; he returned obediently some days later with the missive still in his hand. The Kalon Lama had refused to accept, convey or even read it.[1]

While this was happening, Colonel Younghusband was sum-moned peremptorily back to the Chumbi valley for talks with his masters, who were disturbed by his conduct. Before dawn on 6 June he crept out of Changlo with a bodyguard of mounted infan-try. They managed to give the slip to a host of Tibetan horsemen, and reached the fort at Kangma late that night. Around 4.30 the following morning the small garrison was awakened by 'the pecu-liar jackal-like yell' of Tibetan soldiers on the attack. Grabbing a rifle and, most uncharacteristically, swearing at his escort, Young-husband ran to the parapet. Several hundred Tibetans were scaling the walls of the fort. Once again the British looked as if they would be overwhelmed by sheer weight of numbers, but soon their weapons gave them the advantage. The besiegers withdrew, leaving seventy dead.

Younghusband rode on hard through hostile territory, reaching Chumbi three days later. On the way he sent an irate telegram to the Indian Government, in which he insisted the Mission should not only advance to Lhasa, but stay there all winter if necessary negotiating a full treaty. He followed this up with a threat to resign if his wishes were not approved. Ampthill, Kitchener and Macdonald were firmly opposed to wintering in Lhasa, and the British Government was becoming tempted to cut its losses by withdrawing from Tibet altogether. The Commissioner's offer of resignation came within a whisker of being accepted. But following consideration of the alternatives, it was decided the political consequences of his recall would be too awkward to handle.

Younghusband himself was meanwhile tempering his views in the comparative safety of the Chumbi valley. Basking among the primulas and rhododendrons he was able to eat adequate food, experience the adulation of his colleagues, engage in discussions with the Tongsa Penlop and chew over his worries with old friends such as 'Curly' Stewart (of Bozai Gumbaz days) and his brother-in-law Vernon Magniac, who was joining him as private secretary. An uneasy diplomatic compromise having been reached with Macdonald and the Government of India, they set off for Gyantse with an expanded relieving force. It consisted of eight big guns, over a hundred mounted infantry, four thousand yaks and mules, two thousand coolies and two thousand infantrymen, including four companies of the 1st battalion, the Royal Fusiliers.

Reaching Gyantse in heavy rain on 28 June, they recaptured the surrounding villages with comparative ease. The siege of Changlo was lifted. The British officers, Indian soldiers and impressed Tibetan camp servants could walk the plains of Gyantse again. A deputation of long-awaited Tibetans arrived on 2 July wearing robes of the finest silk; yet discussions proved as fruitless as ever. Remembering perhaps the effect of imperial ceremony on the Mir of Hunza fifteen years before, Younghusband called a durbar for noon the following day. It was to be his final attempt at negotiation.

Boots were polished, fine carpets laid out and a guard of honour assembled. The Commissioner's full-dress uniform and camp chair and cocked hat were dusted down. But five past twelve came and ten past twelve came and still no delegates appeared. Finally at around half past one the Tibetan officials rode over to Changlo at a leisurely pace, oblivious to the British obsession with punctuality. An irate Francis Younghusband responded by keeping them waiting until four o'clock, but it is doubtful whether his chronometrical

retaliation was understood. The meeting proved frosty and incon-
clusive, the Tibetans remaining unmoved by Younghusband's
threats. So on 5 July an assault on the vast *dzong* at Gyantse began.

General Macdonald, who was now suffering from insomnia and
gastro-enteritis on top of his surfeit of cigarettes, proved characteristically indecisive in his command, many of the key decisions being
taken by the company commanders. 'Col. Y. asked the General to
fire but he refused as he is afraid to take the fort,' wrote Eric Bailey,
a young lieutenant whose father was a friend of Younghusband. 'I
wish they would change him as he is no good at all.'[2] Eventually
a diversionary attack was launched on the northern edge of
the *dzong*, followed the next morning by a bombardment of the
southern face. By midday the British controlled the area below the
huge outcrop of rock, but the fort itself was looking impregnable.

A new attack was launched on another of its walls, volleys of
explosive shells eventually blowing a hole in the stone. Then a
direct hit was scored on the fort's powder-magazine, which
exploded with a dull rumble. According to British histories of the
battle this was the result of pure luck, but one Tibetan account
offers a different version of events: 'At this point a kitchen water-
carrying maid was lured at night into the British camp. She then
pointed out the ammunition store, and the following day artillery
fire was directed there and it was blown up. A strong attack was
made on the Dzong which then was captured.'[3]

As the Tibetan response slackened, Gurkhas and Royal Fusiliers
scrambled up the sheer rock face. Some were knocked flying by
boulders and masonry which tumbled down the slope, but they
picked themselves up and kept on climbing. As the soldiers
approached the breach in the wall the shelling halted. Younghusband watched anxiously through his field glasses as the dust
began to clear. Finally a trail of soldiers broke through, led by
Havildar Pun and Lieutenant Grant of the Gurkhas, who later
received a Victoria Cross for his actions. Ten minutes later Gyantse
Dzong was in the hands of the British. By 19 July they had re-taken
the Karo Pass and marched as far as Nagartse, a fortified town on
the banks of the beautiful turquoise lake called the Yamdrok Tso.
The climate was improving, and the exhausted troops found themselves amidst fields of oats, barley, mustard and peas.

It was only at this point that the Tibetan Government appreciated
the gravity of the threat they were facing. They were accustomed
to border skirmishes, but this was beginning to look like a full-scale
conquest. Previous invasions, such as the Mongol capture of Lhasa

in 1705, had been lightning manoeuvres, swiftly executed. Now after a year of lumbering violence and procrastination, the British troops looked set to march on Lhasa. Overwhelmed by this sudden advance the Tibetan army scattered 'like feathers in the wind'. Its new Commander-in-Chief, the Kalon Lama Chamba Tenzin, retreated to Lhasa in panic but lost his way and found himself, appropriately enough, in the Rong district.[4]

It was left to the Gyantse negotiators to try to effect a settlement. There was a long meeting on 19 July between Younghusband and Lobsang Trinley, the Chief Secretary and 'evil genius' who had been at Khamba Dzong the previous year. With him was the Kalon Yutok Phuntsog Palden and a 'grave and foolish' monk-official from the Panchen Lama's court at Tashilhumpo. Also taking part in the talks was the Tongsa Penlop of Bhutan, Ugyen Wangchuk. Although his entourage was dangerously unruly, looting anything they could lay their hands on, the Tongsa Penlop's grasp of both imperial realpolitik and the Tibetan outlook made him an invaluable mediator. He was the only player who enjoyed the trust of both Younghusband and the young Dalai Lama.

It was clear the Tibetans were willing in principle to acquiesce to the British demands. After the capture of Gyantse Dzong the Dalai Lama had written personally to the Tongsa Penlop saying that 'negotiations for establishing friendship should begin quickly'. Another letter of 16 July asked the Bhutanese leader to 'request the English privately not to nibble up our country. Please use your influence with both the English and the Tibetans.'[5] Despite these indications of compromise, and coaxing from Retiring Mac, Younghusband was in no mood to negotiate outside Lhasa itself. Like most of his escort he was itching to reach the Forbidden City, and thought discussions on the banks of the Yamdrok Tso would serve only to delay a settlement. His dilemma was solved when the mounted infantry conveniently captured the Tibetan officials' mule train on 20 July; the delegates fled and further negotiations became impossible.

Up and down the passes and round and round the lakes marched the army, shooting teal, catching fish and bayoneting badgers. Younghusband's popularity was high and his spirits had lifted. At the end of July they reached the banks of the River Tsangpo at Chaksam, the last natural defence the Tibetans had left. During the following week, through skilful use of metal ropes, wooden barges and inflatable goat-skin coracles, nearly four thousand soldiers (and their livestock and supplies) crossed the fast-flowing river. The arrival of new plenipotentiaries armed with a letter from the Tsongdu did nothing to check Younghusband's advance, despite further blandishments from Macdonald. He 'wished me to stop and negotiate', wrote Younghusband to Dunlop-Smith. 'Fancy a General saying this, when with a loss of less than 40 killed in action we have killed 2700 Tibetans.'[6]

But as he approached Lhasa, the Commissioner was quietly aware that his problems were just beginning. He had seven weeks before the onset of winter in which to produce a treaty that satisfied not only his own pride, but also the governments of Tibet, China, India and Britain. On leaving Chaksam he had learned that the Dalai Lama and his entourage had plans to flee the capital, which created the further difficulty of finding somebody with whom he could negotiate. Nor were Lord Curzon's letters from home encouraging.

'Govts. in England are very timid and very ignorant,' the profoundly irritated Viceroy told his friend after a meeting with his colleague the Prime Minister. The Foreign Secretary had assured the Tsar's Government, as part of a reciprocal arrangement over Egypt, that there would be no 'permanent interference' in Tibetan affairs. In Curzon's view this was no way to run an empire, particularly at a time when Russia was tied up fighting a war with the Japanese. 'All that HMG as a whole know or care about Tibet', he fulminated to Younghusband in a mutinous mood, 'is that it is a nuisance and an expense.'[7]

Yet these worries must have floated away as Younghusband and O'Connor cantered their ponies along the fertile banks of the Nyi river, passing apricot, peach and cherry trees, swathes of wild delphiniums, marigolds and asters. General Macdonald followed, coughing and spluttering, carried on a litter by a squad of *dhooly* bearers. Before and behind stretched the trail of soldiers, servants, advisers and coolies: Pathan, Parsee, Balti, Dogra, Sikh, Irish, English, Tibetan, Scottish, Sikkimese, Bhutanese, Ladakhi and Gurkha, all with their own strange tales to tell. As they rounded the brow of a steep hill on the first day of August, the riders came face to face with the holy city of Lhasa, sweeping away into the distance below them. Above it loomed the stately glory of the Potala, the Dalai Lama's thousand-roomed winter palace, its golden roof pavilions shining in the sun 'like tongues of fire'.

Frank Younghusband was home at last, looking down through the crisp air at the city he had dreamed of visiting as he bounded over the crest of the Rhotang Pass in 1884, and again as he schemed with Ney Elias in 1889, and again as he kicked his heels in Hunza in 1893. 'Little did we think as we camped together in the valley of Chitral,' wrote George Curzon a few days later, 'that you would be the first Englishman to enter Lhasa since Manning, and that I should send you there.'[8]

Shortly before dawn on the fifteenth day of the sixth month of the Year of the Wood-Dragon (otherwise known as 30 July 1904) His Holiness the Thirteenth Dalai Lama, Thubten Gyatso, holder of the White Lotus and earthly manifestation of Chenrezig, Bodhisattva of Compassion, left his dusty private apartments at the top of the Potala. The Nechung Oracle had gone into trance, and advised him to interrupt a three-year meditative retreat known as the *nyen-chen*.

The Dalai Lama's official hagiography, *A String of Wondrous Gems, a Drop from the Ocean of Liberated Life of the Great Thirteenth, the Incomparably Kind Lord of All Buddhas, He of the Highest Stage, Crown Ornament of Samsara and Nirvana*, is less than revealing about his thoughts at this time. It says the Tibetan leader left the Land of Snows because Buddhists in foreign lands wished to receive teachings, and 'because the demon-masked ones from England came to the border and invaded with an army . . . Not long after they came to Lhasa making a clamour of meaningless noise about meeting His Holiness.'[9] Although the Dalai Lama was inexperienced, he is described by independent sources as being intelligent and politically astute, with a fiery temper. He felt it would be unwise to risk direct dealings with Younghusband, while his advisers feared he might be taken hostage.

As it grew light the twenty-eight-year-old incarnate deity rode north towards the Go La. He was a man of striking appearance, already sporting the distinctive Hercule Poirot moustaches that can be seen in later photographs. His piercing eyes and large pointed ears must have given him at least a passing resemblance to his opponent Colonel Younghusband. Accompanying the Dalai Lama were eight attendants, including his Chikyab Khenpo or Lord Chamberlain, Yutok Jamyang Tenzin (whose brother had tried to negotiate with Younghusband at Nagartse) and the ubiquitous Buryiat monk Agvan Dorzhiev. The fleeing ecclesiastics were riding fast, heading for Mongolia.

Behind them Lhasa lay in turmoil. The Dalai Lama had left his seals of office with a hurriedly appointed Regent, apparently with the intention of repudiating any forced treaty that damaged his country's long-term interests. Orders were given to release Shatra and the other Kalons who had advocated a policy of negotiation. The government, such as it was, tried to formulate a strategy for dealing with the British. Some monk-officials feared they would loot the monasteries and destroy Buddhism. Being an essentially nomadic society, it was natural for many Tibetans to depart the city in the wake of their Precious Protector the Dalai Lama. Aristocrats fled to their estates, traders packed up their wares and headed east, and ordinary people set up camp in the fields on the edge of the city.[10]

When the British reached Lhasa they were unimpressed. Dogs, ravens and pigs scavenged in heaps of stinking refuse and pools of stagnant water. The streets were filthy and almost deserted, those people who did show themselves appearing 'ill bred' or even 'idiotic-looking'. For all the beauty of the Potala and the Norbulingka, much of the Forbidden City was a depressing anti-climax. Most disappointing of all for the hawkish Great Gamers of the Mission was the total absence of any evidence of Russian influence. Younghusband had to accept reluctantly that his detailed theories about Tsarist conspiracy in Tibet were mistaken: there were no Russian arsenals, no lurking Cossacks. Yet as recently as 12 June he had written to Louis Dane: 'We should appreciate the fact that we are now fighting the Russians, not the Tibetans. Latter were easily knocked out on the way to Gyantse. Since Karo La we are dealing with Russia.'[11] The Russian bogey had turned out to be a phantom.

It is clear that Curzon's fears about the 'insinuating Dorjieff' were wide of the mark: there is no evidence that he was a Tsarist agent. Rather he was a roving ambassador for the Dalai Lama who attempted to gain support for Tibet among the higher echelons of Russian society. This is one of the many absurdities and contradictions of the Younghusband Expedition. Lord Curzon sent an army into Tibet on the pretext of discussing border disputes, boundary pillars and yak thefts. But his true worry was that the security of British India was being endangered by the activities of a Russian agent, Dorzhiev. Yet Agvan Dorzhiev was in fact a Tibetan agent seeking Russian support; support which did not prove forthcoming. Ironically, the result of the Expedition was further confusion about

Tibet's status, rather than a new stability in Asia. The most significant consequence was not Younghusband's Treaty of Lhasa, which
was largely disowned by the British Government, but the precipi-
tation of Curzon's own resignation from office.[12]

'On the very day after our arrival,' wrote Francis Younghusband,
'I and all my staff donned our full-dress uniforms, and with an
escort of three hundred men, including some of the Royal Fusiliers
and a sort of band from the Gurkhas, we marched right through
the city of Lhasa making all the noise we could.'[13] The people of
Lhasa were most impressed, Helen was told, clapping and cheering
at the sight of this 'grand show'. Kalon Shatra's son gives a different
interpretation of events in *The Unadulterated Copper of My History*.
He notes that Tibetans clap their hands in order to drive out evil
spirits – a perfect representation of the gulf between the two
cultures:

> When the British Officers marched to the Tsuglakhang
> [Jokhang] and other places, the inhabitants of Lhasa were
> displeased. They shouted and chanted to bring down rain,
> and made clapping gestures to repulse them. In the
> foreigner's custom these are seen as signs of welcome, so
> they took off their hats and said thank you.[14]

Having made a half-hearted attempt to take over the Norbulingka
Palace as his personal quarters, Younghusband and his Mission
installed themselves in the Lhalu family's compound, at the centre
of which sat a 'very large commodious house' on three storeys,
with clean rooms and glass in the windows. It belonged to the
nephew of the Twelfth Dalai Lama, referred to by the British as
'the premier Duke of Tibet'. By tradition the father of each Dalai
Lama (the Yabshi Kung) was ennobled and given substantial property in perpetuity. Lhalu House was soon renamed 'Younghusband
House', while the illustrated papers christened the Barkhor 'Piccadilly Circus' and the Potala 'Windsor Castle'. 'For sheer bulk and
magnificent audacity,' noted Regimental Sergeant-Major Percy

Coath in his diary, 'Lamaism could do no more in architecture than it has done in this huge PALACE-TEMPLE of the GRAND LAMA.'[15]

Mr Coath wrote elsewhere in his diary that the Tibetans had little respect for Chinese authority. Younghusband found this to be a serious problem: the only official who was willing to talk to him was the charming but incompetent Chinese Amban, Yu-t'ai. Although the Amban plied the British with flour and sheep, and even gave Younghusband some Huntley & Palmer biscuits, it was clear that his influence was minimal, arrogance towards Tibetan officials being no substitute for genuine power. 'The Tibetans hate the Chinese,' Younghusband told his far-off wife, 'and the Chinese know nothing of what goes on here and are completely out of touch. Nor do the Tibetans obey a single word they say. If only we were going to keep a Resident here, we could run the whole show.'[16]

The Amban tried to bring pressure to bear on the remains of the Tibetan Government, but in the end it was the Tongsa Penlop of Bhutan who broke the deadlock by persuading the Regent to visit the British Commissioner. 'Afterwards, the Regent summoned the Kashag [Cabinet] and informed its ministers that his meeting with the British had not impaired his well-being in any way. He said Younghusband was a human being like anyone else and was amenable to reason. The Kashag now lost its shyness and, according to custom, sent presents of meat, fruit, and eggs to the British camp.'[17] The Regent, Lamoshar Lobsang Gyaltsen, was an astute, elderly man who soon became the chief negotiator. In *India and Tibet*, Younghusband compares him favourably to the Lama in Kipling's *Kim*. As Ganden Tripa (the Throneholder or Abbot of Ganden Monastery), he held one of the few senior positions in the Tibetan hierarchy that was attained through ability rather than birth.

Soon the Kalons Yutok and Tsarong were also talking to Younghusband, although the Kalon Lama Chamba Tenzin remained hostile to the last. There were long discussions about the various British demands, which included the establishment of trade marts in western Tibet and the payment of a huge indemnity to defray the cost of the invasion. 'The Tsarong Shape said we were accustomed to fish in the ocean,' wrote Younghusband, 'and did not understand that there were not so many fish to be got out of a well as could be caught in the sea.'[18] Yet the negotiations were conducted in a surprisingly friendly atmosphere. Younghusband liked the Ganden Tripa, whom he refers to as the Ti or Tri Rimpoche, the honorific title by which the office-holder is addressed. 'The Tibetans are excellent people – quite polished and polite and genial and well-mannered,' he told James Dunlop-Smith, 'but absolutely impossible on business matters.'[19]

One imperial demand was complied with easily: the release of those most unlikely justifications for the invasion of Tibet, Captain O'Connor's pair of Sikkimese spies. On 16 August, wrote Candler of the *Daily Mail*, '360 miles from the confines of our Indian Empire and beyond the stupendous barrier of snow-clad mountains, the sacred liberty of the British subject was vindicated with a pomp and ceremony well calculated to impress the simple and the wily Tibetans alike.' Blinking in the sharp sunlight, the astonished, nameless men were brought before Colonel Younghusband, who 'sat in state' and told them 'they were free under the British flag once more'. Their imprisonment, he announced to the assembled Tibetan dignitaries with a flourish of humbug, was a most serious offence, and it was largely on their account that his government had decided to advance to Lhasa.

> Then Colonel Younghusband turned with a kindly smile to the prisoners . . . and told them it was by the command of the King Emperor that they were free. The poor fellows bowed their faces to the ground, and when they rose again their countenances were lit up with delight and gratitude.[20]

But two days later the calm of Lhasa was shattered when a Sera monk with 'the chest and arms of a professional prize fighter' set out to avenge the death of his brother, who had been killed at Gyantse. He broke into the British camp and wounded Captains Kelly and 'Cookie' Cook-Young of the Indian Medical Service, before being overpowered by Sikhs wielding picks and shovels. The monk was 'securely bound hand and foot, but he spat at his captors like a wild cat'.[21]

'I also see my way to getting you some fine silks,' Francis Younghusband wrote to his wife the next evening. 'A beastly lama ran amok and slashed at two officers with a sword. So besides having the man hung I demanded a fine of Rs 5000 from the Tibetan Govt and hostages for future good behaviour. The fine I said could be paid in either cash or kind so today they brought me masses of the most beautiful Chinese silk dresses. I am putting them up for auction . . . and will buy some in for you.' Power had made him assertive, a flippant self-confidence replacing his usual earnestness. Every decision was his. 'Retiring Mac' had faded into subordinate insignificance, and been re-nicknamed 'The Chowkidar', the Hindi word for a guard or nightwatchman. When the General tried to exercise some control, Younghusband had him summoned to Lhalu House. 'As soon as he really runs up against me I am quite capable of putting him in his place,' Helen was assured.[22]

While the diplomatic negotiations ground on, and the beastly lama dangled menacingly from his gibbet on the banks of the Nyi Chu, the Indian and British soldiers entertained themselves. It was clear the Tibetan army were no longer a threat. The men arranged wrestling matches and wheelbarrow races, played polo in the lush meadows at Tsesum Thang, or went in search of camp followers. One day there was a race-meeting, with Colonel Younghusband ensconced in a specially constructed Judge's Box wearing his solar topi. The people of Lhasa, who were starting to return cautiously to their homes, watched in astonishment as the mounted infantry's shaggy ponies galloped round an improvised race track. 'Hatter' Bailey's private diary for late August 1904 gives a fair impression of life in occupied Lhasa: 'Thur 18. Went to Drepung [Monastery] with White & Wilton. Lama ran amok. Gymkhana. Fri 19. Hung lama. Football . . . Sat 27. Races. Sun 28. Auction of silks. Football. Out fishing.'[23]

Despite the entertainment, Younghusband knew he was facing a supremely difficult task. Within the next three weeks he had to negotiate a binding diplomatic settlement with the Tibetans. The internal machinations of the Kashag, the Tsongdu and the Ganden Tripa were one thing; the hesitant pondering of Balfour and Brodrick quite another. The British Government simply had no coherent policy on Tibet, never having been particularly keen on his Expedition in the first place. Curzon was still on leave, fighting his own battles with the Cabinet, and the acting Viceroy Lord Ampthill appeared to have no strong views on the subject. Prime Minister Balfour even sank to suggesting that they might blow up the walls of Lhasa, capture a few hostages and come home again if a settlement did not prove forthcoming.

The caution of General Macdonald was a further complication. He told Younghusband that the troops were not equipped to survive the cold of a Lhasa winter, producing Doctor Waddell of the India Medical Service to support his case. The Commissioner was less than convinced, writing to his father, 'I have never felt such contempt for any man as I did for him when he came up whining to me about the cold, and sheltering himself behind an old woman of a doctor.' To his wife, 'The Chowkidar wired to Simla that whether I had finished or not he would go back on Sept 16th. I wired that if he went back I would put myself under Chinese protection until my work was completed.'[24] There are even indications that a coup against the sickly Macdonald was contemplated by officers of the escort. But in the event there was no need, for by 4 September Colonel Younghusband, aided by his indefatigable Irish interpreter, Captain O'Connor, had managed to reach agreement with the remnants of the Tibetan Government.

The Tibetans accepted his terms comparatively easily, aware that they had no cards left to play. Chinese soldiers were harassing the eastern border areas of Nyarong and Lithang, their leader had fled to Mongolia and the Manchus offered no support or protection. With the military might of the British bang in the middle of Lhasa, they simply had no option but to accept Younghusband's demands. According to W. D. Shakabpa, the Tibetan negotiators based their approach on two proverbs: 'If you have two enemies, you should make one of them your friend,' and, 'Poison can sometimes serve as a medicine.'[25] Under the agreement their Government would refrain from making treaties with foreign powers, sanction the opening of trade-marts at Gyantse and Gartok, respect the terms of the 1890 Anglo-Chinese Convention, and pay an indemnity of an astonishing 7.5 million rupees (over half a million pounds sterling).

It was this last stipulation which had caused the greatest argument, the Kashag suggesting that it was the British who should be paying them money to compensate for the inconvenience of being invaded. Younghusband was not amused, but agreed to the Ganden Tripa's request that the indemnity be paid in instalments over seventy-five years. He also included two further provisions that his masters in Simla and London had never demanded: the stationing of an Agent at Gyantse, with rights to visit Lhasa if necessary, and the occupation of the Chumbi valley by the British until the indemnity had expired. The thruster knew he was exceeding his brief by a long, long way, but he counted on his Government's indecision to let him get away with it.

On 7 September 1904 the Lhasa Convention was signed in the Potala Palace, ten-pounder guns trained on its walls in case trouble arose. The Sishi Phuntsog Audience Hall was lit by flickering butter lamps, its beams draped with silk banners and *thangkas*, its walls lined with curious Tibetan monks and rowdy British soldiers. Along the right-hand side of the huge chamber sat the Kashag: Kalon Tsarong, Kalon Yutok and Kalon Serchung, each wearing a long ceremonial earring in the left ear and beautifully embroidered yellow silk robes. The Kalon Lama Chamba Tenzin was wrapped in a plain maroon monk's robe, but carried an elaborate brocaded water holder known as a *chablug*. Beside them sat the stout Nepalese representative, Jit Bahadur, and the leader of Lhasa's small Muslim community, both of whom had mediated between Younghusband and the Tibetans. The Tongsa Penlop came next, having forsaken his usual grey homburg for an elaborate, bejewelled crown, brought specially from Bhutan.

Opposite them were the rows of British officers in their khaki uniforms, armed with box cameras and magnesium flashes. Their ascent to the Potala had not been dignified, nailed boots and protruding spurs slipping uneasily from the smooth stones which led up to the great building. At the head of the hall sat Younghusband in all his finery, cocked hat at the ready, his camp table covered with a large Union Jack marked with the maxim: 'Heaven's Light Our Guide'. Beside him was the Manchu Amban Yu-t'ai, perched on a painted chair. Although he was not signing the treaty, the Amban's involvement had boosted his own position in Tibet. Five days earlier he had deposed the absent Dalai Lama on the orders of the Chinese Emperor, but proclamations to this effect around Lhasa were promptly torn down by the Tibetans, who regarded the Dalai Lama's position as non-negotiable.

Several copies of the treaty had been prepared in English, Tibetan and Chinese, each one nine feet long since the Ganden Tripa insisted he could not affix his seals to disparate pieces of paper. They were carried into the hall on a large silver tray by Mr Mitter of the Indore Residency Office. The ceremony began with the serving of tea and a translated reading of the Convention. It was over an hour before the seals of the Dalai Lama, the Tsongdu and the three great monasteries had been added to the various documents. Then Colonel Francis E. Younghusband, British Commissioner, picked up a long metal pen and signed the treaty, witnessed by the behatted Amban.

At this point, noted Shenkhawa Gyurme Tobgyal, 'one of the British took a photograph with a flash fire, and some of the members cried out in fear, for until that time a camera had not been seen in Tibet'.[26] Order was soon restored, but before departure Younghusband made a short speech, released the Tibetan prisoners of war and gave 1000 rupees to the monks of the Potala. 'It was the first present,' he noted, 'which I had given since my arrival in Lhasa. My motto had been: the "mailed fist" first and the sugar-plums afterwards.'[27] It is not clear whether the monks appreciated their sugar plums; certainly they laughed and shouted when the

British officers tumbled out of the Potala, slithering and sliding inelegantly down the long stone incline towards the town.

When Emmie Younghusband heard news of the treaty, she wrote at once to her brother telling him that, 'every paper was full of you and the splendid way you had carried it through . . . On Sunday the anthem was "Peace" and it seemed so appropriate when you had just brought peace to Tibet.'[28]

'The Tibetan Government', wrote the author of *The Annals of the All-Revealing Mirror*, 'signed the Treaty of Lhasa in the seventh month of the Year of the Wood-Dragon, as helpless as if the sky had hit the earth.'[29]

The sun rose suddenly over McLeod Ganj, bouncing the distant mountains into life. People were strapping packages to the roof of the bus while the driver roared the engine vigorously. I had emerged from my stint in the Library of Tibetan Works and Archives and was now embarking on a wild goose chase across India. During a crackling long-distance telephone call from the village Post Office to Kathmandu, I had been told there were incomparable documents in Calcutta: telegrams from Younghusband to the Viceroy which were too controversial to have been published at the time. Somehow I knew I would do better to return to Britain and make do with the material I already had, but a sort of pointless obstinacy drove me onwards. After all, this might be the missing link, the crucial piece of evidence that made the jigsaw of the Younghusband Expedition complete.

The bus wormed down the hillside, throwing up a haze of dust with every twist and turn. I had spent the previous day with a very old Tibetan man known simply as 'Shengo' or 'Sergeant'. He sat cross-legged on his bed, smiling and murmuring prayers, his arthritic fingers kneading a wooden rosary. It was a refugee's room, home to a thermos, an umbrella, a small trunk, a prayer wheel and a picture of the present Dalai Lama draped with a ceremonial white scarf. The old *shengo* told me what he had heard.

'I remember my mother when I was a young child, telling me that our country was like a plate of meat. Around the plate sat three greedy cats: the British, the Russians and the Chinese, all watching and waiting to pounce, ready to grab the pieces of meat. That's what Tibet was like.'

'What did you hear about the British invasion when you were a child?'

'Some people said the Inji were afraid of us, because we were so accurate with our sling-shots. In Tibet even a child can make a stone whistle through the air. That was why your army went home again so quickly, out of fear.'

'But didn't the British win?' I asked.

'Well, some people say that. But if they did win, why didn't they stay in Tibet? Nobody worries about their invasion any more. There's a saying: "When you have seen a scorpion, you look on the frog as divine." You see, we've seen the Chinese scorpion now.'

The *shengo* was leaning forward, wheezing heavily, clicking his rosary.

'I have respect for the British, even though they abandoned Tibet when the Chinese came. It was they who taught me how to fire a gun. I was trained at Gyantse by the British officer in the 1930s. Yessah, Atten-shun. When the Chinese invaded I was able to join the Chushi Gangdruk, the Resistance. My British training helped me to fight, to kill Chinese soldiers.'

When I came to leave his room he took my hand and said he was both happy and proud to meet a Britisher again. Then he gave a lop-sided salute. I felt embarrassed as I stumbled outside.

Down in Calcutta it was burning, burning hot and crowded. It took a few hours of queuing to get inside the Writers' Building, home to the State Archives of West Bengal. The place had all the bizarre regulations I had come to expect, and more. 'Non-Indians: Rule 7 (b). In no circumstance is it permitted to light a fire in the Research Rooms. No person shall chew paan or take food and drinks . . . Any research worker must support his/her bona fides.'

I started to go through the files, unsure where to begin. Quite soon I found a reference in the 'Home (Confidential) Section 1904': 'This bundle consists of telegrams and political information in connection with Young Husband's Expedition to Tibet.' I filled in a requisition slip and gave it to the Supervisor. 'Loose copies,' she said thoughtfully. 'I think three days minimum.' I tried to remain calm while absent-minded *babus* shuffled files, examined paperweights, shouted into telephones, took tea-breaks and did all they could to do little. For days I sat and read dusty old copies of the

Weekly Digest of Native Newspapers of Bengal, produced laboriously by the British in search of seditious material. The interesting thing about the Indian (as opposed to British Indian) reports on the Younghusband Expedition was how vigilant and critical they were compared to the British press.

Lord Curzon had invaded Tibet for reasons of pride, said *The Bengalee*, because 'he hankered after the Earldom of Lhasa'. His fears about Russian influence had been proved groundless. Younghusband's negotiations were 'simply a solemn farce enacted in order to throw dust in the eyes of the public' while his settlement was nothing more than 'a useless scroll of paper which they have been pleased to term a treaty'. 'If Colonel Younghusband had been a firm, strong-minded and generous statesman,' wrote the *Daily Hitavadi* on 23 August 1904, 'if instead of being blinded by imperialism, he had calmly tried to accomplish his real object, the Mission would not have led to the shedding of so much innocent blood.'

A news-sheet called the *Hindi Bangavasi* praised Germany, America, France, Italy and Japan for raising doubts about the invasion. The *Indian Mirror* carried several reports from a Darjeeling correspondent claiming that the town was flooded with booty, looted from the monasteries of Tibet. It also made a biting attack on the Church of England's support for the Expedition. 'Dr. Weldon [an English Bishop] has been telling the world that the massacre at Tuna [Chumi Shengo] will be the means of lighting up the torches of enlightenment and Christianity in Tibet ... Will Dr. Weldon tell us if it was the torches of enlightenment and Christianity which were used on this occasion for burning the doomed villages?'

Although the British press was not unfailingly complimentary about the invasion, there was little of this kind of criticism except in a handful of left-wing journals. Most newspapers were steadily supportive. For example, *The Times* of London wrote a fairly representative leading article on 10 September, praising the 'patient and unfailing tactfulness with which the British Commissioner has refrained from hurting in the least degree the religious or social susceptibilities of the Tibetans'. Their former correspondent's achievements 'were the fruits of steady suasion, untiring perseverance, and an intimate knowledge of the Oriental character'.

On the third day, to nobody's surprise, the papers failed to appear. 'This may be a sensitive information file,' said the Supervisor. After another day of waiting I talked my way into the Director's office. I was becoming convinced that the whole of the Calcutta administration had been invented by Franz Kafka in collaboration with Thomas Pynchon.

'I'm so sorry,' said the Director. 'This file may relate to frontier matters.'

'It probably does. Frontier matters ninety years ago.'

He spread his hands apologetically. 'The Ministry makes our regulations. I must tell you this file has been . . . officially mislaid.'

On the way back to my hotel I vomited and collapsed. The next morning, my body feeling heavy and my head feeling light, I went to the Asiatic Society in Park Street. They had nearly all Younghusband's books, first editions. I sat at a long table looking at the plates in *Kashmir*, wondering what to do, feeling irritable and exhausted. As I stared into space a gawky, kind-looking man introduced himself.

'Excuse me, sir, but might I ask you a question? Do you believe in the existence of extra-terrestrial beings?'

Oh God, I thought, this is all I need.

'Um, no, not really. What makes you ask?'

'I noticed you were reading the work of Sir Francis Younghusband. I am a great admirer of his *Life in the Stars*.'

So this was where things were going, towards the heavenly realm. Soon Younghusband would be the mystic, not the soldier, the guru, not the imperialist. Here he was, transforming before my eyes. It was his departure from Lhasa which seemed to herald the change, the epiphanic marker from which the second half of his life could be charted.

After the grand signing ceremony in the Potala they drank whisky and champagne and made toasts and played charades and held another race-meeting. General Macdonald gave a speech, saying that whatever else you might think about Colonel Younghusband, nobody could deny his boldness. Clear-the-line telegrams arrived from Brodrick and Ampthill, from Curzon and Kitchener. The King Emperor sent the troops his highest praise and commendation, and Francis Younghusband beamed with pride and exultation. On their last day in Lhasa the Ganden Tripa arrived with a present for the British Commissioner. It was a small, bronze statue of the Buddha. Over the weeks the two men had discussed religion and philosophy, and developed a certain, rather unlikely, rapport. 'When we Buddhists look on this figure we think only of peace,' said the old monk, 'and I want you when you look at it to think kindly of Tibet.' Younghusband took the bronze Buddha. He was deeply touched.

The next morning he rose early, tucked the little statue into his saddle bag and rode off towards the mountains. The unclouded sky was of the clearest Tibetan blue, the distant peaks bathed in a purple haze. When he was quite alone he dismounted from his pony, sat down on a rock and gazed out over the Himalayas. Suddenly he found himself suffused with the most intense, inexplicable, 'untellable joy. The whole world was ablaze with the same ineffable bliss that was burning within me.' It was one of the most significant experiences of his life, he wrote many years later:

> There came upon me what was far more than elation or exhilaration . . . I was beside myself with an intensity of joy, such as even the joy of first love can give only a faint foreshadowing of. And with this indescribable joy came a revelation of the essential goodness of the world. I was convinced past all refutation that men were good at heart, that the evil in them was superficial . . . in short, that men at heart are divine.

Colonel Francis Younghusband was 'boiling over with love for the whole world'.[30]

SEVENTEEN

Fame in Disgrace and Diversion in Kashmir

On a wet December evening, Francis Younghusband steamed into Charing Cross railway station on the whistling Indian Mail. 'The gallant officer's friends crowded around his carriage, and for a few minutes the Colonel was the only calm figure in an excited group,' recorded the reporter from the *Western Daily Press*. 'His well-knit figure, keen eyes, and strong jaw, denoted strength and determination, two characters which he demonstrated so effectively in the recent campaign. He repelled all the efforts of the journalists to extract copy, by a courteous declaration that nothing would induce him "to say anything about himself, Tibet, or the atrocious weather."'[1]

A day or two later Younghusband was chatting with Edward VII, who had taken a keen interest in Tibet throughout the previous year. 'The King himself was most cordial,' he wrote in a private letter. 'He rose from his chair when I came in and he offered me a chair to sit in which I believe is unusual.' The meeting had been arranged by Sir Dighton Probyn, an equerry to the King who acted as the Younghusband family's conduit to Buckingham Palace. Probyn was a white-bearded veteran of the Mutiny (where he had won the Victoria Cross) and one of John Younghusband's oldest friends. Francis had given him an unexpurgated account of events in Tibet, and Probyn 'promptly pumped it all into the King'. When he arrived for his private audience the first thing Edward VII said was: 'I am sorry you have had this little difference with the Govt . . . I approve of all you did.'[2]

Younghusband's problem was that he was receiving reverential praise from every direction – except Whitehall. Letters were arriving in their hundreds from all over the world: a letter from Austria (addressed simply 'Colonel Younghusband, Tibet, Asia') asking for his autograph; another from Mr Dolch, Bone Meal and Fertilizer Merchant, St Louis, USA, with detailed questions about Lhasa; a letter from the King of Chitral; a long poem praising his exploits from Henry Newbolt; letters of congratulation from his erstwhile loves, Nellie and May, from Indian officials requesting a signed photograph, from Harry Cust (of South Africa days) saying his advance to Lhasa was the most interesting thing to happen for two hundred years.[3] However, the Swedish explorer Sven Hedin spoke out strongly against the invasion of Tibet, while writing privately to Younghusband to assure him of continued regard. 'Fancy it is 15 years since we met in Kashgar,' Hedin exclaimed in a letter. He had recently received a card from Petrovski who 'is now in Tashkent old and broken down. I saw him last in Kashgar in 1902 a couple of weeks after his son had shot himself; the old man seemed not to feel his possible sorrow very deeply. He was as you know a very funny fellow.'[4]

From Younghusband's own government there was little but suspicion and hostility. It was felt that he had deliberately disobeyed instructions, in particular over the question of permanent interference in Tibetan affairs. The European powers had been assured in November 1903 that this was not intended, but his terms clearly implied a long-term involvement. The Government's standing was weak, and its ministers had no wish to be accused by the Opposition of pursuing a 'forward' frontier policy. They were especially worried by the possible repercussions of occupying the Chumbi valley.

Shortly before he was due to leave Lhasa, Younghusband had received a telegram asking him to remain and renegotiate the treaty. He declined on grounds of practicality, and rode off into the mountains with the Ganden Tripa's bronze Buddha. As he approached the forests of Sikkim, a head of steam was building up among the politicians. It burst shortly before he got to Darjeeling, in the form of a telegram to Lord Ampthill from the Secretary of State for India, St John Brodrick, which spoke of 'our representative's disobedience to orders'. Once Younghusband reached Simla he was able to read the official correspondence relating to his Mission, stretching back to the summer of 1903. It was a bitter blow. There had been a 'regular set against me', he wrote to his father, which 'saddened me much'. He realized that his assertive conduct and wildly opinionated telegrams had alienated his masters. 'Kitchener was more severe than any one – though he is most cordial and appreciative now . . . The only true man was Ld. Curzon.'[5]

This was part of the problem. In the minds of the Cabinet, Younghusband was so closely associated with Curzon and his policies that he became the inevitable scapegoat. They thought, justifiably enough, that Younghusband was himself partly responsible for turning a small diplomatic mission into a military advance to the heart of Tibet. Added to this were the heady tensions which existed between Curzon and Brodrick. Like many members of the Cabinet, 'the Brodder' was a friend of Curzon from their Eton schooldays. The rift between them over Tibet and other matters was probably more psychological than political in origin, but it introduced what Harold Nicolson called a 'tortuous malignity' into an already complex affair. Curzon's unwillingness to submit to the Government over matters of policy brought both Brodrick and Balfour to a point of exasperation.

Younghusband had left India in an angry mood, the dust of Tibet still fresh on his heels. When his ship, the SS *Mongolia*, docked at Port Said on the way home he was able to meet up with his mentor, who was heading out to begin a second term as Viceroy. The encounter between the two men was intense and emotional. Curzon had no doubts about the treaty, praising it as 'a most striking tribute to your knowledge of Asiatics, infinite patience and undeviating composure.'[6] Younghusband told Dunlop-Smith that Curzon had 'kept pouring out his gratitude to me with such emphasis I was almost overwhelmed', and wrote to Helen:

> He was so nice, and his thanks to me as he said good bye was one of the experiences of my life time. It was quite overpowering. He shook my hand with such force and for so long and said he could not express to me how grateful he was. 'You may through all your career' he said 'rely absolutely upon my unfailing support' . . . and he said he had told both Brodrick and Balfour what he thought of their behaviour in censuring me . . . He is something of a man and we are faster friends than ever.[7]

Then they sailed their separate ways, both convinced they had been betrayed by a spineless administration. As Curzon pointed out, the arbiter of the Government's India policy, St John Brodrick, had never even been to India. Younghusband reached Britain with a determination to state his case.

His sense of grievance at the way he had been treated, probably assisted by his new-found celebrity, made him react in an ill-considered way. He took an aggressive line when summoned to the India Office. Instead of apologizing for those areas where he had exceeded instructions, he sat sullenly justifying each of his actions. His supporters began a concerted campaign against Brodrick. 'He is just one of those pig-headed thunderers who ruin the Empire,' Younghusband assured his father, 'and the sooner they get rid of him from English politics the better.'[8] Curzon, Probyn, Cust, Earl Roberts of Kandahar and Helen's half-brother Douglas Dawson all tried to use their influence in royal and political circles to improve Younghusband's position.[9]

Although Brodrick's behaviour was in many ways unfair – he was a notoriously tactless man – Younghusband's claim of injured innocence was disingenuous. When he agreed the Treaty of Lhasa he knew full well that he was risking official repudiation. On the evening of the magnificent signing ceremony in the Potala, he had written to Helen: 'What I am most anxious about is to hear how Govt. will take the treaty, and I am fully expecting a great wigging for I put in that the indemnity shd. be paid in 75 years and we can by another clause occupy Tibet till the indemnity is paid. The Secy. of State had contemplated only 3 years and I expect will be horrified.'[10] Brodrick was indeed horrified, but Younghusband lacked the political nous to beat a tactical retreat. He believed he had risked his life for his country, only to be thrown over by a pig-headed thunderer with no comprehension of Indian or imperial interests.

Inevitably, the campaign backfired. Sir Arthur Godley, the Permanent Under-Secretary at the India Office, told Ampthill that several Cabinet ministers were out for Younghusband's blood. 'It is unlucky that he and his wife apparently belong to the race of wire-pullers: this may perhaps be useful to him in the long run, but the immediate effect of it is to create a strong reaction against him in the minds of those who are not accessible to his influences, but are aware of his (and her) tortuous proceedings.'[11]

The immediate area of dispute was not the treaty, but that favourite British obsession, the question of Honours. Streams of letters flew between Downing Street, the India Office and Buckingham Palace, arguing over the relative merits of the KCSI, KCIE and KCB. 'Papa has been overwhelmed with congratulation on all sides,' Emmie had written to her brother in September. 'Mr Townshend thinks they can give you nothing less than a baronetcy.'[12] But her 'dearest Frank' had to make do with becoming a Knight Commander of the Indian Empire, an honour said to be reserved for 'Indian clerks'. To Helen's fury, the Chowkidar Macdonald was given the same award. She 'burst into tears and had a severe heart attack' at the news, being 'thrown into profound melancholy'.[13] Still, it was a knighthood, and from 19 December 1904 the names of Sir Francis and Lady Younghusband could grace the doors of Edwardian society.

On the diplomatic front, the British Government set out to undo the concessions which their representative had so laboriously gained. With Captain O'Connor's assistance the Lhasa Convention was adjusted, the Chinese making skilful efforts to gain control of the negotiations by having them moved to Peking. The article appended to the treaty which allowed British access to Lhasa was torn up, and Younghusband's hard won indemnity reduced by two-thirds to a more manageable 2.5 million rupees. It was to be paid over three years, and the Chumbi valley was to be vacated by 1908. Had Younghusband's original terms been left intact, British soldiers might have been lurking in Tibetan territory until 1979, the year of Margaret Thatcher's ascension to power.

All that remained of the Treaty after the Government's renegotiation was a clarification of existing agreements about the Sikkimese frontier, some vague assurances on tariffs and the onward transmission of letters, and a declaration that foreign powers would not be permitted to exercise influence in Tibet. In the final version, agreed in 1906 when a Liberal Government had come to power, British India was classified as a foreign power but China was not. The net result was that Chinese suzerainty over Tibet was strengthened, while Britain's only substantive gain from the invasion of Tibet and 3000 deaths (95 per cent of them Tibetan) was the right to keep a pair of trade agents and a telegraph wire inside its borders. As Valentine Chirol of *The Times* wrote in a private letter in the same year: 'The end of it all will be that China will have climbed back into Lhasa on Younghusband's shoulders!'[14] He was to be proved right.

A year later in 1907, the status of Tibet was clarified in the Anglo-Russian Convention. Following the crushing defeat of the Tsar's army and navy in the Russo-Japanese war, and the consequent loss of territory in the Far East, Britain and Russia decided to settle their differences in Central Asia. The cold warriors of both sides were appalled by the prospect, but problems in Europe made the governments keen to resolve their century-old clash. Without consulting the rulers of the relevant countries, they carved up the region and brought the Great Game to an end, each side being given defined spheres of influence. They agreed to keep out of Tibet, and only to deal with the Tibetans through Peking. The Lhasa Government was not consulted, with the result that it was not inclined to respect the treaty. China had now realized how vulnerable its western border was, and Tibet's chances of future independence were greatly reduced.

As the European War approached, the Younghusband Expedition

came to look like the last great adventure of the Victorian age. In its scope and execution, it was closer to the forays of Sir Charles Napier than the consolidation of Lord Minto. It had a sort of random, epic grandeur, which belied its historical insignificance, what with the hardship, the cavalry, the grainy photographs, the plumed hats, the camaraderie, the plant hunters and the sixty-seven shirts. The trail of misconceptions and misunderstandings between civil and military, hawks and doves, Simla and Whitehall, British and Tibetans, and the Mission's ultimate failure to achieve anything of lasting substance, embodies the British Empire at its overstretched zenith, a handful of high-collared men in London trying forlornly to square the logic of imperialism with the needs of the British elector. As for the eponymous hero of the Younghusband Expedition, he went on exploring, seeking new dimensions, his name forever linked with the land called Tibet.

The other players in this bizarre drama were beginning their own adventures.

After fleeing Lhasa, His Holiness the Dalai Lama and his ecclesiastical entourage galloped and galloped towards Mongolia. After four exhausting months they found themselves in Urga, now known as Ulan Bator. He remained there for over a year, giving teachings to Mongolians and, according to Dorzhiev's autobiography, answering questions on Buddhist scripture with such skill that he 'was praised with immeasurable admiration and respect as an omniscient being'. Before returning home he made a detour to Kumbum monastery in eastern Tibet and then to Peking, where he met the young Chinese Emperor but refused, like Lord Macartney, to perform the *kowtow*. When he finally made it to Lhasa in 1909 he began to reorganize his government, but within a couple of months the Chinese invaded. The unfortunate lama had to flee again, heading west across the Himalayas to India, in a curious precursor of his reincarnation's flight in 1959. He remained there for two years until the Chinese were driven out by the Tibetans. From then until his death in 1933, Tibet enjoyed a period of comparative stability, establishing good relations with the British after such an inauspicious start.

The members of the Kashag who had dealt with Younghusband were supplanted by the original Kalons who had been sacked in 1903 for advocating a policy of negotiation. Yutok escaped with the Dalai Lama to India, but died soon afterwards. Tsarong remained in Lhasa and was assassinated in 1912, suspected of being in league with the Chinese. His daughter Rinchen Dolma Taring (who is still alive at the time of writing) is the author of *Daughter of Tibet*, the first book to be written by a Tibetan in a European language. As for the Chinese Amban Yu-t'ai, he was later impeached by his government, charged with cowardice, embezzlement and corruption.

That sagacious old monk the Ganden Tripa continued as Regent until the Dalai Lama returned, making the best of an extremely difficult job. Before he died he said that his meeting with the British had taught him the importance of contact with other countries. It was his intention to be reborn not as a Tibetan, but in a country which would help Tibet. When the British Political Officer Sir Charles Bell visited Tibet in the 1920s, people noticed he spoke good Tibetan and had a sympathetic air. Some called him Lonchen (Great Minister) Bell, and said he must be the reincarnation of the Precious One, the late Throneholder of Ganden himself, conveyor of a bronze Buddha to Colonel Younghusband.

What the average Tibetan felt in the aftermath of the invasion is hard to assess. Probably there was a degree of puzzlement as to why an occupying army had gone home with so few gains. According to Shenkhawa's *The Pure Unadulterated Copper of My History*, the Chinese put about a rumour that the British had fled Lhasa in fear, worried that the Chinese would attack them with a huge army. One interesting footnote on the Tibetan perception of the British hangs in The Hermitage in St Petersburg. It is an eighteenth century *thangka*, a Tibetan religious painting, depicting Yama the Lord of Death. In its bottom right-hand corner there is a later addition, showing two figures being dragged into the Hell Realm by a blue demon. On closer inspection they can be seen to be a pair of sahibs, wearing solar topees and spectacles, smoking fat cigars. One of them looks a little like Colonel Younghusband.

As for the mysterious Buryiat monk who had inadvertently helped to spark the invasion, he went on with his covert diplomacy, trying to establish ties between Tibet and Russia. He had some success, the Tsar agreeing in 1909 to the Dalai Lama's request that a Buddhist temple be built in St Petersburg. After the Russian

Revolution, Dorzhiev was sentenced to death, but reprieved following intervention by prominent Petersburg Orientalists. However, his new temple was plundered, and his personal archive of unique secret documents traded for use as cigarette papers. After an accommodation with the Communists in the 1920s, he fell victim to Stalin's purges and was charged with treason, being accused of spying for both the Mongolians and the Japanese. Khambo Agvan Dorzhiev died in police custody in 1938 aged eighty-five, after a life of incomparable variety.

One character who did well out of the Younghusband Expedition was that tough, sharp Bhutanese go-between, the Tongsa Penlop, Ugyen Wangchuk. If unswerving devotion to national self-interest is the hallmark of the good diplomat, he can scarcely be faulted. He exploited the Tibetans for his own benefit, allowing his entourage to loot their way to Lhasa in a fashion which astounded even the British. For his pains he was given a healthy reward. By 1907 he was the unchallenged ruler of his country, a Knight Commander of the Indian Empire and the proud possessor of an annual subsidy of 100,000 rupees. His position became hereditary; his great-grandson is the present King of Bhutan.

On the British side, things were a little less colourful. General Macdonald never recovered his health, and retired into well-deserved obscurity. O'Connor rode off to Shigatse, accompanied by Vernon Magniac, to woo the Panchen Lama. He had some success, and even persuaded the Incarnation to come to Calcutta and meet the Prince of Wales. Bailey carried the Treaty of Lhasa back to India in a specially constructed metal box, and was later appointed Trade Agent at Gyantse on Younghusband's recommendation. But many of the officers who had careered so freely around the Himalayas in 1904 were to face a more equal enemy a decade later in the trenches of Belgium and France. This was also the fate of a handful of Tibetans (including Bailey's camp servant) who enlisted in the Indian army, and died fighting for the British Empire in Mesopotamia in 1916.[15]

Helen Younghusband proved to be an unsung victim of her husband's Mission. Heaps of Chinese and Tibetan silks did not bring her happiness. She took it upon herself to avenge the injustice wrought by what she saw as a Government conspiracy, and sent heady, indignant letters to anybody she thought might intervene. Many years later she was still pursuing the case, when Francis had all but forgotten about it, regarding it as water under the bridge. In the India Office Library there are several boxes of Helen's intricate, scarcely legible jottings on the subject made in the 1920s, many of which make only intermittent sense.

St John Brodrick was the particular focus of her enmity. When the official papers relating to Tibet (the 'Blue Books') were published, Brodrick had sent a confidential letter to London's newspaper editors, denigrating Younghusband's pursuit of an 'adventurous policy' in Tibet. Several of them objected to this behaviour, and one told Younghusband the contents of the Minister's insinuating letter. Helen's own copy of the Blue Book is riddled with pencil notes, and has a typed notice affixed firmly to the front: 'This is "cooked" to an extent wh. I am assured by those who know is quite unusual . . . The arrow over-shot the mark; the Editors warned the Commissioner's friends and well-wishers, by whom this chicanery was divulged.'[16]

Sir Francis Younghusband, meanwhile, is exploring different avenues. During his first months back in England in 1905 there are countless social invitations, even from people who are opposing him politically. According to the *Society Pictorial*, the Younghusbands 'are being much fêted in spite of the view taken of Sir Frank's services by the Government'.[17] They spend glamorous weekends with the Duke and Duchess of Devonshire, Lord Lansdowne, Princess Christian of Denmark and the Balfours. But although Helen finds these events unbearably enticing, Francis feels a little oppressed, stultified even, by the brilliance of the Edwardian social whirl. He escapes alone to the Welsh Revival, attending prayer meetings and singing hymns. 'Men prayed aloud with all self-consciousness completely swept aside,' he wrote. 'They poured out their whole souls in utter disregard of other men's existence.'[18]

When he speaks of his adventures at the Royal Geographical Society that winter the crowds stretch into the street. His talk proves so popular that a repeat has to be arranged a fortnight later. 'The monsoon was just bursting,' he begins, 'the rain coming down in cataracts . . .' In front of him are rows of faces, his family, the geographers, the stalwarts. He steps back to that day in Darjeeling when his destiny came together. 'Few knew of the enterprise upon which I was embarking, but a little knot of strangers who had assembled in the porch of the hotel had got an inkling, and shouted "Good Luck" as I rode off, covered with waterproofs, into the mist . . .'[19] And he tells them his story.

Although there are weeks when Francis and Helen and young Eileen live quietly together in Gilbert Street in Mayfair, he is still in a restless mood. In April he spends a week in Edinburgh staying with 'Hatter' Bailey's parents, giving lectures on Tibet and receiving an Honorary Doctorate from the university. When it is awarded, he tells Helen, he gets more cheering than any of the other recipients, more 'even than Conan Doyle'.[20] Two months later there is another degree to collect, this time from Bristol University, followed by a dinner at his old school. The boys ask him what it was like in Tibet, and in his guest-of-honour speech he pulls out all the stops, praising 'that trait so characteristic of Clifton . . . of playing the game'.[21]

Then he is off again, to be made an Honorary Doctor of Science at Cambridge. He gives that year's Rede Lecture, choosing 'Our True Relationship with India' as his title. There are hints at spiritual union, and frequent exhortations towards healthy comradeship, but much of the lecture is taken up with an apologia for his conduct in Tibet: 'In the development of the human race the use of force and the caning of schoolboys seems inevitable.'[22] More awards, banquets and lectures follow; to his delight he is made an honorary member of the Alpine Club. But the crowds and the lionizing exhaust him. After a brief visit to Bognor Regis with Helen, Emmie and his old father, Francis escapes to the green pastures of Ireland, where he wanders the countryside, reading, looking, making notes, watching birds and plants, pondering his experiences, contemplating his new-found status.

Out in India, George Curzon was having a difficult time. He worked harder than ever, long into the night, trying to gain control of the decisions which had been made in his absence. His wife was still unwell, his back caused him excruciating pain and his three hundred million subjects were restive. As for his colleagues and officials, they were not always as co-operative as he would have liked. If only they could be a little more, well, a little more like Younghusband, with his solid admiration and his belief in the imperial vision. Curzon suggested that his friend should return to India: 'There is nothing that I think worthy of your power,' he wrote feelingly in July. 'I should like them to give you the Residency in Kashmir. It is in my view one of the nicest billets in India for it combines a frontier charge . . . with administrative work of the most important kind.'²³

Younghusband was tempted by the prospect, although his immediate concern was with Lord Curzon's own position. A power struggle was taking place with General Kitchener over the administration of the Indian army. Curzon's case was a good one – the Commander-in-Chief would be given remarkable leeway under new proposals – but the Viceroy's reputation for intransigence and arrogance inclined the British Government against him. In August 1905 he offered his resignation, and A. J. Balfour accepted it. 'I have been miserable all this year seeing how things have been going against you,' wrote Younghusband in desolation. In his view, future generations would regard 'the driving of you from India as one of the greatest crimes England has inflicted on India'. He backed up this unlikely prognosis with a paean to the most superior person:

> I know that through all my life I shall regard it as my greatest honour that I was privileged to serve under your orders in one really great enterprise. The confidence you placed in me at its commencement and all through its execution, and the gratitude you showed me at its conclusion . . . have left an impression on me which will never fade.

'I have found in the letter from you – one of my ablest and most trusted lieutenants for so long – the greatest encouragement,' wrote Curzon in response.²⁴

He trailed back to England, indignant at the way he had been treated. When his boat docked beneath the white cliffs of Dover none of the expected friends and colleagues were waiting to greet the returning Viceroy in the traditional fashion. Balfour, Brodrick, Elcho, Salisbury and Lansdowne were all otherwise engaged; nor were they waiting at Charing Cross the following day. But Lord Curzon's trusted lieutenant was there, ready to lick his wounds and stroke his ruffled feathers. 'I met him at Dover on his return,' wrote the faithful Frank Younghusband, 'and spent that night with him at the Lord Warden Hotel.'²⁵ Within a year Curzon's wife had died.

Although he had initial doubts about working under the new Viceroy, Lord Minto, Younghusband took up the offer to become British Resident in Kashmir. It was too good an opportunity to miss, a posting to India's most beautiful state with its mountains and water gardens. As he sailed to India in March 1906, there was still strong opposition to the appointment from within the

administration. Why should a political officer who had been cen-
sured by the Government be given one of the most coveted positions in the civil hierarchy? 'Col. Y. is a Political Agent of 3rd class,'
an internal memorandum pointed out, '& wd. go over the heads
of 18 senior Political Agents & 10 Residents 2nd class.'[26] But the
appointment was confirmed. The reasons for this are unclear: perhaps the authorities wanted to give Younghusband a reward for
being the scapegoat of the Tibet Mission, or thought it wise not to
alienate a man who was perceived by many as a national hero.

Kashmir was India's largest Native State, with around 80,000
square miles of territory extending from Jammu to Gilgit. Since
1846 it had been ruled by a British-imposed Hindu dynasty,
although 90 per cent of its three million subjects were Muslim. It
often proved more effective for the Maharajah (through the Council
of State) to employ British officials, which gave the Resident substantial indirect power on top of his statutory duties. Younghusband
was responsible for the construction of roads, the conservation of
forests, the administration of justice and the collection of land rev-
enues, but what interested him most was the protection of the
frontier. This involved liaising with the Gilgit Agency and receiving
intelligence reports from as far away as Sinkiang. His Great Gaming
companion George Macartney was still ensconced in Kashgar: any
information he sent down to Simla was examined by the Kashmir
Resident.

Younghusband was also required to keep a sharp but unofficial
eye on the Maharajah of Kashmir, and ensure he was supporting
the British line faithfully. His Highness Major-General Maharajah
Sir Pratap Singh was a story-book Indian prince, vacillating and
oppressive, bedecked in silk pyjamas, pearls and a diamond-
encrusted turban. At a welcoming banquet in June 1906, Younghusband amused him by apologizing for the unceremonious way
he had arrived in Baltistan nineteen years before: 'I first entered H
H's dominion neither in a tonga, nor on horseback, nor even on
foot, but was let down into Kashmir territory from the top of the
Mustagh Pass at the end of a rope formed of turbans and kammer
bands.'[27]

Before he was fully installed in his new position in Srinagar, the
capital of the Kashmir valley, Younghusband received several visits
in rapid succession. The first was from the Swedish explorer Sven
Hedin, whom he had last seen in Kashgar in 1890 on the day of
the plum-pudding explosion. Hedin was on his way to southern
Tibet to begin a long process of exploration, accompanied (on

Younghusband's recommendation) by the legendary caravan man Mahmood Isa. As Hedin was preparing to leave Kashmir, the British Government tried to stop him from going to Tibet. But with Young-husband's tacit connivance a crucial telegram was delayed, and he dodged his way up to Ladakh, pretending he was heading for Chinese Turkestan. 'Sven Hedin put his arms round my neck when he left,' Younghusband wrote to Helen, 'and if I had given him the slightest encouragement wd. have embraced me!'[28] A couple of years later came the sad news came that Mahmood Isa, that most resourceful of travellers, had died of a stroke on the banks of the Tsangpo river.

Horatio Herbert Kitchener was a less demonstrative guest, prefer-ring to pass the time killing bears and ibex. The Commander-in-Chief was 'a great big man', Younghusband told his young daughter. 'He has 220,000 soldiers and a great red face and big moustache.'[29] Despite his host's close links with Curzon, Kitchener treated him affably. After the visit his Military Secretary, the Old Cliftonian William Birdwood, wrote that 'the Chief told me he had enjoyed his time with you at Srinagar better than he had in any house . . . in India'.[30] Although Younghusband felt no great liking for Kitchener as a person, he admired his gruff, domineering style of leadership. In *The Light of Experience* he defends him against charges of coldness, providing an unwitting indication of Kit-chener's homosexuality in the process:

> His personal staff he treated as his own sons. He had such affection for his A.D.C.'s that when one had to leave he was for days after like a bear with a sore head. One of them, Fitzgerald, he managed to keep with him long after he left India. The two went down together in the *Hampshire* . . .[31]

Younghusband's rather unfortunate wording refers to the ship in which Kitchener met his doom during the First World War.

Close on the General's heels came the Mintos. For nearly a month the Residency staff had to provide picnics and ceremonial dinners, while Younghusband juggled the awkward protocol of entertaining the Viceroy of India on land which was technically under the con-trol of the Maharajah of Kashmir. Lord Minto toured the state with a city of tents, reviewing guards of honour and opening an experimental farm, but much of his time was spent relaxing. In the customary fashion he fished and shot birds. (The eggs of English brown trout had been brought over to colonize Kashmir's rivers some years earlier.) Although Younghusband never enjoyed shooting game, he accepted the practice as part of his social inheritance, writing proudly in Kashmir that Lord Minto's party had shot over 1500 ducks in one day.

The Viceroy and his entourage returned to Calcutta in late November, and early in 1907 Helen and Eileen arrived in Srinagar. They were accompanied by a nanny called Miss Higham, who had been nicknamed Shortie on account of her diminutive stature – she was a good six inches shorter than Sir Francis Younghusband. Shortie was to remain with the family for many years, acting as a surrogate mother to Eileen, maternal affection not being one of Helen's strong points. Despite the formality which existed between mother, father and daughter, the three years in Kashmir were in many respects their happiest together as a family. Helen would look back on them as a golden age. She revelled in her status as Lady Resident Sahib, opening gymkhanas and awarding the prizes at the tennis tournament. The role of stately society hostess was one of the few in life that she felt equipped to play.

It was a time of lavishness for the British in India, a time of ease after the formality of Victoria's reign. They arrived in idyllic Kashmir in their thousands every summer, escaping from the heat for a month's poodle-faking in the hills. Political Officers up from Rajputana rented villas above the Bund and strode the golf links. Fresh chaperoned girls wandered the Mughal Gardens with feverish young subalterns. Gangs of box-wallahs concocted shooting expeditions to Gulmarg (provisioning at Cox and Co.), the richer ones even hiring a motor car for the first stage of the journey. And who could fail to be impressed, sipping gin-and-lime on the banks of Dal lake, by the sight of the Resident's barge slipping past, powered by thirty-six scarlet-clad oarsmen with heart-shaped paddles, the leader of the '04 Tibet Show standing pensively on the upper deck?

An invitation to the Residency was a coveted prize. Every June, Lady Younghusband gave a 'Moonlight at Home' in her exquisite garden amidst the climbing roses, gladioli, lilies, apricots and scarlet salvias. Her party on 23 June 1907 was the Success of the Season, according to the *Civil and Military Gazette*. 'The trees were all illuminated with countless Chinese lantern and electric light, and the effect was truly fairylike . . . Captain Giles treated us to a display on the banjo and was uproariously encored.' There were singers, actors, musicians and a soothsayer from 'the underground caves of Wild Tibet'. Imperial society danced all night, and things were only marred when 'a young lady habited proper in full evening dress

tripped off the edge of her houseboat into the rushing river
Jhelum.'³² The Resident did not feel entirely at home in the social
whirl, although he enjoyed entertaining visitors such as the Duke
of the Abruzzi, who was lucky enough to be heading north to
explore the Karakoram.

It was at this time that Younghusband learned of his father's death.
He had died in Haslemere in Surrey on 20 July 1907 after years of
tender devotion from Emmie, assisted by Ethel during the final
months. As a lonely spinster in her late forties, Emmie was left
with no support for the future. So to Helen's irritation she came
out to India to join her darling brother Frank, and accompanied him
on an official trip to Calcutta and Jammu. 'You have not written to
me for ever so long,' Francis told his wife, 'because you are stuffy
at Emmie being here. But you have absolutely nothing to be stuffy
about.'³³ Emmie departed the following month in an uncertain
mood.

Francis was thrown by these events. His father's knowledge and
experience had provided a sheet anchor, a standard against which
achievements could be measured. During the Tibet Expedition he
had been an invaluable long-distance confidant. But Francis also
felt a certain liberation, knowing that he could now pursue the
spiritual path without facing his father's quiet disapproval.
Although his job was challenging, there were days when his mind
wandered. 'I must not give myself up too completely to God and
Nature,' he wrote one morning in Gulmarg after a 'very earnest
communion with God . . . I wondered whether I was wise letting
myself go so much.'³⁴ He joined the Society for Psychical Research
and made extensive notes on telepathy, experimenting with his
own ability to pick up spiritual vibrations. 'The longing at the
bottom of my heart', he recorded in January 1908, 'is to help mankind with a new religious impulse.'³⁵

Alongside his spiritual search ran a preoccupation with self-
improvement, an Edwardian fad which has recently enjoyed something of a revival. 'Breathe deeply for 5 mins 3 times daily,' he told
himself. 'Learn to enjoy life. Hearty hand shake. Keep up an open,

straight confident alert bearing.'[36] 'My chief defects', he wrote in December 1908, 'I take to be shyness, timidity, touchiness, sensitivity, peevishness, too little warmth of heart and true sincerity, fear of giving myself away, letting myself go, meagre capacity for enjoyment.' To remedy these faults he proposed to: 'Mix with manly men to learn virility and power. Mix with womanly women to learn tenderness and sympathy. Seek especially full blooded men and women.' On another occasion he wrote a long list of 'men I have got to imitate in various ways'. With the exception of three relations, everybody on the list was either a peer of the realm or a member of the royal family.[37]

His particular concern was the passivity he witnessed among Christians. He wanted to find 'robust spiritual people' who shared his own curious brand of vigorous, masculine mysticism. Interestingly, Younghusband's religious ambitions during this period were closely allied to early-twentieth-century ideas about eugenics, colonialism and racial supremacy. He merged social and philosophical conceptions which would normally be seen as contradictory. His ambition at this time was nothing less than the creation of a religion (drawing from Islam and Christianity) based on his own vision of Empire.

A draft letter to Henry Newbolt written around 1908 explains his 'important Mission':

> For years past I have felt there is something wrong with our present religion . . . Christianity itself is puny and childish – not great enough for strong healthy full blooded Northern races. All that meekness and humility and peace and submission is only fit for a subject race such as it sprang from . . . We have to realise we are in the veriest infancy of our race and that the greatest men are to *come*.[38]

This vision of a new religion can be contrasted with the conventional idea of 'Eastern' spirituality embodied in the Theosophical movement, with its notions of ancient wisdom and universal brotherhood. Although Younghusband had expressed the greatest admiration for the Theosophical campaigner Annie Besant when he met her at Indore in 1903, within five years his view had altered radically. Now he believed that her religious ideas were doing grave harm by encouraging Indian nationalism, and even suggested to Dunlop-Smith, who had become Lord Minto's Private Secretary, that the Government of India should watch her closely.

Besant's emphasis on 'Hindu thought' and her support for Indian self-government was part of a growing opposition to British rule, which was reinforced by the 50th anniversary of the Mutiny in 1907. There was a new politicization in Indian society. Elements within the Government, most notably the Secretary of State for India Lord Morley, realized that pragmatic changes needed to be made swiftly if India was to remain under control. To officials such as Younghusband, such an attitude was tantamount to treason, since it struck at the heart of the doctrine of imperialism. Curzon led the charge against the Morley–Minto reforms in the House of Lords. 'We are running a very fair chance of spoiling the Natives,' Younghusband wrote to him in April 1908. 'I don't think they are yet sufficiently advanced & altered to be ready for soft easy generous treatment.' In his analysis, 'the root of the whole evil' was that Morley believed 'we have no business in India at all'.[39]

The limitation in Curzon and Younghusband's perception sprung from the world in which they moved. They had no balanced contact with Indians, so the desire for self-rule could be dismissed as a misguided aspiration. Those Indians whom they met tended to support, officially at least, their own perception of British rule. The Maharajah of Kashmir, for instance, suggested to Younghusband that the courts in Calcutta were too lenient towards sedition. In the Prince's view, some prominent Bengali anarchists should be strung up. 'His Highness said . . . that hanging was the proper punishment for them,' Younghusband reported to the Foreign Department. 'He would hang them in public.'

Lord Minto included this report in a bundle that he sent back to the Secretary of State in London. His comments on it are indicative of the official attitude towards the Kashmir Resident: 'I cannot say I value highly the opinions of his Maharajah, and quite between ourselves Younghusband with his curiously reserved manner, is underneath it all, nervous and inclined to exaggeration.'[40] Ever since the Tibet Mission – some memories may even have stretched back to Bozai Gumbaz – there had been doubts about Younghusband's judgment, and his advice on matters of policy was often dismissed. To his great irritation, he was not even consulted by the Government of India about the succession to the Kashmir throne. It was decided unilaterally that the childless Maharajah would be succeeded by his nephew, Hari Singh.

One consolation was the reverence in which Younghusband was held by the Kashmiri ruling family. When the Maharajah's brother died of what the newspapers called an 'internal complaint', the Resident became closely involved in the murky world of royal politics. 'The real cause was a syphilitic affliction of the brain,' Young-husband told Curzon in one of his long letters, 'though this we do not mention. Before he died he handed over his son to my guardianship saying that his wife was an illiterate fool so he could not leave him in her charge and the Maharaja was so weak and surrounded by vultures he could not trust the boy to him. He begged me to keep him from evil influences and loyal to the British and said he wished me to remain guardian even after I had left Kashmir.'[41]

Younghusband managed to prevent Hari Singh from being poisoned – a common fate of heirs to a princely throne – but his efforts to have the boy's character built by Mr Tyndale-Biscoe, a Baden-Powell disciple and prominent local headmaster, were unsuccessful. In her old age, Eileen Younghusband remembered Hari Singh as a 'most tiresome boy' who had persecuted her pet fox-terrier. In the 1920s the gullible prince became the victim of a blackmail plot which contained all the ingredients of a good scandal: a crooked army officer, a fancy-dress ball, a lewd Cockney seductress, an aeroplane with silver chasing, shaved pubic hair, a Paris hotel and a complex court case. When independence was gained in 1947 the unfortunate Maharajah decided his land should accede to India rather than Pakistan; thereby incurring the histori-cal odium of many Kashmiris.

When the job he had been coveting as Commissioner of the Frontier Province went to a rival in July 1908, Younghusband real-ized that his time was up. 'I have decided to leave India and to go into Parliament,' he wrote in his notebook a few months later.[42] As a 'military political' there were simply no new openings available to him after the Kashmir Residency. Although his social relations with Lord and Lady Minto were perfectly friendly, it was clear that the Viceroy had no intention of seeing him promoted. It seems probable that Minto knew Younghusband was feeding Curzon with ammunition to be used in House of Lords debates, and reacted accordingly. 'Really the wire pulling is terrible,' wrote Morley to Minto early in 1909. 'The "fossils" beat anything I ever imagined possible.'[43]

Against his wife's advice, Sir Francis Younghusband left govern-ment service to pursue his incongruous ambitions. He was forty-six years old and healthy, still climbing mountains whenever he got the chance, his hair a little thin but his moustache still fluffy. Whether he would become a politician, a writer or a freelance imperial mystic was as yet uncertain. His underlying intentions were unchanged. 'I wish to enrich the blood of mankind,' he wrote, 'to put good heart into men: and to imbue them with the impulse of a truer, greater, nobler, more virile religion drawn from life itself.'[44] In December 1909 he sailed out of Bombay on the SS *City of Glasgow*, after a deluge of farewell dinners in Kashmir. It would be nearly thirty years before he returned to Asia.

A couple of days before his boat reached England, Younghusband picked up his pen and made an entry in his private diary, noting that he was now beginning 'the new and greatest phase' of his life.[45]

I left India too, still reeling from the illness I had acquired in Calcutta. The State of Jammu and Kashmir was exploding in anger, Kashmiri separatists detonating bombs and Indian paramilitaries responding violently. Each day the papers carried reports filled with unconvincing detail. '22 suspected militants were killed yesterday in a shoot-out in Srinagar Old Town. There were no police casualties.' This was one of the most depressing legacies of British rule – the inevitable running conflict which followed the drawing of such hurried, uncertain boundaries. India and Pakistan both want Kashmir, while Kashmir is not sure if it wants to belong to either of them; and even China claims a bit of Maharajah Hari Singh's old territory.

When I had visited Kashmir a couple of years before, the conflict was only simmering. The valley was a pastoral idyll, packed with fellow tourists but as beautiful as it must have been a century ago. There was certainly an underlying discontent, dark mutterings against Indian rule, but it was easy to forget the tension when you lay on a carpet of spring flowers above Gulmarg. As for Srinagar, it was dusty and crowded, home to houseboats with ancient Monarch-of-the-Glen prints dangling from their wooden walls, even if the pukka sahibs had made way for their year-offing grandchildren who relaxed on Dal lake in the sun discussing the putative death of Tony Wheeler. I found Sir Francis and Lady Younghusband's stately Residency still in place, transformed into a government 'handicraft centre' to bring in foreign currency.

'To think such a thing should happen,' an old Kashmiri had said. 'My father worked here as a cook: cook-cooking in the British time.' He had shaken his hennaed beard in disbelief. 'Now look at it! The Residency! A handicraft centre! To think they should do such a thing.'

I did not want to go back to Kashmir, did not want to destroy a fragile memory with the sight of guns and roadblocks. I trailed Younghusband's footsteps away from the Himalayas to the shores of Kent, exhausted by the cold of the mountains, the heat of the streets, the languor of the bureaucracy and the sheer scope of his travels. Things would become calmer now, if less exhilarating than the path across the Rhotang Pass and the Gobi Desert. But I felt a new thrill at the immediacy of the chase. I knew people who were alive in 1909 when Francis Younghusband sailed away from Bombay: there might even be some who remembered him at the end of his life, a sprightly old man who preached a mystical vision. As I tracked him through space and time, I drew away from history and closer to ourselves, almost believing I might catch up and grab hold of him, shaking out answers to unsolved riddles.

PART THREE

EIGHTEEN

Playing Politics, Brushing Death, Preaching Atheism

Within hours of stepping off the boat in January 1910, Young-husband had plunged into the General Election campaign. 'My Political Programme,' ran the entry in his diary: 'I wd. oppose abstract socialism as likely to emasculate the individual . . . I wd. deal with unemployment by facilitating means for the worthy to go to the Colonies and the wastrels to be put under control.'[1] He stumped the country for the Conservatives, jumping in and out of trains, speaking on successive days at Halifax, Norwich, Ramsgate, Gloucester and Warrington before ending up at Hackwood, an impressive country house where Lord Curzon was living. It is not known what the guests at this outpost of the Tory hierarchy thought of Frank Younghusband's proposals on the employment question.

Curzon acted as his political patron; a rather unwise choice given the former Viceroy's inability to get on with his colleagues. 'I mean now to have a seat in the cabinet,' Younghusband had assured him. 'A good many very inferior men get into cabinets and I do not see why I should not,' he continued with unconscious self-deprecation. 'My idea is to enter English public life with a name well known to Englishmen.' During a brief leave from Kashmir in late 1908, Curzon had arranged for Younghusband to meet Balfour and Lansdowne, who expressed non-committal support for his plans to become a Member of Parliament. The constituency of Plymouth wanted him as a candidate, but his immediate obligations prevented him from accepting the offer. Yet when he began to make speeches in January 1910, he found that he lacked the verbal dexterity of the politician, and concluded he had been a 'dismal failure' on the hustings.

His trouble was that his years in Asia had left him with little direct knowledge of life in Britain. His conception of his home country was an imaginary one, the product of nearly three decades abroad. To an extent this was true of all White Sahibdom: the specific 'Britishness' of the British Empire was constructed by men who rarely visited Britain. 'I can appear before the British public as an Imperialist who for a quarter of a century has been engaged in the practical work of the Empire,' he told Curzon.[2] But the demands of India's northern frontier were of marginal interest to the average Norwich voter. Although Younghusband convinced himself that the 'working man' was 'an Imperialist to the core', he was mistaken.[3] The siege of Chitral and the march to Lhasa caught the public's imagination, but imperial adventure was never likely to overtake food prices and self-interest as a vote winner.

Younghusband's political ideas had gone through a radical transformation since his pronouncement in Chitral in 1894, 'that Government, capital and private property are evils'. His latest opinions were a mixture of George Curzon's brand of grand Conservatism, and an abstract faith in the Crown. 'I should stand as a Conservative,' he had told Curzon the previous year, 'for the Monarchy not democracy which I have no opinion of. I would stand for my own class – the middle class.'[4] Built into these ideas was a paramount devotion to the imperial ideal. 'I am no politician,' he told the voters, but 'it is because I consider the Empire is in a very grave crisis at the present time that I am taking part in this election.'[5]

At the end of 1910 there was a second General Election, following the Lords' decision to reject Lloyd George's budget. Both sides presented it as a crucial turning point in the way Britain would be governed. With revolution brewing abroad and Socialism growing in popularity at home, traditionalists tried to play on the electorate's fears. This was where Younghusband came into his own. He toured the country in the guise of an apolitical celebrity, fresh from Asia, denouncing the 'astounding levity' of the Liberal party's proposals. 'When I was negotiating the Treaty of Lhasa in Tibet,' his speeches would begin, and the crowds roared their approval. 'All of a sudden someone shouted out three cheers for Sir F.Y.,' he was able to report to Helen from Taunton. 'They are all most awfully enthusiastic & nice but by jingo they are thick headed & it is quite tragic to think that it is they who have to decide these tremendously important & intricate Constitutional Questions.'[6] He electioneered for Leo Amery in Bromley and Gervase Beckett in Whitby; but on polling day the Liberals were returned with an increased majority.

Younghusband went off in search of new adventure, making tentative excursions into journalism and writing a series of articles for *The Times* about the Dalai Lama's flight from the Chinese. The *National Review* was treated to a dissertation on 'The Emerging Soul of England', advocating a new spirituality in Europe. 'We virile races of the North require a religion of *our own*,' Younghusband wrote, 'evolved from our midst and fitted to our character.'[7] Plans were made for a new book incorporating the various issues and ideas which were swimming around his head: his notes mention foreign policy, race, Ireland, the army, evolution and the nature of matter. But he remained uncertain quite what it was that he wanted to say, or how he should say it.

He had published two successful books during the previous twelve months. The first was *Kashmir*, a beautifully produced history cum guide book, created in collaboration with his colleague Major Edward Molyneux. Seventy of Molyneux's delicate water-colours of Kashmir were included as coloured plates, while Young-husband put together a readable but unremarkable accompanying text. The second book was *India and Tibet*, which he completed after the first 1910 Election. It was his response to the rash of publications which had followed his expedition, ranging from Landon's magis-terial *Lhasa* to MacCallum Scott's *The Truth About Tibet*, a fervent attack on Younghusband's Mission.

India and Tibet begins with an account of the historical relation-ship between the two countries, before proceeding stage by stage through the events of 1903–04. With hindsight the book is more remarkable for what it leaves out than what it includes, although it does give important information on Younghusband's own atti-tude to the Tibet question. There are few insights into his personal feelings, and he felt unable to mention his battles with General Macdonald, or what he saw as his betrayal by the British Govern-ment. The nearest he comes to criticism is in the suggestion that the India Office might be better run if it was staffed by officials who had visited India. Yet the book was Younghusband's first full pronouncement on his Mission, and it was bought eagerly by the public.

The title-page ran: TO MY WIFE ON WHOM FELL THE ANXIETY AND SUSPENSE OF DISTANTLY AWAITING THE RESULTS OF HIGH ADVEN-TURE I DEDICATE THIS BOOK IN THE HOPE THAT FROM IT MAY COME SOME RECOMPENSE FOR THE SUFFERING SHE ENDURED. Helen was in a disturbed state when *India and Tibet* was published. She had not wanted to leave Kashmir, and now spent much of her time alone while her husband roamed the country on his various esca-pades. She had bought a London flat and a house in Lansdown Crescent in Bath with the remains of her inheritance; her muslin dresses sat in packing cases in the hall. 'I am so distressed at yr.

saying you are sad and lonely,' Francis would begin his daily letter, only to divert to his own concerns before signing, 'Yr. ever loving Dodo', the pet name with which she had christened him.

For the last ten years Helen had been concocting a book about Marie Antoinette, an historical personality with whose plight she identified. Her research involved the purchase of a great many books, intricate correspondence with her Magniac cousins in France, and the dispatch of heavily stylized letters to anybody she thought might prove helpful. *Marie Antoinette: Her Early Life* was published by Macmillan in 1912, and dedicated to: THE UNFADING MEMORY OF A MISTY DAY ON THE FAR BORDERLAND OF THE EMPIRE. The reviews were not flattering, and it sold 350 copies. 'With a prolixity that becomes exasperating,' wrote the *Times Literary Supplement*, 'the author wanders into digression after digression. Not a person appears upon the scene without bringing in his train his entire family tree.' A furious letter from Lady Younghusband followed in its wake, asking how it was that the paper dared to 'attack a Lady by name in the Public Press'. She set to work on a novel, provisionally titled *Tempest Town*.

The truth was that Younghusband simply had no idea how to deal with a depressed wife. Although he felt a broad sympathy for her unhappiness, their preoccupations and interests were too divergent for bridges to be built. Besides, he had worries of his own. The plight of his sister Emmie was a continual concern. He took her out to the theatre in London, but it made no difference; she seemed to have lost her will to live. On top of this, Younghusband still felt a terrible uncertainty about what he should be doing with his own life, as well as a lack of social confidence. 'Look up my list of friends,' he told himself, 'and whenever I have some spare time on my hands go round calling or looking up men in their Clubs.'[8] Yet when he did meet them, he often felt uncomfortable.

'Dinner at Lady Zetland's,' he wrote in May 1911. 'Duke of Richmond and his daughter, Lord and Lady Cadogan . . . It was a typical aristocratic dinner. People spoke out their minds freely, but personally I felt so stilted and stuffed up and self-conscious in comparison.'[9] After years in the wilderness he found himself at the centre of a social whirlwind which gave him no pleasure or security. As so often, the reality failed to live up to the theory behind the social aspiration. The people around him did not share his own dilemmas. Dining with the Crown Prince of Sweden, Lord Minto, Robert Baden-Powell and the indomitable Sven Hedin did nothing to cheer his spirits. Even George Curzon began to irritate him. 'I wish he could grasp the fact', wrote Younghusband, 'that he is not so superior to the rest of humanity as he thinks himself to be.'[10]

Convinced that the meaning of life lay within his grasp, Francis Younghusband journeyed up to Cambridge to seek out 'leading men' from the world of philosophy. The Old Cliftonian John Ellis McTaggart was his first stop: where, Younghusband wanted to know, could he find a 'metaphysical demonstration of the truth of immortality'? McTaggart responded with a puzzled silence and a reading list. In his view, debate was the route to philosophical discovery. 'He says', Younghusband noted earnestly, 'that the main idea is to get the students to think for themselves . . . They discuss things out with each other.'[11] Armed with books and papers, a confused Younghusband left Bath and took a boat to the Continent to join his wife, who was taking the waters at Spa in eastern Belgium.

On the morning of 20 June he rose early and made some notes on the nature of virtue, reminding himself that 'conscience does not always tell us the truth about what actions are right'.[12] Then he set off to watch a display of flying machines, those remarkable contraptions that had first risen from the earth while he climbed the Dzelap La into Tibet.

Returning to his hotel that afternoon, a motor car hit Younghusband side on, carrying him forward, up and onward, as he whirled his arms and flailed his legs in a wild struggle with the uncontrollable machine. He was still conscious when he hit the road and saw a haze of faces and a gendarme, and his own left leg curled beneath his body, protruding at a bizarre angle. Then people lifted him into a motor car and drove him over the cobbles, his bones grating against each other with every bump. As Helen was leaving the hotel she saw a figure borne aloft by a crowd, walked over, and found it was her mangled husband.

It took a doctor three long hours to arrive from the nearest town. He checked the patient's pulse and held a wad of chloroform over the nose and mouth until Younghusband drifted away, shouting with pain and laughter through the oblivion. There was bruising and grazing all over the body. The doctor strapped the leg on to a rough splint, two bones still protruding through the flesh. The bones in the left foot and ankle were found to be smashed, and a deep exposed wound ran down from the right knee.

It was a long, long night that Solstice, the patient drifting in and out of consciousness, blood still pumping out on to the bandages. The next morning, lying on a stretcher and strapped to the roof of a car, Sir Francis Younghusband was bumped twelve miles over cobblestones to a sanatorium. Amputation was considered, but the surgeons decided to give it a chance. There was more chloroform and another operation, the leg being encased in a thick layer of white plaster. The pain continued undiminished, growing more acute, infection thriving beneath the plaster. Younghusband subsided into pleuro-pneumonia, living off milk and brandy, his face a haggard greenish yellow.

Feverishly he gasped for breath for three long nights, straining his frail lungs, sucking shallow breaths, hovering on the edge of life. Helen, terrified, summoned Sir John Broadbent, an eminent London surgeon. Remedies were applied, and the pleuro-pneumonia subsided. But soon the leg was producing a terrible discharge. Belgian nuns and an English nurse applied leeches, mustard leaves and fomentations, and Younghusband battled with the fever, gasping tiny, desperate gulps of air. The local doctor gave him three days to live, so Helen called for Sir John once more. The great man scuttled over from London, and despite the patient's perilous state, suggested a return to England.

On a baking hot day the unfortunate, collapsing body was taken across the Belgian cobblestones to a train, then a boat, then across the sea to Dover, and finally up to London in an invalid carriage. Younghusband relapsed into a feverish stupor, his temperature rising to its highest level yet. The plaster was removed, and the whole festering wound opened up again. The Belgian surgery had not been a success. The bones in Younghusband's leg had failed to join together; instead the stumps had begun to rot. For weeks he scarcely slept, drugged by morphia, unable to turn on to his side. It was September now, and still the leg was producing a foul discharge. The surgeons considered amputation, for the bones refused to join.

Again the wound was pulled apart and the leg bones reset, stretched out on to a long steel splint and bound with leather bandages. There was another operation to remove splinters of rotting bone, but this time his luck began to turn. Some weeks later the

nurses could wheel the patient outside in a bath-chair. Finally at
the end of January 1912, Francis Younghusband was able to take
his first tentative steps since June of the previous year. In time he
was able to walk, though always with a limp, this fearless explorer
who had come through adventures in the Pamirs and the Himalayas
with scarcely a scratch, only to brush death in a Belgian country
lane.

For eight months Helen had tended him, summoning specialists
with indomitable style while Shortie looked after Eileen down in
Bath. There were countless letters of sympathy, many of them
from unknown people. For as Younghusband had told Curzon some
years earlier, he now had a reputation throughout Europe: 'the
name I have made − & which you so greatly helped me to make −
is a great passport.'[13] Even the new Mir of Hunza sent a letter,
declaring that the accident had occasioned 'much shock, but I am
very glad and thank God that you are now convalescent'.[14] A telegram arrived from Sir Dighton Probyn, who was fast approaching
eighty but still working in the service of Edward VII's widow:
'Queen Alexandra has desired me to telegraph Her Majesty's sorrow
at your accident and her hope that you are fast recovering.'[15]

George Curzon came in person of course; it was during a crisis
like this that his self-importance evaporated in favour of a surprising
tenderness. Younghusband described his appearance at the
sick-bed:

> He almost crept into the room, and coming up to my bed,
> said in the most moving way: 'My dear Younghusband,
> how are you, my dear fellow? . . . Now as soon as ever you
> can move you are to come to Hackwood and bring your
> wife and your nurses and anyone you like with you. And
> you shall have rooms on the ground floor, so that you can
> get out easily into the garden. And whenever you want to
> see me I shall be there to see you.'[16]

But Younghusband did not go to Hackwood, for he was far too
busy concocting his next book. He wrote it at great speed with the
Ganden Tripa's bronze Buddha sitting in front of him on his desk.
Although the accident had brought prolonged pain and suffering,
it had the benefit of providing the material for *Within*, a remarkable
excursion into the realms of heretical mysticism. It exposed a side
of Younghusband's character which until then had been known
only to the readers of his private notebooks. *Within* was the book
which changed his public image, alienated certain friends and

relations, and prefigured the search for the God-Child that was to occupy his final years.

Poor Helen was trying hopelessly to pick up the pieces. When her mother died in 1903 she had been left £10,000, and invested it rather unwisely in fine eighteenth-century furniture. Now all the money seemed to have disappeared, leaving them badly in debt. In 'A Plain Statement of Accounts', Helen wrote how they had arrived in Kashmir almost penniless, only to vastly overspend their durbar entertainment allowance. They left India with a deficit of £2,000, and bought the house in Bath almost by mistake. So in 1912 she had to sell her furniture: a great auction was arranged for 13 March. While her husband convalesced and scribbled *Within*, Helen careered about in a great fluster, berating any potential buyers who were foolish enough to come and view the sale. While her treasured possessions were dispersed to the citizens of Bath, she trailed hopelessly from relation to relation. Eileen and Shortie remained in the half-empty house in Lansdown Crescent with a small dog for company and most uncertain prospects for the future.

The book was completed in four months, and published by Williams and Norgate in September 1912. *Within: Thoughts During Convalescence* by Sir Francis Younghusband KCIE, LLD, DSc carries no dedication, but the epigraph refers back to his concussive revelation in Chitral: 'The Kingdom of God is within you'. *Within* begins with a detailed description of his accident and subsequent agonies on the operating table. Why would an omnipotent God permit such suffering; or illness, or battles, or the Rajputana famine? Even the remarkable General Gordon, who had placed such trust in Him, was not spared an unjust death. Yet it was the accident, Younghusband wrote, which showed him that a traditional God could not exist. 'How in the face of such an experience can I be expected any longer to believe in the theory that I was being looked after by a Benevolent Being?'

Having established God's absence and shown there is no evidence of Christ's Resurrection, Younghusband replaces deism with a belief in the 'inherent impulse', a variation on Bergson's idea of the *élan vital*. The True God can only be found within each person, he insists, in the form of an inherent impulse or 'Spirit which animates all living things'. In a bizarre excursion into the world of scientific theory (perhaps his honorary DSc had given him confidence), he proves that the smallest 'specks of protoplasm' contain this animating force. It is this universal 'World-Spirit' which makes humans cohere at crucial moments. By way of example, Younghusband suggests that the death of Edward VII made the whole world unite:

> The natives of India forgot their sedition and joined in the general grief and have ever since had a deeper feeling of unity with England. While the Germans and ourselves sank our differences, and appreciated the closeness of the ties which united us.

This unity would ultimately develop into a state of intense love, possibly as a result of contact with aliens from another planet, for 'we may in time, by telepathy or otherwise, get into communication with them, and they may tell us of something higher than love.' Then the human race would be able to develop in a new spiritual direction. One means of reaching the new state would be through overturning conventional ideas about marriage.

'Eugenic fitness is important for the progress of the race,' he writes. 'But alone it will not raise the race.' To achieve spiritual fitness, 'lovers must no longer feel that society is against them . . . Unions for love must be favoured.' In his opinion, the marriage laws are the consequence of outdated custom, for they were 'made when the woman was still considered to be the property of the man, like his ox or his ass'. In the heady language of the 1960s' sexual revolution, Sir Francis Younghusband espouses: 'liberated love; opportunity for love; freedom to unite when and how a man and woman please; freedom to separate; and entire equality.' He looks forward to an end to 'the present coercive marriage system, the social conventions, and the matrimonial habits which deter men and women from marriage'; for in the future there would be 'no necessity for making a man and woman bind themselves together by oath in public'.

In the final chapter he gives a glimpse of life in the future. There would be an atmosphere of liberation on earth, characterized by music, virtue, beauty and Great Love. Younghusband's last paragraph reveals his ultimate hope – the appearance of a new spiritual leader, the God-Child:

> Then, generations hence . . . when we have given up the habit of incessantly looking without rather than within . . . then, may be, a pure God-Child will arise, more perfect even than Jesus. Intuitively he – or perhaps she – will see into the innermost core of things . . . With the hot glow of Love this divinely-human Being will transfigure all the sordidness of life: make life's beauty shine forth in untarnished radiance; and send a note of poignant sweetness singing through the souls of men.[17]

Within received a mixed reception. The magazine *Votes for Women* praised its espousal of the suffragettes' cause, and called it a 'brave book' which showed 'how the "Woman's Movement" is in truth only an integral part of humanity's progress towards a higher plane'.[18] But most newspapers either ignored it, or carried non-committal reviews that summarized its salient points in bland language.

Younghusband did however receive many letters of praise from the readers of *Within*. It seemed that his transparent rejection of a benevolent deity in favour of the inherent impulse and free love struck a chord with others who had abandoned religious faith. H. G. Wells sent a letter saying that he had read *Within* 'with admiration and sympathy', and that it had helped him in his own work. 'The only sensible philosophy and religion', he told Younghusband, 'is this sort of personal working out that you (&I) are doing.'[19]

The most significant response to the book came from Younghusband's own family and friends. His relationships altered significantly with its publication; social invitations dried up, elderly relations refused to see him and friends such as Curzon drifted away in consternation. 'I was astounded at the reception of the book,' he wrote some years later. 'I received some most wounding letters from those whom I had hurt.'[20] His aunts denounced him as a blasphemer, while 'others wrote in violently abusive terms; and one – a relative – said that she had consigned the book to the fire.'[21] Helen regarded its observations on marriage as outlandish and insulting.

It seems that the experience of coming close to death had made Younghusband recognize the futility of living a life that did not conform to his own most deeply held beliefs. The spiritual ideas he had been pondering for thirty years came to a head, and were poured into *Within*. The source of his ideas about liberated love is harder to fathom. His private notes give no indication of his revolutionary ambitions: certainly he was dissatisfied with his own marriage, but he seems to have been resigned to its limitations. Like most aspiring social philosophers, it may have been the failings he saw in his own experience that made him invent a more satisfying alternative for others.

In early May 1912, Younghusband limped back to Belgium with his brother-in-law Vesey Dawson for a court case over the accident, where he received limited financial compensation. He then travelled alone to Ethel's house in Norfolk. The siblings avoided any discussion of spiritual matters (Ethel's husband was a regular vicar) but concentrated instead on the fate of their elder sister, the unfortunate Emmie. Since their father's death she had become vague and despairing, unable to cope with the sheer grind of living from day to day. With George and Leslie's consent, Francis and Ethel installed her in a Provincial Licensed House: the dumping ground for unmanageable relations. 'She has settled down better than we had expected,' Helen was told, 'and we are sure it is the best thing we could have done for her . . . I think my personal visit will make the doctors & nurses take more interest in the case.'

Younghusband returned to Bath, but two months later he was back at Yelverton Rectory in Norfolk. 'Ethel & I have just come back from seeing Emmie's Home,' he wrote to Helen with measured detachment. 'We did not see her except in the distance. She just walks up & down all day long.' The Darling Girl to whom he had once written 'you cannot know the joy I felt that night when you first showed that you loved me', was drifting away from reality, away into her own sad world. Younghusband buttoned up his emotions, afraid to exhibit the liberated love that he was preaching to others. 'The doctor said it was quite a normal case,' he thought, 'but might take some time to get well.'[22]

When he returned from India in early 1910, Younghusband had been determined to make the acquaintance of Britain's leading philosophers. He had a rather touching belief that by meeting 'the best men of the day', he would be brought closer to an understanding of the meaning of life. His first move had been to join the Aristotelian Society, whose eminent members presented papers and discussed philosophy weekly at 21 Albemarle Street. With knitted brows, Younghusband listened to Bergson, Moore, Whitehead, Haldane, Shaw, Inge, McTaggart and Russell contemplating Mathematics and the Spirit, Creative Morality and the Ideal. Sometimes he would venture an opinion, particularly on questions of love, but generally he sat in silence, listening intently. At times he wondered whether all the sparkling debate might destroy 'that feeling of awe and reverence' which philosophical contemplation should bring.

As a retired imperial administrator, it was not easy for Younghusband to feel at home in this academic world. After an initial coldness, the cat-loving Jack McTaggart was friendly and helpful, but most of the Aristotelians, many of whom were also Cambridge 'Apostles', seemed to come from a different, unapproachable world. Younghusband took to sending copies of *Within* to those he most admired, such as Henri Bergson and A. N. Whitehead. 'My own belief', he wrote to George Moore, the Bloomsbury philosopher and author of *Principia Ethica*, 'is that you and others who are now engaged in wrestling for the Truth are doing work of the very highest value for the race ... I hope you will accept the thanks of one whose practical experience of life is able to recognise and appreciate the value of the great work you are doing'; a rather peculiar compliment given Moore's belief that a life of action held no inherent value. But Moore did not even bother to read the copy of *Within*.[23]

Younghusband had more luck with Bertrand Russell, with whom he established an immediate rapport when they met at the Society in the autumn of 1912. Russell liked the enthusiasm of *Within*, and an unexpected friendship grew up between the two men based on a respect for each other's latitude of thought. *Within* was 'atheism implanted by a motor car', Russell told Lady Ottoline Morrell, with whom he was engaging in a bout of liberated love at the time. 'It is a very amateurish book, but has a quality of simple sincerity which makes one like him. He goes on to build up a religion of atheism, interlaced with irrelevant things such as free divorce.' Before long Younghusband was making frequent pilgrimages to Cambridge to see his new friend, and meeting other intellectuals with whom he could discuss philosophical questions. 'Test all metaphysical conclusions by Russell and McTaggart,' he wrote in his notebook.'[24]

It was around this time that his mystical ruminations began to develop a strong sexual charge. 'Vision of young and beautiful girl so holy in her innocence, tender beauty beaming from her,' Younghusband wrote in a notebook in December 1912. He felt that he could 'almost see the beautiful spiritual fountain playing within her' and 'feel the glow and sparkle of that white and glistening radiance. The set conventional exterior can hardly keep it in . . . How one longs to be able to give what these beautiful young souls are thirsting for!'[25] Fans of *Within* were treated to similar expressions of passion, Younghusband responding keenly to letters of appreciation from readers. However, one woman with whom he was corresponding saw the opportunity to make a profit out of the eminent explorer's spiritual ecstasy, and wrote to Lady Younghusband threatening to disclose the contents of his letters.

'I wrote to her in an intimate and affectionate way,' Francis was forced to confess to Helen, who had summoned the doctor in a fit of 'nerves'. After several extracts from the letters had been sent to her by the blackmailer, the issue was resolved without money changing hands. Younghusband was left chastened by the experience. 'The unpleasant part is that I literally thought I saw the divine in her,' he wrote in April 1913. But he was not entirely deterred from pursuing further erotic dalliances by letter. Six years later there was a similar debacle. 'Little sweetie,' he wrote to his wife afterwards. 'I want to ask one thing of you very much indeed – that you should not ask me any more about it or say or do anything . . . Nothing that has passed has altered in the least what I feel towards you.'[26]

Bertrand Russell was at this time a respected philosopher, having just published the celebrated *Principia Mathematica*, but had not yet gained a reputation as a national luminary. Having lived in a relatively closed world all his life, he was captivated by Younghusband's tales of adventure in High Asia. 'I love him,' Russell told Ottoline Morrell, 'he is very full of universal love . . . and his stories of his life are thrilling.'[27] In his autobiography, he describes Younghusband as 'a very delightful and liberal-minded man, for whom I had a great regard,' and in a BBC report praised his 'immense candour of thought'.[28] As a popularizer himself, Russell liked Younghusband's straightforward approach to complex questions, and his ability to reinforce his opinions with the practical experience of life that academic philosophers often lack.

Younghusband was equally complimentary towards Russell in his own distinctive way. 'A more brilliant intellect I never met,' he wrote in *The Light of Experience*, 'and he had a peculiar charm of his own . . . We differ profoundly on politics, but one of my most delightful experiences was a voyage to America with Russell in February 1914, when we talked together for the best part of five days. He is a socialist, and I know from his conversations has a very deep and genuine sympathy with the labouring classes.'[29]

The sea voyage had come about following one of Younghusband's trips to Cambridge. While staying at McTaggart's house, where he met the writers E. M. Forster and Goldie Lowes Dickinson, it was suggested that he should go to America on a lecture tour. Arrangements were made, and on 7 March 1914 Younghusband and Russell departed together on HMS *Mauretania*, an elaborate Cunard Liner with 'rather the atmosphere of Claridges'. On day two of the voyage Helen was informed that Russell was 'a curious combination of being highly critical and very exclusive – and of being very simple and very genial,' but by day four he was receiving the highest ratings. They strode the promenade deck, walking hard in the 'splendid' Atlantic air: 'Russell is an extraordinarily nice fellow – such good feeling and real refinement. I am very glad indeed to have done the voyage with him and he stays with me all day.'

When they reached New York, the younger man departed for Harvard to teach philosophy, while the elder made the sad discovery that there had been no bookings for his mystical talks. Younghusband found himself at a loose end, pacing the streets, short of money. As ever, he fell on his feet. A contact at the Geographical Association arranged a lecture on Tibet, for which he was paid a good fee. This led to a deluge of social engagements, including an invitation from Teddy Roosevelt's sister, who told him that the former President had always admired him 'so much'. He loved New York ('Perpetual sunshine. Clear bracing air . . . buildings magnificent') and relished the relaxed gusto of Americans, in particular their willingness to strike up informal conversations. Lunch with 'Graham Bell, inventor of telephone' gave way to dinner with the publisher Frank Doubleday, to whom he had been given an introduction by Rudyard Kipling. At the end of March, Younghusband took a train down to Washington to give more lectures on his Tibetan adventure.

Although he had intended to discourse on spiritual matters, he was flattered by the stir he could cause as a famous explorer. 'Though the hall was packed twice – and they all had to pay too –

there were crowds who could not get in,' he wrote to Helen in the dutiful daily letter. 'All the chief people of every kind political, social and scientific were there.' His wife's unhappiness was the only drag on his joy. 'Poor Darling. You seem to have been very sad and depressed'; but it could soon be forgotten in the whirl of excitement. A Senator invited him to lunch, where he fell into conversation with the head of the US army. They discussed India and Tibet, and the General asked him whether he had been on the Younghusband Expedition. On discovering that he was talking to the great man himself, the General was quite overwhelmed: 'He most kindly offered to give orders to the officers wherever I went to give me any assistance.'

The fifty-year-old Sir Francis Younghusband capered across America, trading on his name. He gazed at Chicago, flirted in Colorado Springs and attended dinners in his honour in San Francisco. At the Grand Canyon he caused a sensation by abandoning his mule at the bottom of the gorge: 'I handed the reins over to the cowboy and went straight ahead of the party on foot and never stopped till I was up at the top of the Canyon – 4466 feet in three hours.'[30] April found him in Canada, lecturing frantically at £60 or £100 a time, his ability as a public speaker improving with practice. On arrival in Vancouver his name was spotted in a hotel register by a local reporter, and articles appeared saying that the town was unaware it had been playing host to 'the distinguished British Officer Sir Francis Younghusband'.

After a visit to Winnipeg and lunch with the 'listless' Governor General, Queen Victoria's son the Duke of Connaught, he travelled down from Ottawa to New Haven to be entertained by the gargantuan William Taft, who had been relieved of the Presidency of the United States the previous year by Woodrow Wilson. An 'immense panorama of Lhasa and the Potala hung in his hall', Younghusband wrote, and he showed a keen interest in Asia. 'It is odd – and very pleasant – to find how much I am known and thought of by a certain class over here. They look on it as a sort of compliment to this country that I should visit it.' Some Americans even suggested he should be employed by the US Government to 'settle the Mexican trouble for them'.

At the end of the month he went to Boston to give a final lecture, and met up with his former travelling companion. 'Poor old Bertrand Russell came to see me and was very depressed,' he informed Helen. Separation from Ottoline Morrell had left Russell in a 'miserable' state. 'He has been at Harvard University all this time and says the intellectual life there is very poor. [He] will be heartily glad to get away.'[31] But Russell had to remain a little longer, while Younghusband sailed out of New York in a jaunty mood on the SS *Olympia*. 'I have been surprised', he wrote in a notebook, 'to find how many people in Boston and New York have read my *Within*, and how much it was appreciated.'[32] Despite the initial setback when he arrived in America, Younghusband now found that he had a small core of transatlantic supporters who considered him a spiritual guide as well as a retired explorer.

The period following the US tour was an anti-climax. Helen was still unhappy, so he avoided her company. At the end of June he went down to Westgate with Eileen and Shortie, finding himself at a loose end, wondering in which direction his life was heading.

Then the Great War broke out. In a blinding flash, Younghusband's aimlessness was replaced by patriotic zeal. He spent 3 August 1914 in the Traveller's Club, listening to the latest news and engaging in urgent discussions with acquaintances. Lord Kitchener was on leave in London, and there were rumours circulating that he was about to be made Secretary of State for War. Younghusband saw that his hour had come: his country needed him. Selflessly he would take on the burden of Kitchener's job as British Agent and Consul General in Egypt. He would become a Statesman once more, and the undignified decline in his official career would be swiftly checked. Curzon himself had said there would be employment for men of his calibre if war broke out. 'You will be amused to hear that I have applied to act for Kitchener in Egypt,' Helen was informed. 'I would very suitably fill this place and I have written to Sir Arthur Nicholson to that effect.'[33]

Over the weeks Younghusband made overtures in various directions. But he was not offered the job in Egypt. He made a personal appeal to Kitchener for employment in the War Office; the word came back that nothing was available. So he decided to return to soldiering. His plan was to raise a 'Travellers' Battalion' by recruiting men with experience of exploration and hardship, veterans of the Great Game, fellows of the Royal Geographical Society. They would be united by a common bond, a shared understanding of physical and spiritual travel. On 14 December he had a meeting with Sir Arthur Leetham, who was on Kitchener's staff. The Travellers' Battalion would be of great usefulness, he assured Sir Arthur; it would contain the pick of Britain's greatest travellers, and be overseen by a Committee containing 'some prominent men of position'.[34] But the War Office could see no place for this new model army. Reluctantly, Younghusband resigned himself to becoming the Brigadier-General of a Yorkshire home defence force, and his brother-in-law Douglas Dawson pulled the appropriate strings. But the post had already been filled.

So in the end he settled for work of less than national importance, and joined the management committee of the Travellers' Club. He ensured that the appropriate newspapers were available in the Smoking Room, and that the membership lists were kept up to date. After careful consideration he expelled Lord Sholto Douglas for failing to pay his subscription despite repeated warnings. 'Most amusing,' he wrote to Helen, 'a complaint from Lord Clanricarde that the beef was tough and the potatoes over cooked.'[35]

All Younghusband's enthusiasms had been stamped on. Power in Egypt, a job in the War Office, the leadership of a Travellers' Battalion, even a position in the Reserves were not to be his. He was over fifty and poor, with a collapsing marriage and a wife who was dangerously depressed. Although there was a war on he was effectively unemployable, for the authorities considered him a liability. The idea of a Travellers' Battalion charging about organizing impromptu Jameson Raids on the whim of Sir Francis Younghusband must have struck terror into the heart of War Office officialdom. Since the publication of *Within*, he had been regarded with suspicion by the Establishment. His promotion of free love and arcane mysticism had put him outside conventional parameters when it came to Government appointments. Coming on top of his censure over the Tibet Mission, it had ensured that he was viewed with official suspicion. But in his dogged way Younghusband was scarcely bothered, for he knew that his important work was as a philosopher. He plunged back into writing.

He had been ruminating over a new book since September 1913, and had discussed its thesis in detail with Russell on the journey to America. Newbolt and McTaggart had both given advice. By October 1914 it was finished, and published the following year under the title *Mutual Influence*. He believed that he had made 'a discovery' about the Nature of Good in the Universe. 'I have to get it so absolutely clear that even Bertrand Russell will not be able to pick a flaw in it,' he informed Helen.[36]

His 'discovery' was that atoms, which he refers to as 'these energetic little entities', are animated by a 'Motive Power'. If they vibrated according to a set pattern – a turn of the century revelation – then it became possible, theoretically at least, to establish what would happen in the future. If the smallest protons and neutrons combined with each other to form the nucleus of an atom, by extension humans must combine with each other since they were made up of atoms. It was this physical force which made humans live together: they should put their trust in 'Motive Power' rather than an 'invisible God . . . They will feel erect and self-supporting, and by a greater reliance on themselves they will have acquired that firmness of purpose so necessary for great achievements.'[37]

Mutual Influence is Younghusband's most explicitly humanist book, a development of what Russell had called his 'religion of atheism'. In a letter to Henry Newbolt, who was reading the proofs, he wrote: 'I have an immense faith in the goodness of things and especially the goodness of Man.'[38] His notes for the book two years earlier make it clear that he was intent on a resolute rejection of Christian teaching: 'Give main cause of men's dissatisfaction with Christianity,' he wrote, '– not only unreliability of its historical data, the crudity of its philosophy but also the imperfection of its ideal. Show that even its ethical principles are unsound.'[39] Having demolished Christianity he makes noises about a 'New Religion', but is unclear what form he would like it to take beyond a general exhortation to trust the 'World-Soul' that flows around the Universe.

In the later sections of *Mutual Influence*, Younghusband diverges to the question of warfare, which he believed had given a new, vital unity to the people of Britain. He tries unsuccessfully to link his vision of patriotism to his earlier observations on the nature of matter. Humans were developing and improving as history progressed; the present war was taking place because men on both sides wanted to fight for the 'good' of their country. So 'good' must come out of it. 'There is not a man taking part in this great struggle who will not come out of it with a scorn of the trivial . . . and with a conviction that his countrymen through all future generations must lead cleaner, saner, healthier, nobler, more self-sacrificing lives.'[40]

Like most of his mystico-philosophical books, *Mutual Influence* is a rag-bag of ideas tightly structured around a Beginning, a Middle and a Conclusion. Anything that threatens the cohesion of his argument – such as the notion that the devastating war taking place might not be a force for good – is swept away with studied illogicality. Soldiers fight for the good of their country; *ergo* good must be the result of the fighting. Younghusband's thought patterns depended on a Victorian faith in the unit: the family, the regiment, the learned society, the country. His own inability to fit into the unit did not alter his theoretical faith in it. Atoms, it had been discovered, stick together, so humans should do the same; individual diversity was a disruption of the natural order and had to be dragooned into line with ruthless enthusiasm.

The book was published by Williams and Norgate, Macmillan & Co. having pulled out at the last moment. But few people bought it. The scarce reviews said it was sincere if a little confused. On 11 May he was the guest of honour at a Royal Colonial Institute dinner, but there was little else to cheer him. Forlornly, he journeyed backwards and forwards between Bath and London out of concern for his wife and love for his daughter. Their financial situation was desperate, and Helen was making arrangements to sell her beloved eighteenth-century house in Bath. Their small flat at Buckingham Gate was too expensive to run, so they let it to a Mr O'Brien to raise cash. Sir Francis Younghusband KCIE had to move, pathetically, into the dingy confines of the Vernon Court Hotel in Victoria.

NINETEEN

Fighting for Right in the Great War

In the summer of 1915 Younghusband took an unpaid job at the India Office, preparing daily news telegrams for the Viceroy on the progress of the war. They were supposed to provide an accurate news summary that the Indian Government could disseminate as propaganda. *The Times* ran a short column suggesting that Younghusband's 'ready understanding of the working of the Indian mind' made him the right person to counter the 'mischievous rumours current in the bazaars' which had been spread in India by 'German influence and money'.[1] But he found the job dull, and took any opportunity to go to Cambridge to see his fellow philosophers.

Bertrand Russell was following a 'violently anti-war line . . . Even McTaggart is very angry with him and Sorley calls him the Devil Incarnate.'[2] Whilst Jack McTaggart was to be instrumental in having Russell expelled from his lectureship at Cambridge for publishing a subversive pamphlet, Younghusband did not allow a difference of opinion to destroy their friendship. 'My dear Russell,' he wrote in May 1915:

> I am so distressed at what you say about feeling a sense of isolation because of your views regarding the war. It should be the other way round. You ought to be feeling the pride your friends feel in you for your independence and honesty of thought . . . as regards the military attitude I know from experience how frightfully dangerous it is when you have the physical means of enforcing your own point of view – how apt you are to disregard any one else's. I have seen that with military commanders on campaign and probably I have been pretty bad myself. This it seems to me is what Germany is suffering from.[3]

This is the only occasion when Younghusband acknowledged, however obliquely, that he had been guilty of military excesses during the Tibet Expedition. Once again his unlikely friend had stimulated a side of his character that usually remained dormant. He wrote to

Helen that 'poor Russell is so upset by the war that he cannot think of his work or anything . . . He has taken [it] very much to heart.'[4]

Younghusband, too, had been disturbed, although for rather different reasons. His principal concern was the state of Britain's spiritual health in wartime, a subject about which he had corresponded with Henry Newbolt for several months. He wanted 'to work up the spirit of the nation', he wrote to Helen from his poky room at the Vernon Court Hotel.[5] On 4 August 1915, the first anniversary of the outbreak of war, he had a letter published in the *Daily Telegraph* under the headline 'A Holy War':

> The future of the world is at stake. If the Germans win, the German spirit will dominate human affairs for ages to come . . . All who oppose will be either poisoned, or, with liquid fire, scorched off the earth . . . We are fighting that the ordinary human rights of defenceless women and children be preserved. We are engaged in a spiritual conflict – a holy war – the Fight for Right.

The solution, it seemed, was that meetings should be held up and down the country each Sunday 'on ground common to the whole community'. The 'spirit of the people' would be aroused by 'music, speech, song, the recital of the great words of others'. Younghusband had seen such things happen in India; now they would happen here in Britain. At the climax of the meeting those clean-limbed patriots 'who are willing to offer themselves for service to their country might be asked to present themselves'.[6]

There was uproar. Younghusband had caught the spirit of the nation. Letters and telegrams poured in. The Bishop of Peterborough gave his whole-hearted support; Mr Kerr, the editor of the *Round Table*, wrote to say he would assist in any way possible, as would Mr Robinson Smith; Colonel Dennis declared that he would happily devote his life to the cause; the composer Ernest Austin said he wanted to write rallying hymns; W. W. Asquith, the Prime Minister's brother, 'talked away so enthusiastically about my scheme and has suggested a Jew millionaire to go to for funds', while the General Manager of Railways appeared and 'very solemnly and deliberately said "Sir Francis, I will take off my coat, and my shirt too if necessary, to work with you in this."'

Younghusband travelled down to Cardiff to address a meeting of crusaders, at the end of which he put the motion 'To Fight for Right till Right is won' and persuaded the assembled company 'to rise and with uplifted hand say Aye'.[7] By the end of August he had substantial funding, fifteen ardent helpers and an impressive office in Cavendish Square.

The group circulated a statement outlining their aims:

1. To impress upon the country that we are fighting for something more than our own defence, that we are fighting the battle of all Humanity and to preserve Human Rights for generations to come.
2. To rouse men and women for enthusiastic service in the sacred cause . . .
3. To sustain the spirit of those men and women who are already serving.

Meetings of a 'definitely spiritual character' would be held on Sunday afternoons 'at which such men and women as are imbued with the spirit of the Movement . . . will, by speech and song and music, communicate the spirit to others'. The pamphlet ends with a characteristic Younghusband flourish: 'The motto of the Movement will be: "Fight for Right" for we will fight . . . not for the Highest but for a Higher than the Highest – for the sky beyond the mountain top.'[8] This sentence was dropped from later versions of the pamphlet, which struck a more staid note: 'We mean to see to it that the code of the gentleman and not the custom of the barbarian shall be the rule among nations.'[9]

The Fight for Right, as it came to be called, had been launched at a necessary time. When war was declared in August 1914, the country was moved by a mood of wonderment. Britain had not known a major war for a hundred years: the horror could scarcely be imagined. Young men with dashing white gloves and plumes in their hair marched off to glory, happy to 'give' themselves to their country. 'Isn't it luck for me to have been born so as to be just the right age and just in the right place,' wrote the poet Julian Grenfell, 'to enjoy it the most.' A few months later a shard of shrapnel lodged itself in his brain and he died, causing him to become something of a heroic paragon to Sir Francis Younghusband. Lord Grey wrote a letter of condolence to Grenfell's mother. 'None of us who give sons in this war are so much to be pitied as those who have no sons to give.'[10]

But by August 1915, it was becoming clear that victory was taking longer than expected. There was a stalemate on the Western Front, and in May the Germans had used poison gas for the first time, causing thousands of soldiers to choke to death. Between April and December 1915, a quarter of a million men were killed or wounded at Gallipoli. Whatever the newspapers might be writing about the comfort of the trenches, it was becoming clear they were cold, wet and stinking. Stories filtered back of lice and rotting horses, of mud and barbed wire, of gigantic rats feeding on the bloated corpses of the dead.

The nation needed reassurance that its initial idealism had not been misplaced. Since the outbreak of war, the Government had done its best to rally public opinion. C. F. G. Masterman, the Minister responsible for information and propaganda, invited eminent writers to Wellington House to arrange 'public statements of the strength of the British case' by 'well-known men of letters'. In an extraordinary display of complicity between Government and the Arts, writers rushed to support the official line. On 18 September 1914 a 'Writer's Manifesto' had appeared in *The Times* supporting the righteousness of the war, signed by the eminent literati of the day, including Thomas Hardy, Gilbert Murray, J. M. Barrie, G. K. Chesterton, Arthur Conan Doyle, John Masefield and H. G. Wells.[11]

Robert Bridges, Henry Newbolt, Rudyard Kipling and Edmund Gosse published keen war poetry, and meanwhile in the universities education became an extension of warfare by other means. Walter Raleigh, Oxford's first Professor of English Literature, pronounced the superiority of British culture over German. At Cambridge, Younghusband's old school friend Arthur Quiller-Couch gave a series of lectures on 'Patriotism in English Literature' in which he suggested that 'if only by the structure of his vocal organs a German is congenitally unable to read our poetry'.[12] Plays, articles and novels were inspired by the war. Twelve anthologies of war poetry appeared in 1915 alone; the poems of Owen and Sassoon were yet to be published.

The Fight for Right offered a vehicle for the opinions of public figures. From the beginning, Younghusband made it clear that he wanted writers, mystics, artists and composers to spread his message. Politicians had other business. 'Rousing the spirit of the country should be in the main the work of its spiritual leaders,' he told Gilbert Murray, the revered Greek scholar who was to become one of the leading speakers at Fight for Right gatherings. 'When it was my good fortune', Younghusband intoned, 'to be doing the active work of the Empire and be representing my country, I felt to a depth which you at home would hardly realise the influence of what was thought and said here, and also an almost crying need for some great moral support from here at the heart.'[13]

Younghusband rallied the cultural celebrities of the day, many of whom he already knew socially. John Buchan was 'perfectly certain that I should warmly support any movement with which you were connected'.[14] He was joined by four Old Cliftonians: Jack McTaggart, W. W. Asquith, Harry Plunket Greene and Henry Newbolt. Thomas Hardy signed up, and Beerbohm Tree offered His Majesty's Theatre free of charge for meetings. Gervase Elwes, the flamboyant society singer – 'an extraordinarily nice fellow,' thought Younghusband – joined the Executive Committee. Like many of the organization's active members, Elwes had sons at the Front. 'Gervase and I prayed for them in a special way,' wrote his wife in her memoir of him. 'Every night he used to wake up, rouse me, and we would both get out of bed and pray to the Blessed Virgin, asking her patronage and intercession for them.'[15] The Poet Laureate Robert Bridges agreed to find a rallying song for the movement. According to the historian Samuel Hynes, the Fight for Right began to 'embody the moral crusade against Germany, and support of the war, at its highest and most respectable level'.[16]

A preliminary conference was held in September 1915, at which it was decided that five Sunday meetings should be arranged. The first took place in the Aeolian Hall on 7 November, chaired by Sir Francis Younghusband. There was an organ recital by Mr G. Thalben Ball, at the end of which everybody rose and rendered 'God Save the King'. The chairman then read a speech that Henry Newbolt had rewritten for him, on the subject of treaty obligations and the need for sacrifice. He told the crowd how he had crossed Central Asia aged twenty-three, and been trusted 'simply because I was an Englishman'. But 'what England has stood for in the past should be as nothing to what she will stand for in the future'. Newbolt himself then gave a characteristically rousing address. 'Many say it is the best speech of the war that they have heard,' Younghusband told him afterwards, and 'our Executive suggest that you should publish it in some periodical'. The meeting concluded with 'a fine singer called Gwyther who is invalided home from the front', singing a specially composed hymn called 'Fight for Right till Right be Won!'[17]

Other meetings followed a similar pattern. There were stirring orations and singing, organ music and recitals of poetry. Maurice Hewlett, a romantic historical novelist who later developed Fabian tendencies, spoke on the struggle for freedom. 'He is an odd-looking fish, but has good stuff in him,' decided Younghusband.[18] Gilbert Murray and L. P. Jacks addressed a meeting in Oxford. Gervase Elwes and Frederic Austin sang patriotic songs. The blood-curdling Professor Caroline Spurgeon, an expert on Middle English, spoke out and was promptly elected on to the Executive. Soon she was joined by Evelyn Underhill, the author of *Mysticism*. In December the crowds were drawn by an announcement that 'Mr. John Buchan will give a WAR address'; Younghusband thought that Buchan was especially effective because he 'commands such respect'.[19] The year ended with a triumphal article in the *Inquirer* by Arthur Boutwood. 'Freedom! To us Englishmen that word is dear . . . We are busy with loans, munition-making and recruiting. Sir Francis Younghusband calls upon us for something more; he calls upon us for a *moral effort*.'[20]

Yet even at this early stage, there were powerful differences between the leading members. Younghusband found that the rest of the Executive Committee put more emphasis on belligerence than moral righteousness. In practice most of the day-to-day work was done by a pair of ardent patriots who had responded to the original summons in the *Daily Telegraph*: Arthur Robinson Smith ('Organising Director') and his assistant Paget Bowman. The decisions were taken by Younghusband and Sir Frederick Pollock, Bart., a crusted legal historian who shared Younghusband's devotion to mountains. He was over seventy and turned out to be autocratic and uncommunicative, with a tendency to take decisions without consultation. Younghusband was soon writing to Helen about yet another 'Fight for Right in committee with old Pollock'.[21]

For all his talk of the glories of England, Younghusband believed that the Fight for Right had a profound spiritual purpose. In a letter to Gilbert Murray, with whom he had struck up a friendship, he complained that 'here in England there is often heard the blatant note of jingoism and brassy imperialism'.[22] In his view, the conflict in Europe offered a magical opportunity for spiritual invigoration and the development of mystical fellowship. 'The spiritual part of warfare is of enormous importance and has never [been] sufficiently recognised,' he once wrote to Henry Newbolt.[23] This sense of unity could extend even to those who opposed the war. When he was visited by the future Labour Party leader George Lansbury, who was a leading supporter of the rights of conscientious objectors, 'we had a long talk. He is a really big man and a good man but he cannot bear the idea of fighting . . . Except for that he is strongly with me and greatly impressed by my pamphlet and is coming to the meeting.'[24]

Younghusband was well aware that the Fight for Right ran the risk of being hijacked. Although in November 1915 he accepted the free loan of a building in Waterloo Place from the Crown Estates Commissioners, he was careful not to allow any direct Government involvement. He also resisted attempts to imbue his movement with an exclusively Christian ethos. When the Cavendish Association suggested they should join ranks with the Fight for Right, he was repelled by their claim 'that the future of our country and Empire rests in the hands of God'. Younghusband wanted to appeal to 'the whole of Humanity', he told Henry Newbolt, 'Hindus, Mohammed-ans, Buddhists . . . I do not want to emphasise the Christian part.'[25]

Helen came to several meetings, and found her husband revitalized by his crusade. 'He is very busy, and very happy, fulfil-ling' his role as 'The Peacemaker', she wrote to a friend.[26] At the end of 1915 she sold the house in Lansdown Crescent, Bath, to her friend Lady Strathcona as a convalescent home for wounded officers. Accompanied by Shortie and the fourteen-year-old Eileen, she moved first to an 'agonisingly cold' cottage in Wimbledon, and then went to live with Miss Wilmot, a gardening expert of legendary meanness and eccentricity. The arrangement was not a success, and she was soon moving nomadically between relations and borrowed houses. Eileen trailed behind her, 'a middle-aged child', according to her biographer, 'dressed in a sailor suit and socks and three flannel petticoats with feather stitching.'[27] Francis spent some of his time with them, but more often stayed at the Vernon Court Hotel or wandered the country to regional Fight for Right meetings.

Helen tried to find some sense of purpose. She set up a committee to supply woollen garments, tobacco and books to sailors; she ran a Refreshment Centre in Parliament Square for wounded soldiers. But it was no use. In the spring of 1917 she had another breakdown and went to Bath alone to 'rest' while Shortie looked after Eileen in London. She had no money, it was war time and Eileen needed a new coat, she wrote to her brother Vernon in June 1917. In another letter written around the same time to 'V' (probably her cousin Vallie Magniac) she admitted, 'I have lost all my money yearly in interest and nearly died of the worry of trying to make both ends meet. Once my Eileen is settled in life, we shall have to emigrate . . . One thing I should be most grateful for. That is, if you will prevent a word being spoken to Frank on the subject. He knows nothing. I tell him nothing.'[28]

Lady Younghusband had been brought up to assume that she would always live in grandeur. There had been a temporary apotheosis in Kashmir, but now things were changing too quickly. Servants were becoming expensive and difficult to find. Her husband had an indifference towards money, and was preoccupied by other subjects. Out of a misplaced sense of Edwardian loyalty, Helen felt she should not bother him with financial problems, so there was no communication. Innocence and arrogance combined to make Sir Francis oblivious to her worries. He ate little, seldom drank and had few possessions; his travel expenses were paid by the Fight for Right. Other people bore the cost of his poverty.

Meanwhile his relationship with Eileen, who was bright and appreciative where Helen was nervous and depressing, became increasingly close. He enjoyed showing off his young daughter at Fight for Right gatherings. 'The dear little Pet enjoyed it all and distributed our leaflets and sold our song,' wrote her loving father. 'She does so well on these occasions.'[29] In old age, Eileen remembered the meetings: 'Of course we really knew extremely little about the horrors of the First World War. It was always how splendid the boys in khaki were and there were patriotic songs and we talked about Germans as the Huns. But it was only long after that we began to know what trench warfare had been like.'[30]

1916 was the Fight for Right's most successful year. Small meetings were organized throughout Britain, and branches of the movement were set up by vicars, mayors and other local worthies. Occasionally a dignitary would do his bit to encourage young men to die for their country. Lord Grey, the former Governor General of Canada, wrote to say he had 'got up' a branch of the Fight for Right in his local village. 'I see in this movement tremendous possibilities; the foundation of a New Church, &c. &c.' The Duke of the Abruzzi,

who had forsaken climbing to command the Italian navy, told
Younghusband that he was encouraging soldiers all over the world
'whose steadfast faith will carry them to final victory'.[31] In July,
Younghusband and Newbolt jointly addressed a meeting in Plymouth, and later in the year another in Southampton. The voices
of the schoolfriends rallied the ranks to play up, play up, and play
the game. The Fight for Right's real test, they both stressed, 'will
come when the nation is tasting of success and will need keeping
to the sticking point'.[32]

Early on Younghusband had identified the need for a catchy
rallying song. Ernest Austin's 'Fight for Right till Right Be Won!'
had not caught the public's attention. Robert Bridges, who was
interested in music as well as poetry, agreed to arrange something
for a meeting he was addressing at the Queen's Hall in April. Tall
and stammering, with an irregular gait, Bridges braved his natural
fear of the public to become one of the Fight for Right's most
popular speakers. Although his poems now seem rather leaden,
and his reputation rests primarily on the fact that he introduced
the world to Gerard Manley Hopkins, he was in 1916 a revered
Poet Laureate. His recent anthology on the theme of the country
in wartime, *The Spirit of Man*, had been an immediate success. In
his spare time Bridges paraded with a home defence regiment called
Georgius Rex — but known as God's Rejected; most of its members
were elderly Oxford dons — accompanied by his friend Gilbert
Murray.

Bridges thought that the Fight for Right would 'get the nation
together in a good patriotic and enlightened spirit'.[33] He decided to
approach his composer friend Sir Hubert Parry. After careful
thought, he sent him a copy of the Preface to William Blake's *Milton*,
with the suggestion that he should write 'suitable, simple music to
Blake's stanzas — music that an audience could take up and join
in.'[34] Parry composed the perfect tune.

The Queen's Hall meeting took place on 28 March 1916 in front
of a large audience. Robert Bridges told them that the country's
safety depended on the spirit of its people and 'an irresistible front,
united in the principles of Order, and Right, and devoted Patriotic
Duty'. By using some quirky textual analysis, he showed that the
idea of building Jerusalem in England's green and pleasant land
was much the same as the principle behind the Fight for Right.
William Blake was claimed as a supporter. Whether Blake, with his
radical views on imperialism and social revolution, would have
agreed is open to question. But Bridges was sure. 'I asked my friend

Sir Hubert Parry to compose a setting of Blake's poem for us,' he told the crowd. 'He has done so, and we shall hear it to-night for the first time.'[35]

A choir of 300 Fighters for Right sang *Jerusalem* with gusto, conducted by Walford Davies, and soon they were accompanied by the congregations of Britain's churches. The Land Army joined in, as did the Officer Training Corps, and the Public Schools and the Suffragettes and the Women's Institute, who have not stopped singing since. *Jerusalem* now appears at the Last Night of the Proms (re-orchestrated and embellished by Edward Elgar), at every society wedding and at the end of Labour Party conferences, to the fury of the Tories who think it belongs to them. Novelists and film directors introduce it as an easy symbol designed to trigger a nostalgic image of Englishness, of chapel at school and cricket and tradition; of *Another Country*, *Brideshead Revisited* and *Chariots of Fire*; of a world which probably never existed outside the conceptual imagination of the late twentieth century.

Perhaps *Jerusalem*'s popularity rests on the very instability of its symbolic value. Nobody is quite sure what it does represent; certainly the meaning that William Blake intended has become irrelevant. What matters is that our second National Anthem seems to belong to a time of certainty, a time when we were sorting out the Hun, helping to keep India British and believed there was honey still for tea.

'The war is looking better now and it is a dead certainty that the Germans [will] come an almighty cropper,' Younghusband insisted in a letter to 'Hatter' Bailey, who was heading for Tashkent on a secret mission. A month earlier the Battle of the Somme had claimed the lives of sixty thousand British soldiers on the first day alone. By the end of 1916 over half a million men had been slaughtered for the sake of a few miles of land. Passchendaele was yet to come. 'It is equally certain', the letter continued, 'that by this time next year we shall be by far the greatest and most powerful nation in the world. No other power will be any where near us.'[36] The Great War had become an alternative to the Great Game; another means of extending the scope of British influence.

MI5 had been watching Bertrand Russell for some time. They intercepted his mail, and commissioned several newspaper articles ridiculing him as a traitor. His summer tour of South Wales on behalf of the No-Conscription Fellowship was accompanied by a stolid detective-sergeant, who lurked dutifully at the back of church halls taking down evidence. In Cardiff Russell suggested there was no reason why the war should continue another day, which gave the authorities the opportunity they were looking for.[37] However, the Public Prosecutor decided it would be difficult to lay charges, and suggested that an instruction be issued to the Official Press Bureau 'that under no circumstances is any meeting attended by BR ever to be mentioned in the Press'.[38] The Home Office wanted more. They knew that Russell intended to visit Haverhill in Suffolk to address a group of conscientious objectors, and so cajoled Colonel Kell of MI5 into issuing a War Office order banning Russell from all prohibited coastal and military areas: a sanction usually reserved for enemy aliens.

At the end of August Younghusband spent a weekend in Oxford with Robert and Monica Bridges, and on his return received a letter dated 2 September:

> The War Office have issued an order forbidding me to enter any prohibited area. They have not deigned to suggest any reason for the order, which causes me the gravest inconvenience, besides depriving me of £180 which I had intended to earn by courses of lectures on the theory of politics (not on the war) ... What I do resent is being treated under an order intended for spies ... I think there must be some complete misapprehension of my views and actions. Could you do anything to see if the order can be rescinded? I should be enormously grateful if you could.[39]

Although MI5 knew Bertrand Russell well, he was not acquainted with them. His impulse was to turn to Younghusband, the only friend he could think of who was likely to be in touch with the intelligence services. They lunched together and Younghusband was sympathetic although, to Russell's disappointment, not in the least inclined to be indignant. But he agreed to do what he could to get the order rescinded.

At a quarter past three in the afternoon on 5 September 1916, an unlikely gathering was to be seen at the War Office. On one side of the desk were two short men with high collars and strong eyebrows. The elder was a mystically minded explorer whose latest mission was to stimulate patriotism in the nation, the younger a respected logician lately turned seditious pacifist. Across the desk sat the Director of Special Intelligence and Great Game veteran, General George Cockerill. According to Eileen Younghusband, her father had visited Cockerill earlier in the day to warn him not to be drawn into an argument, since 'Bertrand Russell has one of the finest brains in the world.'[40]

The General did not heed this sound advice, and embroiled himself in an argument about the nature of conscience. He suggested that if Russell believed the war was wrong, he would not want to say so in public, to which Russell retorted: 'You do not apply this principle to those who write and speak in favour of the war; you do not consider that if they hold their opinions in secret they are conscientious men, but if they give utterance to them in the Press or on the platform they are mere propagandists. There seems some lack of justice in this differentiation.'[41] The conversation continued in this vein, General Cockerill becoming increasingly irritated at being made to look foolish. Younghusband listened uneasily to the dispute, having expected Russell to beat a tactical retreat. The General offered to lift the banning order if Russell would agree to abandon political propaganda and return to philosophy, but received a negative response. The meeting ended inconclusively.

When the order had been served on 1 September by two plain-clothes men from Scotland Yard, Russell's reaction had been one of weary resignation. He had already been fined £100 in June for writing an anti-conscription leaflet, and was reluctant to begin another battle with the authorities. His letter to Younghusband in which he refers to a 'complete misapprehension of my views and actions' gives the impression that he felt misunderstood and was anxious to have the restriction lifted. But soon he realized that he occupied the moral high ground. The *Manchester Guardian* announced that the War Office had lost its common sense, and the *Daily News* pointed out the absurdity of pretending that Russell's words were 'a danger in Brighton but not in Birmingham, in Hull but not in Halifax'.[42] The banning order was clearly illogical since he was still permitted to make speeches outside prohibited areas.

At this point in his life, Russell was well known as a logician and philosopher. It was the War Office banning order that launched him into his parallel career as a public thorn in the flesh of the Establishment. The white-haired icon who sat on the pavement outside the House of Commons in the 1960s, preaching civil disobedience in a clipped voice, was fashioned by the events of the

First World War. He relished his new position as martyr to a righteous cause. Lytton Strachey observed that during this stage of the war, 'Bertie . . . is at last perfectly happy – gloating over all the horrors and the moral lessons of the situation.'[43] 'I am thoroughly enjoying it, & think I shall get the best of them in the end,' Russell wrote to Ottoline Morrell on 7 September. 'I am flattered by their making such a dead set at me.'

His introduction to the intelligence services gave him a fresh line of attack. He fired a volley of carefully honed letters at General Cockerill. The banning order, he claimed, implied that he was seeking information that might be of value to the enemy. Might he refute this idea by releasing an account of his War Office meeting to the Press? General Cockerill pre-empted him by obtaining a letter from the Army Council which denied that Russell was suspected of spying. He also reiterated his willingness to lift the order if Russell would agree not to speak about politics. This gave Russell an opening for a salvo of ethical queries, concerning what would and would not count as 'political': 'May I say that I consider homicide usually regrettable?' he inquired. 'If so, since the majority of homicides occur in war, I have uttered a pacifist sentiment. May I say that I have a respect for the ethical teaching of Christ? . . . Or would such a statement be prejudicial to discipline in His Majesty's Forces?'[44]

By the end of the month MI5 and the General were tangled in a philosophical web. Their position was clearly ridiculous, but they could not be seen to back down. Each letter from the damnable egghead made Cockerill's hackles rise a little further. By 2 October he could stand it no longer and brought the exchange to a close. 'I think I must remind you', he crowed at Russell, 'that our correspondence originated in an interview which I accorded to you on being informed by a friend of yours that you were desirous to abstain in future from illegal propaganda, and to devote your attention to logic and philosophy, and that you would be prepared to give an honourable undertaking to this effect.'[45]

The friend, meanwhile, felt he had been manipulated and betrayed. He had arranged the War Office meeting under the impression that Russell wanted to return to academia. Instead Russell had used the favour as a launching pad to ridicule the actions of Military Intelligence, thereby putting Younghusband in a most embarrassing position. As so often in his life, Russell had allowed his crusading ambition to trample on a personal relationship. Although in old age Younghusband would write fondly of the journey together to America, their friendship was at an end.

Younghusband was made a Knight Commander of the Star of India in the New Year's Honours list of 1917: 'a most gracious act,' he told Gilbert Murray.[46] Letters of congratulation appeared from friends and acquaintances. 'I particularly appreciate your warm recognition of my work, for you know better than almost any one what it has been,' he replied to the explorer Sir Aurel Stein, adding that 'the honor came as a complete surprise to me'.[47] It was 'intended to make up for what was thought scant recognition – not to mention censure – which I got when I came back from Tibet,' he told his fellow mystic Sir James Frazer, author of *The Golden Bough*.[48] Lady Younghusband always claimed that Austen Chamberlain had arranged the award as a belated official recognition for the injustices of the Tibet Expedition. But there is no firm evidence to support this, and it seems more likely that the Government wanted to thank Younghusband for the public support they had been given by the Fight for Right.

There were several successful rallies at the Aeolian Hall in the spring of 1917, attended by Belgian and French cabinet ministers. Gilbert Murray made an important speech which he later included in his book *Faith, War and Policy*. He was adamant that war should not be motivated by blind anti-German prejudice, but only by the quest for 'Right'. But it was around this time, while Younghusband's banjo-strumming friend Charlie Townshend presided over the memorable British defeat at Kut in far-off Mesopotamia, that the movement started to fall apart. Sir Frederick Pollock was furious about some mildly pacifist articles from the foreign press which the *Cambridge Magazine* had printed. He drafted a spluttering letter to *The Times* which Younghusband agreed to sign, reluctantly.

The linguistic philosopher C. K. Ogden, who edited the *Cambridge Magazine*, then asked Gilbert Murray to intervene, since 'this "Fight for Right" business is proving disastrous for us'.[49] Although Murray approved of the war he was always anxious to support the moral convictions of his friends such as Ogden who did not. After consulting with friends, Murray organized a letter of protest against Younghusband and Pollock. It stressed the importance of the freedom of the Press, and was signed by many previous supporters of the Fight for Right, including Clutton Brock, Quiller-Couch and Thomas Hardy. A letter was also sent to Younghusband by Sir Hubert Parry, withdrawing *Jerusalem* as the Fight for Right's rallying tune. The idealists and the jingoists had finally split. Men such as Gilbert Murray, whom Younghusband greatly respected, had withdrawn, and the movement was now in the hands of the militarists. At this point Younghusband sided with Murray and broke with Frederick Pollock, refusing to endorse his vision of the Fight for Right.

As ever, Younghusband went off in search of an outlet for his energies. He took up with an organization called the United Workers, who were campaigning against Government secrecy over Foreign Policy. Under the sponsorship of Newbolt, William Inge and the official man of letters Edmund Gosse, he was elected a Fellow of the Royal Society of Literature, and joined a committee 'for promoting an intellectual entente among the allied and friendly countries'.[50] He returned to the India Office to write news telegrams, where he was visited by the young Arnold Toynbee, 'a cleverish kind of fellow'.[51] The Royal Institution invited him to give three lectures on 'The Himalaya', in which he told anecdotes about his exploring days. 'My dear Murray,' he wrote in November 1917, 'Yes I am sorry the Fight for Right will be winding up . . . You have always been most good to us and there was no one who contributed more than you did to any little we were able to accomplish.'[52] On 9 December he went to the final meeting, and afterwards wrote a letter to Helen about the iniquities of Sir Frederick Pollock: 'He really is the biggest ass there ever was!'[53]

One consequence of the Fight for Right's inimical disintegration was that its papers and records were never collected, but presumably dispersed into dustbins and attics. Younghusband's accounts of it in his later writings concentrate on the obvious achievements such as 'the one relic of our work', Parry's *Jerusalem*.[54] Most books about the First World War usually relegate the Fight for Right to the footnotes, while Frederick Pollock avoids the subject altogether in his blimpish memoirs *For My Grandson*. The only regular and detailed archive consists of twenty-six letters which Younghusband wrote to Henry Newbolt between 1915 and 1917. They chart the origins and development of the organization, and provide an unmatched insight into the personal ideals behind the Fight for Right.

The letters came to light almost by chance. I had been corresponding with a Japanese academic, Tamio Kaneko, who was writing about the Great Game. We discussed the various Japanese secret agents who had ended up in Tibet, and the purpose of Count Kozui Otani's mission to Chinese Turkestan. Then at the end of one of his letters, amidst the unwarranted cross-cultural compliments, Tamio Kaneko mentioned some manuscript letters he had bought many years before in London. Would I like to see them?

Over the next few months batches of neatly photocopied letters would appear in the post. I discovered where the Fight for Right lived, and that it used exquisite writing paper: 'Telegrams – "Fiteforite, London". Telephone no. Gerrard 1088. All communications to be addressed to the Secretary.' Often the ancient letters would arrive alone in the envelope, as if Sir Francis himself was posting them to me through the ether. In them he wrote of his hopes for the movement, and the ways in which he knew it would inspire the nation. It was the time of the Gulf War, and the parallel between the justifications put forward for fighting were extraordinary. The *Sun* newspaper's last headline before the bombing of Baghdad could have been plucked directly from a Fight for Right pamphlet: 'WHEN THE BRITISH LION ROARS WE KNOW THAT WE HAVE RIGHT ON OUR SIDE.'[55]

Newbolt was Younghusband's most consistent friend. While others were addressed by their surname in Victorian fashion – 'Dear Hedin', 'My dear Curzon' – only Newbolt was greeted with 'My dear Henry'. Their friendship endured from schooldays together at Clifton to Newbolt's death. They shared a fascination with Britain's moral and spiritual influence, and a sense of the historical importance of the era. There was also great mutual admiration. Younghusband longed to be a literary figure, while Newbolt regretted the lack of adventure in his own life. In an account of a train journey he made in the 1920s with the Speaker of the House of Commons, Francis Younghusband and Field Marshal Haig, Newbolt wrote that, 'Dear old F.E.Y. sat hunched and silent in his corner, with large coal-like eyes. Interesting as the other two were, I couldn't forget that it was he, and not they, who started on that wonderful boyish journey across the illimitable plain of flowers in a Turkestan April morning, and after years of adventure out-mystified the Lamas in the Thibetan Hall.'[56]

It is hard to establish what influence the Fight for Right had at the time, or to what extent it succeeded in rousing people 'for enthusiastic service in the sacred cause'. According to Young-husband's letters to his wife, over a thousand 'Fighters for Right' would regularly attend the London rallies. Yet as a movement it was probably more significant for what it represented than for what it achieved. Symbolically, it seems to carry the gaudy, desperate patriotism of the First War, a patriotism that was unaware of the extent to which bad news from the Front was being temporarily deleted from history. Although its intention was to persuade all the people of Britain and the Empire to unite and reach for 'the sky beyond the mountain top', it was almost exclusively an English, male, upper- and middle-class organization. *Jerusalem* is a suitably contradictory legacy. An ode to the destruction of industrial capitalism becomes a monument to stability and tradition, having to double as a revolutionary anthem and Eton's leaving song.

'Dear old F.E.Y.' spent the rest of the war thinking about India. Edwin Montagu, the Secretary of State for India, asked him to make suggestions on the planned constitutional reforms there. He busied himself with details of agriculture, natural resources, caste, culture and the benefits of the *panchayat* system, and extolled the virtues of the village as a seat of native power. Control of government should gradually be handed over to the Indians, since for too long 'we have tended to emasculate the people'. He had still not grasped the speed with which the British would have to move. 'I am dead against precipitate action such as that demanded by Mrs Besant . . . It will take nearer a century than a decade to reach.'[57] Backward though his ideas seem now, they were at the time considered radical by many of his generation. He wrote a letter to *The Times* supporting Montagu's moves towards Indian self-government, and was derided by retired colonial servants. 'I received twenty pages of very closely typewritten rubbish from a lunatic,' he wrote to his wife from a cottage in Minehead, where he and his daughter were staying. 'He signs himself the Sword of the Lord.'[58]

The notion of a book about India had been in his mind for some time. It would be called *Imperial Development*, or perhaps *The Reconstitution of India*, and would show the need to revert to traditional Indian values. Western ideas about education and religion had been shown to be flawed. During 1918 he filled three notebooks with detailed jottings and chapter outlines. India needed a spiritual revival, which in turn would inspire the spirit of other countries. But his heart was not in it, so he made plans of garden layouts instead. Some days he resorted to the traditional British response to having too little to do: '9th October 36°. Dull day, heavy clouds. Drizzling all day,' he wrote in his diary.[59] But at the beginning of November he was revived. Earlier in the year he had given morale-boosting talks (assisted by slides exhibited on an 'A 1 lantern') to wounded soldiers in Plymouth and Hull. Now the War Office asked him to go to France and lecture. He would excite the troops with tales of his adventures in Tibet and the Himalayas, and then encourage them to keep up their peckers.

It was only a few days before the Armistice and the streets were crammed with soldiers and ill-dressed, malnourished refugees of war. Children dodged through the devastated buildings, 'parading about with flags and singing the Marseillaise'. Younghusband relished it. 'Last night I was lecturing to the Flying Corps. I was motored out about twenty miles and dined with them and lectured in a huge hangar to about 2000 of them with the slides looking most effective,' he wrote excitedly to Helen. 'It was a huge success.' At a Thanksgiving Service in Amiens Cathedral the candles fell over and the priest's vestments caught on fire. He went from Hallencourt to Vignacourt to Oisemont, speaking twice a day to audiences of several thousand. Younghusband's moustaches, determined air, checked suit and gaiters meant that he was frequently mistaken for the French leader, Monsieur Clemenceau. People stared at him in the street and a British soldier saluted him saying, ' "Bonjour monsieur." Great fun it is.'

Reading through the letters that Younghusband wrote during this journey, I was reminded of the hero of a picaresque novel who manages to bounce back from every misfortune. He was as untroubled by his own lack of money and prospects as he was by the physical devastation all around him. The vision of a generation had been blown apart on the battlefields of Europe, but his own idealism was scarcely dented. He marched on, firing arrows from his bow of burning gold. The battered remnants of the Australian Corps delighted him. 'There is not a trace of rowdyism or loudness or boasting about these men,' he told Helen, 'but only manly cheeriness. Such a clean lot they are.'[60]

TWENTY

The Quest for a World Leader on
the Planet Altair

During the 1920s, Francis Younghusband's spiritual ideas passed through another series of bizarre and dazzling transformations. It was a time of social change and experimentation, and he was willing to risk the most peculiar notions in his quest for mystical truth. He had been brought up an Evangelical Christian, read his way into Tolstoyan Simplicity, experienced a revelatory vision in the mountains of Tibet, toyed with telepathy in Kashmir, proposed a new faith based on virile racial theory, then transformed it into what Bertrand Russell called 'a religion of atheism'. His move away from Cosmic Humanism began with the publication of *The Heart of Nature*.

He wrote it during a fallow period following the Great War, intending to appeal to a wider audience than he had reached previously. By mixing philosophy with poetic descriptions of Tibet, Sikkim and the Himalayas, he aimed to draw admirers of his Eastern adventures into his mystical orbit. *The Heart of Nature; or The Quest for Natural Beauty* was published by John Murray in 1921 to an enthusiastic reception, the *Evening News* even claiming (under the headline 'EXPLORER – POET') that Younghusband's descriptive powers rivalled those of Coleridge and De Quincey. 'He talks about the loveliness of the hills and valleys and woods . . . with beauty of language which has seldom been surpassed.'[1]

The Heart of Nature is broken up into alternate chapters of description and philosophizing. Younghusband's contention is that the world needs 'a Naturalist-Artist – a combination of Julian Grenfell and Darwin', to reveal the inherent spirituality of Nature. Using the Himalayas as his starting point, he writes of dripping forests and glistening orchids, 'glorious sunsets' and 'billowy mists'. For the first time, he gave a public account of his mystical vision at Lhasa, defining it as a moment when he was 'intimately in touch with the true Heart of Nature'. Strangely, he then devotes the end of the book to showing that the 'Naturalist-Artist' he has just created will be inadequate, since 'the finest pitch of all is only

313

reached in the union of man and woman'. An ethereal sexual unity becomes his ideal, through which 'we can enter unreservedly into the Spirit of Nature', since in 'the womb of to-day is contained the promise of a Love and Beauty still more glorious.'[2] Throughout the book his language and ideas are correspondingly vague and amorphous.

It may have been a recognition of the limitations of *The Heart of Nature* that made him choose a new form for his next offering. *The Gleam: Being an account of the life of Nija Svabhava, pseud.* ('pseud.' standing for 'pseudonym' in this case) is an odd book, comparable only to the later *Wedding* in its bizarre combination of Edwardian heartiness and unquantifiable mystical rambling. It purports to tell the true story of Nija Svabhava, a north Indian Brahmin whose destiny it is to be 'a follower of the Gleam'. He is a man of 'deep earnestness and sincerity', marked by a 'spirit of daring and high adventure'. 'With these many tastes in common,' wrote Younghusband, 'it was natural that Svabhava and I should quickly come together when I arrived at Kangra in 1884 on my first wild rush into the Himalaya.' Together they strode the mountain passes, discussing religion.

Nija Svabhava is, of course, Younghusband himself; or rather his alter ego – 'svabhava' is a Sanskrit philosophical term used to denote the exclusive properties of a particular idea or person. Whether this was appreciated by the average reader seems unlikely. The *Daily Telegraph* reviewer did not spot the true identity of the hero, preferring to commend 'a book of a subtly esoteric character steeped in the mysticism of the East . . . of a lofty and ennobling outlook'. *The Times* responded in similar tones, choosing *The Gleam* as its 'Book of the Day' and saying it gave 'a very full presentation of the workings of a typical Oriental mind seeking a pure religious philosophy'.[3] In the final chapter, 'The Vision', Younghusband describes the ultimate realization using a trickle-of-consciousness technique:

> And these starry angels may carry the Godhood supremely
> compared with all others, and, lovingly tending mankind
> as we tend our flowers . . . His wonder more wonderful
> grew. Admiration unbounded . . . Divine gift, too, he had
> not merely of shining himself, but of making the others
> shine also . . . Oh! my God, I do thank Thee![4]

When *The Gleam* was published at the end of 1923, he was tempted to reveal his hero's identity to the world. He even wrote a melodramatic letter to *The Times* on the subject ('Sir, He whom I have described in "The Gleam" as Svabhava is myself, and how continuously I have strived may be seen in that book . . . England! I beseech you to hear my last words.'); but he lost his nerve and forbade its publication at the last moment.[5]

It was around this time that Younghusband began to refer to himself as Svabhava in his private writings, often with comic results: 'Svabhava would indeed have agreed with some of the speakers at the Modern Churchmen's Union . . . Svabhava would have been quite at one with Canon Rashdall . . .'[6] His use of an alter ego is an interesting development, since it shows the gulf between the different faces he presented to the outside world. It became easier to think of Nija Svabhava, 'follower of the Gleam', as a separate aspect of his own identity, one which could not always be fully united with the retired explorer called Sir Francis Younghusband. Although he was now willing to publicize his mystical ideas, he did not yet feel able to display them on every occasion.

The Younghusband family trailed from house to house after the war, until at the end of 1921 they came to rest in Kent at Currant Hill, a tall, modern, red-brick building perched above the village of Westerham, about thirty miles south of London. Helen bought it with the remains of her inheritance. Their financial situation was still perilous, but Francis kept his feet firmly off the ground as far as money was concerned. He had his £500 a year Political Service pension, and erratic royalties from his books. Helen sold her pearls, bought more French furniture and convinced herself she had been swindled by her brother Oswald.

> Statement by me, Helen Augusta, Lady Younghusband, the first day of May, 1920 . . . No one seems to know, or can or will give me any information whatever . . . I have begged, and implored and entreated, and written till I am weary and sick of it all.[7]

Somewhere along the line her fortune seemed to have disappeared, but she could not establish quite how, or where. So she busied herself arranging for Eileen (now a handsome, rather shy nineteen-year-old) to do a cut-price 'season', with a view to finding a suitable husband. Shortie acted as Eileen's chaperone. Helen enjoyed berating the iniquity of the Modern Girl: 'My dear you really would not know the difference between their nightdresses and their evening dresses,' she told another grand old lady. So one evening Eileen and a friend came down to dinner in their nighties. 'But no one noticed.'[8]

Otherwise Helen ate a good deal, continued to work on her melodramatic novel and, like most members of the bookish upper-classes, wrote frequent letters to the *Spectator* which were never printed. She had more luck with *The Times*. Something should be done, she insisted, about the decline of the stately homes of England. They should be preserved for those 'whose lot it is to be cast in Greater England beyond the seas' as a reminder of 'green glades where deer shelter beneath forest trees' and 'the voices and laughter of generations of happy English children'.[9]

Helen was discontented. 'I don't believe you'd notice if my head was hanging on by a thread,' she said to Francis one morning, 'nor if they built the Eiffel Tower one night in our field.'[10] Her irritation manifested itself in endless reprimands on matters of social protocol. The Secretary of the RGS was rebuked for addressing an invitation incorrectly ('Sir Francis never uses his second name as a signature: still less as an initial'), and later for neglecting to include his KCSI on an envelope.[11] While her husband wandered off into the realms of the spirit, Helen did her best to instil a sense of society into her daughter. She told Eileen how as a child the steward of Chesterfield House had asked her 'whose task it was to clean the looking glasses in the drawing-room. I replied the fifth footman, which was perfectly correct.'[12] But Eileen was more interested in social justice than social propriety, and moved out to a Settlement in Bermondsey. She patrolled the tenements of Stepney and ran a play-group – to the distress of her mother, who saw such activities as most improper. Francis ignored the tension between mother and daughter.

Although he still wrote to Helen every day when he was away (which was often), the warmth had gone. 'We are going through a bad time just now,' he would write to her, 'but I really do think things are better ahead.' A few months later there would be another letter in a similar vein, but it made no difference; the marriage was dying. Francis had developed a technique of remaining aloof from the problems of everyday life. As his love for humanity grew, so his concern for individuals declined. His sister Emmie was another abandoned remnant. In 1923 he went to visit her in Norfolk, but could not face a meeting. 'I said I wd. not see her as it wd. only upset both her and me,' he admitted to Helen. The nurses told him that Miss Younghusband 'just sat and did nothing all day long. Nevertheless, Emmie cd. not be in a better place,' he convinced himself.[13]

That was the last anyone ever heard of Clara Emily Younghusband. All references to her in her brother's many notes and letters cease on 10 August 1923. The indications are that she had been suffering from sporadic depression, loneliness and low self-esteem from the 1890s onwards, losing her faith in life, living for nothing but the distant concept of her beloved Frank, her 'darling boy'. There was something about Emmie's representative plight that held my attention. I imagined her drifting in and out of lucidity, remembering her childhood in Murree, the teenage years in Bath, the Evangelical instruction and the religious doubts, her mother's death, the suicide attempt, her father's death, the awkward trip to Kashmir and then the years of utter, utter despair before being decanted into a mental institution where she could be safely forgotten.

Emmie was the personification of the desperate Victorian daughter, hemmed in by family and convention, who took to illness as a substitute for living. I found myself in the Norfolk Record Office searching through the registers of county mental institutions, determined to locate her, to discover the fate of this discarded legacy of an outdated approach to mental health. Finally I did, in the books of The Grove, a 'Provincial Licensed House (females only)' on the outskirts of Norwich, run by the Misses McLintock and 'limited to quiet and harmless cases'.

Emmie had remained there for thirty-four lonely years before dying of 'senile decay' in the winter of 1945.

Mother World (in Travail for the Christ that is to be) was Francis Younghusband's next contribution to the canon. Like *Within* it was published by Williams and Norgate, John Murray preferring to keep away from another mystical excursion. Yet the book stands out from his earlier work, for its theories are surprisingly close to present-day ideas: Mother World is a forerunner of 'Gaia' theory, by which the Earth is perceived as a self-regulating entity which seeks an optimal environment for the maintenance of life. The Gaia hypothesis, proposed by the scientist James Lovelock, has recently been taken up and embellished. Gaia has come to embody the idea of ecological inter-dependence, whereby the planet can be seen as a living organism which defends its own physical integrity. This embodies a spiritual dimension, since God and Nature become indistinguishable, which has a decided appeal to today's New Age mystics.

Younghusband's belief was that the world should be seen as a benevolent deity. People are 'in God and God is in them just as the ovum is in the mother and the mother is in it'.[14] Although his feminization of the divine principle now seems unremarkable, in 1924 it was disturbingly radical. His 'pantheistic tendencies' were attacked by the *Tablet*, who thought his 'Christ that is to be . . . from a Catholic point of view, could be none other than Anti-Christ himself'.[15] Yet there was praise from the physicist J. S. Haldane, who felt Younghusband's work broke new ground since it recognized that the universe was spiritual rather than mechanical.[16] Mother World became an amorphous, caressing reconstruction of the traditional male God. Her natural glories could provoke the strongest sense of joy: if the Pope and a group of staunch Protestants were to go walking in the Himalayas they could not fail to be struck by a 'common bond'.

In the final stages of *Mother World*, the purpose of his latest notion is revealed. It was Younghusband's conviction that the world was 'groaning and travailing to bring forth a leader': the 'Christ that is to be', a development of the God-Child he had first prophesied in *Within*. Soon a baby would be born 'at one with World Mother', enabling the human race to undergo a religious rebirth. In the last paragraph, he drops his guard and enters a state of mystical ecstasy:

> And so tuned, he touched closest revered Mother World and far into her mingled, as lover with homeland, in sacred communion. His being expanded to infinite measure . . . in rapt adoration, he let himself flow.[17]

Such excitement might have surprised readers of *Wonders of the Himalaya*, which was published in the same year. Sir Francis had considered writing it as 'a book for boys', but decided that boys prefer 'books written for men'. It gave a breathless account of his adventures in India and Central Asia, avoiding the Gobi Desert journey which had already been covered in *The Heart of a Continent*. He wrote of his first trip over the Rhotang Pass and the taming of the Mir of Hunza five years later. It was a well-paced book, and the critical reception was enthusiastic. Younghusband evoked 'some lost legendary golden age', wrote the *Manchester Guardian*: 'There is no trace anywhere in his writings of the dull, incurious insolence of mind which smears repulsively so many English books about India.'[18]

The success of *Wonders of the Himalaya* persuaded him to produce *Peking to Lhasa: Journeys made by the late Brigadier General George Pereira*. His friend Pereira was a veteran of the Boxer Rebellion who had made a remarkable expedition across China and eastern Tibet in the early 1920s, but died of a gastric ulcer as he approached its end. Younghusband wrote an account of the journey, mixing extracts from Pereira's journals with his own commentary. It was published in 1925, and followed in 1926 by *But In Our Lives: A Romance of the Indian Frontier*, the mawkish autobiographical novel which has been referred to in earlier chapters. It tells the story of the heavenly Evan Lee, who introduces sporting activity to his regiment in an attempt to ward off VD, only to die from a Gulistani's sword blow on the frontier.

But Younghusband was not satisfied with writing stories of physical adventure; he wanted to return to the spiritual realm. 1927 was a year of compromise, for he published both *The Light of Experience: A Review of some men and events of my time* (an interesting but conventional set of memoirs, covering India, Tibet, South Africa and his friendship with a variety of eminent figures) and the more outlandish *Life in the Stars: An Exposition of the View that on some Planets of some Stars exist Beings higher than Ourselves, and on one a World-Leader, the Supreme Embodiment of the Eternal Spirit which animates the Whole*. To his disappointment, it was *The Light of Experience* which received the more exuberant response from public and critics.

Under the headline SIR F. YOUNGHUSBAND'S GOSPEL, the *Yorkshire Post* called it his 'greatest contribution to literature' and 'certainly one of the remarkable books of these days'. British newspapers were equally complimentary, comparing Younghusband to Marco Polo and describing him as a 'symbol of adventure' for more than a generation. The response of the American reviewers is more intriguing. Although he had a strong popular following in the United States – where the book sold well – there was a far greater willingness to dissect his activities and opinions. The *New York Times* felt he was a 'perfect empire builder' who managed to combine an unusual range of ideas; although to call him 'a Dr Jekyll and Mr Hyde would be discourteous'.

The *Herald Tribune* was less flattering, opening its review with a sharp barb:

> He, like Ulysses, is a legendary hero, for what he did in Tibet and the Himalayas; but, unlike Ulysses, he was not content to be merely a hero. He wanted also to be a writer, and not merely a writer, but an 'author'. He has been writing books for thirty years – and they have been getting steadily worse.

The reviewer claimed that although Younghusband's knowledge and experience could not be matched, he was incapable of communicating his ideas through prose. His philosophical works were dismissed as being naive and 'more or less pathetic', and as for *The Light of Experience*: 'Its amiable puerility is almost incredible.'[19]

Yet although some reviews were hostile, at least the book was noticed. *Life in the Stars* suffered the indignity of being ignored, except in the United States where it was treated with some seriousness. It was given the lead review in the *New York Times*, which felt it was interesting despite being naive and scientifically inaccurate. The greatest compliment however came from the British *Quarterly Review*, with the claim that, 'Of all people, living or once alive, none would have appreciated Sir Francis Younghusband's book more than William Blake.'[20] It was a bizarre book, even by the standards of his recent work, involving another change of style and theory. The first section marked a return to the pseudo-science of *Within*, complete with complex accounts of nebulae and star clusters. Younghusband claimed that whether you took a biological or philosophical starting point, you would arrive at the same conclusion: there must be intelligent beings on other planets. 'What was before a speculation is now for me a conviction.' By wrapping up his fantastic notions in scientific garb, he hoped to make them more convincing to his readers.

In the latter part of *Life in the Stars* he moves from science to science fiction, by elaborating on Boodin's theory that for the human mind to have developed in the way it has, there must be higher levels of intelligence elsewhere in the universe. Extraterrestrials 'may be exercising an influence on our lives just as surely as members of the Houses of Parliament in debate exercise an influence on the lives of remote savages in the forests of Central Africa'. Younghusband then strays into regions of true absurdity as he tries to envisage the inhabitants of distant planets. Despite his willingness to postulate the most outlandish theories, he is unable to make the mental leap away from his own limited environment. Alien beings 'must be born, grow up, come to maturity, earn a living, marry, produce offspring, rear their offspring, and die'. Although they may grow wings and have non-verbal methods of communication, they would certainly be sensitive, polite, charming and animated by 'strong *esprit de corps*'.

He then makes a decided move away from the embracing feminine anima of *Mother World*, imagining a strict hierarchy among the aliens. At the pinnacle is the 'World-Leader', a universally influential figure selected on a rotating basis by the 'higher beings'. 'He would be Holiness itself made manifest,' wrote Younghusband, 'the very embodiment of the Holy Spirit of the World: a hallowed Presence in which all would bend the knee.' Contact between him and his subjects would be through 'heavenly music', telepathy or 'ether waves'.[21] Like a flock of birds, they would move as a group, united by an elevated vibration 'springing directly from the essential nature of the Genius of the Whole through the closeness of their contact with it'.[22]

One unexpected admirer of *Life in the Stars* was the Chief Scout, Lord Baden-Powell, who took the book with him on a voyage to New Zealand. 'My dear Younghusband,' he wrote:

> I have . . . been greatly impressed by it. Indeed I reckon myself a disciple . . . as you may possibly recognise from my remarks in my little book 'Rovering to Success' . . . I only hope that someday I may persuade you to come and see our training camp for scoutmasters in Epping Forest and possibly – if you would care to – to speak a few words to them, since you are the very type that I put before them as my ideal 'Peace Scout'.[23]

Although he had admired the Scout Movement when it was set up in 1908, as the years went by Younghusband became increasingly doubtful about its militaristic regimentation. Further invitations from his disciple were turned down: 'That old Baden-Powell rang me up wanting me to make a speech to some Boy Scouts,' he wrote to Helen in April 1928. 'I said Nothing doing!'[24]

As if *Life in the Stars* was not enough, Younghusband soon went off on another tangent in *The Coming Country: A Pre-Vision*. It is a bizarre kind of novel cum moral fable, a cross between Morris's *News From Nowhere*, Bunyan's *Pilgrim's Progress* and his own *But In Our Lives*. Its blend of saccharine piety, unconvincing characterization and vapid moral platitudes is truly astonishing, especially since it had been rewritten under the instruction of Henry Newbolt. Most newspapers and magazines avoided *The Coming Country*; although the *Daily Herald* ran a rather uncertain review, unsure whether the book was intended as a joke. The idea that one should 'devote one's energies solely to the organisation of Sacred Dramas, Community Singing and Nature Festivals' was surely ridiculous.[25]

Each character has a name that is intended to reflect her or his outlook on life. There is Golden Promyss ('a straight, clean-living young man with an alert, fearless look'), Vera Love (his kindly auntie), Manew Fakchurer (a manufacturer), Vicker (a vicar), Frank Kritik (a reasonably frank critic), Fyre Brand (a Communist revolutionary), Messrs Scoff and Croker (who ridicule the staging of religious drama), and the self-explanatory Clere Lyte, Vapid Worldling, Percy Veerance, Blak Enmytie, Gay Kurridge, Fikkel Kapress and Earnest Interest.

Francis Younghusband first met this remarkable cast of characters when he was wandering in the Himalayas, and chanced to stumble on a remote place called Ourownland. It was there that he developed Endsight, 'a kind of spiritual television' (Baird had invented the television two years before) which enabled him to see into the depths of people's hearts. The book has no firm plot, but for over three hundred exhausting pages the reader is told of holiness, co-operation between clergy and laity, singing and the joys of family life. The citizens of a town called Towne form both a 'Truth Society' and a 'Zenith League', at which significant questions are debated. How reliable is Henri Bergson's theory of the spirit? Was Jesus divine?

About half-way through *The Coming Country*, the staging of religious plays becomes the primary activity. First there are 'sacred tableaux', in which religious scenes are mimed behind a gauze screen while Vicker reads from the Bible. Then they act scenes from the life of Jesus, such as his encounter with John the Baptist (played by Mr Flaming Zeele). Some villagers are impressed, but Frank Kritik is not, so a new, finer production is staged, starring Vera Love and Golden Promyss. People burst out in spontaneous prayer and the cynical Sekuler Kulcher is spotted 'running over with the milk of human kindness'. Overwhelmed by 'the choir-spirit and a passion for holiness', the message of Ourownland travels far and wide, as lark-like singers start 'flooding the heavens' with 'glorious paeans of praise'.[26]

The development of Younghusband's theoretical spirituality had almost reached its climax. He had one more step to take. In 1933 he would publish *The Living Universe*, a book replete with asexual aliens, ether vibrations and a far-off planet called Altair:

> It is different with this planet of Altair, because here are beings far higher than men – beings reputed to be the highest in the whole universe – beings who in the highest degree embody the Cosmic Spirit . . .

In it he makes a firm challenge to prevailing scientific thought, claiming that in a benevolent universe there must be a 'winding-up' of energy rather than a 'running-down'. It is his contention that a living force is attempting to evolve highly developed creatures, such as those on the planet Altair. Like similar ideas in *Life in the Stars*, his suggestion is both brave and ridiculous, as he attempts to articulate his vision. Why he chose to name his planet Altair is unclear (he had chosen 'Stellair' in the past): it may have come from the Latin altus meaning 'high', or from the Altai mountains on the edge of the Gobi Desert.

He suggests that Altairians are translucent beings who communicate with one another 'on the pinions of the ether', assisted by 'delicate organs of perception . . . They would have windows to the world around them where we have only dense walls of the flesh.' On Altair '*Esprit-de-corps* would be at its most fervent pitch', enabling them to live in harmonious communities. Highly evolved Altairians would be an asexual combination of male and female, and the 'supreme leader' would 'really be a pair, a "man" and a "woman" so united as to be reciprocal in their activities, so mutually stimulative and responsive as to act as one – as indeed we have an example in General and Mrs Booth, the great founders of the Salvation Army'.

Younghusband's rampant optimism endorsed a rhythmic, pulsating cosmos 'that men can trust' and 'lay hold of'. As ever, he felt compelled to cast his amorphous ideas in stone. The inhabitants of Altair had to have a firm physical form and an assured structure of leadership, which could be compared to something as stolid as the Salvation Army. Only then did he feel happy with his flights of fancy, dreaming of the day when: 'As reptiles developed into birds, homo sapiens may develop into *homo mysticus*.'[27]

Reaction was predictable: newspapers ignored the book or

politely dismissed it as nonsense, while his British and American devotees applauded. 'That some reviewers should consider it "too fanciful" I can well believe,' wrote one, 'but the Sun will always Gild the mountain top before it touches the plain, and from "penny a line-ers" one cannot ask [for] that conception of Evolution of Nobility of Life that grants that: "Veil after veil shall lift." '[28]

'Was he barking mad?' This was the question that I found myself being asked whenever I tried to explain Sir Francis Younghusband's mystical theories. The first part of his life was easy enough: anybody could understand a young thruster crossing the Gobi or spying in the Karakorams. But how on earth (or on Altair) could I explain cosmic vibrations, World-Leaders and God-children? Indeed what were Younghusband's theories? They changed and developed and contradicted each other so frequently that it was hard to pin him down with certainty. But on one thing I was sure: he was not 'mad' or mentally unstable. In many respects he was saner at this stage of his life than he ever had been before; certainly he was more at ease with himself and his own aspirations. What is harder to fathom is how seriously he took his own ideas, and where he found them.

While writing books like *The Gleam* and *The Coming Country*, Younghusband was leading a perfectly conventional outward life, organizing the Everest Expeditions, going to church on Sundays and attending Buckingham Palace garden parties. Somehow at the same time he managed to dream up a plethora of bizarre conceptions. He would take the work of philosophers he admired, like Sorley, Moore or Bergson, and elaborate their ideas into fresh proposals. These would be mixed with the extensive jottings he had made in his notebooks under headings such as Homo Mysticus, Cosmogony and The Governance of the Universe, and then rewritten. *Life in the Stars*, for example, began as a work of comparative philosophy, and only in its third draft did it come to concentrate on distant planets. The actual manuscripts were written at great speed. Between 1920 and 1930 Younghusband published no fewer than twelve full-length books; like many of his generation, he was astonishingly prolific.

As for the theories, they seem to have been projections of spiritual possibility rather than definite statements of 'fact'. Younghusband often wrote in the subjunctive in the first person plural ('We now see that the divine spirit would rise . . .') in an effort to convince his readers that his meanderings were part of a shared experience. Although at the time of writing he may have believed there was a World-Leader on a distant planet who communicated with the rest of the universe by ether waves, it was probably a temporary conviction rather than an absolute belief. It was an attempt to grab hold of his life-long spiritual intuition and embody it in physical form. He had an endless need to expand and stabilize the intangible realization with which he believed he had been blessed.

Younghusband's problem was that his means of communication was seriously flawed. His attempts to make his message comprehensible succeeded only in making it absurd. As the *New Statesman* wrote of his theorizing in 1923: 'It presents an ill-assorted mixture of religion, modern science, philosophy, patriotism and love; it is illogical, it is inconsistent; it shirks difficulties, it is over-credulous of anything vaguely altruistic, it breathes a too easy optimism; and much of it is sheer nonsense. Nevertheless, its naive sentimentality disarms criticism.'[29] Aware that his books had limitations, Younghusband tried other means of putting across his spiritual message during the 1920s.

One of his earlier methods had been the private publication during the Great War of short pamphlets with titles like *Religion and Empire* and *England's Mission*. These were dispatched optimistically to his acquaintances, but had a tendency to disappear without trace. Newspapers and magazines seemed a better way of reaching the people of Britain. Younghusband went to see the editor of *The Times*, Geoffrey Dawson, with a radical plan to transform the paper. Golf, racing and political news were all very well, but what really mattered was religion. Throughout the Empire, Younghusband said, followers of Islam despised the irreligious ways of the British. Dawson parried with a suggestion that he write a short article on the subject: Younghusband responded with a great series under the heading 'Savages or Saints?', but Dawson rejected them as unsuitable. 'I mean to see the idea through,' runs a note on the manuscript, 'and the day will come when the Times will regret turning this down. F.E.Y.'[30]

Younghusband's theories of religion were published in any publication that would take them. Usually the articles elaborated on ideas he had already included in his books: 'The Faith of the Future',

'This Lovable World', 'God and the Universe', and so forth. These were supplemented by book reviews and frequent letters on anything from the connection between shell shock and the divine spirit, to a denunciation of the British mandate in Palestine on the grounds that it would increase conflict between Christians and Mohamedans. Popular papers such as the *Daily Herald* and the *Daily Express* usually turned down his religious pronouncements, although they were happy to publish innocuous recollections of his early years with titles like 'The Spirit of a Boy'.

Public speaking was another method of propagation. The need for unity between religions was a theme with which he became increasingly preoccupied. Many of the world's problems came from a particular faith believing it had an exclusive hold on truth, he told the Conference of Living Religions. Younghusband spoke in schools and colleges and town halls; to learned societies and obscure outfits; in London and the provinces; to huge gatherings and to audiences of three; to a Guildhouse meeting on 'The Riddle of the Universe', to his local parish church on 'The England To Be', and to the Autosuggestion Institute on 'Better and Better – and Best'. Each speech was carefully prepared in the library of the RGS or the Travellers' Club. Although he was not a naturally gifted public speaker, he recognized his own limitations and overcame them by relying on a written text and a steady delivery. Often his audiences would receive a surprise. University College London expected a lecture on geography, but found it extended to Natural Beauty and the gender of the planet: 'Now the Earth I regard as a lady – as dear Mother-Earth. A real living being – live enough, at any rate, to give birth to mankind.'[31]

Throughout this period Younghusband had an overwhelming need to express and rationalize the religious impulse he could feel within himself; each day his vision drove him forward. The certainty of his ambition was increased on the last night of September 1925, when he had a mystical experience more forceful and profound even than the one in Tibet. It convinced him that he had been granted a degree of spiritual perception that set him apart from others. 'I had a strong premonition that the Power of the Spirit would come on me again,' he wrote in a precise hand the following morning.

> In the middle of the night – about three – I awoke and I immediately knew the Power was coming. I made one desperate effort to resist and then it was on me. I felt it in

my legs first. They were convulsed and shook violently.

Then it came all over me till I was filled with it. And I gave great puffs – as it were to blow the spirit out of me before it could overwhelm me. But I was filled and filled with it and could no more fight against it. It took absolute possession of me and I just settled down and lay there. And then a wonderful peace came on me – most beautiful and sweet.

Fortunately Helen was not sharing his bedroom by this stage of their marriage; Sir Francis lay alone, 'collected and composed', trying to take in and comprehend the experience.

'I feel like the clear sky after a storm,' he wrote.[32]

TWENTY-ONE

Running the Jog and Climbing
Mount Everest

'I sometimes think of this expedition as a fraud from beginning to end,' wrote George Mallory from the snow-swept slopes of Everest, 'invented by the wild enthusiasm of one man, Younghusband; puffed up by the would-be wisdom of certain pundits in the Alpine Club; and imposed upon the youthful ardour of your humble servant.'[1] It is the Everest expeditions of the 1920s that mark Younghusband's most prominent excursion into public life after his supposed retirement. They were a relaxed, post-Edwardian complement to the Great Game: adventures in the Himalayas with great risk but no strategic purpose. The mountaineers, or Everesters as they called themselves, followed Younghusband's trail from Darjeeling to the Dzelap La and Phari, before turning benignly west towards the foothills of Everest. Their expeditions were the peaceful successor to his invasion of 1904.

During the time that he was writing about Cosmic Spirits and the God-Child, Younghusband was leading an active parallel career. In June 1919 he was appointed President of the Royal Geographical Society in succession to Sir Thomas Holdich, author of *Tibet, the Mysterious*. It was a fitting climax to his involvement with the RGS (or the 'Jog' as he called it), which had begun with his election as its youngest Fellow in 1888. The Presidency was a position of substantial public clout, with influence extending well into the Colonial Office. The late nineteenth and early twentieth century marked the height of the Royal Geographical Society's fame. It was the stamping ground of explorers and officials from all over the Empire, including many both eminent and retired, who were often happy to irritate those in power by conducting an alternative foreign policy from the steps of Number One Kensington Gore.

In 1913 the RGS had moved to Lowther Lodge, an imposing building between Hyde Park and the Royal Albert Hall. Under Lord Curzon's Presidency (1911–14) 'the finest country house in London' had been refitted and refurbished. By 1919 the Jog was

well installed in its new premises. Younghusband was stepping into
a plum position, and could decide for himself how much time he
devoted to his Presidential duties. Curzon had been a working President (as he was a working everything — he terrified the Oxford
dons when he was Chancellor of the University by ruling the place
'like an Indian province'), but other incumbents had taken a purely
ceremonial role. Younghusband proved to be fairly active in the
job, although he allowed Arthur Hinks, the pedantic Secretary, to
make most day-to-day decisions.

Hinks was a clever, awkward cartographer who maintained effective control over the Society from 1913 until his retirement in 1945.
He had prolonged, scalding disputes with many of his colleagues,
but Younghusband avoided conflict by teasing him and letting him
get his own way. When Hinks wanted to name the long hall of the
RGS the 'ambulatory', Younghusband said: 'If that is the ambulatory, then you shall be known as the perambulator.'[2] The Younghusbands treated 'Hinkie' as a running joke. 'The Jog function yday.
was a huge success,' Sir Francis wrote to his daughter after one
official event. 'There were very nice little Japaneses and a Turk &
a Serb in full uniform like a Fireman & Armenians & heaven knows
who else . . . Hinkie not a bit swollen [headed] & in great glee . . .
Mrs Hinkie surpassed herself.'[3]

Younghusband attended to his duties at the RGS, but was 'determined to make this Everest venture the main feature of [his] three
years' Presidency'.[4] It was an activity that some of the Society's
professionals saw as a distraction from the real business of geography. He raised the subject in his inaugural Presidential Address in
May 1920, his speech being reported in every daily newspaper. 'If
I am asked what is the use of climbing this highest mountain,'
Younghusband announced, to the chagrin of the scientific geographers, 'I reply, No use at all: no more use than kicking a football
about, or dancing, or playing the piano, or writing a poem, or
painting a picture.'[5] Unlike his fellow Victorians he was moving
away from a rigid, empirical approach to geographical exploration
towards a looser definition, in which experience and personal fulfilment were as important as bald statistics. The press were keenly
excited by the project, although the *Evening News* thought it would
be a great shame if 'trespassers' were allowed to tread upon the
pinnacle of the Earth.

Younghusband had first considered an Everest ascent while walking across the Chitral polo ground with Charlie 'Bruiser' Bruce
three decades before.[6] The idea was resurrected in 1919 when a

young adventurer, Captain John Noel, spoke to the RGS about his experiences in the foothills of Mount Everest. In the discussion that followed, several big names such as Younghusband, Freshfield and Captain Farrar of the Alpine Club supported the idea of an attempt on the summit. The press ran reports and opinions on the feasibility of an ascent. *Punch* printed a parody called 'Himalayans at Play' which caught the tone of the debate: 'Sir Francis Oldmead' said his preferred route to the summit was 'up the Yulmag valley to the Chikkim frontier at Lor-Lumi, crossing the Pildash at Gonglam, and skirting the deep gorge of the Spudgyal'. Having discussed 'manlifting kites and trained albatrosses, the assembly dispersed after singing the Tibetan national anthem'.[7]

Three weeks after his Presidential Address, Younghusband led a delegation of dignitaries to the India Office for a meeting with the Under-Secretary of State, Lord Sinha. After some per-suasion, the authorities agreed to allow Colonel Howard Bury – an Anglo-Irish landowner who had never climbed a mountain in his life – to proceed to India for some preliminary diplomatic and geographical reconnaissance. Although Everest straddled both Tibet and Nepal, the political situation meant they had to settle for an approach from the Tibetan side. The Lhasa Government issued an early mountaineering permit, informing the regional Dzongpons that 'a party of Sahibs are coming to see the Cha-mo-lung-ma mountain and they will evince great friendship towards the Tibetans. On the request of the Great Minister [Charles] Bell, a passport has been issued requiring you [to supply transport] as required by the Sahibs.'[8]

Younghusband sent an unsolicited letter of thanks to the Dalai Lama, his first attempt at correspondence with the Holder of the White Lotus since the Gyantse ultimatum of 1904. He avoided any mention of his invasion of Tibet, concentrating instead on express-ing his gratitude to the Tibetan leader for granting permission to climb 'the great mountain which we call Mount Everest'. The clim-bers would take all necessary steps to comply with the demands of Tibetan officials, and avoid interfering with local customs, he insisted, before signing himself: 'With great respect and much con-sideration, Believe me, Your Holiness' very sincere friend, Francis Younghusband.'[9] As ever, the Dalai Lama did not respond to the importunities of Colonel Younghusband.

So it was that the myth was born of the Everesters, those lithe and romantic young Englishmen with their Chamonix caps, thick tweed coats and stout walking boots, who pitted their wits and their character against Chomolungma, the Goddess Mother of the World. George Bernard Shaw compared their adventures to a picnic in Connemara surprised by a snowstorm; James Morris thought an Everest expedition consisted of 'a group of English sportsmen, attended by their native servants, trying to climb an impossibly difficult hill in a ludicrously distant place, and quietly risking their lives in doing so'.[10] The Everesters reached their physical and spiritual apotheosis in George Mallory, who died on Everest in 1924, and their practical climax when Tenzin and Hillary reached the summit in 1953, the news breaking on the day that Queen Elizabeth II was crowned.

A Mount Everest Committee was formed under Younghusband's chairmanship, with Hinks as Secretary, consisting of RGS and Alpine Club officials, and a representative from the War Office. There were to be strong rivalries and innumerable conflicts within the Committee over the coming years, but Younghusband proved to be a perfect Chairman. He had no interest in internal politics, floating serenely above the disputes in a mystical cloud. Yet he was utterly determined that the expedition would succeed, and used his innumerable contacts to ensure its progress. His own achievements as an explorer meant that his pronouncements were obeyed, and at fifty-seven he was old enough to be revered while young enough to be energetic. He also had experience as a journalist, and was surprisingly adept at using the press to the expedition's advantage, to the consternation of Hinkie, who had 'a pathological distaste for publicity'.[11]

Younghusband's popularity among the mountaineers remained strong throughout; to an extent he acted as a foil to the sarcastic Hinks. His boundless optimism and mystical belief in the significance of the expedition was a continual encouragement to the climbers. 'I could not have had a more delightful and understanding chief,' wrote Howard Bury after the 1921 expedition was over.[12] 'I

had the greatest admiration & affection for the old man,' declared
Edward Norton, the pig-sticking enthusiast who led the fateful 1924
expedition: 'He was the very salt of the earth, & if there were
more like him the world would be a very different place.'[13] To Jack
Longland, of 'the '33 show', he was simply, 'a historic hero, to
whom we looked up'.[14]

As news of the forthcoming ascent became public, suggestions
poured in on the necessary involvement of kites, balloons, Bovril,
aircraft, meta-stoves and ski lifts. The offers of equipment were in
some cases accepted, but unsolicited applicants turned down by the
Committee in favour of upper-to-middle-class young-to-middle-
aged men, most of whom had a military or a medical background.
The star was a public schoolmaster and minor Bloomsbury groupie,
George Leigh Mallory. He was, according to Younghusband, 'certainly good-looking, with a sensible, cultivated air', although 'slim
and supple, if not broad and beefy'. The essayist Lytton Strachey
was less restrained: 'Mon Dieu! – George Mallory! – When that's
been written, what more need be said? My hand trembles, my
heart palpitates, my whole being swoons away at the words – oh
heavens! heavens! . . . he's six foot high, with the body of an athlete
by Praxiteles, and a face – oh incredible . . .'[15]

While the halls of the Jog throbbed with activity, and the Committee did its best to raise funds from the notables of Britain, Younghusband negotiated the sale of photographic and telegram rights
with the help of John Buchan. *The Times* was the principal benefici-
ary, and was to remain so into the future. Younghusband busied
himself sending wires to civil and military officials out in India, and
persuaded the Indian army to assist in the organization of mules
and supplies. As the Party of Sahibs set sail from East India Docks
in the spring of 1921, he presided paternally over the proceedings.
'Younghusband amuses and delights me more than anything – grim
old apostle of beauty and adventure,' wrote Mallory in a letter to
a friend. 'The Everest Expedition has become a sort of religious
pilgrimage in his eyes. I expect I shall end by sitting at his feet,
hearing tales of Lhasa and Chitral.'[16]

Younghusband's public image was revived by the expeditions. Newspapers dredged up stories of his Himalayan exploits, portraying him as the embodiment of the Everest spirit. According to the *Children's Newspaper*, he was 'the hero of dazzling adventures in hazardous exploration, a writer of noble English, a daring soldier, and a great gentleman'.[17] The *Englishman* commended his understanding of Eastern beliefs, while observing that he had 'qualities that are not usually associated with Englishmen'. It recounted an anecdote from his Great Gaming years. While sitting beside a camp fire in the mountains, a group of officers had been choosing the historical figures they most admired. When Younghusband's turn came, he astonished them by naming not Nelson or Sir John Lawrence, but the Bengali revivalist Ram Mohun Roy and the Hindu religious leader Ramakrishna, a man derided by most Britishers as a wild fakir.[18]

During the 1920s and 1930s, Younghusband came to be perceived as Britain's international geographical ambassador, even when he had given up the post of President of the RGS. He was given honours and awards by the Geographical Societies of Paris, Vienna, America, Italy, Canada and Belgium, often being summoned to the relevant country for a presentation.[19] Sometimes his high profile could have embarrassing consequences for others. When a delegation of Jog bigwigs were visiting Buckingham Palace in 1928, George V asked to speak to the President of the Society. Sir Charles Close, who by then had taken over from Younghusband, 'meekly said that he was the President'. But the King was not interested in 'Poor Close', and simply demanded: 'Where is Younghusband?'[20]

During this time Younghusband gave many lectures and talks, and wrote two definitive works on the early expeditions: *The Epic of Mount Everest* and the shorter *Everest: The Challenge*. Both books gave an insider's account of the adventures, touching briefly on mystical matters, and sold well in Britain and abroad. There were many perks to be gained from his status. In March 1925 he was invited to an International Congress of Geographers in Egypt as head of the British delegation. Arriving in Alexandria he was met by a man from Thomas Cook's who asked: 'You are Sir Husband?' and whisked him off to Cairo to attend the opening of the new Opera House. 'I was given a ticket,' he told Helen, 'but had not the least idea where my seat was. To my astonishment it was on the platform in the seat of honour immediately next to the Prime Minister, a very fat determined old gentleman.'[21]

That evening there was a reception at the King's Palace, followed by a fortnight of pyramid-visiting, speech-making, banquets and entertainment. 'We are having a roaring time,' he wrote to Eileen. 'I am the "haute personalité dans le monde geographique".'

> I tell them all I was here sixty-one years ago before the Suez Canal was built . . . In my speech at the Jubilee Celebration of the Egyptian Geographical Society I said that Egypt had only one defect – it had no Mount Everest. They took this quite solemnly at the time and thought I really meant it was a defect. But several hours afterwards they came up to me beaming and said 'C'était le humour anglais!'[22]

The head of the French delegation was Paul Pelliot, the controversial Sinologist who had obtained unique ancient manuscripts from the Caves of the Thousand Buddhas at Dunhuang. Younghusband thought him 'a good little man', although 'like so many Frenchmen he broke down badly when he got excited'.[23] There were numerous other well-known figures to meet. While dining with the High Commissioner Lord Allenby, Younghusband found himself seated beside Howard Carter who was busy excavating Tutankhamen's tomb.

Sailing back towards Brindisi, he wrote to Eileen telling her how much he had enjoyed the trip. 'Those old Gyppies produced a gold medal . . . so I have brought back some loot after all. We had a huge banquet on the last night in a perfectly gigantic hotel – the Heliopolis – about eight miles out of Cairo. There was a band and speeches galore . . . Among the first to leave the gay scene was Sir Francis Younghusband accompanied by a friendly Pasha who thinking he would copy "le humour Anglais" said he hoped that in another 61 years I would come again!'[24]

The following April Younghusband found himself in Rome with that ardent Alpinist, Pope Pius XI. The meeting had been set up by his fellow Vice-President of the Royal Society of Literature, the Bohemian diplomat Rennell Rodd. Having been introduced to a swathe of Swiss Guards in 'purple coats and knickerbockers', Younghusband was summoned to the Papal presence. His Holiness asked 'about Lhasa and the Himalaya and was very kindly and appreciative'. According to a Reuter's Special Service report (under the headline: EVEREST CLIMBERS AND THE POPE: SIR F. YOUNGHUSBAND RECEIVED IN AUDIENCE), the Pontiff 'was greatly pleased and expressed his very keen interest in the Expedition, he himself being a lover of mountaineering'.[25]

Out in the Himalayas things were proceeding satisfactorily. Having been photographed in school-team fashion on the verandah of the Planter's Club, in Darjeeling, the nine British men and several hundred porters set off for the mountain. After three exhausting weeks they reached Khamba Dzong, the desolate spot where Younghusband had bided his time in 1903 before the main invasion of Tibet. From there all was speculation: as Mallory put it, they had to 'walk off the map'. They engaged in reconnaissance for several months, taking photographs and assessing the northern approach to Everest from their base camp near the Buddhist monastery at Rongbuk. Then the climbers returned home.

The following year they tried again in earnest, the expedition being led this time by 'Bruiser' Bruce, now known as Burra (Big) Sahib on account of his status and his corpulence. They intended to attempt an assault on the summit. Accompanied by glass bottles of champagne, steel bottles of oxygen, leather waistcoats (to wear under their woollen coats) and tins of quail-in-aspic, they set off into the Himalayan snow. At Rongbuk, Bruce managed to secure a meeting with the 'Great Lama'. He was a figure who crops up in the memoirs of several of the Everesters, who regarded him with some reverence and sought his blessing before climbing; Bruce found him 'full of dignity, with a most intelligent and wise face'.

At first the Tibetan monks were wary of the climbers, having heard tales of Younghusband's 1904 invasion. As on that occasion, there was a profound cultural gulf between the British and the Tibetans: Chomolungma was sacred, and the monks were puzzled as to why the foreigners wanted to climb it and disturb the mountain spirits. Burra Sahib claimed in *The Assault on Mount Everest* that he got round this problem by telling the Lama they were mountain worshippers on a pilgrimage, a statement not far from the truth given Younghusband's ideas on the subject. The Rongbuk Lama, Ngawang Tenzin Norbu, records a slightly different version of events in his autobiography:

'Where are you going?' I asked.

'As this snow peak is the biggest in the world, if we arrive on the summit we will get from the British Government a payment and high rank,' said the ja-nan [general] . . . 'We will not harm the birds and wild animals of this area. I swear our entire weaponry consists of this little penknife.'

Then relying on ingenious devices such as iron spikes, wire threads and iron claws they strove to climb the mountain.

Three separate assaults were made during the 1922 expedition, as a series of camps was installed at different levels on the mountain. The second attempt reached a height of over 27,000 feet, but on the third there was an avalanche, and seven Sherpa porters were swept to their death. The Rongbuk Lama organized several religious ceremonies in memory of the dead men, one of which was intended to deal with the bad karma they had accumulated by climbing the mountain. 'I was filled with great compassion,' wrote the monk, 'that they underwent such suffering in unnecessary work.'[26]

Mallory believed his decision to set off in poor weather had caused the disaster. 'I'm very much to blame for this terrible accident and I'm very sorry,' he wrote to Younghusband from the mountainside.[27] One of the climbers – Howard Somervell, who later became an ardent Indian nationalist – wrote: 'Only Sherpas and Bhotias killed – why, oh why could not one of us Britishers have shared their fate?'[28] Younghusband took a less commendable view of the calamity in a letter to Helen: 'They have done so splendidly it is particularly bad luck. But thank goodness no European life was lost.'[29] The charitable interpretation of this remark would be that it was made in haste, and that Younghusband was relieved none of his friends had been killed.

The expedition reached England in dribs and drabs, to the indignation of the meticulous Hinks who expected such things to be conducted in a more orderly style. Lecture tours and film shows were arranged, and another series of newspaper features and profiles written. 'I came up to see Mallory who is not at all cross,' Younghusband told his daughter from Brooks' Club, 'the first one ever back from Everest who was not. He is only a little sad, and I rather gather does not want to go again. He is all for younger men – who don't know anything at all about it.'[30] But under pressure from the Mount Everest Committee George Mallory did go back, with a premonition, some said, of the fate that awaited him.

They reached Rongbuk Monastery again in April 1924. It was now becoming a permanent outpost of the Jog and the Alpine Club, a sort of spiritual and practical starting point for assaults on the great mountain. Two attempts to reach the summit were made that year, Norton the pig-sticker attaining a height of over 28,000 feet without oxygen. Then on the morning of 8 June, Mallory set out from his camp with the twenty-one-year-old Andrew 'Sandy' Irvine. A little after midday they were seen ascending the first, or possibly the second, step below the summit. Then the peak of Everest became enveloped in cloud, and the mystery of Mallory and Irvine could begin. However many monographs are written in the *Alpine Journal* about the probable course of events on that fateful day, nobody will ever know for certain whether Mallory and Irvine reached the top before they died; and that, of course, is the enigmatic excitement of it.

Sir Francis Younghusband, optimistic as ever, had firm views on the subject. Mallory 'knew the dangers before him and was prepared to meet them', he wrote in *The Epic of Mount Everest*. 'He could imagine the thrill his success would cause among all fellow-mountaineers; the credit it would bring to England . . . Of the two alternatives, to turn back a third time, or to die, the latter was for Mallory probably the easier. The agony of the first would be more than he as a man, as a mountaineer, and as an artist, could endure.'[31] After all, the two climbers had last been seen 'going strong' for the summit. Mallory's wife took a different line. 'I know George did not mean to be killed,' she wrote in a private letter.[32]

There were no more attempts on Mount Everest for another decade. The cause of the delay was not the death of Mallory and Irvine, but the activities of a group of chanting, dancing, horn-blowing monks from Gyantse. They were brought over to Britain in January 1925 by John Noel, whose talk at the RGS had sparked the first expedition, to provide accompaniment to a silent film called 'The Ascent of Everest'. In the most appalling conditions, Noel had lugged his clockwork cameras up the mountain, shot yards of film and developed fragile photographic plates in a darkroom-tent at

21,000 feet. The finished product was distributed by Explorer Films Ltd (Chairman: Sir Francis Younghusband), a company which had been set up by Noel to buy the film and photographic rights to the 1924 expedition.

The monks caused almost as much stir as the footage when they popped up in the cinemas of London. Tibet still had a powerful hold on the popular imagination, and there was great excitement at the prospect of seeing mysterious 'holy men' engaging in cacophonous 'devil dances' while George Mallory climbed Everest with jerky steps. Younghusband ran the head monk around the country, taking him to St Paul's, the India Office, the Jog and Lambeth Palace, where the Archbishop of Canterbury presented him with an illustrated edition of the Bible. According to the Archbishop, 'the visit of the Tibetan Lama to England' was 'a unique thing in the story of the world'.[33] Since Tibetan books are not bound, the monk promptly dismembered his new scripture and distributed the loose pages to his comrades.

Problems arose when the Tibetan Government heard about the monks' antics. An angry letter was sent to the British Political Officer in Sikkim, who had responsibility for relations with Tibet, objecting to certain scenes in Noel's film, its frivolously offensive captions and the fact the monks had been enticed to London 'deceitfully'. Charles Bell had retired, and the new PO in Sikkim was the 1904 veteran F. M. Bailey. The Tibetans' letter was one of several pieces of evidence he assembled against the Everesters. Since arriving in Sikkim, he had found the expeditions an unwarranted irritant to Anglo–Tibetan relations, and so developed a slightly irrational antipathy towards them. When John Noel told some injudicious lies to the India Office about the monks' passports, a furious row blew up between Hinks, Bailey, Noel and the Secretary of State for India.[34]

Although 'Hatter' Bailey had begun his career as a protégé of Younghusband's, he had no qualms about helping to stop the expeditions. As the sole mediator between Tibet and India, he was able to ensure there were no more attempts to conquer the mountain. Supplications were made by the Everest Committee, and a yellow silk bag (embroidered by Eileen Younghusband) was dispatched to the Dalai Lama, stuffed with photographs of the Himalayas. But it made no difference: mountaineering on Everest was now forbidden. Younghusband did however remain on good terms with Bailey, and still saw him occasionally during the 1930s. 'I ran up against Colonel Bailey in the street,' he wrote to Eileen in

October 1929, 'and got him to lunch. He was most amusing. He has brought home thirteen Tibetan dogs and is going to make a fortune by them.'[35] This was how the celebrated Lhasa Apso found its way into British society.

Another expedition took place in 1933, but Younghusband played no active part beyond arranging the sale of newspaper rights. It did however bring him together with a replacement protégé in the form of Frank Smythe, a rising star in the world of mountaineering. Smythe was a complex character, rather like Younghusband in some ways. He was physically slight but immensely resilient, with a strong spiritual streak; his fellow climbers considered him arrogant and irritatingly self-contained, while admiring his mercurial talent as a mountaineer. His father having died young, Smythe chose Younghusband as a surrogate paternal guru, a role which the older man was happy to accept. Frank Smythe made three attempts on Everest, developing an obsessive determination to reach the top. Younghusband always felt a great disappointment that the summit was not reached in his lifetime. Unlike some of his contemporaries, he was convinced it was possible. 'The mountain now stands there proud and erect and unconquered,' he wrote in *The Epic of Mount Everest*, but 'in the end man will have his way'.[36]

Younghusband sailed into the 1930s on board the SS *Adriatic*, bound for Boston. At the age of sixty-six he was still small and remarkably sprightly, happily walking five or ten miles a day, examining plants and flowers as he went. His hair had become very white and thin, but his moustache and eyebrows were bushier than ever. He wore a soft felt hat and a baggy tweed suit, its pockets stuffed with pencils and note-books, and carried a cheap umbrella which he usually forgot. Helen solved this problem by giving him one with a silver band inscribed: 'Stolen from Sir Francis Younghusband. Travellers' Club'.

As he dressed for dinner in his cabin one evening – the Ganden Tripa's bronze Buddha packed safely in his suitcase – Younghusband found his waistcoat would not meet in front. 'However by pulling very hard,' he reported to Eileen, 'I did just manage to button it up and then marched off to dinner, when to my astonishment I found that no one had dressed.' For the next six weeks he toured the USA and Canada giving lectures, staying with the Governor-General Lord Willingdon while in Ottawa. Wall Street was crashing, unemployment booming and Britain had just come off the Gold Standard, but Younghusband was as cheerful as ever. 'Pretty – fairly – hectic . . . I ran down to the American Jog at New York, and to speak at Philadelphia where I raked in 200 dollars,' he informed Eileen from Montreal. A couple of days later he told the Prime Minister of Quebec 'what an ungrateful little thing' Eileen was to have voted for Ramsay Macdonald when it was Baldwin who had given her the vote. The PM said 'what a kind father I must be not to have made you be Conservative. So you see what a lucky gel you are to have such a nice parent.'

At this stage of his life it was his twenty-seven-year-old daughter who was his closest friend and confidante. For the first time, he had discovered a woman with whom he could laugh, chat, debate and relax. Eileen was quick and intelligent, doing a course in Social Studies at the London School of Economics despite her lack of formal education. Her mother regarded this as bad enough (the Director of the LSE, Sir William Beveridge, had a high rating in Helen's demonology), but worse, Eileen was showing no interest in men or marriage. Francis was less worried, and perfectly happy to appropriate Eileen for himself. 'It is all very well watching other girls being married,' he told her. 'It would be quite a different kettle of fish if it was you. I suppose it must come some day – but it is a dreadful thing to think of.'[37]

By now he had lost touch with many of his old acquaintances. Some had drifted away, alienated by his mystical absorption, while others such as Dunlop-Smith, Haig, Cust and Roberts had died. There were occasional meetings with his brothers – George had become Keeper of the Crown Jewels while Leslie had retired from the army as a Major-General – and every year or so he would exchange letters with Nellie Douglas. In 1924 the last link with his father's generation had been severed when Sir Dighton Probyn died aged ninety-one. Probyn had worked as Queen Alexandra's Comptroller up to the final moment, once nearly choking to death because nobody could open the stiff collar of his courtly uniform. From that day on, Queen Mary invariably carried a penknife in her reticule. But the strangest ending was that of Captain B. L. Grombtchevski, the man who had once been Russia's answer to Captain F. E. Younghusband.

Thirty-five years after their bizarre meeting in the freezing, dust-blown Pamirs, a letter arrived out of the blue at the RGS. 'The revolution in Russia bereaved me of all I possessed,' wrote Grombt-chevski, 'and yet I worked hard and honestly for it during 37 years of service . . . As you see, my dear General, my long life is ending very sadly.' The Russian was now living in bitter poverty in exile in Warsaw, unable to leave his room on account of 'a grave heart disease'. His one hope was that his old rival might find a British publisher for a book he had written, *Kashgaria*. Younghusband replied promptly, and arrangements were made for a Polish priest to deliver it. 'As to the state of my health,' wrote Grombtchevski, 'I do no more have any illusions.' He was dependent on injections of morphine, and knew his life was 'a question not even of weeks, but of days'.[38] Then came a letter saying the Russian explorer had died; the fate of *Kashgaria* is unknown.

A month later, while on his way to Egypt for the Congress of Geographers, Younghusband heard of George Curzon's death. 'I bought a French paper in Nimes and was dreadfully shocked,' he wrote to Helen. 'It was a sad life in a way for he missed what he had set his heart on.' Since 1910 their relationship had cooled; they no longer had the urgent demands of India's northern frontier to bind them together. Curzon had become increasingly taciturn, and by the time of his death had quarrelled with almost everybody he knew. Despite his monumental achievements, he had never managed to become Prime Minister. Yet Younghusband still felt a strong bond, for he knew his own career had depended on Curzon's patronage and their shared vision of the Empire. 'Poor man,' he went on, 'he was always a good friend to me, and I have an idea he showed me a better side of himself than he showed to anyone else.'[39]

Younghusband's best side was reserved for Eileen. He showed her an aspect of his personality which scarcely escapes in his published books: witty, observant and self-mocking. 'I had a roaring time at Oxford,' he wrote to her in 1927. 'Told guileless undergraduates yarns about the Himalaya and showed them my old boots which the scout nearly took away to clean.' A French Marshal he met at an official luncheon was 'very cordial indeed shaking hands like the diggins, while I did the heavy "vainqueur du Tibet" touch, and crowds of little Frenchmen looked on – all very nice indeed.' On his trip to Italy to see the Pope he claimed to have 'discovered a brand new lake between Rome and Florence which no European had ever seen before – because no one ever looks out of the window

... It was a great find. I could not find out what the natives call it. I shall call it Lake Eileeno.'

She was his 'Rogie' (a diminutive of 'little rogue'), his 'Rog Pog', 'Little Scampie' or 'Baby'. 'So what shall we do?' he asked her in the spring of 1926. 'I am ready for anything so suggest what you like. I have £50 to bust so let us make the most of it.'[40] Like a pair of excited children, Rogie and Sir Francis scampered off to Switzerland while Helen remained morosely at Currant Hill. 'I know Darling it is a great grief to you that she is not more with you,' Francis wrote to Helen a few months later, 'but I don't know any other girl who is a patch on her.'[41] Father and daughter formed a union of frivolity, playing practical jokes on each other, but Helen found it exasperating. 'Mummy,' he wrote to Eileen, 'has just said "You and the Baby may be very clever but neither of you has any common sense." I will not be bracketed with you, when I am full of common sense but have no more brains than Bernard Shaw.'

He was safe with Eileen; he could drop his guard and say what he liked. Even Royal Geographical Society stalwarts were up for ridicule. 'We had an enormous Jog meeting last night,' he wrote in November 1924. 'Sir Aurel Stein droned away for nearly two hours . . . and Hinkie was slinking about more impressively than ever.' On another occasion he went to listen to 'the wretched [Kenneth] Mason', who had recently returned from 'that Shaksgam Valley which I explored just before the Peninsular War'. Younghusband brought along William Inge – the reactionary journalist and Dean of St Paul's known as 'the Gloomy Dean' – as his guest:

> I introduced Charlie Bruce to him. Charlie came up all beaming and it was a toss up whether the Dean's gloom or Charlie's cheeriness would win. The Dean won hands down and Charlie went off discomfited. The only thing that defeated the Dean was K2. Mason went on putting on pictures of K2 and the Dean gradually succumbed.
>
> Poor Mason was full of humility and dragged my name such a lot in the lecture that [Tom] Longstaff said it was the canonisation of Younghusband and poor [Martin] Conway who was only mentioned once went off in a huff.

Eileen loved his letters; her enthusiasm encouraged his new-found frivolity. 'Hinkie writes that the Amsterdam Jog are bringing over a Gold Medal for me. Shall I say make it diamonds and I will accept it? Be kind . . . except to Beveridge. Yr. loving Daddie.'

It was a buoyant Sir Francis Younghusband who sailed into the next decade, fizzing with plans, theories and ideas. His latest proposal was that the world should be animated through the staging of monumental religious plays. 'Perhaps even now', he told himself, 'the golden age of drama may be beginning to dawn.'[42]

TWENTY-TWO

Religious Dramas, Peculiar Swamis and Indian Sagas

For the first fifty years of his life, Younghusband was shy, nervous and introverted. As he grew older he became less concerned with other people's judgments and more at ease with himself, relaxing into the identity he had created. He knew now that his remaining days had to be devoted to preaching his spiritual message. Although its contents varied from time to time, the essence remained true to the mystical revelations he had been granted in Lhasa in 1904 and in bed in 1925. To the last, he remained in full control of his mental and physical faculties, inventing new ways of reaching out to the people of Mother-World.

During his time in India, he had been greatly impressed by huge festivals like the Kumbh Mela, when hundreds of thousands of pilgrims, yogis, gurus, sadhus and swamis would congregate for weeks of colourful devotion. The festivities would often culminate in stagings of the Hindu epics, the crowds being thrown into a state of intense religious excitement. As an Evangelical, he had been brought up on the notion that actors and acting were somehow improper, but with the revival of the theatre at the end of the nineteenth century his opinions changed. He came to see religious drama – combining Western-style acting with Hindu fervour – as a possible means of re-launching spirituality in Britain.

Younghusband joined forces with Olive Stevenson, a rather stern member of the Congregational Union who had similar ambitions. Together they called a public meeting, which took place in London in February 1929. It began with a lecture by Laurence Housman, the radical playwright (and brother of A. E. Housman) whose plays such as *Bethlehem* had been banned by the authorities. Housman pointed out that the social and legal restrictions on religious drama were still strict, and that any attempt to promote it would certainly be met with strong opposition. Depictions of Christ on stage, for example, had been forbidden since the Puritan Revolution of the seventeenth century. Younghusband was undaunted, and plans were made to hold a conference that summer.

Several eminent actors and directors attended, including Lillah McCarthy, Barry Jackson (the Shavian philanthropist who founded the Malvern Festival), Frank Benson, Sybil Thorndike, Geoffrey Whitworth (representing the BBC) and 'clergymen of all kinds'. 'The conference went off first-rate,' Eileen was told. 'A fine free fight at one time between the religionists and the dramatists – the latter furious at being regarded only as a means. But in the end they were happy and all agreed to come on the Council.'[1] The 'Religious Drama Society of Great Britain' was formed, with the aim of focusing on 'those truths of the Christian Religion which were common to all branches of the Christian Church'.[2] Younghusband was unhappy with this specifically Christian emphasis, but allowed himself to be elected Chairman, with Olive Stevenson as Honorary Secretary.

Objections began immediately. Protesters petitioned the Archbishop of Canterbury, complaining of 'graven images' and 'acts of sacrilege', while the Protestant Truth Society picketed a production of *The Marriage of St Francis* in a Brighton Church.[3] Scribbling away with his usual alacrity, Younghusband wrote *The Reign of God*, a play in seven scenes, hoping that it would be performed 'by expert readers in public'. 'Yea, verily, I am Mother-Love itself,' says a voice from on high, 'I am as near to you as England is to the sons of England. As they are born out of her so are ye born out of me.'[4] But no producer could be found for his offering, or for the large number of unsolicited plays (such as *The Best Kept Secret in History*, a rambling diatribe on the numerical significance of the Talmud by Mrs Lotus Dudley of Frome) which poured in to the new offices of the RDS. So a Summer School of Religious Drama was established.

Its first meeting was held in Bournemouth, with the young actor-director E. Martin Browne as 'Chief of Staff'. Browne was an idealistic, charismatic, pacifist old Etonian who had recently been appointed Director of Religious Drama to the Chichester Diocese by the controversial Bishop, George Bell. While Browne organized mime classes and readings of the Mystery Plays, Younghusband told ancient Hindu stories and described the stunning Passion Play he had seen a few months earlier at Oberammergau in Bavaria. During subsequent years Browne took the leading role in the RDS, commissioning T. S. Eliot to write plays like *The Rock* and *Murder in the Cathedral*. Younghusband faded into the background, remaining Chairman but allowing others to take over the running of the organization. He had different subjects on his mind. Since the late

1920s, he had become increasingly preoccupied with the fate of
India.

'That India is in revolution is the startling discovery just made by
Fleet Street,' he wrote in the *Spectator* in November 1930.[5] Since
Mahatma Gandhi's salt march earlier in the same year, India's political temperature had been nearing boiling point. From Chitral to
Cape Comorin there was a massive campaign of civil disobedience
as nationalists tried to persuade the Britishers to go home. The
Government responded with the Simon Report, an elaborate but
unsatisfactory proposal for gradual moves towards self-rule. Even
this was too much for many of the older generation.

One of Francis Younghusband's most remarkable (and rare)
qualities was a willingness to change his mind in the light of fresh
information or changed circumstances. Between the end of the
First World War and the beginning of the Second, his opinions on
Britain's Indian Empire went through an impressive transformation, partially under the influence of his daughter Eileen. Once a
noted Curzonian imperialist, he became a supporter of the Indian
National Congress and an advocate of immediate British withdrawal
from India. While Winston Churchill resigned from the Shadow
Cabinet denouncing Gandhi as a seditious half-naked fakir, Younghusband praised him as 'a true national hero' whose 'name will be
honoured in all Indian history as one of India's greatest saints'.[6]
He recognized the inevitable and embraced it wholeheartedly, with
the hopeful aspiration that the transition to independence would
be achieved without partition or bloodshed.

In 1918 he had thought it would take at least a century before
India was ready to govern itself. His ideas were closely bound up
with a belief in racial hierarchy, whereby the 'higher races' had
a duty 'to protect and guide and inspire the lower races'.[7] This
paternalistic racialism was at the time being challenged both
by prescriptive pseudo-scientific theories of 'race hygiene' (which
were soon to be adopted by the Nazis), and by the growth of nationalism and anti-colonialism. As late as 1925, in the (Harry) Cust
Foundation Lecture, Younghusband was promoting a Victorian

vision of Empire, in which the colonized had to 'prove' themselves before being given freedom. Indians were 'a sensitive, impressionable people' whose 'pain would be greater if we withdrew than if we remained'. Instead, Anglo–Indian unity should be strengthened by a 'Dharma Durbar', a monumental religious ceremony presided over by the King.[8]

The change came in 1930 when he published *Dawn in India: British Purpose and Indian Aspiration*, which proposed a gradual British withdrawal. He believed that the British faced a stark choice: 'We must trust India . . . or else regard our Army as a garrison, increase it, and rule by force.'[9] The book ranged from the trading origins of British rule to the practical difficulties of creating an independent country, and was well received. '*Dawn in India*', wrote Francis Yeats-Brown, the yoga enthusiast and *Spectator* editor, 'should be read and reread by every European who goes East of Suez, and studied by all of us who presume to have an opinion on India.'[10] In *An Essay on India*, Robert Byron commended Younghusband and Yeats-Brown for a willingness 'to mature their conclusions by thinking on the evidence rather than to accept, like bats and sheep, the occult sovereignty of a detestable convention'.[11]

Younghusband was soon in demand as that rare commodity – a white-haired India hand of progressive opinions. The BBC commissioned a talk on 'India: The Future', in which he stressed the need for an un-Westernized India, where 'the saint and the sage are honoured above the richest industrialist'.[12] Newspapers like *The Times* and the *Manchester Guardian* wanted to know his views, and the Viceroy Lord Irwin wrote to thank him for supporting a policy of conciliation. Beset by critics within his own party, the Conservative leader Stanley Baldwin invited him to the House of Commons for discussions.

'You and I know each other not intimately,' he told Younghusband before a meeting in March 1932, 'but I think we understand and have some regard for each other. We can talk intimately at any rate and without reserve.'[13] Baldwin was reassured by his support for coercive measures in the short term, provided that the urgent goal of Indian freedom was maintained. A couple of years later the two men had a chance conference in the unlikely setting of the Travellers' Club urinals. As they washed their hands in adjacent basins, Younghusband commended Baldwin's stand on India: 'He had been taking up a line which for the leader of the Conservative Party was considered very advanced, and as we parted I said: "Stick to it, Sir." He replied: "I will, but it is becoming increasingly difficult." '[14]

It was not only the Tories who sought Younghusband's advice. The Labour Government's India Secretary, William Wedgwood Benn, summoned him in July 1930 when unrest was at its height and Mahatma Gandhi had just been imprisoned. 'Said he wanted to have a talk with me to comfort him,' Younghusband told Eileen, and 'asked me to tell him what I thought of the situation . . . He is a very good little man – the best Secty. of State I have struck. Mummy told me before hand to have plenty of bounce when I saw him. I said "Shall I be very grandiose". She said Yes to grandiose.' It may have been the bouncing grandeur that persuaded Benn to shelve an extraordinary plan to send the retired imperialist on a secret mission. He wanted Younghusband to go out to India as an ostensibly neutral peace envoy, and somehow 'get round Gandhi' in his prison cell. 'I was jolly glad I had not been asked to go out,' Younghusband wrote some months later when he heard of the plan, 'for Gandhi's mind was quite made up and I could have done nothing with him'.[15]

Gandhi and Younghusband did meet the following year during the 'Round Table' discussions on India's future, when the Indian leader attended a Buckingham Palace reception clad only in a *dhoti* and a symbolic *kadhi* shawl. Younghusband had great respect for Gandhi's spirituality, but believed his political judgments were short-sighted. Other delegates were given a better rating, such as the Begum Shah Nawaz, 'full of grace and refinement . . . glowing with the intense inner fire of the new patriotism', and the Maharajah of Bikaner, who had 'the born ruler's instinctive knowledge of the feelings of his people'. 'Less sedate, less balanced, less mature yet also typical of the new India', wrote Younghusband, 'is the younger Nehru – Jawarihal Nehru. Educated at Harrow he has known Western influence. But he has also known Bolshevist influence.' At the instigation of the India Office, Younghusband took Gandhi on a tour of London, pursued by a crowd of scallywags who asked the Mahatma where he had lost his trousers.[16]

Flitting between his different identities with greater confidence than ever, Younghusband took up with an assortment of sages, visionaries and cranks. They ranged from Rabindranath Tagore to Paul Brunton, Ph.D., but were all treated with a touching degree of reverence. Some came to him through personal contacts or through his writings, while others were picked up at public meetings. Younghusband kept up his schedule of talks, speaking at the Mothers' Union on 'Social Needs', to the Aristotelian Society on 'Religious Experiences and Philosophy', to the Indian Students' Union on 'Stars as the Abode of Life', and giving the Hibbert Lecture on 'The Destiny of the Universe', in which he held forth on Stellarians, the Organic Whole and the Cosmic Spirit. His breadth of interests and ideas seemed to invite the attention of the outlandish.

Tagore first floated into Younghusband's line of vision during his time as Resident in Kashmir. He admired the Bengali poet's attempts to fuse Eastern and Western culture, and helped persuade the India Society to publish the flowing translations and re-creations of *Gitanjali* in 1912. He was glad when Tagore won the Nobel Prize for literature the following year, but began to have doubts when he actually met him. With his diaphanous robes and impressive white beard, Tagore was fast becoming the darling of London's progressive intellectuals, playing on his status as a colourful, exotic rarity. To Younghusband, this was all a little suspect. 'Last night great meeting of India Society,' he wrote to Eileen in June 1930. Tagore was 'in his best form' as the guest of honour, attending an exhibition of his latest paintings.

> Between you and me if you or I had painted them people wd. have said 'What awful monstrosities.' But last night we said 'What marvellous creations of this amazing many-sided genius.'
> Tagore was quite the gracious gentle poet. The only difficulty was that he flowed about the room quite unmanageably at the start and it took me all my time to steer him into his chair and get him seated.[17]

Younghusband liked Rabindranath Tagore, and praised his commitment to India's cultural traditions, but he never took him entirely seriously. Tagore was a flamboyant showman, and Younghusband was always suspicious of theatricality: this was why he mistrusted people he might otherwise have admired, such as Lawrence of Arabia and Winston Churchill.

Along the way Younghusband picked up numerous oddities, like

Verrier Elwin, an Oxford academic who had rejected a strict Christian upbringing to search for alternative ways of living. He was that most troublesome of characters – a sahib who agitated for Indian freedom. Elwin investigated police brutality against the Red Shirts on the North West Frontier, smuggling his findings out of the area in an impeccably pukka accoutrement: a box of 'Force' wheat flakes. Returning to Britain in 1932 he gave lectures on India's struggle and, strangely, sought Younghusband's advice on intimate matters. At Gandhi's Sabarmati Ashram he had shared a room (chastely) with an Admiral's daughter, but now . . . ? Younghusband advised sexual liberation, and Elwin promptly married a Gond woman called Kosi. 'I do treasure your friendship and your counsel more than I can say,' he told Younghusband later that year.[18] After Independence he became an Indian citizen and a respected expert on tribal culture; a stayer-on with a difference.

Younghusband was a little less discerning when it came to religious showmen like Paul Brunton, entertaining him to tea at the Travellers' Club and corresponding at length. Brunton had begun life as Raphael Hurst, changed his name to Brunton Paul, transposed it to Paul Brunton and then awarded himself a doctorate (from the Astral University) for good measure, before disappearing off to a jungle ashram. His later disciples knew him as PB or Philo S. Opher, and he preached a bizarre message of meditation, dietary fads and oriental mysticism. In the foreword to Brunton's *A Search in Secret India* in 1934, Younghusband wrote that the doctor had found his way through 'an innumerable crowd of mental acrobats and contortionists', including some with 'occult powers', to 'The Maharishee – the Great Sage . . . the very embodiment of all that India holds most sacred.'[19] Brunton lived until 1981, busily collecting acolytes and prophesying disaster from his base in Los Angeles.

There were many others from all over the world: letter writers, searchers and pilgrims, seeking guidance, friendship or endorsement from Sir Francis. He tolerated, even revelled in, their rambling solicitations. Miss Dorothea Spinney of Hertfordshire told him of her spiritual experiences, how she had become removed from time and space and experienced 'being' without the 'I'. Paramahansa Yogananda arrived to discuss 'cosmic joy'. Frank Smythe was plied with advice on apparitions. A Midlands industrialist called Harold Whiston kept up a prolonged barrage of letters: Younghusband was his 'dear Elder Brother'. 'May I say,' he asked, 'I love you very much for keeping me in touch with the Infinite.' For a time Younghusband even toyed with the idea of forming a Society of Mystics. 'The world is in a bad way just now,' he wrote in a circular letter to his correspondents. 'And to a peculiar degree it is up to us who have been favoured with direct experience of God to set it right.'[20]

His own spiritual guidance during this time came from an elusive figure called Swami Bon. Between 1932 and 1935 the Swami's name occurs in Younghusband's engagement diary as often as twice a week, and occasionally in letters to Eileen and Helen: beyond that there is no mention of him. There is no clear reason for this, although it is possible that as an aspiring spiritual leader himself, Younghusband did not want to be seen seeking advice from someone else. Alternatively, Swami Bon may have been another name for Purohit Swami, an intriguing character whom he saw from time to time.

Gurus are hard to pin down, and it is difficult to know whether Shri Purohit Swami was a saint or a charlatan; or, as sometimes happens, an inescapable combination of the two. Younghusband was introduced to him in early 1931, probably by Paul Brunton Ph.D., and took an interest at once. The Swami was clearly on the make: within months of his arrival from India he had organized public lectures on the Bhagvad Gita and gained access to both William Butler Yeats and John Masefield, the Poet Laureate. His autobiography, which he began to write in conjunction with the poet and illustrator Tom Sturge Moore, reads like an alluring work of fiction, directed at a European audience hungry for oriental mystery. It tells of spiritual realization at the feet of his Master, the apparition of a red-lipped yogini on Mount Girnar, the growth of a sacred lump between his eyes, and the tale of how he survived for months on end on nothing but a daily ration of half a pint of milk.

When the book was nearly finished, the Swami brought the manuscript to Younghusband, who suggested it should be simplified in places. A copy was also sent to the ageing W. B. Yeats, provoking an ecstatic response: 'The Swami's autobiography is beautiful,' he told Moore, 'and I think of great importance, almost certainly the first clear and simple life of such a man . . . Lady Gregory read the MSS and said she thought it would make a sensation.' Realizing on which side his bread was buttered, the Swami sent Moore a cheque for £10 ('to pay me off', Moore wrote later, 'as you might tip a railway porter') and abandoned his ghostwriting talents in favour of the celebrated Irishman. A monumental row ensued, letters flying furiously between the three men until the Swami asked Younghusband to intervene. After several attempts he managed to call a meeting at the Travellers' Club on the last day of March 1932, but it did not resolve the crisis.

Yeats went on to pen a deeply flattering introduction to *An Indian Monk*, as the book was to be called, saying he had been waiting for the book since he was seventeen years old, and comparing its author to Tagore. This did not improve matters, and Moore's bitter tirade continued, denouncing Purohit Swami as a fraud, a cheat and a womanizer, full of 'absurd gibes against worldly people' and 'nauseating stuff'.[21] Yeats was undaunted, and the Indo–Irish relationship prospered under the disapproving eye of Mrs Yeats. The Swami spent much of 1935 and 1936 with him in Majorca working on a translation of the *Upanishads*, saving Yeats from a heart attack and fending off unwelcome visitors. By 1937 he was back in India inviting Yeats to the Parliament of Religions, but the great man refused on the curious grounds that he had recently undergone the Steinach operation, and feared he would be unable to keep his sexual desire under control.

Shri Purohit Swami is an easy figure to mock, with his flowing pink robes and his mystical stigmata nestling beneath his carefully constructed orange turban. In photographs he certainly looks a little plumper than one might have expected given an exclusive diet of milk and mountain water. But it should be remembered that Sir Francis Younghusband thought his spiritual adventures worthy of a chapter in *Everest: The Challenge*, and that the celebrated W. B. Yeats revered him as a 'figure of wisdom'.[22]

'Harry, whose curly head is fathoms deep beneath the great rollers of the Pacific,' wrote Lady Younghusband, sitting at her mahogany escritoire in Currant Hill. 'Dermot, who was hauled up alive from a deep well in the Mutiny, only to die from small-pox . . . Fatality after fatality removed the band of strong cheery boys, who set out with brave hearts and high hopes to help build the Empire.'[23] *Tempest Town* was not progressing well. There were too many diversions. Her work with the National Equine Defence League, the need to sort out her Indian lace collection, her correspondence on historical matters with the Comte de Pimodan and the continuing pain in her leg (following an encounter with a London omnibus in the winter of 1932) conspired to distract her. And then there was the constant worry about Eileen.

Her unmarried daughter suffered from appendicitis and polio, yet persisted in consorting with slum dwellers from Stepney and socialist blue-stockings. She even went on an excursion with them to France. 'I know a little of the Continent,' wrote Helen in a private note, 'and protested (as usual over-ridden). I begged to be allowed to arrange hotels etc . . . I prophesied that I and I alone wd. be blamed for this risk.' Was it any surprise, then, that the girl caught a 'terrible microbe' on her travels?[24] Yet what was worse, worse than any of this, was Eileen's pursuit of a career. Not only did she have a diploma in sociology from that hotbed of vice, the London School of Economics, but she was now employed there as a tutor. Moreover Eileen seemed to prefer evenings with her unsuitable friends, chattering and drinking cocoa, to the smart social events that her mother arranged so carefully.

Sir Francis, on the other hand, was perfectly happy with their daughter's occupation. Personally he had little interest in the plight of the people of Stepney – he viewed earthly suffering with a fatalistic detachment – but he admired Eileen's commitment to her vocation. When she was made a Justice of the Peace in 1933 he was both impressed and amused. 'I am having a nailing time here parlez-vous-ing with the best of them,' he wrote to her from a geographical conference in Anjou. 'Expect me at nineish in the evening on Sunday and be a good little J. P. Your loving Daddy.'[25] His frivolous letters continued through the 1930s, although they were a little less frequent than before. He told her of dinner with the Prince of Wales (who took a 'violent liking' to him), tea with the Swami ('thinks he has been fearfully badly treated') and lunch with Verrier Elwin ('not "breathing" about Gandhi as I had expected').

The tale of a grand luncheon party in Kent was recounted, at which the Marchioness of Anglesey was found to have 'only one fault – picking her nose all the time she was talking to me. I thought of asking her to pick someone else's for a change now and then.' Later that afternoon Younghusband put his foot in it with Clemmie Churchill:

They were all discussing what to do with young men at Oxford and she asked me what she ought to do with her boy. I said 'Put him into the Army: he will learn much

more than at Oxford and get some discipline too.' She
looked rather blue and said that certainly Randolph did
require some discipline as Winston had never been able to
do anything with him. And then I tumbled to it who she
was! That is the way I get so beloved in society.[26]

Younghusband told Eileen stories of his travels and encounters, the
language becoming more exuberant and closer to caricature as he
relaxed into old age. A foreign tour was 'a razzle dazzle', his fellow
delegates 'mostly scallywags', rich food 'dodged-up stuff', while a
travel guide managed to 'excel himself in devilment'. Letters to
Helen were never as adventurous as this, although he maintained
a dutiful two sides a day whenever he was away from her. Despite
the breakdown in their marriage he retained a certain tenderness:
'Good night darling. Mind & keep yourself warm. Your ever loving
Dodo.'[27]

During the 1930s he spent several nights a week in London,
usually staying at the Prince of Wales Hotel in Kensington at: '9/6
bed, bath & breakfast which is not bad.'[28] Sometimes they managed
to borrow a London flat for the summer from one of Helen's
brothers. When this happened a variety of servants were engaged,
although Lady Y's impetuous demands meant they often gave
notice within days unless pacified by Eileen. A pantry maid called
Gladys Aylward whom they employed in 1930 went on to become
a famous missionary in China. The story of her life was later filmed
as *The Inn of the Sixth Happiness*, in which Younghusband is depicted
as a rich, gruff character who wears a blue suit. As Miss Aylward
(Ingrid Bergman) leaves Victoria station on her way to Peking, Sir
Francis reveals his heart of gold by giving her his overcoat, and
advising her to keep her passport in her knickers, 'Foreigners being
what they are'.[29] This event did not occur in real life.

The Younghusband family's most important collective find of the
1930s was Nona Miller, a young, attractive, socially ambitious New
Zealand nurse who came to look after Helen. (Shortie had died a
lingering death from cancer some years before, supported lovingly
by Eileen.) Almost at once Nona was incorporated into their lives,
being called 'dear child' or 'sister'. She was unique in that each
member of the family got on with her well, although for different
reasons. To Eileen she became a close friend, the 'sister' she had
never had; Francis liked her flirtatious efficiency and plum cake;
Helen enjoyed her company and her genuine interest in society.
For hours on end Nona would listen in awe while Lady Young-

husband lay stretched on a sofa giving her the Eliza Doolittle treatment, instructing the girl from the Colonies on social protocol, fine art and the history of the British aristocracy. Here at last was a daughter who understood what really mattered in life.

In December 1932 Nona married a London businessman called Bob Guthrie, rather to the disapproval of the Younghusbands, who thought she could have done better. Despite the marriage, which proved unsatisfactory from the start, Nona came down to Westerham several times a month. She took Helen for walks and went to smart tea parties as her companion; she typed the manuscript of *Modern Mystics* (a guide to spiritual 'masters' like Thérèse of Lisieux and Vivekananda) and teased Sir Francis for neglecting his appearance. Politics and religion held no interest for her, but she was always cheerful and affectionate, making a conscious effort to avoid what she called 'controversial' subjects. Throughout the mid 1930s her name crops up continually: 'Nona came down today and was a great success,' is a frequent refrain in the family's letters.[30] She liked the atmosphere and the company at Currant Hill: it became her home from home.

What drew Nona particularly was the frequent presence of Frank Smythe. He had taken to spending weekends there, chattering away about mysticism and the Himalayas with Younghusband. By now Smythe was becoming well-known as a mountaineering writer and photographer, although his popularizing tendencies did not endear him to the climbing establishment. He was a taciturn man, prone to tantrums, but in his mentor's presence he became suffused with a feeling of calm. He was at his best at Currant Hill. Nona found him amusing and endearing, and they took to spending a lot of time together. To the stern disapproval of Helen and the keen enthusiasm of Sir Francis, a love affair began.

In the spring of 1934, Younghusband raced around North America, lecturing on everything from the Dalai Lama and the Holy Himalaya to the Rhythm of the Universe. 'I am having a fairly fizzing time,' he told his daughter from New York on 16 May 1934, 'but have already trousered £20 in solid hard paper.' A spate of newspaper interviews had been followed by a fifteen-minute live radio broadcast across the United States on 'How to Lead a Noble Life', in which he advised the people to follow the fine example set by President Roosevelt.[31]

A talk on mysticism the following day was warmly received. 'The common conception of a mystic', he began, 'is of some misty, musty, dreamy unpractical person utterly lacking in vigour or in any clearness of intellect.' This was wrong: a mystic was someone with 'direct and immediate experience of the . . . Creative Spirit of the Universe − of God.'[32] His ideas found a ready audience, and several talks were turned into booklets. The Church of the Truth published a discourse on alien beings, while a disciple called Angelica C. Kaufman arranged for a speech called 'The Value of Joy' to be printed with an introduction describing it as 'an imperishable document of inspired love'.[33]

'The day of the Great Mystics is dawning,' he wrote on board the Cunard Liner *Berengaria* as he sailed out again in April 1935.[34] This time New York was 'about as New Yorky as ever, but colder than usual', while the people were 'really most appreciative and nice: a few bores and faddists but on the whole extremely good'. His lecture tour had been organized by Kedarnath Das Gupta, an inter-faith enthusiast whom he knew well from England, and involved a fervent gallop from east coast to west. Younghusband's ideas were as outlandish as ever, yet they seemed to be growing in popularity. He had 'a most topping time' discussing the loveability of the world in Massachusetts, while in Chicago he was surrounded by a 'maelstrom of reporters and photographers. This is a regular ritual on arrival in a place and seems to amuse them,' Eileen learned, 'but has no other results.'[35]

His love affair with the United States was almost at an end, until he was invited out in September 1936 for the 300th anniversary of the founding of Rhode Island. Back he went, to tell the Americans to love religious liberty, learn lessons from Asia and rule their country through 'theocratic democracy'. According to the *Newport News*, the huge celebration's 'world-wide atmosphere' was shown by 'the presence of the principal speaker, Sir Francis Younghusband, British author and philosopher . . .'[36] The philosopher had published only one significant work during the 1930s, *The Living Universe*, with its notions of a unisex world leader on the Planet Altair. Yet his promotion of religious understanding was touching a popular nerve.

As his life neared its end, Younghusband used the knowledge he had gained as a thrusting young imperialist to try and mediate between East and West. The apex of this process of change came when he was invited to represent the League of Nations Union at the Parliament of Religions in Calcutta. 'You are returning to India after 27 years,' he was told by Sarvepalli Radhakrishnan, the philosopher who later became President of India, 'with your mind deeply mellowed by spiritual reflection'.[37]

He sailed out at the beginning of February 1937, feeling elated but 'a bit off colour'. During the voyage his sculptor friend Rom Landau made the practical travel arrangements, for Younghusband was 'too much preoccupied with his own dreams to turn willingly to the sudden complexity of life'. One day at breakfast a steward addressed Landau as 'Sir Younghusband junior', to their intense amusement, and while taking tea on deck with some Americans, a Marconigram arrived:

> I opened it in a casual way while the conversation was going on and then said: 'Oh it's only a message from Lindbergh saying he will fly me from Bombay to Calcutta.' That gave them a pretty good start![38]

Charles Lindbergh had flown into Younghusband's life the previous year. The dashing, steely young airman had made his name ten years earlier with the first non-stop solo flight from New York to Paris, but the glamour turned to tragedy when his baby son was kidnapped and murdered. In an effort to distract himself from the death and the publicity, Lindbergh began a study of 'supersensory phenomena', writing to Younghusband out of the blue, asking for his help. While stressing the need for total secrecy, Lindbergh expressed a wish to find fakirs and fire-walkers and 'squat with a yogi'. Younghusband was surprised but sympathetic, so it was agreed they should meet in Bombay in the spring. 'If it will be possible for me to have the opportunity of meeting even a few of the Indian mystics and religious men,' wrote Lindbergh, 'I feel that alone would be worth the trip.'[39]

India's newspapers ran pictures of Colonel Lindbergh and Sir Francis Younghusband (an 'authority on India and the Near East', apparently) clambering in and out of the cockpit of a single-engine Miles Mohawk, but nobody picked up the story of the aviator's search for an avatar. Younghusband found his first trip in an aeroplane 'huge fun', skimming over the jungle:

> And Lindbergh is such an awfully nice fellow and laughs away – except when we land and there are press people about. Then he is frightened as a hare. If they press very hard he shakes them by the hand, smiles and says: 'I have nothing to say.'[40]

Down in Calcutta, Younghusband was installed at the Great Eastern Hotel, surrounded by swamis, showered with papers, soaps, scents and silk scarves and driven around Bengal in a grand yellow motor car. He introduced Lindbergh to every holy man he could lay his hands on, and when Mrs Lindbergh arrived she too was swept up in the excitement. They dined with a rich Bengali who dressed Anne Morrow Lindbergh 'in Indian fashion as a bride with a crown of flowers on her head and armlets and wristlets of flowers'; her husband pronouncing himself 'well satisfied'.[41]

Two days after his arrival Younghusband had lunch with a fat monk he had known in Lhasa, who introduced him to two remarkable characters: Gedun Ch'omp'el and his master Geshe Sherab Gyatso. Sherab Gyatso was an erudite companion of the Thirteenth Dalai Lama who later collaborated with the Chinese (only to be tortured to death during the Cultural Revolution), while Gedun Ch'omp'el was a mercurial, subversive monk who wrote erotic verse, spoke thirteen languages, smoked opium and joined the Tibet Revolutionary Party before being thrown into jail. In March 1937 Sherab Gyatso, already suspected of having Communist sympathies, was on his way to China by boat, and persuaded Younghusband to make a speech at the Calcutta docks. According to the Tibetan newspaper *Melong* ('Mirror'): 'The Tibetan and Chinese communities of Calcutta held a farewell celebration. On this occasion Sir Francis Younghusband addressed them.'[42] Sadly there is no record of what he said, or of his opinions on this pair of notorious Tibetan revolutionaries.

The Parliament of Religions aimed to promote inter-faith dialogue, and marked the centenary of the birth of the influential Hindu leader, Ramakrishna. For a week fiery Christians, inspired Sikhs, intense Buddhists, studious Muslims and half-naked ascetics made zealous speeches. Younghusband chaired two sessions and spoke on 'The Indian Spiritual Revival', his speech being broadcast live on the radio. In the evenings there was more entertainment: a huge gathering at the Sikh Gurdwar in Kalighat and a festival of religious plays and celebrations organized by swamis from the world's Ramakrishna ashrams, 'in which from 150,000 to 200,000 people must have taken part', rather more than the usual quota at Religious Drama Society productions.[43]

Younghusband raced from speech to speech, from temple to temple, from *chota hazri* to dinner, overwhelmed by the hospitality and by India, land of his birth, 'having a pretty strenuous time' – 'but these Indians', he confessed to Eileen, 'are so fearfully keen and intelligent.'[44] He was sketched by the artist Mukul Dey, had meetings with the great Tagore and eminent Congress wallahs, and caught the impassioned mood of nationalism that was sweeping the country, realizing for the first time how much had changed in thirty years, and how urgent the need was for British withdrawal. Wherever he went he was honoured; maybe Indians appreciated his spiritual transformation more than the British ever would. 'Thrice great thou art as a Peace Maker, as a Warrior, as one interested in others' good,' ran a citation from one admirer, 'Sir FRANCIS YOUNGHUSBAND, of untarnished fame, all the gifts of Fortune be thine.'[45]

On his last day in Calcutta the College of Pandits awarded him the title 'Krama Kesari' or 'Lion of Enterprise' – an award never before bestowed on a European. It meant more to him, he wrote, than any medal he had ever received. Sailing back through the Mediterranean he told Eileen the voyage was the best he had ever had, and that he was 'just bursting with health'. India had exceeded his wildest dreams.

Things were a little chaotic back at Currant Hill. Their precarious financial situation had finally tottered to the brink, so Helen was arranging to sell the house and auction its contents. Younghusband's bank statements show that they were surviving on no income at this time except his tiny Political Service pension, the remains of Helen's legacy, the dwindling royalties from his books and occasional stipends from Eileen. The Pita Fibre and Rubber Company – he had sat on the board since 1924 – does not appear to have generated any cash. Overwhelmed by this sudden intrusion of worldly affairs, Sir Francis went for a long walk across the fields, invited the Lindberghs to tea and read some P. G. Wodehouse. There was nothing else for it. A few weeks before his seventy-fourth birthday his heart stopped beating and he was admitted to a Sevenoaks nursing home.

TWENTY-THREE

The Remains of His Day:
Inventing Societies

If Younghusband had died from a coronary occlusion in May 1937, his life would have lacked three important excitements: his most amusing book (*Wedding*), his most enduring group (the World Congress of Faiths), and his final, startling love affair, indeed the only love of any real substance or significance to him. In his last five years, many of his lifetime aspirations came true. By the mid 1930s he had realized that books and pamphlets were a flawed means of communication. Genuine success as a religious leader would depend on human contact. He also came to accept that the number of people willing to make a life-changing spiritual leap was strictly limited, and that he had to unite existing devotees of different faiths in 'a spirit of fellowship through religion'.[1]

The concoction of new organizations had become his favoured route to the elusive mystics of Britain. During his life, Younghusband founded or helped to found no fewer than six societies, and attempted to found another four. It may have been his difficulty in establishing close relationships with individuals that drew him to the fraternity of institutions. They combined a structured sense of 'fellowship' – that essential Edwardian ingredient – with the possibility of tangible influence and swathes of disciples. The first two groups that he started (the Central Asian Society and the Fight for Right) had a specific purpose, but the rest were fan clubs in various shapes and guises. His belief in his own spiritual destiny was so closely bound up with their identity that success or failure depended on him.

As a tireless activist, he was also happy to accept a role in other people's organizations, from the eminently respectable to the inescapably comic. After retirement in 1909 he was a ceremonial Vice-President of the Public Morality Council, the Royal Empire Society, the Over-Seas League, the Indian Village Welfare Association, the Royal Society of Literature and the Himalayan Club. He was also an active Chairman or President of the India Society, the Royal Geographical Society, the Sociological Society, the Men of the Trees, the International Executive of the Moral Education Congress, the Mount Everest Committee, the Society for the Study of Religions and the New Life Movement.

At the end of the Great War he founded the Quest Society, which promoted Honour, Nature and the Ideal. It spluttered briefly into life before disappearing without trace; nor did he have much luck with the Natural Beauty Association. When he first moved to Westerham, Younghusband was captivated by the butterflies and flowers, just as he had been in Kashmir. Each morning he would set off down the lanes 'with zest, swinging his walking stick, his hat rakishly on the side of his head and whistling or singing as he went, shouting for joy indeed'. According to Eileen, he knew 'every one of the village children in Westerham intimately', and would introduce them to the joys of hunting for white violets and wild roses. 'He would give them sweets and walk hand in hand', an activity which in the 1920s was doubtless regarded as an innocent diversion.[2]

In an attempt to reproduce this pastoral idyll, he invented an organization that would send 'photographic artists and landscape painters . . . in search of beauty, and to bring back pictures of physical nature, plant, animal and human life'. The Chairman would be Sir Francis Younghusband ('the idea being mine'), and in time 'branches wd. be established in the British Isles and in the Empire − perhaps also in foreign countries'.[3] Helen organized a luncheon at the Guards' Club to promote the idea, but it failed to generate much enthusiasm. Then Younghusband decided to link his quest for the zenith with the fate of the City of London's churches, many of which were in imminent danger of demolition.

In 1923 a public meeting was held at the Mansion House, the official residence of the Lord Mayor of London. According to the *Morning Post* it was a success: the City's churches 'long islanded in a gloomy sea of commercialism, may again glow with light and be thronged with worshippers'. There would be daytime literary appreciations, musical performances and readings by eminent figures on 'the ideal man, mother and child, tillers of the soil, patriotism, flowers, sunsets, public spirit' − a whole host of characteristic Younghusband specialities. With the backing of the Lord Mayor and several rich businessmen, the Zenith Society (or 'Excellence-Worship Society') looked set for great things. It would bring 'refreshment of the spirit for City men'.[4]

There was unfavourable reaction from the start. The social reformer Lord Knutsford ridiculed Younghusband's whimsical proposals and pointed out that money from the sale of old churches would help suburban parishes. 'Lord Knutsford contemplates me waking from my dream,' he responded in *The Times*. 'But I have no intention of waking. I intend to dream still deeper, for I have found that if I dream deep enough my dreams come true.'[5] His dream did come true, in a small way. There were well-attended talks by John Masefield, Alfred Noyes and Walter de la Mare. Members paid their five shillings subscription and a magazine called the *Beacon* was started. But by 1927 the Zenith Society had fizzled out. Although in the short term it publicized the City of London's historic churches, its alternative ambition – the extension of Younghusband and his theories by other means – did not catch the public mood.

Never one to be outdone by circumstance, he founded the Religious Drama Society the following year. If anything, it was too successful: by attracting committed, inspirational figures like Martin Browne, Younghusband's own influence was reduced. So he moved to the realm of mountain sanctuaries. He would seek out sacred sites from Wales to Tibet where pilgrims could experience 'that ineffable bliss which springs from deepening union with the spirit'. People who had been touched by spiritual forces would receive 'the full impress of the mountains'. A Guardian of the Gate and a Leader of Pilgrims would be appointed to assist visitors to commune with mystical, spotless, heavenly snow peaks.[6]

In 1933 Younghusband set to work with a vengeance, writing to mountaineers like Tom Longstaff, society figures like Lady Susan Hicks Beach, Great Gamers like Eric Bailey, and of course to that ubiquitous Himalayan holy man, Shri Purohit Swami. Some of them responded, and some even responded favourably, yet to his surprise the creation of mountain sanctuaries did not set fire to his correspondents' collective imagination. For a time it looked as if the organization might soar to the sky beyond the mountain top, but soon the practical and financial difficulties took over, and it flopped to the ground. Like the Natural Beauty Association, the Fight for Right, the Quest, Zenith and Excellence-Worship Societies before it, the Mountain Sanctuaries Association faded away into history.

Above His Holiness the 13th Dalai Lama of Tibet, an incarnate deity who developed into an astute politician.

Right The incomparable Agvan Dorzhiev, seen here in St Petersburg with a boy monk in attendance.

Above Yeshe Dolma, Queen of Sikkim: 'an uncommonly slim little thing,' thought Colonel Younghusband.

Left A senior Tibetan officer, almost certainly Depon Lhading who was killed in the massacre at Chumi Shengo in March 1904.

Above Divide and Rule. A Sikh Pioneer flogs a Tibetan camp servant under the watchful eye of a British military policeman; he had probably been caught pilfering supplies.

Above George Curzon as a young Member of Parliament. The talented, arrogant Viceroy of India was to exert a crucial influence on Younghusband's life.

Right The Tongsa Penlop Ugyen Wangchuk, soon to become the hereditary ruler of Bhutan.Ugyen Kazi stands to his left.

The four Tibetan Cabinet Ministers who negotiated the Treaty of Lhasa in 1904. Their long silk sleeves signify high social status and unavailability for manual work.

Below British troops march into Lhasa through the West Gate, a landmark which the Chinese authorities have recently pulled down. The Potala rises in the background.

Above Sir Francis and Lady Younghusband, their daughter Eileen, and the syphilitic Maharajah of Kashmir in 1908.

The Kashmir Resident with Shukar Ali, a formidable Ladakhi who saved his life on at least one occasion.

'Slim and supple, if not broad and beefy': the delectable George Mallory on his way up Mount Everest.

Above Younghusband clutching the Ganden Tripa's bronze Buddha

Doctor Sir Sarvepalli Radhakrishnan, the revered philosopher who later became President of India.

Sir Francis Younghusband in the
1930s with: a look of wisdom, a giant
lily, a commendable flat cap on his
way to New York.

Above The Religious Drama Society in action.

Nona, the New Zealand nurse who so captivated Francis Younghusband, Frank Symthe and the Earl of Essex.

Right Younghusband in Oxford with Herbert Samuel and Gilbert Murray at a 1941 meeting of the World Congress of Faiths.

Above Madeline Lees flanked by her husband and seven children, a year before she met Sir Francis Younghusband.

At Ease With The Universe. Younghusband reclines in an armchair, contemplating the realms of the spirit.

At the time of Younghusband's death in 1942 three of his societies were still in existence: I decided to see which of them had made it into the 1990s.

In worldly terms, the Central Asian Society has been the most successful, although strictly speaking it is not 'his' creation since the original proposal came from Alfred Cotterell Tupp. It has an office in Belgrave Square, a respected journal called *Asian Affairs*, the patronage of the Prince of Wales and a new name: the Royal Society for Asian Affairs. I walked along Piccadilly in the drizzling rain past the fruit stalls and the smoking buses to Burlington House, where a lunchtime meeting was being held. Pushing open a mahogany door of immense stature I found myself in a magnificently panelled room amidst umbrellas, dark suits and smartly pressed shirt cuffs, with long portraits dangling from the walls. There were no Asians present, but I could see some grand old ladies, merchant bankers, late colonial servants and gentleman writers. I took a seat at the back.

The lecturer was speaking on Younghusband's role in the geopolitics of the Great Game. He began with a ringing declaration of his intentions: 'In this talk I will not endeavour to engage in psychological analysis of Sir Francis Younghusband. Indeed, it would not be proper for me to do so.' Since the talk covered the period in the early 1890s when Younghusband was capering about in the Himalayas, dreaming of that splendid colonel Nellie Douglas and a Tolstoyan renunciation of his worldly goods, this constraint was formidable. The founding members would have been heartened by such a wondrous Victorian vision of historical duty, in which human interest had to be subordinated to propriety. I had no doubt that Frank, Algy and George would have felt at home in the timelessness of today's Royal Society for Asian Affairs.

Down in that bleak, grey area between Lambeth and Waterloo I moved past full dustbins and heavily defended off-licences until I found what I was looking for – a door tucked away behind an unprepossessing parish church. The Religious Drama Society was not conspicuous. It had taken me some time to run it to ground, involving several returned letters from addresses around the country before I found it had changed its name from the RDS to RADIUS. I rang the buzzer which buzzed and crackled back at me defensively, and after ten minutes a face appeared behind a glass panel with a scraping of keys. Gwen told me there had been a bit of trouble lately with young boys pressing the intercom and you really had to be careful. We went up flights of stairs past Shelter and Samaritans notices.

'We had five thousand members in the early '60s,' said Gwen. 'We were doing ever so well. There was opposition from the church hierarchy but that didn't stop us. We had a nice office and a donation from the Rockefeller Foundation.'

'Although prices weren't so high in those days,' cut in Helen. 'The Summer School was very popular too. We had a lady physical-training instructor who used to organize it.'

Gwen went to put the kettle on. The room was small, crowded with piles of brown envelopes, curling typescripts and old packages. I squinted at the faded spines that lined the bookshelves. There were hundreds of copies of dusty plays with titles like *He Is Risen* and *A Man Called Jesus*. Gwen came back with a tray of tea and biscuits.

'I'll leave the door open,' she said. 'That way I'll be able to escape when the telephone rings. It's not so easy these days, there's only me and Helen and sometimes Doris in the office now since Mrs Evans went. We're looking for a part-time administrative secretary with keyboard skills and a sense of humour, that's what we put in the advert.'

'We do still have the script competition,' Helen insisted. 'A lovely little Jewess won it last year. And we're holding a Summer School up in Ripon on the theme 'Time to Share', if you're interested in coming. It's residential – there'll be workshops on dance and movement and a lot of creative drama. All ages.'

'I know Sir Francis was very keen on Temple Dancing and Eastern Drama. There's not much demand for that these days, although we do have some Hindus who take part in the youth groups. Young people like drama. Then there's Bill and Sylvia from Theatre Round-about. You've heard of them. They travel round in a camper doing shows. *Glory Be!* and popular plays like that. She was in the Pilgrim Players.'

'There's not much call for big-cast religious plays now. Gospel narration up at the altar tends to be more popular.' Helen began thinking back. 'We've had all sorts of famous people on the Council: Athene Seyler, T. S. Eliot, Sybil Thorndike, Christopher Fry. Martin Browne was our President. He was a wonderful man, most inspiring.'

'But we do still have Judi Dench. She's our Patron, you know, Dame Judi – a lovely lady.'

It was getting dark outside. I left with a handful of newsletters and some RADIUS pamphlets. By the door there was a box of yellowing plays called *Christ's Comet*. As I went out I thought I heard Gwen's telephone ringing, but it was a burglar alarm from the street below. She walked with me down the stairs and unlocked the front door. I was out on the pavement with the youth and the drama of Lambeth.

In another part of London, somewhere behind Paddington Station, I found myself on the trail of the World Congress of Faiths. Armed with an ancient newspaper cutting and an *A to Z*, I paced past cheap hotels and over-lit deep-pan pizzerias until I found Norfolk Square. According to the cutting, the new headquarters of the organization had been opened there in 1956 by Younghusband's successor, Herbert Samuel, the former Home Secretary and Liberal party leader. 'Younghusband House – and we could of course have called it by no other name,' Viscount Samuel was quoted as saying, 'will, I trust, be a centre of incessant and vigorous activity which is second to none in its urgency.'[7]

There was some vigorous activity going on in the 'No Alcohol' garden opposite the building, as two homeless-looking men threw empty cider bottles at a third, shouting insults in an affable sort of way. I went up to a big door with a long steel knocker and dark green peeling paint. Above it was a grey glass fanlight with YOUNG-HUSBAND HOUSE painted in bold letters. There were dirty net curtains covering the ground floor windows, but they did not twitch.

Once the place had been full of bustling people, preparing for the opening of the new WCF office and the launch of its inter-faith crusade. There was Miss Eileen Younghusband CBE, Viscount Samuel OM, Miss Holmes and Miss Sharples (two of the keenest acolytes), Bishop Bell, Mr Rudra of the Brahmo Samaj, the Rt. Hon. J. Chuter-Ede, Baroness Ravensdale and Mr Abdul Majid of the Woking Mosque. Now it had been turned into a dozen bedsits. A woman with an anxious look and a pushchair shot out of the door. She had never heard of the World Congress of Faiths and, as far as she knew, there were no mystics at all in the building.

I did run it to ground some time later, lurking in a dumpy bunker opposite the end of the All Saints Road. The old building had been given up in the 1970s, so now the WCF had to cope with the dealers and the wildness on the fringe of Ladbroke Grove. Even so the organization was impressive, with the present Dalai Lama as its Patron and nearly a thousand members. There are meditation weekends, joint religious services and the annual Younghusband Lecture. Although the WCF was created in the image of its founder, it is now much like any other inter-faith group, battling against the self-righteous exclusivity of fundamentalism.

'We might have begun as a Younghusband fan club,' they told me, 'but we've gone beyond that now. Look at Ireland, look at the Middle East – that's why we're here. Even in Britain you get vicars trying to ban non-Christian prayers from their church. Nothing's going to change until the world's religions stop preaching fear and hatred of each other.'

'My dear Rogie,' Younghusband wrote to his daughter in a shaking hand. 'You have been so good all this time & I love you for it.'[8] For six weeks he lay in bed in the Sevenoaks nursing home while doctors listened to his heart and ordered him to rest. There were visits from Eileen and Nona, bringing the Ganden Tripa's bronze Buddha to put by his bedside. But nothing could stop him: by the time he was released in July 1937 he had completed a short book called *The Sum of Things*, containing 'the cream' of his thoughts. It was similar to his earlier work, if more accessible, explaining how he had forced himself to challenge assumptions after his Tibet vision ('How should I have the courage to say things so contrary to all that was expected of a soldier and explorer?') until he reached a point of mystical rapture and 'deep, sweet, ineffable peace'.[9]

A little heart trouble was not enough to keep him in check. By late July he was at a World Congress of Faiths meeting in Oxford, and a fortnight later was taking the air in Switzerland with Eileen, telling his wife (with perhaps less than total sincerity) that he looked forward to the day when they were installed in their new home and he could devote all his time to looking after her. To Helen, alone in the shell of Currant Hill, it must have seemed a distant prospect. By then much of her precious furniture had been auctioned, and they were waiting to move to a poky London flat. Her husband travelled around the Italian and Swiss Alps until September, feeling fitter by the day and 'looking more & more the choleric retired Indian Colonel', he told Eileen.[10] Then he returned to promote religious unity.

The first stirrings of the WCF had come when Younghusband

attended a World Fellowship of Faiths Congress while on his trip to New York in 1934. Although the idea of different religions talking to each other now seems unremarkable, at the time it was considered radical and potentially dangerous. Yet there was support from the start, the concept catching an idealistic mood that was current in the 1930s. The horrors of the Great War had made people determined that international relations should be guided by dialogue rather than mutual antagonism. Many of the WCF's founding figures were also involved with the ill-fated League of Nations, which shared this optimistic approach to potential conflict. Younghusband was joined by the pacifist rector of St Martin-in-the-Fields Canon Dick Sheppard, Kedarnath Das Gupta, Nancy Astor, Lord Ullswater, Swami Purohit, the Rani of Sarawak and Evelyn Wrench, founder of the English Speaking Union and the Over-Seas League. They touched millionaires for funds, receiving a friendly brush-off from Dorothy Elmhirst at Dartington, and a big dose of goodwill from the famously wealthy Maharajah Gaekwar of Baroda.

By the end of the year Younghusband ('Founder and Chairman') had secured an office in Bedford Square, the devotion of a Miss Beatrix Holmes (the 'maid-of-all-work of the WCF') and a salaried 'organising secretary' called Arthur Jackman. Jackman was an interesting choice, since he was closely involved with the Theosophical Society. In 1907 Younghusband had seen Theosophy as a malign force. It was, he wrote, a doctrine for 'neurotic and partially educated ladies, and not a wholesome, healthy, religion which can be confidently encouraged. It has enlisted the support of no single man of any real eminence, and any thinker of even moderate ability would very soon knock the bottom out of it.'[11] But thirty years on, his own ideas were close enough to the tenuous notions of Besant and Blavatsky for him to feel happy with an unwholesome Theosophist in charge of his brainchild.

With a little secretarial assistance from the glamorous Nona, Younghusband sent letters to Krishnamurti, Aldous Huxley, H. G. Wells, Gilbert Murray, Herbert Samuel, G. B. Shaw, Joseph Needham, J. S. Haldane and Paul Brunton, asking for their support. Shaw's response was suitably forthright. While admitting that he had 'found in the east a quality of religion which is lacking in these islands', he doubted the practicality of uniting 'men of burning faith'. In his view, all potential members should be asked a number of questions, including: '1. On what public grounds would you shoot your next door neighbor, excluding those already recognised by our criminal court?' Shaw believed that talk of faith and love and unity was all very well, but that spiritual types were 'extraordinarily quarrelsome':

> Get them round a table to agree on a basic manifesto or spend half a crown of public money, and most of them will make frantic scenes and dash out of the room after hurling their resignations at you.[12]

Shaw's predictions proved accurate. Within a year the key activists of the World Congress of Faiths were busy falling out with one another, and challenging the Chairman's assumption that his own decisions would automatically prevail. Younghusband came to think he was being 'constantly hindered' by Jackman and the Executive Committee. There was also a split between the idealists and the groupies: the leading public supporters like Gilbert Murray and Herbert Samuel had an inter-faith agenda, but many of the office volunteers were simply fans of Younghusband. Personally he was devoted to the aim of religious fellowship, yet craved the praise and support of his admirers. As he wrote to Helen: 'It is quite wonderful what appreciation I am getting – far better than any peerages and things.'[13]

The first big public meeting was held at the Queen's Hall in July 1936. Sandwich-board men traipsed around London advertising the joys of WORLD FELLOWSHIP THROUGH RELIGION, but fewer than a hundred members of the public were attracted, some of whom had to be ejected for misbehaviour. Far more impressive were the internationally renowned speakers. They sat on a dais in their robes and turbans, surrounded by a hymn-singing choir and potted shrubs (courtesy of Captain St Barbe Baker of the Men of the Trees, who had also arranged for Younghusband to be driven around in a Rolls Royce). The Gaekwar presided with Sir Francis perched by his side, bearing a message of support from King Edward VIII. The previous month Younghusband had given a talk on the BBC – despite objections from the Faith Defence League, an especially virulent Catholic group – in which he promoted his 'fellowship of fellows', predicting that 'the great day of religion' was yet to come.[14]

For a fortnight talks, discussions and meditation sessions were given by Jews, Confucians, Muslims, and Bahais, and even a Communist in the form of the absent-minded physicist J. S. Haldane. He was keen to argue a scientific view of religion, but died before he was able to deliver his paper, so it was read on his behalf by his daughter, the novelist Naomi Mitchison: 'I was told by two people that they saw my father beside me,' she wrote half a century later, 'but I think one can imagine things; though we were very fond of one another.'[15] The Marchioness of Aberdeen gave way to Sir Abdul Qadir and Nicolas Berdiaeff, but the high point for many was a talk by the frail Japanese Buddhist scholar D. T. Suzuki, who slept through the preceding speeches and when woken said he had no idea what was meant by Younghusband's phrase 'The Supreme Spiritual Ideal'. Instead he told the Zen story of Joshu's Stone Bridge, which was but a wooden plank over a stream.

The Church of England remained deeply suspicious of the meeting, although individual clergy did attend. No Roman Catholics went near it. Press coverage was mixed, the greatest hostility being restricted to the letters pages, with talk of heathen temples, fish-god idols and Our Lord bruising Satan under His feet. Some papers were actively supportive, such as the *Inquirer*, the *Jewish Bulletin* and a magazine called *Great Thoughts*, which described the WCF's founder as being bronzed and grizzly with the eyes of a Himalayan eagle.[16] He succeeded in arranging a government reception at Lancaster House, but did not have enough support to create an inter-faith church service. However, the delegates were invited to a Christian ceremony at St Paul's Cathedral, provoking a demonstration on the steps at which leaflets were distributed depicting Younghusband as the Devil.[17]

Once the excitement had died down he wrote a book called *A Venture of Faith*, which told the story of the Congress and preached the need for World Fellowship. The following summer there was a smaller meeting in Oxford concentrating on the society's growth in Britain, and in June 1938 they met in Cambridge to call for a worldwide religious revival to combat Fascism and Godlessness, hearing speeches from the Imam of Woking Mosque and Sir Sarvepalli Radhakrishnan. Requests for a linked BBC broadcast were treated cautiously, the Director of Talks declaring in an internal memo: 'I should not be in favour of Sir F. Younghusband giving a talk on his own system of belief – if that is the idea.'[18]

In the event he was allowed to speak on 'The Renascence of Religion', provided that no references were made to Italy, Germany, dictators or alien ideologies. Younghusband's fight against Nazism at this time was in marked contrast to 1934, when in a pamphlet he had commended the 'valiant spirit' and 'stern discipline' of the Nazis as being preferable to laxity and cynicism.[19] Like many of his generation, his first reaction to the rise of the Right in Europe tempered disapproval with admiration. It was only when he saw Mussolini's blackshirts in action in 1937 that he became a trenchant critic of the Fascists. As he said in his BBC broadcast, the diplomatic crisis was at heart a spiritual one, and all religions needed to unite to 'give the world a lead to peace'.[20]

In the months before the outbreak of war he scurried around with unflagging energy promoting fellowship and dialogue, hoping against hope that Edwardian amateurism might secure a late triumph over the forces of darkness. Although he was not a pacifist, Younghusband worked with many people such as George Lansbury who were, in an attempt to avert conflict. He was now operating in a curious area beyond militarism or pacifism, in which mystical love became a route to a deeper universal peace. War was simply a 'fit of bad temper' which could be replaced by friendship and unity. In July 1939, six weeks before the German invasion of Poland, he opened the inaugural meeting of the 'Congrès Mondial des Croyances' at the Sorbonne. It had been started by an Agnostic turned Muslim turned Catholic, Louis Massignon, with the unofficial backing of the Jesuit mystic Pierre Teilhard de Chardin, and the hopeful ambition of encouraging 'l'esprit de cooperation humaine'.[21]

With the Paris meeting well underway, Younghusband dashed across to Holland. 'A local Jackman met me on arrival,' he told Eileen, 'and [has] followed me like a dog ever since.' The Dutch Foreign Minister turned out to be 'a quite amiable gentleman ready to eat out of my hand', who was willing to lend official support to the WCF. A quick skip to Geneva followed before Younghusband returned to London for a royal garden party, busily reading P. G. Wodehouse on the boat train. During August he wrote introductions to religious books for the World Classics, informing Eileen joyfully that he hoped he had not 'imparted any of the Wodehouse spirit into the life of the Buddha'. Nona ('the one and only') was coming on a walk with him that afternoon: 'Every day and in every way I am getting better & better and if a ray of sun did come it wd. probably explode me,' he wrote.[22] Three weeks later his country declared war on Germany.

For a while I became convinced that Sir Francis Younghusband was having an affair with Nona. My hunch was based on three things:

a misplaced letter, an attorney's letter and a lack of letters. The first was in a file of discrete papers in the India Office Library, and had clearly been put there by accident. It was written in loving tones ('. . . thinking – oh! so much of my Darling. What wouldn't I give for you to be here with me', and so on) by Younghusband in the autumn of 1935 while on holiday in Northumberland with his wife.[23] The references in it seemed to point to Nona as the recipient. My suspicions were strengthened when I found out that she was still alive (aged about eighty-five) and I attempted to make contact. A hostile letter came back from her attorney stating that 'any intrusion into her private life would cause her distress'.[24]

Around the same time I was told by a different source that Nona had burnt her correspondence: 'I also had many letters from Sir F.,' she wrote to a friend in 1983, 'but destroyed them all as I consider private should be private.'[25] She also made an effort, as executor of Eileen Younghusband's will, to destroy all Sir Francis Younghusband's papers, with the exception of those relating to the Tibet Mission. It was this that convinced me: why would Nona have made the effort to destroy them unless there was something she needed to hide from a prying biographer? Then nearly a year later, after some tenacity, I was told that I would be allowed to visit her. Nona was now the dowager Countess of Essex, living in a private residential home, her state of mind fluctuating from day to day. I set off on a crisp February afternoon.

I had already visited some of Eileen's friends to listen to their tales of the 1930s; fierce, likeable women who had battled against convention to reach senior positions in the field of mental health or social policy. We met in upright sitting rooms and small hotels around the country. Mugs of cocoa, felt hats and soft shoes had generally given way to dry sherry, white hair and the bulky trainers favoured by street-wise ten-year-olds and the elderly. Sir Francis was courteous and wonderful; Lady Younghusband was a difficult character; the food at Currant Hill was terrible and the rooms were cold. Interviewing Nona was likely to be rather different: she had seen things from the heart of the family.

'Of course Lady Younghusband was a Magniac,' she announced.

'A maniac, Lady Essex?' said the nurse, depositing a tray of coffee and biscuits beside us.

'A M-A-G-N-I-A-C. An important family. Now this boy,' she declared, swinging round and patting me fondly on the hand, 'is a *great* friend of Sir Francis Younghusband.'

'Well,' I coughed, 'friend is . . .'

'Sir Francis Husband?' wondered the nurse as she closed curtains. *'Younghusband!* He made friends with the Tibetans.'

'Is that right?' said the nurse.

Nona sat neatly on a long-legged chair between her bed and her television, looking dignified and stylish in a soft pink cardigan. The walls were covered with good paintings.

'Of course I was his greatest girlfriend,' she proclaimed. 'Sir F was very much in love with me – made a dead set from the start. I was a bright young thing, you see. But I wouldn't have it, I said to him Sir Francis it won't do, Lady Y wouldn't like it at all and nor would Frank Smythe. He was crazy about me. Lady Y was a funny old body, you know, her hair used to get terribly frizzled at times but Eileen didn't worry a bit.'

This was more than I had ever expected.

'Oh, it was a dreadful sorrow for her the way Eileen went off slumming it in the East End, doing good works and so on with some *vivid* Socialists. She had plans for her, you know, plans for a good marriage into the social world.'

I asked some questions, but with few definite results.

'Sir Francis was a great walker. His suits were scruffy but that wouldn't stop his love for me. All that mysticism, you see, though he was never a churchie sort of chap.' She leant forward coquett-ishly. 'They're all the most frightful old dodderers here, you know. I *lead* the exercise classes.' Very suddenly Nona stood up and started opening doors around the room. 'I'm afraid I have to go to the country now,' she said, picking up her handbag and walking outside.

I felt puzzled as I drove away in the thin grey light. She had kept to the recurring theme of Sir Francis's wild love. Was it in his character to make a 'dead set' at a woman a third of his age? Was it anything more than an old man's flirtation? Would Lady Younghusband have tolerated such conduct? The weight of the revelation was lightened by Nona's tales of ardent advances from several other people, including Lord Curzon, who, I calculated, had died five years before she left New Zealand. She was hardly a reliable witness. Might she have destroyed the correspondence for entirely different reasons? Disentangling truth from the distortions of time and memory was looking more difficult than ever. Besides, I had a bigger story on my mind.

On Saturday 2 December 1939 at 3.45 in the afternoon, Madeline Lees (44) met Francis Younghusband (76) at the World Congress of Faiths office in Bloomsbury. She was to change his life.

'Madeline,' he wrote. 'I go about all day in a lovely dream with an exquisite little figure in blue with radiant eyes making sunshine all around. And I am absolutely possessed by this vision. And the glory of it is that it is no ethereal Angel that I could not touch but only see. It is a nice human Angel that actually loves to come to me and be folded in my arms and be pressed as close to me as ever I can get her. That is how I look on you my beloved.'[26]

Madeline Annie Pamela Lees was small and compact with compelling violet eyes and pale brown hair. There was an attractive, eccentric dynamism about her, a tactless determination that could be infuriating to those who expected women to be more docile. To Younghusband she was nothing less than perfection: maternal but girlish, devoted to the teachings of the Bible, yet with a miraculous, unflinching faith in the wildest spiritual fantasy. She had been born into one upper-class Dorset family and married into another, escaping from a strict mother who had stopped her from nursing when she found out she had seen a naked man. Her husband, Sir John (Jack) Lees, Baronet, DSO, MC, Croix de Guerre, was eight years older than her, an affable landowner with a bad stomach. They married in 1915, and soon produced Katharine, James, Rosamond, Thomas, Anne, Jane and Mary Gabriel.

Seaver's bland biography of Younghusband makes a couple of very tentative references to the subject. It is possible to deduce that the great man died while staying with his friends Sir John and Lady Lees, but not much else. What made me inquisitive was an indication at the end of the book that Younghusband was in Dorset against his family's wishes – there is a clear impression that Eileen disapproved of the arrangement. This niggled in my mind for some time, until I remembered Helen Younghusband's injunction – if in doubt, consult *Burke* or *Who's Who*. There was a Sir Thomas Lees listed: 4th Bart, landowner, born 1925, former High Sheriff of Dorset, discharged from RAF after losing eye. Could there be a connection? A quick computer search revealed a publication called *Another Man*; when I got hold of it the blurb alone was enough:

What happens when a baronet is filled with the Holy Spirit?
Sir Tom Lees' Dorsetshire country house is now the base
of the Post Green Community, a centre of renewal where
God is healing, bringing love, making people whole. This is
the story of Tom's encounter with Christ and his vision for
the Church.

It all seemed faintly familiar. So it was that I found myself driving
down twisting country lanes in a rattling Morris Traveller, heading for
an encounter with a one-eyed Dorset baronet who had been filled
with the Holy Spirit.

Stalking around Lytchett Minster, I wondered what on earth to
expect. A woman at the village shop said the people in the Community were 'normal types mainly, not like they used to be'. This
seemed to refer to a period in the 1970s when some Americans,
Canadians and New Zealanders lived there ('like a commune, six
to a bedroom, some said'). I walked along the road in the damp
mist, feeling strangely calm. Up at the big house a pair of nuns
were wandering serenely through the garden. They smiled but did
not speak. I waited in the hall looking at religious pamphlets while
a very earnest young man went off to find Sir Tom.

He materialized in a rust-coloured guernsey and stout shoes, cordial but brusque, insisting that he remembered little. I should realize, he said, that I was hunting a very cold trail. No, he didn't have
any strong recollections of Younghusband, although he knew he
was friends with his mother and used to come to stay at Lytchett
occasionally. Further questions were parried in an amiable way
while he hustled me down the road to see his sister. If there were
any old papers, Sir Tom said, she would be in possession of them.
Perhaps he was just busy, but I had a sense that the last person he
wanted to talk to was a sleuthing biographer.

Jane was in her sixties, round and vague in a mauve tracksuit.
She lived in a pink house a few hundred yards from her brother,
surrounded by dogs. 'Oh, hello,' she said. 'Tom told me you might
turn up. I brought this down from the attic – it's got some of
Mummy's old stuff in it.' On the table was a battered suitcase,
stuffed with books and papers. I took a deep breath. 'There might
be something on Sir Francis in there,' she went on. 'He was a
wonderful man, you know, very small but full of joy. A great friend
of Mummy's, although the relationship was never like that of
course.' I spent the whole afternoon working my way through the
suitcase and sneezing at the dogs. There were newspaper cuttings

about Younghusband and a pile of his circulars to World Congress of Faiths members. By the end I felt half dead: one WCF pamphlet reads much like another after a time. Feeling despondent I wandered through to the kitchen. Jane was cutting up a giant mushroom the shape of a football.

'I don't suppose there could be anything else left in the attic?'

'No, I think that's the lot,' she replied. 'I really don't know why I eat these things – they're so jolly disgusting.' The mushroom flopped open into the sink with a hollow thud. 'But I do like to try them. Well, I suppose I can go and have another look in the attic.'

With that she trundled off up the stairs, returning a couple of minutes later with a collapsing cardboard box. On the top was a copy of Younghusband's play *The Reign of God*, and underneath it a stack of paper bound with a faded green ribbon. *In his handwriting!* As I saw it my heart leapt and Jane's dog leapt with it, grabbing a mouthful of letters between its teeth and trotting off into the garden. 'Oh, you silly old thing,' said Jane, quite unconcerned. I had a brief struggle between social and biographical duty as she tried to interest me in a copy of *England's Resurrection*, then ran outside as fast as I could.

It was getting dark and starting to rain. There was no sign of the dog. Suddenly I spotted it at the end of the garden and set off in pursuit, chasing up and down as a trail of letters flew from side to side, caught by the wind, blowing away into the hedges. The dog was wagging its tail delightedly as it ran. When I finally managed to catch it most of the bundle was still there, locked between its foul jaws, the green ribbon dripping with saliva. I tried to prise open its gums with no success, and then, forgetting the Buddhist prohibition on causing gratuitous pain to any sentient being, put my fingers to its throat and pressed as hard as I humanly could. With a strangulated yelp the dog released its prize and scurried back to the house. I stood there with an armful of sodden letters, the warm rain pouring down my face, exultant.

TWENTY-FOUR

Love in the Blitz

The letters were astonishing. It was as if everything I had always known about Younghusband but been unable to prove was here before me. Prolific as ever, he had written to his Beloved nearly every day for two years. The style and the language were familiar, but for the first time he seemed truly to have let himself go. His other writings had a sort of staged liberation about them, as if he found his mystical destiny hard to live up to in practice. The reserved enthusiasm of his earlier love letters ('Oh Nellie Nellie you are so kind and good') was replaced by ecstatic, tumultuous revelation. This was his grandest passion yet: he had been waiting all his life for a woman like Madeline.[1]

As well as these letters, I found Madeline's letters to him, which had been returned to her after his death. Some were missing, but all Younghusband's were there, despite the occasional hound's tooth-mark. At some point Madeline had gone through them with a pen, crossing out delicate sections in an arbitrary way, so it was often possible to make out the obliterated words. The censored passages left me intrigued. They had also used acrostics as a form of code, which I was able to crack fairly easily after immersion in their writing. What could M.V.O.M.V.D.S.F.I.L.Y.M.M.E.M.M.B.O. mean other than: 'My Very Own My Very Dearest Sir Francis I Love You More And More Ever More My Beloved Own'?

When Currant Hill was sold in late 1937 the Younghusbands had moved to a dingy flat in Ashley Gardens, tucked behind Victoria railway station. Around the same time Eileen had met Helen Roberts, another pioneering woman who had given up a privileged background for the social services, and moved in with her at Lansdowne Road. The outbreak of war saw her desperately busy setting up a Citizens' Advice Bureau in Kensington while her parents moved to a relation's house near Henley. When it became clear that German bombs were not yet falling, they returned to London. Lady Younghusband was now eighty years old and scarcely able to walk, so Nona came to visit several times a week. During this period – the 'Phoney War' – Younghusband walked across St James's Park each morning to the WCF office in Bloomsbury, determined that his plans would not be disrupted.

On 19 April 1940 he took a slow, blacked-out train down to Dorset, arriving in a state of exhaustion. His destination was a Conference to promote a 'unifying principle of World Peace'. When he was invited the previous December he had accepted because the organizer, Madeline, Lady Lees, was 'so open and genuine and candid' that he could hardly refuse. At South Lytchett Manor he was installed in front of a huge log fire, while Lady Lees sat at his feet and talked about her plans. To his delight her teenage children and their cousins ran around the big house in an atmosphere of friendly chaos. He enjoyed meeting her husband (an admirer of Tibet 1904), and Miss Deal and Miss Dacombe ('Dealer' and 'Dakes'), her secretary and lady's maid turned housekeeper. There was an inspirational, welcoming feel in the air; somehow he knew at once that he had 'come in contact with a kindred soul'.

The Conference itself was not entirely successful. To the horror of Sir John Lees Bart, a host of Communists ('some of them complete cranks in sandals', according to his daughter) came to express their support, followed closely by a deputation from the Ministry of Information. Although Lady Lees insisted that a 'false armistice' was not her ambition, her activities were regarded as subversive and she was placed on a government black-list until the end of the War. To Sir John, who was busy setting up a local platoon of the Home Guard, all this was supremely embarrassing. When one delegate asked him about his own religious views he shuffled off stiffly with the answer: 'You'd better ask my wife – she's the one who deals with those sort of matters.'[2]

Her peace proposals were an odd confection of the idealistic and the irrelevant, such as a worldwide religious revival, educational reform, free trade, a pooling of the world's mineral resources and an overthrow of 'the present Economic and Financial system of usury'. Like Younghusband, she was not a pacifist, but rather a believer in the idea that war would become outmoded after 'the establishment of God's Kingdom on Earth'.[3] After two days of talking the meeting broke up with World Peace still some way off: the Communists and the men from the Ministry went on their way. Before Younghusband left, Lady Lees took him through primroses and camellia trees to the prayer grotto she had built in her garden. That was the moment, he wrote later, at which their communion in spirit began.

Afterwards they wrote each other warm letters of thanks, and corresponded busily through the summer. To Lady Lees, the labours of the World Congress of Faiths offered hope for the future and gave 'fresh courage to thousands'. To him, the raising of a large family on progressive religious principles seemed the most practical way of changing the world. Younghusband anticipated 'an unheralded outbreak of peace'; but Denmark fell to the Nazis, and Norway, Holland, Belgium and France. He was undaunted, just as he had been undaunted by the horrors of the Great War: 'The war does not depress me. I like the feeling of everyone going about in dead earnest and being so much more ready for religion.'

Despite the imminent possibility of an invasion, he managed to hold a five-day WCF conference at Bedford College on that elusive concept, the New World Order. Speakers included the Chief Rabbi, Curzon's biographer Lord Zetland, the Islamic scholar Yusuf Ali, a renegade Catholic named Maud Petre, a Buddhist Bikkhu and Bishop George Bell. The staunch old Fighter for Right Gilbert Murray was unable to attend. Herbert Samuel, who had been Home Secretary during the last war, gave an eloquent denunciation of Nazism and spoke of the need to abandon the restrictions of religious dogma. When the conference was over Younghusband felt 'strangely elated' and sent Lady Lees a copy of his recent book *Vital Religion*, which restated his familiar spiritual theories.

The Battle of Britain began in earnest; the railings outside the Jog were uprooted to help with the war effort; Eileen wrote urgent Ministry of Health reports. Down in Dorset Lady Lees could hear the bombs dropping by the coast: IS YOUR JOURNEY REALLY NECES-SARY? asked the posters. In this world of grave austerity and careless abandon, her journey was necessary, somehow, if it meant love might triumph. On the first day of August 1940, Younghusband met her at Waterloo station. 'I was as happy as a child at being with you again,' he admitted to her later; he even asked permission to call her Madeline. They strolled through St James's Park, arm in arm, past ducks and pelicans, talking of God and watching a butterfly fluttering around a buddleia bush. They sat on a bench (their bench, it became) and Sir Francis plucked up his courage to ask whether she too had ever experienced a mystical vision.

The answer was yes – twice. She had been 'suddenly suffused with unutterable joy', and summoned to 'the other side'. Subsequent experiments with a Ouija board had produced no comparable feeling. Sir Francis realized then that she had shown him 'the very sanctuary' of her soul. 'This communing with you in the spirit',

Madeline told him, 'is bringing a new and marvellous joy . . . into my life.' They met again and braved a visit to Ashley Gardens. Helen was in a cheerful mood, regarding Madeline as a more suitable luncheon guest than most religionists. The love birds parted that afternoon, but four days later Sir Francis found himself back at the station. 'At last I caught sight of you,' he explained, 'running so gaily down the platform and when we met you threw your dear arms round me and kissed me and pressed me to you and I caught you to me and we were utterly happy.'

He knew then that there had 'never been anything quite like this spiritual communion and companionship of ours'. Yet Madeline had a husband and seven children and he had an ailing wife. The Blitz was nearly upon them. It was simply impossible to be together for any length of time. 'Beloved,' he cried out at the end of August. 'Oh! how I miss you!':

> I am so relieved and happy . . . For five hours last night we were down in the basement and I would keep repeating to myself what you had said in your letter which I received this morning: 'My arms are round you blessing and thanking you for ever.'

What worried him most was the news that his Beloved was unwell, having suffered a minor stroke. For days on end she remained in bed: like Teresa of Avila and Hildegard of Bingen she experienced frequent migraines. Madeline seems to have been overwhelmed by physical and emotional stress, floored by the impracticality of her spiralling love affair and the demands of her family. South Lytchett Manor had been requisitioned by the army and they were moving to a nearby house called Post Green. She wrote to her 'perfect knight' sporadically while he showered her daily with compliments and ideas.

'The womanly in you makes great appeal to me and rouses all the most manly in me,' Sir Francis announced. 'You are a remarkable illustration of the essential Creative Spirit of the World. You are a perfect manifestation of Mother Love.' It was even possible, he believed, that she might be the Messiah he had prophesied in *The Coming Country*, or the incarnation of the fictional Vera Love. There was no reason why the new Christ should not be a woman, although 'we will keep [this] absolutely sacred and secret between you and me alone . . . And, except by me, you will not be recognised in your life time. But your influence will grow and grow till it becomes one of the great influences in the world.' Madeline's reply does not survive, but the indications are that she viewed the prospect of divine realization calmly and sincerely. She began to feel better.

They discussed everything from mountains and religious drama to the propriety of Madeline having given a cup of tea to a shot-down enemy pilot. Both agreed with Bishop Bell that it was wrong to bomb German cities. 'On no account must we come down to the Hitler level,' Sir Francis declared. 'We must preserve the English Nelson tradition.' Nona, Baden-Powell, Bertie Russell and Mah-atma Gandhi were all forked over; Russell was deemed to have been in need of 'a woman like you' all his life. As for Gandhi, he had admitted in a recent speech that he had never found God, despite years of seeking. 'I have spoken with him and listened to him several times,' Sir Francis confirmed, 'and I could feel that. Things would be a good deal better, and India would be a good deal better, if he had.' Experience of the Divine was limited to the exclusive few: 'I bless you and love you . . . so determined to make use of our wonderful gift for the service of God.'

Postal love was one thing: physical contact was another. Some-how they arranged to see each other in Droitwich, on the pretext of attending a religious gathering. It would be harder to get there in the Blitz than it had been to reach Lhasa in the snow, he told her, but he was animated by an 'indomitable spirit' that nothing could quench. They met in a hotel on the afternoon of 21 October for the first time in two months. 'Oh! How thankful I am that I was so crystal [?] pure of heart when we were on our Honeymoon,' he exclaimed afterwards. 'But you and I did prove ourselves the perfect Bride and Bridegroom':

> How is your poor neck, and your eyes, and your face, and your jaw. I am afraid I may have hurt you through not realising your suffering enough and not being gentle enough in my touch . . . So we kneel together facing each other and folding ourselves closely and lovingly together, and then I give you the gentlest sweetest kiss and off I go into life with you running through me in every pore.

They were united in wonder; forced apart by circumstance. During November the correspondence continued, but the explosions did too. Doodle-bugs and incendiary bombs rained down on Britain's cities night after night until it seemed there could be no more left to fall. Equipped with a stirrup pump and a tin hat, Sir Francis paraded London's streets in his new capacity of Fire Warden. In the middle of December 'the Madeline–Sir Francis Fellowship' snatched a night in London. 'The whole atmosphere of this flat is full of the delicate fragrance you have left,' he told her afterwards:

> Oh! my Madeline, oh! my precious precious Madeline how can I bear the joy . . . Oh! what a blessed, blessed time that was – to feel that you were always there – just at the end of the passage and that at any time we could go to each other. And when we did go to each other. Oh! what happiness we had – unbelievable!

A fortnight later he was revelling in her description of Christmas at Lytchett, marred only by Sir John's recurring stomach pain. Sir Francis could picture hordes of children opening their stockings. 'Do you know,' he told her, 'we children never once went into our parents' bedroom neither at Christmas or at any other time. Their bedroom with its double bed was kept as a kind of sanctum. And I never once saw my dear mother even in a dressing gown.' On the last day of 1940 he went to their 'trysting place' (the St James's Park bench) and 'communed' with his lover. He felt it had been the happiest, most glorious year of his life.

In the first week of January his life was turned upside down when, during a daytime raid on Westminster, an incendiary bomb crashed through a skylight in the roof. Sir Francis approached the fizzling device carefully, threw a bucket of sand at it and retired into the street. Lady Younghusband, who was starting to lose her mental faculties, was equally forthright, refusing to leave the building until she was properly dressed. Although the fire in Ashley Gardens was extinguished swiftly, Eileen decided her parents would have to move. She was herself now involved in what she described to her biographer as 'a very close partnership of living together' with her friend Helen Roberts.[4] A flat near Park Lane was offered by the Roberts family, so the elderly couple packed their suitcases and set off on a new adventure.

Nomadism suited Sir Francis. It gave him a good excuse for a three-day visit to Lytchett, which passed off happily, his relations with Sir John remaining cordial throughout. Whatever the baronet may have known or suspected about his wife's relationship with the retired explorer, it is clear that he tolerated it. Sir Francis did his best to be enthusiastic with Sir John, telling Madeline that it was 'a great treat to me to have talks with him about soldiering & birds & local life, and as I told you once before, I am much more at home with him than with some of my Congress people.'

During his stay he planned the 'work' that he and Madeline had to do together. It covered a vast range of things from education and peace promotion to the post-war administration of the world. For her part, Madeline was happy to defer to his authority: it is clear that she saw him as a figure of wisdom. He accepted the role gladly, keeping her to himself with the manipulative skill of the experienced guru: 'I am more certain than ever', he explained, 'that you had better, for the present, concentrate upon our dear union all the time and energy you can spare from yr. family and local duties.' By loving him she had 'done something of incalculable value. Through our most intimate and sacred communion you have enabled me to reach the solution of that vitally important man-woman [question].'

With a stroke of genius, he decided it was their duty to tell the world of this 'solution'. They would write a book together called *Wedding*, outlining the joys of love for the benefit of the younger generation. It proved essential for Madeline to make several visits to London to discuss the project, and at the end of March they both went to a World Congress of Faiths meeting at Downe House near Newbury to listen to a trail of titled figures hold forth on spiritual reconstruction. Having herself run a small private school at Lytchett before the War, Madeline made a short speech on the need for religious education to begin at the mother's knee. This was their first joint public appearance: Sir Francis was determined that their 'soul union' should become 'the very nucleus of the Congress', which did not help his relations with WCF workers like Mr Jackman.

Blinded by passion, he had a naive assumption that everybody would derive as much joy from her company as he did himself. On the night of the great air-raid of May 1941 (in which the House of Commons was bombed) he crouched in the cellar with his wife and his lover. When the 'all clear' sounded, Madeline went upstairs to prepare some food. She made tea on a spirit stove and sliced sandwiches into neat triangles. 'Humph,' announced Lady Young-husband when she saw them. 'Cut like a parlour maid.'[5] Eileen was openly resentful. She felt that her father's relationship with a woman six years older than herself was humiliating and ludicrous. On the day of the raid she was barely courteous, a social lapse that Sir Francis tried to explain away: 'I have never seen her before like she was on Saturday. She had made Helen angry & Helen had made her angry,' he suggested to Madeline, 'and all this came on to you & me.'

When a land mine fell opposite the flat a few days later 'and the concrete wall buckled in like warm icing', the Younghusbands were left homeless again.[6] First on the scene was the needlework expert Dorothy Thorold, who lived nearby. 'I remember leaning out of the window with a cushion on my head,' she said, 'watching the bombs drop':

> I climbed up the stairs and found the old lady sitting on a small settee covered from head to toe with broken glass. She was quite, quite senile by that stage. There was a foreign maid who'd gone hysterical and couldn't do a thing. I'm not sure where Sir Francis was.[7]

While Eileen tried to find a new home for her parents they took a slow train to Dorset. The trip was not a success, the Lees family finding Helen less than endearing. 'She was an awful old thing,' one of them recalled, 'grossly fat and bigoted, like a great big waddling pillow. She hated Roman Catholics in particular, and didn't like all that religious work Sir F. was doing with Mummy. But he was always sweet to her.' Four days into the visit, Sir Francis was able to write to Eileen that her mother had, so far, been on her best behaviour, although 'whether we shall survive [until departure] without a catastrophe only Providence knows'.[8]

Had Providence been able to speak, the celebrated mystic would have learned that a catastrophe was looming the very next day. With the inscrutable, ambiguous logic of the nearly demented, Lady Younghusband made her way to the drawing room, picked up a copy of the *Catholic Herald*, placed it carefully on a sofa, and lowered her vast bulk on to it. Then, while a Papist housemaid looked on in disbelief, she began to urinate. It was her last message to the world.[9]

Younghusband was busier than ever in the last year of his life. With Helen settled first at Lansdowne Road, and later in a nursing home in Holland Park, he was able to devote himself to his destiny. His friends and contemporaries were disappearing fast: Newbolt, Bergson, Yeats, Baden-Powell, Tagore, Buchan, Bruce and the Gaekwar had died within three years of each other. Caught in a world of motor cars and bombs, he began to divest himself of his worldly goods. Under Nona's supervision his books and silver were sold. Trunk loads of Chinese silks were given to Madeline: she wrote to thank him from her bed, 'covered with the spoils of the East'. The gold medals of four Geographical Societies, as well as one from the King of Bhutan, were presented to the Chancellor of the Exchequer to help with the war effort. He was reaching a position of total, Tolstoyan simplicity.

The mountaineer Frank Smythe was to be his biographer. Sir Francis hoped that he would take on the task 'almost as a religious duty', since it was 'most exasperating . . . that such a second rate man as H G Wells should be looked upon as a major prophet'.[10] Although Smythe's own spiritual ideas were at least as peculiar as those of his subject, his personal devotion made him a natural choice for the task.[11] They spent several weeks together going through papers and preparing an outline of the book. Asian exploration would be covered in detail, but the focus would be on his work as a religious leader. Sir Francis told Madeline that the story of their love would have to be left out, since 'anything about that is far too sacred to publish in my life time or in an ordinary biography'.

Wedding was to be his last will and testament, a definitive guide to sex, love and religion. Sir John Lees Bart had forbidden Madeline to co-author the book when he found out its intended subject, so she could only make suggestions. Sir Francis purchased booklets from the Alliance of Honour with titles like *The Hygiene of Marriage* and *Simple Hints to Mothers of Little Boys*, illustrated with line drawings of well-scrubbed Aryan youths. He spent a long time writing the book, producing drafts on betrothal and the creative urge. Advice on the delicate issue of contraception was given by his Beloved: 'I had not realised the hideousness of the whole thing,' he told her. 'In fact I know precious little about it & have never even seen a contraceptive apparatus.'

In *Within* he had preached free love from a theoretical standpoint: now in *Wedding* he would show how it could be put into practice. Like a flushed teenager, he wanted to tell the whole world about his experiences. 'I <u>have</u> made [the] discovery that bodily union does not impair soul union but heightens and tightens it,' he exclaimed to Madeline. 'And this is a very, very important discovery which shd. have enormous influence for good on the future of the race.' She shared his conviction, writing: 'It is a perversion to believe that there is something ultra spiritual in not having bodily union. Why, if spiritual marriage is so blissful, shd. it not penetrate the realms of earth + spiritualise the bodily union. <u>We</u> know that it can.'

The manuscript of the book was sent to Sir John Murray, who reacted with astonishment. In a rather bewildered letter (written by hand for he felt too embarrassed to dictate to his secretary) he pointed out that it failed to condemn pre-marital sex. 'I must confess', he added, 'that I think there are some physical details which would better be left to purely medical books; and to me it comes as rather a shock to find within a few pages so-to-speak of these physical chapters a glowing account of the King and Queen's war work, Empire tours etc.'[12] Editorial guidance was then taken over by young John Murray and his wife Diana, both of whom Sir Francis had known since they were children. Diana was ' "modern" but in the very best sense', Madeline was told, and most helpful with her advice on *Wedding*.

The final version of the book was an unsatisfactory jumble, with appendices attached. Diana had made various proposals, tactfully suggesting that he cut particular chapters, but Madeline insisted they were retained. *Wedding* ended up as a guide to religious love for the young, praising marriage, patriotism, sexual joy, happy home life and the customs of Indian forest tribes. It condemned prostitution, self-abuse, contraception and smutty talk, the last being a vice that 'may also easily lead to homo-sexuality which, if allowed to become prevalent may become a cancer eating into the life of a people, as it is already eating into the life of great cities like Berlin, Paris and London'.

Like Queen Victoria, the possibility of lesbianism does not seem to have occurred to him, although he believed the consequences of male homosexuality were severe: 'When a man wants children – as for instance a Chief a son and heir – he finds to his disgust that he cannot have them. The habit takes such a grip upon a man that he becomes impotent with women . . . And he becomes an object of scorn and reproach among men – a bugger.' Heterosexuality and 'the marriage act' were keenly promoted, although in thoroughly oblique language. For all his intentions, Sir Francis found himself quite unable to cast off his Victorian shell and speak candidly. Having apologized repeatedly for the need for frankness, he confined himself to vague talk of sensitive flesh, indrawing actions and 'a simple piston-like operation'.[13] Whether this description was helpful to the guileless newlyweds at whom the book was aimed seems doubtful.

Young John Murray had reservations about *Wedding*. (He had become Old John Murray by the time I went to see him fifty years later.) It had all been rather embarrassing, he remembered. He sat in an armchair wearing a shambolic old tweed jacket and the customary bow tie, giggling slightly:

'He wrote it with that Lady Lees woman, you know. I thought to myself what a strange thing for Sir Francis to have done. I'd gone with him to a couple of Congress of Faiths meetings but he'd never struck me as cranky.'

'But what about his earlier books?' I asked.

'Well, they were a little odd. Yet as a person he was always very upright. Very direct and gentle in his mysticism. *Wedding* never sold of course. We had to publish it – he'd been with us for ever. It was only the travel ones like *The Heart of a Continent* that sold.'

As we walked slowly down the stairs at Albemarle Street he observed that the book had been all the more surprising since Sir Francis had never struck him as a libertine.

'There probably wasn't much of a marriage there with Lady Younghusband, I shouldn't have thought. I'd imagined he was slightly John Ruskin in his sexual inclination.' Here the eyebrows were raised. 'There was a time when biographers didn't have to deal with all that side of things, but now with the Kitty Cat woman writing about Mrs Reagan and so on, I think they rather expect it of you.' He opened the old front door with exquisite pre-war courtesy, eyes twinkling.

I was left perplexed by this. Did Sir Francis share Ruskin's predilection for young girls or his fear of pubic hair? Did old John Murray know something I didn't? Sadly he died soon after our meeting, so I was unable to follow up the matter. It did however bring me back to the question of Nona, 'the adopted daughter' as one friend of the family described her.

The puzzle was largely solved by the letters I found at Lytchett Minster. It became clear that there had been an understanding of some kind between Nona and Sir Francis, although it was probably an amorous flirtation rather than anything more serious. When her affair with Frank Smythe began, Sir Francis complained, she refused to take part in affectionate cuddling. Nona, for her part, felt that the old man's charm had been dented by Madeline. 'He hadn't been in the house five minutes when he asked me if he could ring Lady Lees,' she told Eileen in 1941 while having him to stay, 'and then when she rang at 8 a.m. before he was up I came to the conclusion it must be "luv"!! . . . I told him that he'd grown up and I like him much better as a boy!'[14]

After reading the letters I became fairly certain why it was that Nona had burnt her correspondence and tried to destroy the rest of the Younghusband papers. I realized that they dealt with a period of great stress in her own life. In 1940 she had taken the dramatic step of leaving her husband and moving in with Frank Smythe, a sure route to social disgrace. Sir Francis was unruffled by such an irregular arrangement, but others were openly censorious. There were also references to financial and marital matters that made Nona's bonfire understandable. By the time I went to see her in the nursing home in 1991, her life had changed dramatically. Frank Smythe had been dead for many years and she was now the Dowager Countess of Essex, with no wish to be reminded of ancient social embarrassment.

If it can be assumed that Nona's relationship with Sir Francis was simply a romantic flirtation, one riddle remains unsolved. Who was the recipient of his 1935 love letter? There is no definite answer to this, although it may have been an American woman called Mrs Brownell whose letters still sit in the restricted-access section of the India Office Library. Some questions have to remain unanswered.

The 'Madeline–Sir Francis Fellowship' managed to secure adjacent rooms at the 1941 WCF summer conference. Oxford had been chosen as the venue, although Sir Francis still felt angry with the university over a humiliating experience at the Union some months before. A speech he was giving on the Nature of the Whole had been interrupted by a facetious undergraduate asking how 'whole' was spelt: 'meaning to be funny he said had seen it spelt H.O.L.E.' To top it all, 'C. E. M. Joad was not only cheap but thoroughly nasty – attacking the Church in the most disgraceful way.' The ordeal, he told Madeline, had made him realize 'the fearful need the country has for what you and I have to give'.

Sir Francis had lumbago and frequent nose bleeds, yet there was no hint of senility. He had managed to arrange a full schedule on 'World Religions and World Order' despite wartime restrictions. Speakers included Lord Samuel, Yusuf Ali, Sir Hassan Suhrawardy, and Gilbert Murray, while the literary critic G. Wilson Knight gave 'a recital showing the religious aspect of Shakespeare'. For all his excitement at seeing the World Congress of Faiths at work, Sir Francis was quite unable to keep his mind off Madeline. He told her afterwards that the five days at Oxford had surpassed even the happiest of their previous meetings. Lodged in his mind was the memory of her watching the sunrise from his window:

> Then how proud I was at breakfast-time taking the photo
> of you and yr. family & showing [it] to the Congress people.
> You are M.V.O. [My Very Own] so why shouldn't I be
> proud. Besides wh. it is very important for the Congress
> that they shd. know about you and yr. work.

What the breakfasting faithful made of this can only be guessed at, but there were certainly tensions developing within the WCF. On top of the fact that it had twice been bombed out of its Bloomsbury headquarters, Sir Francis seemed set on ruling by personal whim. His frequent references to Lady Lees and her views on family life were not appreciated by Arthur Jackman, who was sacked later that year from the post of Secretary. The WCF office was put under the control of a Miss Anderson.

Madeline was a little more cautious, yet equally convinced that they had a unique message of spiritual love and joy that should be shared with others. She really did feel that he was leading her to 'the real + great work' of her life; everything else had 'only been the preparation – the training ground'. Back at Lytchett she wrote him a letter, 'So comf. propped against a tree in the hay with 3 cushions at my back + the sun on my chin.' John's stomach problems were worse than ever (he needed X-rays and oil massages) and her beloved son James was going away to war, but still she felt joyful. 'How can we ever thank God enough,' she asked.

He responded with ecstatic letters, digressing over many different subjects. He praised her body, and issued an edict prohibiting her from referring to it as a 'husk'; it was, after all, 'the most divinely beautiful of all God's creations . . . And how sweet and lithe and lissom it is! So perfect in its lines and curves! So exquisite to the feel!' Madeline insisted that her body was nevertheless a husk, but agreed to take care of it. 'We are getting on aren't we!' she exclaimed. 'Such heavenly letters . . . One morning early as I was lying v. still God entered me + I was transfigured into the Spiritual World which is always so close to us.'

Sir Francis kept the compliments coming, comparing Madeline to other religious promoters he knew. Dorothy L. Sayers and the Bishop of London had 'not in their whole bodies as much spirituality as you have in your little finger'. Indeed Sayers had 'no profundity of religious feeling or thought, and is very cheap & vulgar at times. In India she wd. be regarded as very amateurish in matters of religion.' As for Curzon's daughter Lady Ravensdale (a staunch WCF activist), 'she is pretty dictatorial and dominating but she is a good sort,' yet even so 'none of her eloquence can touch people like you do'. All in all, his Beloved had 'a practical wisdom and a sane common sense such as neither Gilbert Murray, Madriaga, Lord Samuel or any other of the high lights of the Congress possesses'.

He cast her as the moon to his sun, the reflection of his own singular personality – the soul partner he had longed for all his life. 'One thing I love & admire in you is that you are both conventional & unconventional,' he wrote one morning. 'You are always tidy in mind as in body but much fuller of spirit & courage & adventure than any towselly Bohemian.' 'I'm going to write a marvellous book with you called "The New Patriotism",' Madeline told him, '+ another called "Brave New Heaven". Gosh they will make people sit up + take notice.' People would take notice, he was sure of it. After he was gone, their mutual influence would spread far and wide. He would abandon the idea of a Himalayan burial in favour of a shrine on Beacon Hill, a remote beauty spot near Lytchett. His grave 'wd. become a place of pilgrimage', he informed her. 'And it wd. commemorate <u>our</u> romance.'

Madeline made the most of his remaining time on earth. 'You do know, don't you,' she asked, 'how I never leave you, how Love + Joy (or as you wld. say Joy & Love) stream out to you from me.

M.V.O.S.F.F.E. [My Very Own Sir Francis For Ever] I feel yr. help to me all the time. It is God's own Power coming to me thro' you.' She loved him for himself and for the dangers he had passed. She even loved him – as true lovers must – for his failings: 'My dearest dearest beloved Sir Francis. Yes I do love yr. very inability to express all you feel – that inability to express it just expresses it better than the most brilliant rhetoric could ever do.'

Backwards and forwards went the letters. In the autumn he managed two trips to Lytchett, loving the chaotic bustle of her teenage children with their ponies and bicycles. He took to dressing in the robes he had brought back from the East. 'I changed into the Indian silk,' he wrote to Helen, whose lucidity was fading fast, 'and Madeline ensconced me under the tree where I slumbered peacefully.'[15] On one visit he brought Suhrawardy and Qadir with him, to the great consternation of Dakes the housekeeper, 'who didn't hold with coloured gentlemen coming to stay'.[16] His ideas on race had gone through a strange transformation, so that 'quick-witted, supple-minded, highly spiritual Hindus' now sat at the top of the racial tree. In a newspaper article in 1938 he had even claimed that Christ's qualities depended on his birthplace, since Asiatics were of a 'finer mould' than Europeans.[17]

Despite the demands of the heart and the flesh, Younghusband remained frantically busy, travelling around the country as best he could, giving speeches and attending meetings. He was now living in the basement of Eileen and Helen Roberts's house. With some effort, he persuaded the Royal Society of Literature to nominate the Indian religious philosopher Sri Aurobindo for the Nobel Prize for Literature. He continued to write articles and book reviews, praising Chiang Kai Shek for his belief in Sino–Indian fellowship and calling for a 'revised and reformed League of Nations . . . inspired by a burning spiritual impulse.'[18] By late 1941 the worst of the Blitz was over. Throughout, wrote a neighbour, Younghusband had remained 'invincibly cheerful' and 'quite imperturbable . . . like a rock'.[19]

The crisis in India continued to hold his attention. Many Indians were unwilling to support the Allies in the War until a fair independence settlement was reached; with Churchill as Prime Minister this was looking like a vain hope. On 25 September Younghusband was sent an urgent telegram by the All-India Congress stating: 'MEETINGS HELD ALL OVER INDIA DEMANDED BRIT GOVERNMENT BY REASON INHERENT JUSTICE . . . IMMEDIATELY UNEQUIVOCAL DECLARATION END WAR INDIA CEASES DEPENDENCY.'[20] The retired imperialist sprang into action at once, arranging a meeting at the India Office with the Secretary of State, Leo Amery. There was no discernible result, but Younghusband hoped 'a Press coverage wd. be started'. The Quakers India Committee even tried to persuade him to go out to India himself, since he 'combined both political & spiritual qualifications'.

A letter to *The Times* of London had some effect, in India at least. His unusual status as a poacher turned gamekeeper meant that his pronouncements were taken seriously by Indian nationalists. '"WE HAVE BLUNDERED" – SIR F. YOUNGHUSBAND'S OUTSPOKEN LETTER', ran the main headline in the *Hindustan Times*. His views made front-page news and provoked leading articles in most Indian newspapers. The essence of his case was that the British had 'blundered badly' and 'caused the deepest resentment' by not respecting the desire of the population of India to be free:

> To myself personally, who was born in India, and have for the last 59 years been closely connected with Indians, it comes as a bitter reproach that we should treat Indians as anything else than the most loyal comrades and affectionate friends.

His hope was that 'the good name of England' would be saved by letting the Indian people decide their own future.[21]

Soon afterwards, he was asked by the BBC to write a radio talk on 'My Debt to India'. He did so, giving a romanticized interpretation of his Great Game exploits, and stressing the exalted quality of Indian culture. Overseas Talks then commissioned a programme, but the draft he submitted was considered too radical. His theme was that European civilization had collapsed and the world's only hope lay in the religious wisdom of the East. When a re-written script was again rejected, he appealed to his friend the Marquess of Dufferin and Ava at the Ministry of Information. The Marquess intervened and Younghusband was sent polite letters of apology by the BBC, but the talk was not broadcast.[22]

In December he ran down to Lytchett to watch a religious play that Madeline was producing. Intense preparation had been going on for months, which he had assisted by obtaining a cautious letter of endorsement from Bishop Bell of Chichester. 'My Lord,' he had assured the Bishop on the subject of His Beloved, 'her one aim is the revival of religion.'[23] The play was 'a perfectly wonderful success', he wrote to Helen. 'Exactly what I had always been wanting in my Religious Drama Society.'[24] As for the RDS, it was now closely connected with the staunchly pacifist Pilgrim Players, and his fellow founder Olive Stevenson had resigned in disgust. Sir Francis was not bothered. Religious drama of any kind was nothing short of glorious, he felt, since it infused the world with religion.

He abandoned the 'perfect pandemonium' of Lytchett in favour of an awkward Christmas in London with his family. Helen's condition was deteriorating and his relationship with Eileen had become badly strained. 1942 began with a lull. He read Aurobindo's *The Life Divine* and made frequent visits to the 'trysting place' in St James's Park, his spirits being kept up by the fan mail he was receiving from India. Mr Dutt of Bengal had told him he was 'indeed great', while Diwan Chand Obhrai of Peshawar introduced himself as 'one of your humble followers and admirers'. 'May you live long and Evermore,' he exhorted, 'as a Salt on Earth to Season with.'[25]

Sir Francis Younghusband KCSI, KCIE spent the first months of 1942 correcting the proofs of *Wedding* and going to religious meetings. He took a trip down to Sussex to discuss plans for his biography with Frank and Nona: Nona was now calling herself Mrs Smythe in a bid for social acceptability, but was plagued by hate mail from Frank's real wife. In the middle of March Sir Francis went to Lytchett for a rest, exhausted by the rigours of wartime rationing. Madeline fed him 'with creamy milk, butter, eggs and every kind of luxury' until he felt himself bursting with health.[26] One afternoon he rode up to Beacon Hill on a little white pony called Misty.

The troubles of war, finance, transport and apathy were all taking their toll on the WCF. Against the advice of his officials, Sir Francis was determined that plans for the 1942 summer conference should push on regardless. He knew the Divine Spirit would come to his aid in a crisis. When he was opposed by the office manager he reacted swiftly: 'Miss Anderson,' he wrote to her. 'You, I know, have the interests of the Congress most deeply at heart and I shall be ever grateful to you for the help you have given us for a long time past. But . . .'[27] She was dismissed, and Sir Francis personally took on the day-to-day running of the office.

Despite constant setbacks his plans went ahead. He worked himself desperately hard, determined that it should be a resounding
success. The meeting would be on the theme, 'Religion Today: The
Mutual Influence of East and West'. Birmingham was to be the
venue, and there would be speeches by Rabbi Georg Salzberger and
Canon Guy Rogers. Madeline and Sir Francis planned to stay just
outside the city with Dame Elizabeth Cadbury, a rather stern 'Con-
gresseur' who had opened the very first WCF meeting in 1936.
'M.V.O.S.F.K.O.G. [My Very Own Sir Francis Knight Of God],'
Madeline wrote a few days before it all began:

> I do hope Dame E. won't squash our liberty too much – I
> rather wish we were going to be in an hotel don't you. We
> shall have to be so frightfully prim + proper. I am going to
> bring a bicycle to wizz about on . . . I suppose you can sit
> on the handle bars in front of me or on my carrier at the
> back. Oh! . . . The thought of Birmingham is uplifting. Love
> forever. Y.V.O.M.A.P.L. [Your Very Own Madeline Annie
> Pamela Lees]

Sir Francis set off from London on the morning of 17 July carrying
fewer possessions than he had taken with him to Tibet. His small
case contained:

> Light vest
> Shirt & Collars
> Drawers
> Socks
> Grey tie
> Alopin pills [for his heart]
> Gasmask
> Nail brush
> Tooth powder
> Razor & blades[28]

He gave the opening address, insisting passionately that there
should be no mood of vengeance when the war came to an end.
'Winning the Peace' should be their ambition, otherwise more conflict would follow in the future. The Congress was sparsely
attended, yet he felt that the atmosphere was more inspired than
he could ever remember. On the fourth day, after listening to
speeches by Miss Picton Turbervill and Swami Avyaktananda, he
felt a little tired and went to a tea shop near Victoria Square. While
he was there he fainted, so Madeline abandoned her bicycle and

took him back to Dame Elizabeth's house in a taxi. He lay on his bed murmuring, 'So happy, so happy,' in a weak voice. The next morning he felt a little better and Madeline took him down to London on a train. He was determined to say goodbye to Helen, his little sweetie, the wife who had never shared his life.

Petrol was rationed and motor cars were hard to come by but Madeline, with customary élan, obtained a large private car and chauffeur to take him down to Lytchett. His remaining earthly possessions – the spoils of his Eastern travels – were placed in the boot. He wished to give them to his Beloved for the promotion of religious drama. Before leaving Helen's nursing home he wrote a pencil note to his daughter in a shaky hand: 'My dear Rogie, The Congress was a huge success. The University, the Lord Mayor and Canon Guy Rogers all played up like Billy oh, and Sir Francis Younghusband . . . was a bit played out at the end so Madeline is motoring him straight to Lytchett today and he is giving the Men of the Trees the go by. Your loving Daddie.'[29]

His Beloved perched him high on pillows and cushions, and they were driven sedately through the ruins of London to the English countryside. As they passed Beacon Hill he looked up and said: 'I should like to be buried there.' She put him in a sunny room facing the garden and plied him with glucose, peaches and cream. A telegram from the WCF was waiting: the meeting had passed a special resolution. 'We, the members of the World Congress of Faiths,' it began, 'send a message of love and sympathy to you, Sir Francis . . .'[30]

The next day he felt too weak to do anything but sleep, but on 24 July managed another note to Eileen:

> All is going A1 here though they are doing their best to spoil a hitherto blameless character. They fed me with creamy milk and raspberries and gooseberries and eggs and a real good bread & butter . . .

He did his best to reassure her that he would be back home soon, certainly by 6 August. It worried him that Helen might be alone for the anniversary of the death of their baby boy, Francis Charles Delaval Younghusband. Although the child had been dead for forty-four years he knew it was still 'the bad day' for Helen.[31] And then there was the BBC talk on India that he had to broadcast towards the end of the month. For a while he sat out on the verandah in the sun, reading lightly and talking with the Lees children. He wrote his last letter to his wife, saying that he 'was being made most splendidly comfortable by Madeline. All I am allowed to do is to lie in a big armchair and eat and drink and sleep all day long and I have started a fresh lot of P. G. Wodehouse.'[32]

Early in the morning on 26 July, Dakes the housekeeper went to bring him a cup of tea and found him in a state of great distress. He had suffered a stroke during the night and his mouth and throat were partially paralysed. Madeline telephoned Eileen, who came down at once from Cambridge, collecting Nona on the way for moral support. There was strong unspoken tension between the mistress and the daughter, and rivalry over questions of diet and treatment. Should he have been brought down to Dorset after his fainting fit? Was the nurse from Poole suitably trained? Had he eaten a surfeit of raspberries and cream? For five days he lay there, the Ganden Tripa's bronze Buddha by his bedside, floating in and out of awareness, speaking little.

Sir Francis Younghusband remained conscious almost to the last. He drifted slowly towards another world, the world of the spirit, the mystical dimension that he had come to live and die for. He was dying, slowly dying. Madeline sat with him, reading prayers while he squeezed her hand to signify he understood. Very early in the morning on Friday, 31 July 1942, she felt that the final moment was approaching. As the sun rose over Lytchett Minster he began to leave her, very calmly and peacefully. A little after six o'clock he died, cradled in Madeline's arms.

EPILOGUE

Creating the God-Child

They put the coffin on a farm cart strewn with wild flowers, and Misty the pony drew it across the fields to the little churchyard at Lytchett Minster. Sir John's uniformed Home Guard turned out as pall-bearers, followed by Madeline and Eileen and Nona. The Lees children wore brightly coloured clothes in accordance with the last wishes of Sir Francis. With the sun shining brightly and the Ganden Tripa's bronze Buddha placed squarely on top of the wooden coffin, some simple prayers were read at the graveside. Then the body of the last great imperial adventurer was buried in the Dorset earth.

'Younghusband, 79, Explorer, is Dead', ran the headline in the *New York Times*. 'He Made Tibet Our Friend', claimed the *Sunday Express*, 'and knew more of innermost Asia than any other white man', while the *Edinburgh Evening News* thought he had been a 'Schoolboys' Hero'. 'He had a fine simplicity of character,' suggested his old employer *The Times*, 'and no more honourable man ever served King and Empire.' The Royal Society of Literature obituary confirmed that he had been 'most happily married' – a hopeful suggestion matched only by the entry in the *Dictionary of National Biography*, insistent that no hint of Atheism or Altairianism should sully his posthumous reputation of such an upstanding public servant. Younghusband had been 'a devout Christian, who had long pondered upon the mysteries of life and explored the religions and philosophies of the East, particularly Hinduism and Buddhism'.

Tributes poured in from all over the world. As Madeline told Helen in a decidedly tactless letter on 6 August: 'He has left me a great work to carry out as a living ever-expanding memorial to him . . . Beloved Helen, amongst all his perfection nothing is so beautiful as his utter devotion to you and yours to him.' There were literally hundreds of letters, praising him as a mystic and a visionary and as 'Saint Francis', calling for the creation of a shrine in his honour. 'I worshipped the ground he walked on,' wrote Miss Mary Gutsell, while another woman expressed a wish to give up

her house 'furnished for hospitality to Indians in memory of Sir
Francis'. Plans were drawn up to establish a 'Chair of Mysticism'
at Oxford. 'He was one of the noblest and wisest of men,' wrote
Sudhin Ghose, 'one whom both Britain and India could – with
equal justice and pride – count among the most devoted standard
bearers and knight-errants.'[1] Some years later the writer Sirdar
Pannikar suggested 'there were only two Englishmen in 200 years
who really penetrated into the soul of India, and they were both
soldiers – Francis Younghusband and Archibald Wavell'.[2]

The World Congress of Faiths arranged a Memorial Service on
10 August at St Martin-in-the-Fields. It was firmly inter-faith, with
readings and representatives from every religion under the sun.
While careful not to speak ill of the dead, the *Church Times* made
it clear that it had been a rather improper performance. There
were readings by Bhikkhu Thittila, Sir Atul Chatterjee, Rabbi Dr
Salzberger and Sir Hassan Suhrawardy. One woman remembered
it as 'truly, truly extraordinary. I had never seen anything like it
at that time. It really was most unusual to have foreign religions
gathered at that kind of service in a Christian church – but quite
appropriate.'[3]

At the end of the month a tribute was broadcast on the Home
Service by Lord Samuel, under the title 'Man of Action, Man of
the Spirit', commending Younghusband's stimulating, energetic
interest in religious philosophy. It was followed a fortnight later by
a talk on the Tibet Mission by Freddie O'Connor, praising the
character of its leader. The Hindu guru Ranjee Shahini gave a lecture at the India Society, pointing out that 'Sir Francis was a very
wise man, far wiser than scholars, or thinkers, or politicians . . .
He understood Asiatics better than most Orientalists and experts.'
Nevertheless 'words cramped his style', since: 'Mysticism can only
be suggested by hints, half-tones, figurative allusions, and best of
all by paradox and self-contradiction . . . Sir Francis forgot this.'[4]

The Presidency of the WCF was taken over by the greatly
respected but undeniably dull Lord Samuel, with Baroness Ravensdale as Chairman. Mindful of the late Sir Francis Younghusband's autocratic methods, the group's constitution was
rewritten to prevent any one person from again assuming a concentrated hold on power. One of the keenest disciples, a railway clerk
called George Harrison, began to give talks in the north of England
on the teachings of Sir Francis. He also compiled a book (as yet
unpublished) called *The Great Adventure: A Younghusband Anthology
of Divine Fellowship*. There were other acolytes too: a Muslim who

considered Sir Francis an Islamic 'mystic saint', a man who called himself 'Francis Younghusband Thompson' and a certain Mr Wheeler who began a cult of Younghusbandry in the Poole area. 'The reason', as their hero had explained a few months before his death, 'is that they can all feel I have touched God.'[5]

Lady Lees set about perpetuating his memory. The Bournemouth branch of the WCF sprang into life with Lady Younghusband (senile in her Holland Park nursing home) as its President. Assisted by a Mrs St Clair Stobart, who was unfortunately prone to take 'astral trips', Madeline trotted around the country with the 'Sir Francis Younghusband Exhibition', consisting of a selection of the artefacts he had given her on his deathbed, including lengths of silk and brocade, sword belts and Yarkandi robes. The most favoured items were the Tibetan and Chinese silk dresses taken – or looted, depending on your point of view – from the Lhasa authorities as a fine for the misbehaviour of the 'beastly lama' with the flailing sword. Lady Lees took a more imaginative view of their provenance: they had been given to her friend 'as tokens of goodwill', she said, 'by wise men of the East, by Chinamen, Tibetans, Indians, and men of various creeds and races, united by the goodwill and sense of fellowship that Sir Francis invariably aroused in them through his own deep spirituality'.[6]

In 1954, a few months before the death of Sir John Lees Bart during an exploratory stomach operation, Madeline set about making a religious film. She wanted to promote the idea of 'World Peace through Religious Drama' using the costumes that Sir Francis had given her. Before he died he had said he would always be there, 'in you and with you ... And perhaps one day God may grant it that I may appear to you in a vision and fill you with an even intenser happiness than I have yet been able to bring you.'[7] With customary zeal she sought out local actors, engaged the services of a film director by the name of Mr Royal Gornold and started a café on the side of the Poole-to-Wareham road to finance the escapade.

'They're not hanging their heads at Lytchett when anyone mentions de Mille,' proclaimed the *Poole and Dorset Herald* three years later when it was finished. *Voice in the Wilderness* told the story of St John the Baptist in glorious Technicolor, shot on location in the sandpits and heathland of south Dorset. 'The film is in the language of modern youth,' Lady Lees told a reporter; its avowed purpose was 'to catch the Teddy boys by surprise'.[8] Some years on came *Messiah*, telling of God's incarnation on Earth in the form of Jesus

Christ. Sir Jack's collection of vintage port had to be auctioned to provide funds, but Madeline knew the story had to be told.

The films are remarkably well made considering the circumstances of their creation, with crowd scenes of up to three or four hundred people. Yet they both bear an unforeseen but undeniable resemblance to Monty Python's *Life of Brian*, as men with funny beards and tea-towels charge about the Dorset countryside on Chipperfield circus camels, singing 'Silent Night' and pretending they are in the Holy Land. If you look carefully you can see members of the cast swaddled in Chinese silk robes and brocade – and one of the Three Kings wears a helmet that once belonged to the Tongsa Penlop of Bhutan's bodyguard, and bears a Tibetan incense burner.

Throughout the 1950s and early 60s there was a running battle between Madeline and Eileen about the ownership of these treasures, complicated further by Sir Francis's failure to have made a will.[9] When Eileen was informed that Madeline was 'cutting up the Dalai Lama's robes to make cushion covers for village sales of work', and that a bolt of rare Chinese silk (obtained Yarkand, c. 1888) had been turned into a trailing mantle for an actor, she began legal proceedings to recover them. She was assisted by Nona, who shared her bitterness at the way in which Sir Francis and his message had been appropriated. (Frank Smythe had died in 1949, his biography of Younghusband unfinished, and Nona was now married to the heir to the Earl of Essex, Viscount Malden.) The conflict was finally resolved when Madeline agreed to deposit the entire collection in Liverpool Museum, home to a substantial holding of Tibetan material.

Only one riddle was left unsolved: the fate of the Ganden Tripa's bronze Buddha. When Younghusband was buried it was taken from the lid of his coffin and installed in the house at Lytchett. Madeline subsequently gave it to Liverpool Museum, only to retrieve it for an exhibition and then hand it to a man with 'a fresh clean young face' called R. A. Wheeler who had 'made a cult of "Sir Francis"' and 'hero worshipped him since the age of 14'.[10] Eileen's attempts to recover it were fruitless, until finally in 1967 (Madeline had died earlier that year) she persuaded Sir Tom Lees to take legal action against Mr Wheeler. This met with little success, Wheeler insisting that he needed it for 'lecturing purposes'. But finally he did agree to return the icon to his hero's daughter – on the condition that he could first meet her to explain the kidnapped Buddha's spiritual significance.

When Dame Eileen Younghusband died in a car crash in North Carolina in 1981, now an internationally famous figure in the world of social work, and a recipient of the René Sand award, she gave the Ganden Tripa's Buddha to the Royal Geographical Society. I went to look for it one August morning, but the Keeper denied all knowledge of the bequest.

When I returned with a copy of Dame Eileen's will, another search was made, and finally the much-travelled bronze deity was discovered somewhere in the basement, nestling in a Peak Frean's biscuit tin. It seemed a fitting resting place, somehow. I was always pleasantly surprised by the Edwardian eccentricity of the Royal Geographical Society – it is the only place I know that keeps its telephone in a large oak cupboard marked: AVAILABLE FOR LOCAL AND TRUNK CALLS.

'Kill that green light,' said the fat man with stubble. 'OK. We'll try ultra-violet and take it on to Monitor 2.'

'Yeah, and pull the plug on the colour screen,' said the tall one with glasses.

'That's a bit better. No, hold on. 1940, you said? Could be censoring ink – wartime and all that. Try the VSC at the Met: that'd soon sort you out. Right, we'll try switching to negative . . . That's a little better, push it a little higher and focus that spot.'

'It's approaching one micron,' whispered the man with glasses.

'Bingo!' said the fat man. 'Now we're talking.'

I was standing in a darkened room somewhere in central London, looking at a large video screen. In front of me were the crucial love letters that Madeline and her ink pen had so haphazardly obliterated. With great difficulty I could make out these words:

> . . . And I am going to have a crowningest in [. . .] bring forth a God-Child . . . who will be greater even than Jesus. You will shrink at my saying this. But why shouldn't he be? Jesus did not fully and completely manifest every side and facet of that Infinite Being who is the Source of all things . . .

And there is no reason whatever why a God-Child fathered by me and born of you whilst we are both buoyed up to best pitch by this fight for the soul of the world should not manifest God more completely than any one who has gone before. Now when War may bring death on any one of us at any moment . . . why shouldn't an exceptionally spiritual woman like you who has already had the idea of giving birth to a Christ and who is now wedded in the spirit [to me?] crown her experience and give birth to a God-Child who will manifest God more completely even than Jesus did? There is nothing inherently impossible in this. And there is everything in it to make it probable.

Younghusband's letters to Lady Lees were the missing pieces in the jigsaw. I had continued to be intrigued by them, and the way that they were so casually censored. Thought-provoking phrases like 'You will shrink at my saying this' and 'giving birth to a Christ' had been left uncovered, tempting speculation. It was as if Madeline and her fountain pen had sought not to obliterate her lover's bizarre fantasies, but merely to hide them away for another day, for a time when strange technology and odd wavelengths of light could reveal her secret to the world. The letter went on:

'My Beloved, whom I so deeply reverence, do take these things and treasure and ponder them in your heart as you feel the little one swelling within you. And then one day in the far future they will be saying of you and me (as Churchill said of our airmen that never in history had so many owed so much to so few) that never had so many owed so much to one godly pair.[11]

I raced down to Dorset in a mad whirl of speculation. Was there a God-Child? Had it been born? Every permutation and possibility presented itself. Could it be Sir Tom or his sister Jane, here in our midst, a Messiah for the new millennium? Down at Lytchett Minster it certainly seemed unlikely. I got out of the car and was ready to ask them, but the sight of such British normality, of dogs, a mauve tracksuit, a sweeping green lawn and a rust-coloured guernsey stopped me in my tracks. For a start, the dates didn't fit. They were a good fifteen years too old to be Younghusband's children. Their mother, they said, as I coughed politely and shuffled my feet, had not produced any wartime babies.

But my mind stayed open to the fantastical prospect. Might there have been a discreet confinement, I wondered as I walked through the shimmering yellow-green fields, a quiet birth in the midst of the Blitz which gave the world a little child to carry forward the vision of Madeline and Sir Francis? Was there an unknown fifty-something incarnation still waiting to be discovered in the depths of the English countryside, a living, guiding deity for our lost generation? 'A pure God-Child will arise,' Younghusband had written in *Within*, 'more perfect even than Jesus.' The new leader would 'make life's beauty shine forth in untarnished radiance' and 'send a note of poignant sweetness' singing through our souls. I continued on up to Beacon Hill, pondering the fantasy. Yet when I got to the top there were no pilgrims, nor any trace of the shrine that Sir Francis had wanted built in his memory. There were some caravans and old ice-cream wrappers, but no disciples.

I went down to the graveyard, through the glittering trees and the long grass. He lay there in the ground, bones now, this source of such thought and speculation. Above him was a stone carving of the Potala and an inscription: 'Blessed are the pure in heart for they shall see God.' Beside him Helen, dead in her nursing home in 1945. Nearby Madeline, and Sir John, and their son James, killed in hand-to-hand combat in the Balkans. After the war, Madeline had set off with a basket and a borrowed flying suit to find his killer. The man was an Italian Fascist called Roberto. Madeline located him, gave him her forgiveness and invited him to Lytchett. Some time later he arrived. 'Was it awkward when he came?' I asked her daughter. 'No, of course it wasn't. Mummy had read in the New Testament that you should love your enemy, and so that's what she did.' It was an extraordinary and deeply impressive forgiveness, embracing the man who had killed your child, hating the sin but not the sinner.

Younghusband came closest to attaining his dreams of true joy during his time with Madeline. His life-long search for love and empathy reached a point close to fruition in the final two-and-a-half years before his death. In a rare way, he found he had attained something close to liberation at a stage in his life when many people have abandoned moral or spiritual development. Rather than allowing old age to encrust him in the damp mould of complacency and tradition, he reached out, seeking fresh answers and a new horizon. At other moments he had glimpsed happiness in the distance and tried to describe it, but been uncertain how to reach out across the final stretch to real bliss.

Younghusband was a maverick. It was his individuality that had launched his journey to Manchuria and his crossing of the uncharted Gobi Desert. It was his unwillingness, even inability, to conform that had stunted his career, and sent him to backwaters like Mastuj or Mount Abu. Yet it was this same characteristic that had marked him out for unusual missions like the Jameson Raid or the invasion of Tibet. Without his defiance of authority his achievements would have been drastically limited. His dynamic, stubborn independence joined with his immense physical resilience to send him to places where others had never been. Once he had retired from Asia, it was this same blinkered determination that drove him along the spiritual path that he saw mapped out ahead of him, leading to creations as diverse as *The Living Universe* and the Fight for Right movement.

Behind his conventional exterior lay a radical impulsiveness and irresponsibility, and a willingness to confound expectations. In Tibet his rebelliousness nearly led him, as Lord Ampthill put it, to go off the rails. Within his shy singularity was an ironic selflessness; he was oblivious of other people's expectations. He was never specious or theatrical, or anxious for social normality; he felt most at home in the wild expanses of High Asia. Yet in order to achieve his ambitions, he behaved in a way that consistently disregarded the needs of others – his wife, his daughter, his superiors and his government. His final espousal of the prophecy of the God-Child was at once an act of intense vanity, placing himself in a pivotal role in human history, and an act of great, childlike naivety.

It was an extension of this optimistic idealism that had enabled him to believe in the value of colonial rule as a doctrine of compassion. In a priggish way he thought it was the duty of the Empire to govern people on the basis of the colour of their skin. It was not commercial greed that animated his actions: his version of imperialism was a theoretical political doctrine, explicitly linked to contemporary ideas about eugenics, heredity and anthropological distinction. Yet when his faith failed, when he saw imperialism falling apart in the way that closely defined creeds tend to do as reality catches up with theory, he moved forward to a new belief. Racial determinism was replaced with a looser vision, in which the peoples of the Empire would be permitted to take control of their own destiny. Although his later attitudes to race and self-rule may now seem patronizing, they were ground-breaking when compared with the views of many of his contemporaries.

Younghusband's life was shaped by his willingness to change his opinions. His detached, bizarre approach to the people around him opened up possibilities that others would never have considered. Although he was not willing or able to change his outward bearing – he remained a paragon of proud, polite, British respectability to the end – he came to realize that his inner voices could never be ignored. After his mountainside vision in Tibet and his near-fatal car accident, he slowly permitted his deeply felt spiritual impulses to come into the open. During the 1920s and 30s he felt his way in the dark, uncertain how to put his mighty religious ambitions into practice. Then in his final years he stepped back from Everest and exploration and the written word, transferring his energy to the process of intense personal transformation with his beloved Madeline, Lady Lees. It was this capacity to evolve that gave his life an epic quality, a kind of representative greatness that mirrored the era through which he lived.

Francis Younghusband belonged in Dorset, not in the Himalayas, I felt by the end. It was his last great joy, the place where he found a love and a peace and an understanding that he never reached elsewhere. It was the right place to leave him, propped up in bed dreaming of improbable schemes for a world conference on mystical experience, or another book, or a new society for promoting fellowship between Asiatics and visitors from the stars, drifting away, a bowl of fresh raspberries and cream by his side. That was where I found Younghusband, I think, in the exquisite haze of an autumn afternoon.

NOTES

ABBREVIATIONS

OIOC Oriental and India Office Collections of the British Library, more usually known as the India Office Library.

FY Younghusband Collection in the India Office Library. (Mss. Eur. F197/).

BL British Library, Department of Manuscripts.

BOD Bodleian Library, Oxford.

NLS National Library of Scotland.

CUL University of Cambridge Library.

RUL University of Reading Library.

BBC British Broadcasting Corporation Written Archives Centre, Caversham.

LPL Lambeth Palace Library, London.

NISW National Institute of Social Work Archives, London.

RGS Royal Geographical Society Archives, London.

NAI National Archives of India, New Delhi.

WBSA West Bengal State Archives, Calcutta.

KC Private collection of Tamio Kaneko, Japan.

LEY Letters from Francis Younghusband to his daughter Eileen Younghusband, in a private collection.

LC Papers of Madeline, Lady Lees, in a private collection.

Extended quotations from Francis Younghusband's published books have not been separately sourced. Where two or more successive quotations are from the same manuscript source, the final one provides the reference.

A BRIEF NOTE ON WORDS

Place names in India and Central Asia are notoriously difficult: they change from map to map, and the spelling is always variable. I have followed no standard system, but usually used the version which was in common usage when Younghusband was alive. Where necessary the modern variant has been included in brackets. Words and phrases which now sound offensive ('coolie' and 'Native State' for example) have been retained in my writing, since I felt it would be inaccurate to substitute later alternatives. Tibetan words have not been fully transliterated, except in the bibliography: any reader likely to appreciate the difference between 'depon' and 'mda'-dpon' (or 'sde-dpon') should be able to consult the source material.

PART I

ONE: Younghusband: 'Damned Rum Name'

1. FY/1–FY/21.
2. Younghusband, Francis, *The Light of Experience*, London 1927, p. 14.
3. FY/43.
4. *Sind Gazette*, 23 July 1907.
5. Ibid.
6. Eleven years later John Younghusband's brother Romer married Clara Shaw's sister Annie.
7. FY/292.
8. FY/37.
9. FY/323.
10. Seaver, George, *Francis Younghusband: Explorer and Mystic*, London 1952, p. 6.

11. Woolf, Virginia, *Roger Fry*, London 1940, p. 31.
12. Seaver, op. cit., p. 10.
13. FY/150 and FY/510.
14. Seaver, op. cit., p. 10.
15. FY/128.
16. Newbolt, Henry, *Admirals All*, London 1897, p. 21.
17. FY/510.
18. Clifton College Library, I, p. 29 and *The Cliftonian*, February 1928.
19. FY/323.
20. FY/152.
21. FY/150.
22. FY/323.
23. FY/151.
24. FY/148.
25. FY/142.
26. FY/152.
27. LC, 29 July 1941.
28. Fleming, Peter, *Bayonets to Lhasa*, London 1961, p. 67.
29. In FY/323 Younghusband wrote that Evan Lee was himself, but that the final scene was based on the death of his friend Major Averell Daniell, to whom the book is dedicated; *Madras Mail*, 14 May 1926, *Spectator*, 12 June 1926, *Pioneer* (Allahabad), 4 July 1926, *Sketch*, 6 May 1926.
30. Younghusband, Francis, *But In Our Lives*, London 1926, pp. 10–125. The book makes no mention of how the women might have come to contract venereal disease in the first place. VD was a continual preoccupation of the military authorities: in 1895 more than half the British soldiers in India had been treated for it.

TWO: Two Journeys to the Mountains

1. FY/36.
2. Younghusband, Francis, *The Heart of a Continent*, London 1896, p. 1.
3. FY/248.
4. Younghusband, Francis, *Wonders of the Himalaya*, London 1924, p. 21.
5. FY/248.
6. Younghusband, op. cit., pp. 14–33.
7. FY/248.
8. Younghusband, op. cit., pp. 42–4.

THREE: Playing Great Games beyond Manchuria

1. RGS Younghusband archive, 29 July 1884.
2. FY/153.
3. See Waller, Derek, *The Pundits*, Kentucky 1990. The phrase 'the Great Game' has recently been used by some political commentators as a general term to cover Superpower diplomacy. Here it refers only to the clandestine war of nerves between British India and Tsarist Russia; for a full and readable account see Hopkirk, Peter, *The Great Game: On Secret Service in High Asia*, London 1990.
4. Kipling, Rudyard, *Kim*, London 1987 (1st edn. 1901), p. 222.
5. Hopkirk, op. cit., p. 4.
6. Kipling, op. cit., p. 248.
7. FY/133.
8. Seaver, op. cit., p. 38.
9. See ibid, p. 41.
10. FY/153.
11. FY/68.
12. FY/153.
13. Younghusband, Francis, *The Light of Experience*, London 1927, p. 19.
14. FY/153.
15. Younghusband, *The Heart of a Continent*, pp. 6–18.
16. James, H. E. M., *The Long White Mountain*, London 1888, p. 262.
17. Younghusband, op. cit., p. 28.
18. FY/69.
19. Younghusband, op. cit., pp. 32–6.
20. FY/69.
21. Younghusband, op. cit., pp. 42–6.
22. FY/68.
23. Younghusband, op. cit., pp. 61–2.
24. KC.

FOUR: Across the Gobi and
Down the Mustagh

1. Younghusband, op. cit., p. 67.
2. FY/251.
3. Younghusband, op. cit.,
   pp. 68–79.
4. KC.
5. Younghusband, op. cit.,
   pp. 78–86.
6. FY/469.
7. Younghusband, op. cit.,
   pp. 93–113.
8. James, op. cit., p. 298.
9. Younghusband, *Wonders of the
   Himalaya*, p. 57.
10. Rockhill, William Woodville, *The
    Land of the Lamas*, London 1891,
    p. 96.
11. Younghusband, *The Heart of a
    Continent*, pp. 116–77.
12. FY/68.
13. Younghusband, op. cit.,
    p. 178.
14. KC, 22 October 1915.
15. FY/148.
16. FY/251.
17. Younghusband, *Wonders of the
    Himalaya*, p. 58.
18. Younghusband, *The Heart of a
    Continent*, pp. 179–83.
19. Younghusband, *Wonders of the
    Himalaya*, pp. 63–5.
20. FY/142.
21. FY/469.
22. Keay, John, *The Gilgit Game*,
    London 1979, p. 180.
23. Mason, Kenneth, *Abode of Snow*,
    London 1987, p. 286.
24. *Nature*, 17 May 1888.
25. National Sound Archives,
    T10272WR, Track R.
26. Younghusband, *The Heart of a
    Continent*, pp. 190–203.
27. Younghusband, *Wonders of the
    Himalaya*, p. 87.
28. The Baltis are a distinct ethnic
    group who, although usually
    Muslim, speak an archaic dialect of
    Tibetan. They are thought to have
    invented the game of polo.
    Baltistan is now part of northern
    Pakistan, but at the time was
    theoretically under the control of
    the Maharajah of Kashmir.
29. FY/654.
30. BBC Radio contributors 910, file 1.
31. Younghusband, op. cit.,
    pp. 102–5. Notovitch went on to
    write a book supposedly detailing
    Christ's activities in Kashmir and
    Ladakh after the resurrection,
    which Younghusband dismissed as
    a 'pretentious volume'.
32. Younghusband, *The Heart of a
    Continent*, pp. 211–13.
33. FY/152.
34. FY/491.
35. FY/152.
36. FY/491.
37. FY/70.

FIVE: 'Impressed by My
Bearing': Bearding the Mir

1. FY/252–FY/253.
2. FY/227.
3. FY/152.
4. FY/252.
5. Francis Younghusband to Jessie
   Elias, quoted in Morgan, Gerald,
   Ney Elias, London 1971, p. 285.
6. Younghusband, *Wonders of the
   Himalaya*, p. 117.
7. Younghusband, *The Heart of a
   Continent*, p. 214.
8. Younghusband, *Wonders of the
   Himalaya*, p. 120.
9. Younghusband, *The Heart of a
   Continent*, p. 219.
10. Descendants of the Shahidula
    Kirghiz fought the Soviets
    following the 1979 invasion of
    Afghanistan, under the leadership
    of Haji Rahman Qul. See M. Nazif
    Shahrani's anthropological study of
    displaced Kirghiz in *Central Asian
    Survey*, (London) volume 5,
    number 3/4, 1986.
11. Younghusband, Francis, *Report on
    a Mission to the Northern Frontier of
    Kashmir in 1889*, Calcutta 1890,
    pp. 9–10.
12. Younghusband, op. cit., p. 228.
13. Younghusband, *Wonders of
    the Himalaya*, p. 140.

14. Younghusband, *The Heart of a Continent*, p. 229.
15. Younghusband, *Wonders of the Himalaya*, p. 140.
16. Keay, op. cit., p. 182.
17. Younghusband, op. cit., pp. 149–151. The pass at the head of the Urdok Glacier was subsequently named Younghusband's Col, although it is now known as Indira Col.
18. Younghusband, *The Heart of a Continent*, p. 253.
19. OIOC L/P&S/8/3.
20. Younghusband, *Wonders of the Himalaya*, p. 160.
21. Younghusband, *The Heart of a Continent*, p. 259.
22. Younghusband, *Wonders of the Himalaya*, p. 169.
23. Younghusband, *The Northern Frontier of Kashmir*, p. 51.
24. Younghusband, *Wonders of the Himalaya*, pp. 170–2.
25. Younghusband, *The Heart of a Continent*, p. 261.
26. Younghusband, *The Northern Frontier of Kashmir*, p. 52.
27. OIOC L/P&S/8/3.
28. Younghusband, op. cit., p. 62.
29. Younghusband, *The Heart of a Continent*, p. 268.
30. 'Relazione del capitano B. L. GROMBTCHEVSKY sul viaggio negli anni 1889–1890 per l'esplorazione delle valli montane dell'Hindu Kush . . . letta nella sessione straordinaria della Societa Geografica Imperiale Russa, il 10 gennaio 1891, p. 19. Translated from Russian into Italian from an original document in the Lenin Library in Moscow by Lionello Fogliano, privately published 1993.
31. Younghusband, op. cit., pp. 268–72.
32. Keay, op. cit., p. 190.
33. Younghusband, op. cit., p. 272.
34. OIOC L/P&S/8/3, 26 October 1889.
35. Younghusband, op. cit., p. 293.
36. Ibid, p. 273.
37. Younghusband, *Wonders of the Himalaya*, p. 188.
38. Younghusband, *The Northern Frontier of Kashmir*, p. 75; *Wonders of the Himalaya*, p. 188; see Fogliano, op. cit., p. 20.
39. Younghusband, *The Heart of a Continent*, pp. 281–2.
40. Younghusband, *The Light of Experience*, p. 47. The Hunza people are Ismaili Muslims, who recognize the Aga Khan as their spiritual leader. The present Mir still exercises substantial power, travelling his kingdom by helicopter.
41. Younghusband, *Wonders of the Himalaya*, p. 196.
42. Younghusband, *The Heart of a Continent*, pp. 283–4. Durand claims to have given the tent to the Mir, but according to Hunza oral history he was relieved of it by force.
43. Younghusband, *Wonders of the Himalaya*, pp. 199–200.
44. Younghusband, *The Northern Frontier of Kashmir*, p. 84.
45. Younghusband, *The Light of Experience*, p. 48.

SIX: That Sinkiang Feeling: Outwitted in High Asia

1. FY/70.
2. FY/153.
3. Galwan, Ghulam Rassul, *Servant of Sahibs*, Cambridge 1923, pp. 37–8. Younghusband wrote the introduction to the book. Ghulam Rassul Galwan also made a journey deep into Tibet with a Mr Littledale, wrote a playlet called 'Testing the Sahibs' and travelled with a man who can only have been an anthropologist, since: 'That sahib's business was to measure the people's face, feet, and hands: everybody's.'
4. FY/155.
5. Ibid.
6. Skrine, C. P., and Nightingale,

Pamela, *Macartney at Kashgar*, London 1973, p. 5.

7. Fogliano, op. cit., p.29. (See note 30 of Chapter 5.)

8. Younghusband, *The Heart of a Continent*, pp. 302–5.

9. See Hopkirk, op. cit., p. 464.

10. Younghusband, op. cit., p. 316.

11. FY/70.

12. FY/155. The Russian consulate is now an expensive tourist hotel called (if a contemporary travel writer is to be believed) 'HOTEL SEMEN: Joint Hotil With Civilation.' See Dalrymple, William, *In Xanadu: A Quest*, London 1989, p. 229.

13. Younghusband, op. cit., p. 321.

14. FY/155.

15. Younghusband, *Wonders of the Himalaya*, p. 210; FY/153.

16. FY/148.

17. FY/142.

18. FY/161.

19. FY/163.

20. Younghusband, *The Heart of a Continent*, p. 316.

21. FY/160.

22. FY/155.

23. Seaver, op. cit., p. 96.

24. Younghusband, op. cit., pp. 321–6. For details of this premature Cold War see Skrine & Nightingale, op. cit.

25. FY/142.

26. FY/155.

27. Younghusband, op. cit., p. 327.

28. FY/142.

29. Younghusband, op. cit., pp. 328–30.

30. FY/142.

31. Verrier, Anthony, *Francis Younghusband and the Great Game*, London 1991, p. 135.

32. Younghusband, *The Light of Experience*, pp. 60–2.

33. *The Times*, 30 September 1891.

SEVEN: Loving a Splendid Colonel and Seeking God's Kingdom

1. FY/155.

2. FY/253.

3. Younghusband, *The Heart of a Continent*, pp. 332–40.

4. FY/142.

5. Younghusband, *The Light of Experience*, p. 63.

6. FY/516.

7. CUL Add.7676/P.189.

8. Younghusband, *The Heart of a Continent*, p. 347.

9. Younghusband, *But In Our Lives*, pp. 182–90.

10. FY/218.

11. NAI Foreign Dept., Frontier B, pp. 371–7.

12. FY/219.

13. See Younghusband, Francis, *Everest: The Challenge*, London 1936; and Chapter 21 above.

14. Younghusband, *The Heart of a Continent*, p. 354.

15. FY/219.

16. FY/162.

17. Younghusband, op. cit., p. 353.

18. Younghusband, *But In Our Lives*, p. 235.

19. FY/143.

20. FY/219.

21. FY/52.

22. FY/225.

23. FY/219.

24. FY/155.

25. FY/220.

26. FY/52.

27. FY/255.

28. *Correspondence Relating to Chitral*, HMSO 1895. (2 June 1894: in FY/71).

29. FY/220.

30. Masters, John, *Bugles and a Tiger*. London 1957, p. 146.

31. FY/255.

32. FY/318.

33. FY/257. Mahatma Gandhi was influenced in a similar way by Tolstoy's book. 'It left an abiding impression on me,' he wrote (in Gandhi, M. K., *An Autobiography*,

Ahmedabad 1927, p. 114), 'the independent thinking, profound morality, and the truthfulness of this book.'
34. FY/220.
35. NAI Foreign Dept., General A, Nos. 1–50.
36. FY/318.

EIGHT: Clubland: Travels with a Most Superior Person

1. Rose, Kenneth, *Curzon: A Most Superior Person*, London 1985 (first edn. 1969), p. 263.
2. FY/257; Younghusband, *The Light of Experience*, p. 70.
3. FY/220.
4. Rose, op. cit., p. 265 and p. 146.
5. FY/516.
6. FY/257.
7. FY/221.
8. Hopkirk, op. cit., p. 492.
9. FY/496.
10. FY/221.
11. *Geographical Journal*, London, 1895.
12. Younghusband, op. cit., p. 78.
13. Younghusband, Francis and Younghusband, G. J., *The Relief of Chitral*, London 1895, pp. 117–19.
14. CUL Add., 7676/P/237.
15. FY/221.
16. Younghusband, *But In Our Lives*, p. 207.
17. Younghusband, *The Light of Experience*, p. 75.
18. FY/221.
19. Younghusband and Younghusband, *The Relief of Chitral*, p. 170.
20. Younghusband, op. cit., pp. 72–3. See also *Roddy Owen* by his sister Mai Bovill, London 1897.
21. FY/318.
22. FY/221.
23. FY/225.
24. FY/260.
25. See FY/155.
26. FY/221.
27. *Financial Times*, 6 July 1991.
28. Seaver, op. cit., p. 35.

29. Showalter, Elaine, *Sexual Anarchy*, London 1991, p. 11.
30. Kipling, op. cit., p. 306.

NINE: 'Not Only a Fiasco': African Intrigue

1. Younghusband, Francis, *South Africa of To-Day*, London 1898, p. 1.
2. FY/221.
3. Longford, Elizabeth, *Jameson's Raid*, London 1982 (revised edn.), p. 218.
4. FY/144.
5. Quoted Longford, op. cit., p. 208.
6. Younghusband, *The Light of Experience*, p. 122.
7. FY/144.
8. Younghusband, op. cit., p. 125.
9. FY/222.
10. Younghusband, *South Africa of To-Day*, p. 95.
11. FY/222.
12. FY/221. See RUL MS. 1089 for contractual details.
13. Younghusband, George, *Forty Years a Soldier*, London 1923, pp. 233–4.
14. Younghusband, *South Africa of To-Day*, quoted endpapers.
15. Gilbert, Martin, *Churchill: A Life*, London 1991, p. 81.
16. Younghusband, *The Heart of a Continent*, pp. 383–400.
17. FY/225.
18. FY/222.
19. Younghusband, *South Africa of To-Day*, p. 104.
20. Rose, op. cit., p. 308. Cust once partnered Curzon in a game of naked lawn tennis, playing against the politician George Wyndham and the poet Wilfred Scawen Blunt. Cust and Curzon won.
21. FY/82.
22. FY/222.
23. FY/156.
24. FY/223.
25. FY/164–FY/166.
26. FY/328.
27. FY/573.
28. FY/583.

29. FY/575. See FY/585–594 and FY/619–643 for the intriguing history of the Magniac family.
30. FY/213.
31. FY/576.
32. FY/542.
33. FY/223.
34. FY/156.

PART II

TEN: An Interlude in Rajputana

1. Byron, Robert, *Letters Home*, ed. by Lucy Butler, London 1991, pp. 125–33.
2. FY/328.
3. FY/223.
4. FY/156.
5. FY/157.
6. FY/213 and Notes by Kathleen Lutyens in a private collection.
7. FY/169.
8. FY/157.
9. FY/70.
10. FY/157, and Younghusband, *The Light of Experience*, p. 147.

ELEVEN: 'A Really Magnificent Business'

1. FY/596.
2. OIOC Mss. Eur. F111/222.
3. FY/170.
4. FY/76.
5. FY/157. In 1919 Curzon was made Foreign Secretary; in 1923 he narrowly missed becoming Prime Minister; whether Younghusband succeeded in his ambition to 'guide the nation' remains open to question.
6. FY/264.
7. KC, 20 January 1901.
8. Royal Society for Asian Affairs leaflet.
9. FY/241.
10. As late as 1927 Younghusband was quoted as saying that the prospect of Bolshevik expansion was 'a very great deal more serious than the old threat to India by the Czarist Government', FY/542.
11. FY/158 and FY/172.
12. FY/160.
13. FY/268.
14. FY/172.
15. FY/268.
16. Younghusband, *The Light of Experience*, p. 154.
17. FY/172.
18. KC, 8 December 1902.
19. FY/158.
20. Younghusband, op. cit., p. 157.
21. Morris, James, *Farewell the Trumpets*, London 1978, p. 62.
22. FY/318.
23. FY/145.
24. FY/173.
25. Younghusband, Francis, *The Heart of Nature*, London 1921, pp. 90–1.
26. FY/472.
27. 'Rough Notes Passing Through Sikkim on my Mission to Tibet 1903', FY/270. There is a typescript copy of Yeshe Dolma's History of Sikkim in OIOC Mss. Eur. E78.
28. NAI Foreign Dept., General B 1903. Nos. 357–60.

TWELVE: The Sikkim Adventure

1. FY/270.
2. FY/145.
3. FY/270.
4. Much of the historical information in this chapter comes from *Sikkim Coronation*, Gangtok n.d. (c. 1970), and Sunanda Datta-Ray's excellent *Smash and Grab: Annexation of Sikkim*, New Delhi 1984.

THIRTEEN: Sixty-seven Shirts, a Bath and an Army

1. FY/145.
2. These comparisons of official rank are inevitably somewhat arbitrary. Tibetans share the British obsession with position

and hierarchy, which gave India Office officials the opportunity to draw up detailed tables of comparison: *dzasa* for earl, *kung* for duke, and so on. See OIOC L/P&S/ 12/4185A.

3. Younghusband, *India and Tibet*, London 1910, p. 122.
4. FY/173.
5. Shakabpa, W. D., *Tibet: A Political History*, New York 1984, p. 207. All quotations from Shakabpa are from the English-language edition of his work.
6. FY/173.
7. NAI Secret E, 1903, nos. 118–58.
8. FY/80.
9. Government Blue Book, cited by Lamb, Alastair, *Britain and Chinese Central Asia*, London 1960, p. 263.
10. FY/78. See also Curzon's June 1904 memorandum to the Cabinet in BL B.P.22/2.(1).
11. *Von Cinggis Khan zur Sowjetrepublik*, quoted by Snelling, John, *Buddhism in Russia*, Shaftesbury 1993, p. 84.
12. See Arash Bormanshinov's 'A Secret Kalmyk Mission to Tibet in 1904', *Central Asiatic Journal*, 1992, vol. 36, nos. 3–4, Wiesbaden, Germany.
13. FY/80.
14. FY/174.
15. Datta-Ray, op. cit., pp. 29–30. See also Dawa Norbu's 'The Europeanization of Sino–Tibetan Relations, 1775–1907', *Tibet Journal*, 1990.
16. FY/80.
17. Fleming, op. cit., p. 76.
18. *Pall Mall Gazette*, 17 November 1903.
19. FY/79.
20. FY/145.
21. See Lamb, op. cit., p. 336.
22. NAI Secret E., January 1904, 358–93.
23. FY/80.
24. FY/212.
25. FY/145.
26. *The Times*, 3 December 1903 and

Westminster Gazette, 2 December 1903.
27. FY/145.
28. FY/328.
29. FY/99–FY/102.
30. FY/271.

FOURTEEN: 'The Empire Cannot Be Run like a Tea Party'

1. FY/580. See also Warwick, Alan, *With Younghusband to Tibet*, London 1962.
2. *Daily News*, 3 December 1903.
3. Buchan, John, *The Last Secrets*, London 1923, p. 18.
4. In 1957 a cousin of Eileen Younghusband arranged for her to have tea with Lobsang Rampa at the Stafford Hotel in London. For obvious reasons, Lobsang Rampa/ Cyril Hoskins cancelled at the last moment. Doctor Rampa claimed to have 'met Sir Francis Younghusband twice, and formed the impression that he had had considerable spiritual enlightenment through Tibetan belief', see FY/544.
5. FY/559.
6. Landau, Rom, *Personalia*, London 1949, p. 216. In another burst of mystical invention, Rom Landau claimed that Gurdjieff and Dorzhiev were one and the same person.
7. Morris, Jan, *The Spectacle of Empire*, London 1982, p. 77.
8. *Blackwoods Magazine*, London, February 1929. The article was written by Lieutenant-Colonel L. A. Bethell under the pseudonym 'Pousse Cailloux'.
9. FY/174.
10. Private collection.
11. FY/145.
12. Younghusband, *But In Our Lives*, p. 301.
13. O'Connor, Frederick, *To the Frontier and Beyond*, London 1931, p. 33.

14. Younghusband, *India and Tibet*, p. 166.

15. FY/495.

16. A variation on this story can be found in both Candler, Edmund, *The Unveiling of Lhasa*, London 1905, and Waddell, L. Austine, *Lhasa and its Mysteries*, London 1905.

17. Namgyal Wangdu of Gyantse, *bod ljongs rgyal khab chen po'i srid lugs dang 'brel ba'i drag po'i dmag gi lo rgyus rags bsdud* [*A Short Military History of Tibet*], Dharamsala 1976, pp. 113–14. See also Petech, Luciano, *Aristocracy and Government in Tibet 1728–1959*, Rome 1973, pp. 181–3.

18. Shenkhawa, Gyurme Sonam Tobgyal, *rang gi lo rgyus lhad med rang byung zang* [*The Pure Unadulterated Copper of My History*], Dharamsala 1990, p. 5. Horkhang had in fact committed suicide by this point.

19. Under a bizarre programme instituted in 1913 by Charles Bell, Kyibuk's son (and three other boys) were sent for education at Rugby, an English public school. The fees were paid by the Tibetan Government, using a single gold bar. In 1919 Younghusband arranged for Kyibuk to be trained in cartography at the RGS. When I was in Sikkim I met Kyibuk's grandson, who lives in exile in Gangtok. See also Tsering Shakya's article in *Tibetan Review*, January 1986.

20. Phuntsog Tsering, ed., *deb ther kun gsal me long* [*The Annals of the All-Revealing Mirror*], Lhasa 1987, p. 402.

21. FY/495.

22. Younghusband, *India and Tibet*, p. 166, and Younghusband, *The Light of Experience*, p. 89.

23. FY/80.

24. FY/318.

25. FY/272.

26. *Daily Mail*, 26 December 1903.

27. FY/549.

28. 'Pousse Cailloux', *Blackwoods Magazine*, February 1929.

29. OIOC Mss. Eur. F166/12.

30. FY/145.

31. FY/175. The Japanese agent Hisao Kimura, who spent ten years travelling around Central Asia disguised as a Mongolian monk in the 1940s, found it inexplicable that such a hostile, wind-swept place as Tuna should have been chosen as an advance base: '[We made] the easy climb to the broad Tang La, and then with Chomolhari on our right the barren plain of Tuna stretched before us . . . I had been struggling through accounts of the Younghusband Expedition, and found it unbelievable that an army would have camped in this inhospitable spot at almost 15,000 feet for the winter.' Kimura, Hisao, *Japanese Agent in Tibet* (as told to Scott Berry), London 1990, p. 160.

32. Lopon Nado, druk karpo [*The Religious and Political History of Bhutan*], Bumthang 1986, p. 195.

33. NAI Foreign E., July 1904, nos. 7–105. Much of the material in the National Archives of India is duplicated in the printed Government Blue Books, but some despatches (such as this one) survive only in the original file.

FIFTEEN: 'Bolting like Rabbits': Blood in the Land of Snows

1. Buchan, op. cit., p. 21.

2. Phuntsog Tsering, op. cit., pp. 398–9.

3. Namseling, Paljor Jigme, *mi tshe'i lo rgyus dang 'brel yod sna tshogs* [*The History of a Man's Life and Related Matters*], Dharamsala 1988, pp. 35–6. The author was almost certainly Namseling's grandson or stepson, although in the text he refers to the General as his father;

Tibetan family relationships are notoriously complex.

4. Unsourced, but quoted in Shakabpa, op. cit., p. 212.

5. Tezur Jigme Wangchuk et al, *A Compiled History of the Tibetan People's Struggle Against the British Invasion,* 'Tibetan Autonomous Region' n.d. (c.1985), pp. 88–9.

6. Phuntsog Tsering, op. cit., pp. 398–9. The suffix '-se' denotes Lhading's status as the eldest son and heir, equivalent to the Scottish title 'Master of'. This narrative is particularly noteworthy since it goes on to blend credible history with what is clearly a piece of fantasy: 'Lhading-se saw a white horse nearby, and mounting it he fled eastward over streams and fields to a mountain. But the British opened fire with a cannon, and it was left to mourn the character of the heroic Lhading-se.' According to British sources, General Lhading was killed at the very beginning of the battle; besides which, the idea of the hero fleeing to the mountains on a white horse is a myth which crops up in Tibetan folk tales.

7. *The Times,* 1 April 1904.

8. Younghusband, *India and Tibet,* pp. 176–7.

9. NAI Secret E., July 1904, nos. 7–105.

10. OIOC Mss. Eur. F111/342.

11. Private collection, 3 April 1904.

12. Candler, op. cit., p. 110. Candler was himself badly wounded in the battle. 'Poor Candler', wrote Lieutenant Hadow in a letter home, 'was looking on when the melée started, & they fell upon him and hacked him about fearfully. He has had his left hand amputated & may lose his other hand as well. However he is doing as well as possible. He is an old Reptonian & left about the time I went there.' Private collection, 3 April 1904.

13. Shakabpa, op. cit., p. 212.

14. Candler, op. cit., p. 110.

15. FY/175.

16. FY/145.

17. OIOC Mss. Eur. F166/12.

18. See OIOC Mss. Eur. F111/342.

19. 'Pousse Cailloux', *Blackwoods Magazine,* February 1929.

20. FY/78.

21. Phuntsog Tsering, op. cit., p. 400. This engagement receives only a cursory mention in British accounts of the invasion, and it seems the attackers were unaware of Nenying's religious significance to Tibetans.

22. Gilbert, op. cit., p. 163.

23. *Overland Mail,* 8 April 1904. A noteworthy account of the battle appeared in *Ladakh News,* a Tibetan-language newspaper edited and published by a Moravian missionary in Leh. The paper reported that sacred amulets worn by Tibetan soldiers at Chumi Shengo had failed to protect them from gunfire; signal proof, thought the Editor, of the failings of the Buddhist faith. But his Ladakhi readers found this story unlikely, and the paper's circulation began to flag. See Bray, John, 'A. H. Francke's "la dvags kyi akhbar": The First Tibetan Newspaper', *Tibet Journal,* Autumn 1988.

24. FY/80.

25. NAI Secret E., July 1904, nos. 258–387.

26. NAI External B., May 1904, nos. 213–15.

27. FY/158.

28. *The Britannia,* Norwich 1933.

29. Private collection, 11 July 1904.

30. Shenkhawa, op. cit., p. 7; and see Shakabpa, op. cit., p. 218.

31. Tezur Jigme Wangchuk et al, op. cit., p. 214. In the absence of newspapers, street songs were an important way of communicating information in Tibet. They are still composed and sung today, often with subversive intent.

32. As recently as 1990 an American Evangelical mission published leaflets describing Tibet as 'a nation long steeped in demonism and Tibetan Buddhism, called Lamaism, a nation in desperate need of sharing the Truth of the Gospel of Jesus Christ', a land where the people use 'rancid smelling yak butter for just about everything'. *Background Papers on Tibet*, September 1992, Tibet Information Network, London.

33. FY/176.

34. FY/158.

35. FY/83.

36. *The New Age*, 19 May 1904. In fact all but a handful of the pursuing soldiers were Sikh.

37. FY/81.

38. OIOC Mss. Eur. E233/37.

39. FY/158.

40. NAI Secret E., July 1904, nos. 258–387.

41. FY/150.

42. NAI Secret E. July 1904, nos. 258–387.

SIXTEEN: 'Helpless as if the Sky Had Hit the Earth'

1. FY/87. I found Younghusband's ultimatum in the bowels of the India Office Library, still unopened, its seals intact.

2. OIOC Mss. Eur. F157/164. Bailey took a primitive 3D camera with him to Tibet.

3. Namgyal Wangdu of Gyantse, op. cit., pp. 118–19.

4. Shakabpa, op. cit., p. 214. By this stage the Younghusband Expedition had clearly become an invasion, but the fiction of it being a diplomatic mission with a small military escort was maintained to the end.

5. WBSA Government of Bengal Political Dept., 1904. Confidential Spare Copies.

6. OIOC Mss. Eur. F166/12.

7. FY/80. Anthony Verrier (*Francis Younghusband and the Great Game*, London 1991) suggests that Curzon 'abandoned' Younghusband on the road to Lhasa. By way of evidence, he claims Curzon wrote to his agent only once between May and September 1904. This is inaccurate. Although the Viceroy was both ill and on leave (with his wife on her death bed), he sent Younghusband several telegrams and at least six letters during this time. See FY/80 and RUL MS. 1391.

8. FY/80. Thomas Manning made a remarkable journey through Tibet in 1811.

9. Purchokpa, Thubten Champa, *A String of Wondrous Gems . . .*' (1940) from *A Jewel Rosary Illustrating the Various Incarnations of Saintly Avalokiteshvara the Bodhisattva of Compassion*, Dharamsala 1984, vol. 5, pp. 287–8.

10. See Snelling, Shakabpa, Petech and Namgyal Wangdu of Gyantse, all op. cit., and Glenn Mullin's *Path of the Bodhisattva Warrior* (New York 1988), all of which offer different interpretations of the Tibetan response and the Dalai Lama's role in it.

11. NAI Secret E., July 1904, nos. 483–619.

12. The information about Agvan Dorzhiev given in Wilhelm Filchner's rip-roaring *Sturm Uber Asien* (Berlin, 1924) should not be taken seriously. Disentangling the real Dorzhiev from the many myths about him is a difficult task, which has been tackled successfully only in the work of Alexander Andreyev and the late John Snelling. Agvan Dorzhiev's autobiography *chos brgyad gdon gyis byas te rgyal khams don med nyul ba yidam chos nor gyis* ('the Story of one who has wandered purposelessly across the Plains, motivated by the Eight Worldly Concerns: may he be overwhelmed by the power of the Protector Deities') concentrates on his religious activities, and reveals

little about events in Tibet during 1903–04.

13. Younghusband, *The Light of Experience*, p. 98.
14. Shenkhawa, op. cit., p. 7.
15. Royal Fusiliers Museum, Tower of London. T14-T15. Lhalu House, one of the 'beauties of Lhasa', was demolished by the Chinese authorities in the late 1980s.
16. FY/177. See also Frederick O'Connor's letter to Helen Younghusband in FY/101.
17. Shakabpa, op. cit., p. 216.
18. Younghusband, *India and Tibet*, p. 285.
19. OIOC Mss. Eur. F166/12.
20. *Daily Mail*, 23 August 1904.
21. *Press Association*, 20 August 1904.
22. FY/177.
23. OIOC Mss. Eur. F157/197.
24. FY/145 and FY/177.
25. Shakabpa, op. cit., p. 217. On the subject of poison serving as medicine, smallpox inoculation was practised in Tibet, China and Mongolia long before the discoveries of Edward Jenner.
26. Shenkhawa, op. cit., p. 6.
27. Younghusband, op. cit., p. 306.
28. FY/160.
29. Phuntsog Tsering, op. cit., pp. 403–4.
30. FY/414 and FY/385.

SEVENTEEN: Fame in Disgrace and Diversion in Kashmir

1. *Western Daily Press*, 12 December 1904.
2. OIOC Mss. Eur. F166/12.
3. FY/90-FY/91.
4. FY/241.
5. FY/145.
6. FY/80.
7. FY/179.
8. FY/145.
9. In *Bayonets to Lhasa*, Peter Fleming confuses Harry Cust with the art historian Lionel Cust.
10. FY/177.
11. OIOC Mss. Eur. E233/37.
12. FY/160.
13. OIOC Mss. Eur. F166/12.
14. Lo Hui-Min (ed.), *The Correspondence of G. E. Morrison*, Cambridge 1976, vol. 1, p. 361.
15. See Snelling, Shakabpa, Petech, Fleming and Hopkirk, all op. cit.; and Swinson, Arthur, *Beyond the Frontiers*, London 1971; Andreev, A. I., *The Buddhist Shrine of Petrograd*, Ulan Ude 1992; Bell, Charles, *Portrait of a Dalai Lama*, London 1946; and Hopkirk, Peter, *Trespassers on the Roof of the World*, London 1982.
16. FY/95 and FY/106.
17. FY/542.
18. Younghusband, Francis, *Within: Thoughts During Convalescence*, London 1912, p. 72.
19. FY/472.
20. FY/179.
21. FY/510.
22. FY/499.
23. FY/225.
24. OIOC Mss. Eur. F111/420.
25. FY/516.
26. NAI Foreign Dept., General B, April 1906, nos. 104–7.
27. FY/111.
28. FY/180. During his time in Kashmir, Younghusband was also reunited with two other veterans of his journey across Central Asia. First came Turgan, the Balti who had descended the Mustagh Pass (ropeless) after being purchased in the Yarkand slave market for 800 tangas. Then Shukar Ali, the man who had saved Younghusband's life on at least one occasion and assisted in the bearding of the Mir of Hunza. In the fastness of Ladakh he had heard about his old employer's promotion, and set off down to Srinagar, where a delighted Sir Francis Younghusband entertained him to tea in the Residency garden.
29. LEY 1906.
30. FY/111.
31. Younghusband, *The Light of Experience*, p. 280.
32. FY/578.

33. FY/181.
34. FY/328.
35. FY/276.
36. FY/332.
37. FY/276 and 278.
38. FY/229.
39. OIOC Mss. Eur. F112/15.
40. OIOC Mss. Eur. D573/16.
41. OIOC Mss. Eur. F112/16.
42. FY/278. See *Highness* by Ann
    Morrow (London 1986) for
    details of the young Maharajah of
    Kashmir's exploits.
43. NLS Minto Papers Mss.12746/132.
44. FY/285.
45. FY/260.

PART III

EIGHTEEN: Playing Politics,
Brushing Death, Preaching
Atheism

1. FY/332.
2. OIOC Mss. Eur. F112/15.
3. FY/512.
4. OIOC Mss. Eur. F112/15.
5. FY/284.
6. FY/183.
7. FY/512.
8. FY/285.
9. FY/289.
10. FY/184.
11. FY/282.
12. FY/289.
13. OIOC Mss. Eur. F112/16.
14. FY/242.
15. FY/226.
16. FY/516.
17. Younghusband, *Within*,
    pp. 21–189.
18. *Votes for Women*, 1 May 1914.
19. FY/244. H. G. Wells quoted at
    length from *Within* in his book *God
    the Invisible King* in a chapter
    entitled 'Heresies'.
20. Younghusband, Francis, *The Sum of
    Things*, London 1939, p. 25.
21. Younghusband, *The Light of
    Experience*, p. 243.
22. FY/185.
23. I found the presentation copy of
    Within which Younghusband had
    given to Moore in a bookshop in
    Kent; most of the pages were
    uncut.
24. Quoted by Clark, Ronald, *The Life
    of Bertrand Russell*, London 1975,
    p. 190, and FY/295.
25. FY/294. A variation on this passage
    can be found in Younghusband,
    Francis, *The Gleam*, London 1923,
    p. 69.
26. FY/186 and FY/199.
27. Quoted by Clark, op. cit., p. 191.
28. Russell, Bertrand, *Autobiography of
    Bertrand Russell*, London 1969,
    vol. 2, p. 47, and FY/559.
29. Younghusband, *The Light of
    Experience*, pp. 219–20.
30. FY/188.
31. FY/189.
32. FY/299.
33. FY/189. Kitchener's job was
    eventually split between Sir Henry
    McMahon, a lugubrious Indian
    Government official who had just
    returned from discussing the
    Tibetan border with Shatra Paljor
    Dorje at Simla, and Sir Reginald
    Wingate.
34. FY/112.
35. FY/191.
36. FY/189.
37. Younghusband, Francis, *Mutual
    Influence*, London 1915,
    pp. 51–141.
38. KC, 31 January 1915.
39. FY/294.
40. Younghusband, op. cit., pp. 90–1.

NINETEEN: Fighting for Right
in the Great War

1. *The Times*, 6 July 1915. In fact the
   Indian 'native press' was usually
   more accurate than the British
   during the First World War.
2. FY/193.
3. Russell, op. cit., pp. 47–8.
4. FY/190.
5. FY/193.
6. *Daily Telegraph*, 4 August 1915.
7. FY/193, and KC, 31 August 1915.
8. KC, n.d.
9. FY/388.

10. Mosley, Nicholas, *Julian Grenfell*, London 1976, p. 231.
11. W. B. Yeats and G. B. Shaw refused; Gilbert Murray suggested that his friend 'Gavin Boosey Shaw, a Scotch literary man in reduced circumstances' might sign with his initials only. See Wilson, Duncan, *Gilbert Murray*, Oxford 1987, p. 220.
12. Baldick, Chris, *The Social Mission of English Criticism*, Oxford 1983, p. 88.
13. BOD Mss. Gilbert Murray, 28–30.
14. FY/242. John Buchan was a keen admirer of Younghusband, praising him in *The Last Secrets*. It is suggested that he modelled the character of Sandy Arbuthnot on him. See Richard Usborne's *Clubland Heroes*, London 1953.
15. Elwes, Winefride, *Gervase Elwes*, London 1935, p. 242.
16. Letter to the author, 10 December 1990.
17. KC, 22 October, 14 November and 16 October 1915.
18. FY/194.
19. KC, 16 October 1915.
20. BOD Mss. Gilbert Murray, 28–30.
21. FY/194.
22. BOD Mss. Gilbert Murray, 28–30.
23. KC, 14 April 1915.
24. FY/194.
25. KC n.d.
26. FY/594.
27. Jones, Kathleen, *Eileen Younghusband: A Biography*, London 1984, p. 8.
28. FY/594.
29. FY/194.
30. NISW Tape-recorded interview with Professor Kathleen Jones.
31. FY/242.
32. KC, 8 July 1916.
33. FY/195.
34. Charles Graves, *Hubert Parry*, London 1926, vol. 2, p. 92. See also Dibble, Jeremy, *C. Hubert H. Parry*, Oxford 1992.
35. *Times Literary Supplement*, 6 April 1916.
36. OIOC Bailey Papers Mss. Eur. F157/219.
37. In fact the detective-sergeant's notes turned out to be illegible; but fortunately the *Western Mail* reporter had the full text of Bertrand Russell's subversive speech.
38. Clark, op. cit., p. 298.
39. FY/242.
40. NISW interview.
41. Russell, op. cit., pp. 72–3.
42. Clark, op. cit., p. 303.
43. Holroyd, Michael, *Lytton Strachey*, London 1979 (revised edn.), p. 623.
44. Clark, op. cit., pp. 300–2.
45. Vellacott, Jo, *Bertrand Russell and the Pacifists in the First World War*, Brighton 1980, p. 96.
46. BOD Mss. Gilbert Murray 33–5.
47. BOD Mss. Stein 15/6&7.
48. Wren Library, Trinity College Cambridge. Add. Ms. c.61/53.
49. BOD Mss. Gilbert Murray 33–5.
50. Royal Society of Literature archives, Younghusband file.
51. FY/196.
52. BOD Mss. Gilbert Murray 33–5.
53. FY/196.
54. Younghusband, *The Sum of Things*, p. 28.
55. *Sun*, 14 January 1991.
56. Newbolt, Henry, *Later Life and Letters*, London 1942, p. 293.
57. FY/113 and FY/497.
58. FY/198.
59. FY/293.
60. FY/198.

TWENTY: The Quest for a World Leader on the Planet Altair

1. FY/541.
2. Younghusband, *The Heart of Nature*, pp. xxv–192. The book was translated into German, and received good reviews from the German press. His message was similar to the *volkisch* nature-mysticism which was popular in Germany at this time, whereby Nature was invested with an

almost divine status as the arbiter of what is right and good.

3. FY/541.
4. Younghusband, *The Gleam*, pp. 14–286.
5. FY/533.
6. FY/521.
7. FY/594.
8. Notes by Kathleen Lutyens, in a private collection.
9. *The Times*, 23 November 1925.
10. Jones, op. cit., p. 18.
11. RGS Younghusband archive.
12. Jones, op. cit., p. 14.
13. FY/202.
14. FY/378.
15. FY/541.
16. See FY/243.
17. Younghusband, Francis, *Mother World*, London 1924, pp. 41 –151.
18. FY/537.
19. FY/540. By coincidence (perhaps), the goalkeeper turned prophet David Icke chose *In the Light of Experience* as the title of his most recent book.
20. FY/539.
21. By 'ether', Younghusband was not referring to the chemical compound, but to a hypothetical substance that was thought to float around the universe. Scientists believed that in order for light or radio waves to travel from one place to another, they would have to be carried through a physical medium: ether was the name they chose for it. Although by this time its existence had been disproved by the experiments of Michelson and Morley, there was still a popular belief in 'the ether'.
22. Younghusband, Francis, *Life in the Stars*, London 1927, pp. 75–162. Younghusband's interest in the stars never extended to astrology, despite being a stereotypical Gemini in many respects.
23. FY/244.
24. FY/205.
25. FY/541.
26. Younghusband, Francis, *The Coming Country*, London 1928, pp. 9–309.
27. Younghusband, Francis, *The Living Universe*, London 1933, pp. 191–247.
28. FY/233.
29. FY/541.
30. FY/437.
31. Younghusband, *The Heart of Nature*, p. 219.
32. FY/318. Most of Younghusband's religious speeches and articles survive in manuscript and typed form. See FY/372–FY/456.

TWENTY-ONE: Running the Jog and Climbing Mount Everest

1. Robertson, David, *George Mallory*, London 1969, p. 162.
2. Unsworth, Walt, *Everest*, London 1981, p. 31.
3. LEY, 15 July 1928.
4. Younghusband, *Everest: The Challenge*, p. 12.
5. Younghusband, *The Heart of Nature*, p. 212. Younghusband's lecture to the RGS had a profound impact on the geographer Vaughan Cornish, who went on to become one of Britain's leading environmental campaigners in the first part of this century.
6. Although this story is now firmly embedded in the mythology of Everest exploration, its veracity is open to question. 'I had Charlie Bruce to lunch today and we had a real good crack,' Younghusband wrote to Eileen in 1932. 'He has a yarn that I had a scheme forty years ago for him & me to go up Everest and that I have thought of nothing ever since! He is going to write an article about it for the Daily Telegraph and if it brings in another twenty quid to the Expedition funds that is all to the good.' LEY, 10 September 1932.
7. Noel, J. B. L., *Through Tibet to Everest*, London 1927, p. 97.
8. RGS EE. 1/19/2.

9. RGS EE. 1/13/4.
10. Morris, James, *Coronation Everest*, London 1958, p. 19.
11. Unsworth, op. cit., p. 31.
12. Seaver, op. cit., p. 305.
13. Private collection.
14. Letter to the author, 8 August 1989.
15. Holroyd, op. cit., p. 417.
16. RGS EE. 3/3/5.
17. FY/542.
18. FY/529.
19. See FY/126.
20. LEY, 15 July 1928.
21. FY/202.
22. LEY, 3 and 6 April 1925.
23. FY/202.
24. LEY, 12 April 1925.
25. FY/203, and *Ceylon Observer*, 24 April 1926.
26. 'dus-mthar chos smra-ba'i btsun-pa ngag-dbang bstan-'dzin nor-bu'i rnam-thar 'chi-med bdud-rtsi'i rol-mtsho' p. 290 a-b. Quoted in Macdonald, Alexander W., *The Lama and the General*, Kathmandu 1973, Kailash vol. 1, no. 3.
27. RGS EE. 3/4/65.
28. Unsworth, op. cit., p. 97.
29. FY/202.
30. LEY, 28 August 1922.
31. Younghusband, Francis, *The Epic of Mount Everest*, London 1926, pp. 276–7.
32. RGS EE. 3/5/19.
33. Private collection, 19 January 1925.
34. See Unsworth, op. cit., pp. 142–57. After four years as Trade Agent in Gyantse, Eric Bailey explored the Tsangpo Gorges, before being sent to Russian Turkestan to spy on the new Bolshevik administration. While there he was recruited into counter-espionage, and ordered to track down a foreign agent ... called Bailey. See also Swinson, Arthur, *Beyond the Frontiers*, London 1971, CUL Hardinge 69 and OIOC Mss. Eur. F157/219.
35. LEY, 8 October 1929.
36. Younghusband, op. cit., pp. 310–11. Given his aversion to the use of oxygen ('the gas', as he called it) Younghusband would probably consider Reinhold Messner's 1978 ascent the first true 'conquest' of Everest, although his greatest reverence might be reserved for Stephen Venables, the first gas-free Britisher to make it to the summit.
37. LEY, 4 January 1930, 27 January 1930, 2 February 1930, 12 November 1924.
38. FY/243.
39. FY/202.
40. LEY, 28 February 1927, 5 December 1928, 15 April 1925, 8 April 1926.
41. FY/203.
42. LEY, 31 August 1929, 4 November 1924, 22 November 1926, 25 January 1927, 8 October 1930, and FY/118.

TWENTY-TWO: Religious Dramas, Peculiar Swamis and Indian Sagas

1. LEY, 15 May 1929.
2. RADIUS pamphlet, in a private collection.
3. LPL Bell/153.
4. FY/427.
5. FY/479.
6. Younghusband, Francis, *Dawn in India*, London 1930, p. 273.
7. FY/514.
8. FY/482.
9. Younghusband, op. cit., p. ix.
10. *Spectator*, 18 October 1930.
11. Byron, Robert, *An Essay on India*, London 1931, pp. 153–4.
12. BBC Radio contributors 910, file 1.
13. FY/244. See also CUL Baldwin 167.
14. FY/485.
15. LEY, 23 July and 7 October 1930. William Wedgwood Benn, later Lord Stansgate, was the father of the radical Labour Party politician Tony Benn.
16. FY/503 and author's interview

with Elizabeth Townsend, February 1991.

17. LEY, 5 June 1930.

18. FY/244.

19. Brunton, Paul, *A Search in Secret India*, London 1965, foreword. It is characteristic of Paul Brunton's disregard for worldly accuracy that he refers to Younghusband in this book as a 'Political Minister' and a 'Brigadier General'. See also Jeffrey Masson's icon-shattering *My Father's Guru: A Journey through Spirituality and Disillusion*, London 1993.

20. FY/233.

21. BL Add. Mss. 45732.

22. Jeffares, A. Norman, *W. B. Yeats*, London 1990, p. 265.

23. FY/584.

24. Private collection.

25. LEY, 25 May 1933.

26. LEY, 5 March 1930.

27. FY/207.

28. LEY, 8 September 1932.

29. *The Inn of the Sixth Happiness*, Twentieth Century Fox, 1958, directed by Mark Robson. Gladys Aylward objected passionately to the film on the grounds that she was played by a divorced woman (Ingrid Bergman) and portrayed falling in love with a Chinese general.

30. LEY, 7 March 1934.

31. LEY, 16 May 1934.

32. FY/417.

33. FY/447.

34. FY/397.

35. LEY, 22 April, 25 April and 9 May 1935.

36. FY/434 and FY/534.

37. FY/116.

38. Landau, op. cit., pp. 207–8, and LEY, 22 February 1937.

39. FY/235 and NISW P47. When Lindbergh flew the Atlantic he took five sandwiches with him, but only ate one and a half; the fate of the remaining sandwiches is unknown.

40. LEY, 27 February 1937.

41. Seaver, op. cit., p. 298.

42. *Melong*, 13 March 1937; quoted by Stoddard, Heather, *Le Mendiant de l'Amdo*, Paris 1986, p. 178. When Gedun Ch'omp'el was arrested in Lhasa in 1947 he was found to be in possession of a black tin trunk containing revolutionary pamphlets, the manuscript of a subversive history of Tibet and a rubber woman. See Stoddard for the fascinating story of his life.

43. FY/488.

44. LEY, 19 March 1937.

45. FY/116.

TWENTY-THREE: The Remains of His Day: Inventing Societies

1. WCF pamphlet, 1937.

2. *World Faiths*, Spring 1966, and Seaver, op. cit., p. 358.

3. FY/275.

4. FY/117 and FY/310–311.

5. *The Times*, 13 February 1923.

6. FY/412. Around the same time that Younghusband was attempting to found the Mountain Sanctuaries Association, mountain symbolism was growing in popularity in Germany. The pure white, solid power of snow mountains had a powerful appeal to the Nazis. The film-maker Leni Riefenstahl, who directed *Triumph of the Will*, began her career making *bergfilm* in the Alps. It is claimed that Adolf Hitler admired the supposed racial purity of the Tibetans, and made contact with the Tibetan government in the early 1940s.

7. *Forum*, WCF newspaper, June 1956.

8. LEY, 20 May 1937.

9. Younghusband, *The Sum of Things*, pp. 24–148.

10. LEY, 19 August 1937.

11. OIOC Mss. Eur. F166/12 and FY/269.

12. FY/244.

13. FY/120 and FY/208.

14. BBC Radio contributors 910, file 1. In *My Life, My Trees* (Findhorn

1985), Richard St Barbe Baker records a 'cosmic experience' that he had in a dentist's chair in Portman Square.

15. Letter to the author, January 1990.
16. FY/532 and FY/122.
17. McConnell, Heather, *A Venture of Faith for all Faiths: Onwards From Younghusband's Vision*, World Faiths Insight, June 1986.
18. BBC op. cit.
19. FY/447.
20. BBC op. cit.
21. FY/120.
22. LEY, 14 July and 9 August 1939.
23. FY/328.
24. Letter to the author, August 1989.
25. Nona Essex to Robin Huws Jones, 13 January 1983.
26. LC, 16 December 1940.

TWENTY-FOUR: Love in the Blitz

1. Since the whole of this chapter depends on the letters I found at Lytchett Minster, I felt it would be confusing to include a trail of virtually identical footnotes. So all unsourced quotations come from the correspondence of Francis Younghusband and Madeline Lees from March 1940 to July 1942, presently in a private collection (LC). Where the date of a quotation is significant, it has been indicated in the main text.
2. Author's interview with Jane Brian, October 1989.
3. LC.
4. Jones, op. cit., p. 36.
5. Author's interview with Jane Brian, October 1989.
6. Jones, op. cit., p. 44.
7. Author's interview with Dorothy Thorold, August 1990.
8. NISW P186.
9. Author's interview with Katherine Rawlinson, October 1989.
10. FY/323.
11. Frank Smythe was a practitioner of automatic writing, and often spotted flying saucers.
12. FY/246 and FY/451.
13. Younghusband, Francis, *Wedding*, London 1942, pp. 14–35.
14. NISW P199.
15. FY/209.
16. Author's interview with Jane Brian, October 1989.
17. Younghusband, *The Living Universe*, p. 45, and *Manchester Evening News*, 12 August 1938. The newspaper printed the article on Christ's qualities beneath a strong disclaimer.
18. FY/461 and FY/448.
19. Martindale, Hilda, *Some Victorian Portraits*, London 1948, pp. 84–5.
20. FY/116.
21. *The Times*, 15 October 1941.
22. BBC Radio contributors 910, file 1.
23. LPL Bell/156.
24. FY/209.
25. FY/246.
26. FY/209.
27. FY/123.
28. FY/326.
29. FY/214.
30. FY/246.
31. LEY, 24 July 1942.
32. FY/210. In Seaver's biography of Younghusband, Madeline and Eileen give conflicting accounts of the circumstances leading up to his death. Although Madeline's version is written in effervescent prose, it does seem to be accurate. My account is based on FY/544, FY/613, Seaver, op. cit., pp. 372–5, pencil notes in George Harrison's copy of Seaver's book, an interview with Jane Brian and some neutral information in the papers of Madeline Lees (LC).

EPILOGUE: Creating the God-Child

1. See FY/545, FY/546, FY/580, FY/613 and FY/614.
2. World Congress of Faiths Younghusband Memorial Lecture, 1976.
3. Author's interview with Dorothy Thorold, August 1990.

4. FY/549.
5. LC, 27 March 1941.
6. LC, speech written by Lady Lees for the Aid to China Fund, n.d.
7. LC, 5 January 1941.
8. *Poole and Dorset Herald*, 4 December 1957.
9. Letters and notes by Miss Elaine Tankard in Liverpool Museum. Francis Younghusband's total estate at the time of his death was valued at less than £100. Eileen Younghusband told inquisitive researchers that many robes and papers had been destroyed in a fire in a shed at Currant Hill. Although the fire definitely happened (and the hill was too steep and icy for the fire engines to get there) there is no evidence that any substantial number of robes or papers were destroyed. After Eileen's death, one commentator described her as a cross between Virginia Woolf and Captain Hook. Her biographer thought this a tasteless remark, but I felt it might have been intended as a compliment. Indian *rishis* in the Himalayan forests, as Sir Francis Younghusband once observed, 'may in their own way be doing as much good as many a busy social worker'. FY/476.
10. FY/551.
11. LC, 4 November 1940. Readings of censored material were obtained with the assistance of a Video Spectral Comparator Mark Two, using infra-red light and a standard infra-red filter with a light length of 830–1000 nanometres.

SELECT BIBLIOGRAPHY

Addy, Premen, *Tibet on the Imperial Chessboard*, Calcutta 1984.

Akiner, Shirin, *Islamic Peoples of the Soviet Union* (revised edn.), London 1986.

Alder, Garry, *British India's Northern Frontier, 1865–1895*, London 1963.

Andreev, A. I., *The Buddhist Shrine of Petrograd*, Ulan Ude 1992.

Bell, Charles, *Portrait of a Dalai Lama*, London 1946.

Biscoe, C. E. Tyndale, *Character Building in Kashmir*, London 1920.

Browne, E. Martin, *Two in One*, Cambridge 1981.

Calvert, Harry, *Smythe's Mountains*, London 1985.

Candler, Edmund, *The Unveiling of Lhasa*, London 1905.

Clark, Ronald W., *The Life of Bertrand Russell*, London 1975.

Cooke, Hope, *Time Change*, New York 1980.

Datta-Ray, Sunanda K., *Smash and Grab: Annexation of Sikkim*, New Delhi 1984.

Dickinson, G. Lowes, *J. McT. E. McTaggart*, Cambridge 1931.

Elwin, Verrier, *The Tribal World of Verrier Elwin*, Bombay 1964.

Fleming, Peter, *Bayonets to Lhasa*, London 1961.

Galwan, Ghulam Rassul, *Servant of Sahibs*, Cambridge 1923.

HMSO, *Correspondence Relating to Chitral*, London 1895.

HMSO, *Papers Relating to Tibet*, London 1904.

HMSO, *Further Papers Relating to Tibet*, London 1905.

Holzel, Tom & Salkeld, Audrey, *The Mystery of Mallory and Irvine*, London 1986.

Hopkirk, Peter, *The Great Game: On Secret Service in High Asia*, London 1990.

Hopkirk, Peter, *Trespassers on the Roof of the World*, London 1982.

Hynes, Samuel, *A War Imagined*, London 1990.

Jeffares, A. Norman, *W. B. Yeats*, London 1990.

James, H. E. M., *The Long White Mountain*, London 1888.

Jones, Kathleen, *Eileen Younghusband: A Biography*, London 1984.

Kawaguchi, Ekai, *Three Years in Tibet*, Benares 1909.

Keay, John, *The Gilgit Game*, London 1979.

Khalfin, N. A., *Russia's Policy in Central Asia*, London 1964.

Lamb, Alastair, *Britain and Chinese Central Asia*, London 1960 (revised 1986 as *British India and Tibet*).

Lamb, Alastair, *Kashmir: A Disputed Legacy*, Hertingfordbury 1991.

Landau, Rom, *Personalia*, London 1949.

Landon, Perceval, *Lhasa*, London 1906.

Lees, Faith, *Love Is Our Home*, London 1978.

Lees, Lady, *Peace Aim*, Poole 1939.

Lees, Tom, *Another Man*, London 1980.

Longford, Elizabeth, *Jameson's Raid*, (revised edn.), London 1982.

Martindale, Hilda, *Some Victorian Portraits*, London 1948.

Mason, Kenneth, *Abode of Snow*, London 1987.

Mehra, Parshotam, *The Younghusband Expedition: An Interpretation*, London 1968.

Moorehead, Caroline, *Troublesome People*, London 1987.

Morris, James, *Coronation Everest*, London 1958.

Morris, James, *Farewell the Trumpets*, London 1978.

Murray, Gilbert, *Faith, War and Policy*, London 1918.

Newbolt, Henry, *Later Life and Letters*, London 1942.

Noel, J. B. L., *Through Tibet to Everest*, London 1927.

O'Connor, Frederick, *To the Frontier and Beyond*, London 1931.

Petech, Luciano, *Aristocracy and Government in Tibet 1728–1959*, Rome 1973.

Purohit, Swami, *An Indian Monk*, London 1932.

Rampa, Lobsang, *The Third Eye*, London 1956.

Ravensdale, Baroness, *In Many Rhythms*, London 1953.

Richardson, Hugh E., *Tibet and its History*, (revised edn.), London 1984.

Robertson, David, *George Mallory*, London 1969.

Robertson, George, *Chitral: The Story of a Minor Siege*, London 1898.

Rockhill, William Woodville, *The Land of the Lamas*, London 1891.

Rose, Kenneth, *Curzon: A Most Superior Person*, London 1985. (1st edn. 1969).

Russell, Bertrand, *Autobiography of Bertrand Russell* (vol. 2), London 1969.

Seaver, George, *Francis Younghusband: Explorer and Mystic*, London 1952.

Scott, A. MacCallum, *The Truth About Tibet*, London 1905.

Shakabpa, W. D., *Tibet: A Political History*, New York 1984.

Shaw, Robert, *Visits to High Tartary, Yarkand and Kashgar*, London 1871.

Sikkim Coronation. Gangtok n.d. (c. 1970).

Singh, Amar Kaur Jasbir, *Himalayan Triangle* (and the companion volume *A Guide to Source Materials . . .*), London 1988.

Skrine, C. P., and Nightingale, Pamela, *Macartney at Kashgar*, London 1973.

Snelling, John, *Buddhism in Russia*, Shaftesbury 1993.

Stoddard, Heather, *Le Mendiant de l'Amdo*, Paris 1986.

Swinson, Arthur, *Beyond the Frontiers*, London 1971.

Switzer, A., *D. T. Suzuki*, London 1985.

Tidrick, Kathryn, *Empire and the English Character*, London 1990.

Unsworth, Walt, *Everest*, London 1981.

Verrier, Anthony, *Francis Younghusband and the Great Game*, London 1991.

Waddell, L. Austine, *Lhasa and its Mysteries*, London 1905.

Waller, Derek, *The Pundits*, Kentucky 1990.

Wang Furen and Suo Wenqing, *Highlights of Tibetan History*, Beijing 1984.

White, J. Claude, *Sikkim and Bhutan*, London 1909.

Winterbottom, Derek, *Henry Newbolt and the Spirit of Clifton*, Bristol 1986.

Younghusband, George, *Forty Years a Soldier*, London 1923.

Younghusband, Helen, *Marie Antoinette*, London 1912.

Yule, Henry, *Hobson-Jobson*, London 1903.

BOOKS BY FRANCIS YOUNGHUSBAND

The Relief of Chitral (with G. J. Younghusband), London 1895.
The Heart of a Continent, London 1896. (Abridged 1898 as *Among the Celestials*.)
South Africa of To-Day, London 1898.
Kashmir, London 1909.
India and Tibet, London 1910.
Within, London 1912.
Mutual Influence, London 1915.
The Heart of Nature, London 1921.
The Gleam, London 1923.
Mother World, London 1924.
Wonders of the Himalaya, London 1924.
Peking to Lhasa, London 1925.
But In Our Lives, London 1926.
The Epic of Mount Everest, London 1926.
Life in the Stars, London 1927.
The Light of Experience, London 1927.
The Coming Country, London 1928.
Dawn in India, London 1930.
The Reign of God, London 1930.
The Living Universe, London 1933.
Modern Mystics, London 1935.
Everest: The Challenge, London 1936.
A Venture of Faith, London 1937.
The Sum of Things, London 1939.
Vital Religion, London 1940.
Wedding, London 1942.

OTHER PUBLICATIONS BY FRANCIS YOUNGHUSBAND

Report on a Mission to the Northern Frontier of Kashmir in 1889, Calcutta 1890.
    (Reprinted as *The Northern Frontier of Kashmir*, New Delhi 1973.)
Memorandum on our Relation with Tibet, Simla 1903.
The Sense of Community, London 1916.
England's Mission, London 1920.
India section of *The Empire at War* (ed. Charles Lucas, five vols.) London
    1921.
Tibet section of *Peoples of All Nations* (vol. 7), London 1922.
Philosophy, Science and Religion, London 1929.
World Fellowship of Faiths, London 1935.

BIBLIOGRAPHY OF WRITINGS IN TIBETAN

Lopon Nado, *druk karpo* [*The Religious and Political History of Bhutan*],
    Bumthang 1986.
Namgyal Wangdu of Gyantse, *bod ljongs rgyal khab chen po'i srid lugs dang*

'brel ba'i drag po'i dmag gi lo rgyus rags bsdud [*A Short Military History of Tibet*], Dharamsala 1976.

Namseling, Paljor Jigme, (ed. Tashi Tsering), *mi tshe'i lo rgyus dang 'brel yod sna tshogs* [*The History of a Man's Life and Related Matters*], Dharamsala 1988.

Phuntsog Tsering (ed.), *deb ther kun gsal me long* [*The Annals of the All-Revealing Mirror*], Lhasa 1987.

Purchokpa, Thubten Champa, '*A String of Wondrous Gems . . .*' (1940) from *'phags pa 'jig rten dbang phyug gi rnam sprul rim byon gyi 'khrungs rabs deb ther nor bu'i 'phreng ba* [*A Jewel Rosary Illustrating the Various Incarnations of Saintly Avalokiteshvara the Bodhisattva of Compassion*], (vol. 5) Dharamsala 1984.

Shenkhawa, Gyurme Sonam Tobgyal, *rang gi lo rgyus lhad med rang byung zang* [*The Pure Unadulterated Copper of My History*], Dharamsala 1990.

Shukseb Jetsun Chonyi Zangmo (ed. Sonam Tobgay Kazi), *gangs shug ma ni lo chen rig 'dzin chos nyid bzang mo'i rnam par thar pa rnam mkhyed bde oter zhes bya ba* [*The Autobiography of Shukseb Jetsun Chonyi Zangmo*], Gangtok 1975.

Tezur Jigme Wangchuk, Serdong Wangyal, Dhezur Rinchen Wangdu, Chabtsom Chime Gyalpo, (eds.) [*A Compiled History of the Tibetan People's Struggle Against the British Invasion*], 'Tibetan Autonomous Region' n.d. (c.1985).

Tsepon W. D. Shakabpa, *bod kyi srid don rgyal rabs* [*An Advanced Political History of Tibet*], Kalimpong 1976.

Yonten Gyatso, *bod kyi rgyal rabs lo rgyus don bsdud* [*A True Summary of the Tibetan Lineages and History*], Dharamsala 1990.

INDEX

429

Younghusband, (*later* Dame) Eileen –
cont'd.
letters 329, 334, 336, 338, 341–2, 345,
348, 349, 351, 354, 355–6, 359, 367,
370, 394; custodian of FY's papers xiv,
89, 121; 371, 400–1; memories of FY 57,
122, 305, 361, 387; death 401; bequests
xiv, 121, 371, 401
Younghusband, Ethel (FY's sister) 6, 88,
156, 267, 285
Younghusband, Sir Francis Edward: birth 3,
7; family background 3–7; childhood 7;
education 7–13; Sandhurst 13–14; sails
for India 14–16; army life 16–17; visits
uncle's house 22–3; Rhotang Pass 24–5,
32–3; mapping and surveying 34, 37;
Great Game 35–7, 67, 119, 144, 363;
Manchurian expedition 37–42, 403;
Peking 42–3; Gobi Desert expedition
43–8, 403; Mustagh Pass descent 56–60;
engagement to May 64–6, *see also* Ewart,
May; Tibetan plans 66–7; Hunza mission
67–80; Viceroy's approval 81; Kashgar
mission 82, 84–92; awarded CIE 92;
Bozai Gumbaz incident 93–5, 96, 98–9;
Political Officer in Hunza 100–1; Chitral
mission 102–10; on leave in England
113–16; *Times* Special Correspondent
116–19, 120, 124–9, 132; studies
biology 118; Jameson Raid 124–9, 133,
404; South Africa 133–5; marriage
135–40; Mount Abu post 144–5, 150,
403; Deoli post 151–3; leave in England
152; Rajputana famine 153, 154;
awarded Kaiser-i-Hind Gold Medal 154;
leave in England 155–8; Indore posting
154, 158–60, 165–6, 206; parliamentary
ambitions 156, 157, 275; Great Durbar
159–60; Tibet Expedition 160–5, 175–7,
183–90, 193–6, 205–17, 220–34,
235–48, 257–8, 404; Chumi Shengo
Massacre 221–7; keeping monks in order
229–30; Changlo besieged 232–5;
capture of Gyantse Dzong 237; arrival at
Lhasa 239–40; occupation of Lhasa
242–8; Treaty of Lhasa 247–8, 256–7;
leaves Lhasa 251–2; reception in
England 253–62, 291; KCIE 256;
Honorary Doctorates 262; Kashmir
Residency 262, 263–71; General
Elections (1910) 275–6; meetings with
philosophers 279, 286–8; car accident
279–81, 405; public response to *Within*

284–5, 290, 291; US tour 288–90; Great
War 290–1; India Office 294, 308, 310;
Fight for Right movement 295–303,
307–10, 404; KCSI 307; lectures in
France (1918) 311–12; religious lectures
326; Everest expeditions 328–39; US and
Canada tour (1930) 339–40; Religious
Drama Society 344–5, 349, 362; Indian
nationalism 346–8, 359, 391; US tours
(1934–6) 335–6; Parliament of Religions
in India 357–9; Krama Kesari title 359;
societies 360–70; Second World War
370, 376–83; relationship with Madeline
376–95; Fire Warden 380; death 395;
funeral 397; tributes 397–8
PERSONAL:
beliefs and attitudes: Evangelical
upbringing 7, 9, 121, 313; imperialist
fervour 9–10, 54–5, 98–9, 131–2,
155–6, 268–9, 391, 404; Russian
threat 15, 37, 42, 99, 106, 156, 187–8,
193, 241; racial views 24, 45, 70,
72–3, 131–2, 144, 155–6, 269, 313,
346–7, 390, 404; interest in evolution
63, 109, 118, 131; studies *Buddhism*
71; religious doubts 87; Tolstoy's
influence 109–10, 113, 119–20, 313,
384; spiritual aspirations 120; vision of
'Universal Spirit' 131; Besant influence 206;
speculations on alien intelligence 214,
283, 320–1, 356; vision in Tibet 252,
313, 344, 405; communion with God
267; telepathy 267, 283, 313, 321;
self-improvement 267–8; creation of
religion 268, 277, 313; eugenics 268,
283, 404; God-Child 282, 284, 318,
401–3, 404; free love 283, 385;
Svabhava persona 314–15;
World-Leader 321, 325; Power of the
Spirit experience 251–2, 326–7, 344
characteristics: appearance 13, 15,
89–90, 119, 140, 196, 215, 240, 253,
309, 311, 339; attitude to pain 50, 281;
'lone agent' 70, 99; reliability 73–4;
risk-taking 40–1; running 8, 13, 37–8;
sexuality 13–14, 118, 121–2, 136–7,
287, 384–7
health: accidents 50, 109; snowblindness
70; illness in Chitral 104; insomnia
104, 107, 112, 113, 152; Belgian car
accident 279–81, 405; heart attack
359, 360, 366–7; old age 388